Revolutionizing the Service Industry With OpenAI Models

Mahmut Demir
Isparta University of Applied Sciences, Turkey

Ali Dalgic
Isparta University of Applied Sciences, Turkey

A volume in the Advances in Hospitality, Tourism, and the Services Industry (AHTSI) Book Series

IGI Global
PUBLISHER of TIMELY KNOWLEDGE

Published in the United States of America by
IGI Global
Business Science Reference (an imprint of IGI Global)
701 E. Chocolate Avenue
Hershey PA, USA 17033
Tel: 717-533-8845
Fax: 717-533-8661
E-mail: cust@igi-global.com
Web site: http://www.igi-global.com

Library of Congress Cataloging-in-Publication Data

Names: Demir, Mahmut, 1970- editor. | Dalgiç, Ali, 1987- editor.
Title: Revolutionizing the service industry with open AI models / edited by Mahmut Demir, Ali Dalgıç.
Description: Hershey PA : Business Science Reference, [2024] | Includes bibliographical references. | Summary: "This book aims to explore how OpenAI models are bringing about revolutionary changes in the service industry"-- Provided by publisher.
Identifiers: LCCN 2024002197 (print) | LCCN 2024002198 (ebook) | ISBN 9798369312391 (hardcover) | ISBN 9798369312407 (ebook)
Subjects: LCSH: ChatGPT. | Chatbots. | Service industries--Data processing.
Classification: LCC QA76.76.C52 R48 2024 (print) | LCC QA76.76.C52 (ebook) | DDC 658/.0563--dc23/eng/20240310
LC record available at https://lccn.loc.gov/2024002197
LC ebook record available at https://lccn.loc.gov/2024002198

This book is published in the IGI Global book series Advances in Hospitality, Tourism, and the Services Industry (AHTSI) (ISSN: 2475-6547; eISSN: 2475-6555)

British Cataloguing in Publication Data
A Cataloguing in Publication record for this book is available from the British Library.

Advances in Hospitality, Tourism, and the Services Industry (AHTSI) Book Series

ISSN:2475-6547
EISSN:2475-6555

Editor-in-Chief: Maximiliano Korstanje, University of Palermo, Argentina

MISSION

Globally, the hospitality, travel, tourism, and services industries generate a significant percentage of revenue and represent a large portion of the business world. Even in tough economic times, these industries thrive as individuals continue to spend on leisure and recreation activities as well as services.

The Advances in Hospitality, Tourism, and the Services Industry (AHTSI) book series offers diverse publications relating to the management, promotion, and profitability of the leisure, recreation, and services industries. Highlighting current research pertaining to various topics within the realm of hospitality, travel, tourism, and services management, the titles found within the AHTSI book series are pertinent to the research and professional needs of managers, business practitioners, researchers, and upper-level students studying in the field.

COVERAGE

- Tourism and the Environment
- Service Training
- Food and Beverage Management
- Travel Agency Management
- Health and Wellness Tourism
- Hotel Management
- Service Management
- Sustainable Tourism
- Service Design
- International Tourism

IGI Global is currently accepting manuscripts for publication within this series. To submit a proposal for a volume in this series, please contact our Acquisition Editors at Acquisitions@igi-global.com or visit: http://www.igi-global.com/publish/.

The Advances in Hospitality, Tourism, and the Services Industry (AHTSI) Book Series (ISSN 2475-6547) is published by IGI Global, 701 E. Chocolate Avenue, Hershey, PA 17033-1240, USA, www.igi-global.com. This series is composed of titles available for purchase individually; each title is edited to be contextually exclusive from any other title within the series. For pricing and ordering information please visit http://www.igi-global.com/book-series/advances-hospitality-tourism-services-industry/121014. Postmaster: Send all address changes to above address.

Titles in this Series

For a list of additional titles in this series, please visit:
http://www.igi-global.com/book-series/advances-hospitality-tourism-services-industry/121014

Mountain Tourism and Ecological Impacts Himalayan Region and Beyond
Soumendra Nath Biswas (Assam University, Silchar, India) and Pradip Kumar (Assam University, Silchar, India)
Business Science Reference • © 2024 • 280pp • H/C (ISBN: 9798369308233) • US $250.00

Promoting Sustainable Gastronomy Tourism and Community Development
Andrea Edurne Jimenez Ruiz (Universidad Autonoma del Estado de Mexico, Mexico) Shivam Bhartiya (Jain University, India) and Vaibhav Bhatt (Central University of Tamil Nadu, India)
Business Science Reference • © 2024 • 287pp • H/C (ISBN: 9798369318140) • US $285.00

Impact of AI and Robotics on the Medical Tourism Industry
Viana Hassan (University of Malta, Malta) Ahmad Albattat (Management and Science University, Malaysia) and Shakeel Basheer (Lovely Professional University, India)
Business Science Reference • © 2024 • 361pp • H/C (ISBN: 9798369322482) • US $300.00

Service Innovations in Tourism Metaverse, Immersive Technologies, and Digital Twin
Surabhi Singh (G.L. Bajaj Institute of Management and Research, India)
Business Science Reference • © 2024 • 295pp • H/C (ISBN: 9798369311035) • US $275.00

Utilizing Smart Technology and AI in Hybrid Tourism and Hospitality
Sanjeev Kumar (Lovely Professional University, India) Mohammad Badruddoza Talukder (International University of Business Agriculture and Technology, Bangladesh) and Ana Pego (Nova University of Lisbon, Portugal)
Business Science Reference • © 2024 • 367pp • H/C (ISBN: 9798369319789) • US $290.00

Innovative Technologies for Increasing Service Productivity
Sridhar Manohar (Chitkara Business School, Chitkara University, India) Amit Mittal (Chitkara Business School, Chitkara University, India) Sekar Raju (Ivy College of Business, Iowa State University, USA) and Arjun J. Nair (Chitkara University, India)
Business Science Reference • © 2024 • 404pp • H/C (ISBN: 9798369320198) • US $290.00

For an entire list of titles in this series, please visit:
http://www.igi-global.com/book-series/advances-hospitality-tourism-services-industry/121014

IGI Global
PUBLISHER of TIMELY KNOWLEDGE

701 East Chocolate Avenue, Hershey, PA 17033, USA
Tel: 717-533-8845 x100 • Fax: 717-533-8661
E-Mail: cust@igi-global.com • www.igi-global.com

Table of Contents

Detailed Table of Contents

The study sought to investigate the service quality of chatbots on telecom service providers' websites and apps. The research model was based on an integration of the expectation confirmation model of IS, the E-S-Qual model, and the technology anxiety construct. The study used a quantitative research design. Data were collected from 263 chatbot users; however, after data cleaning, 255 responses were retained. Data analysis was done using structural equation modelling. The results show significant relationships between confirmation and perceived usefulness, as well as confirmation and satisfaction. Additionally, efficiency and privacy constructs of the E-S-Qual model have significant effects on satisfaction. Post-use confirmation, efficiency, and privacy have the most significant impacts on chatbot usage satisfaction of customers on telecom service providers' websites and apps. Technology anxiety could not significantly mediate the relationship between the E-S-Qual model constructs and post-use confirmation.

This study explains the pros and cons of using ChatGPT in the tourism industry. Data obtained from interviews with professionals and consumers in the tourism industry have revealed that ChatGPT should not be evaluated solely from one aspect. Although using ChatGPT in the tourism industry offers significant advantages such as personalized holiday and travel recommendations, instant language translation, and the ability to provide 24/7 customer support, significantly enhancing the user experience, providing cultural information, increasing customer satisfaction by assisting in travel planning, etc., it also leads to potential disadvantages such as real-time and limitations in current data, inaccuracies in some cases and lack of a human touch to ensure the processing of sensitive information, ethical and security concerns, etc. As a result, the findings were compared and discussed with the results of the studies in the literature.

This research focuses on data privacy and security in ChatGPT systems, which have gained popularity in various industries. It aims to identify potential risks and propose effective strategies to ensure data privacy and security, fostering user trust. The chapter explores privacy-preserving techniques like differential privacy, federated learning (FL), secure multi-party computation, and homomorphic encryption to mitigate risks. Compliance with data protection regulations, for example, CCPA and GDPR, is essential for ensuring data privacy. Implementing a secure infrastructure with encryption, data access controls, and regular security audits strengthens the overall security posture. User awareness and consent are also crucial, with transparent data collection and usage policies, informed consent, and opt-out mechanisms. A well-structured incident response plan, communication strategies, and learning from security breaches enhance system resilience. The chapter presents case studies and best practices for secure ChatGPT systems, drawing insights from past privacy failures.

Artificial intelligence (AI) and technology's possibilities and influence on marketing are crucial and well-known. ChatGPT is a new AI-powered technology that has caused a worldwide boom since its release, with substantial ramifications for all business practises. While acknowledging the growing body of work on ChatGPT, this study attempts to contribute to the ongoing debate by identifying the numerous prospects for employing ChatGPT as an enabler in marketing research and practise. It also highlights the difficulties associated with employing ChatGPT in marketing research. The chapter also discusses the potential for incorporating ChatGPT into other disciplines of marketing, including consumer behaviour, advertising, branding, and sales, as well as the practical consequences for managers. Finally, the chapter recognises the need for more study to better understand the scope of ChatGPT and offers a future research strategy. The chapter concludes by emphasising the significance of incorporating ChatGPT into marketing research and practises with human interaction.

In today's world, the presence of artificial intelligence applications is observable in various aspects of life. One of the artificial intelligence-based applications, ChatGPT, has been employed in many fields. Scientific research has delved into the potential applications of ChatGPT in different domains. In the realm of tourism education, research studies focusing on ChatGPT are increasingly emerging. This study investigates the impact of case studies created through ChatGPT on tourism students, in addition to the theoretical knowledge provided in tourism education. Interviews were conducted with 32 tourism students, and the detailed results are presented.

The study sought to examine the task-technology fit of ChatGPT for healthcare services. The research model was based on an integration of the task-technology fit (TTF) model and the technology acceptance model 2 (TAM2). The study used a quantitative research design. Data were collected from 265 health workers who have used ChatGPT in the performance of their work. Data analysis was done using structural equation modelling. Six of the seven hypotheses were accepted. The results show significant positive relationships between task characteristics and task-technology fit, task-technology fit and ChatGPT usage, ChatGPT usage and performance impacts, social influence and perceived usefulness, perceived usefulness and usage intention, as well as usage intention and ChatGPT usage. There was an insignificant positive relationship between task-technology fit and performance impacts.

Artificial intelligence (AI) is essential in all aspects of life. One crucial area to examine is the integration of artificial intelligence in education. The true essence is in providing individuals with the necessary knowledge, skills, and values needed to have a fulfilling and meaningful life. Education must adapt to equip students with essential abilities to navigate life's challenges while upholding integrity in a dynamic world. Artificial intelligence (AI), shown by technologies such as ChatGPT, exhibits significant promise in educational environments. This chapter explores personalized learning enabled by artificial intelligence (AI). Furthermore, intelligent tutoring systems are also analyzed. The text delves into various facets of the educational system where ChatGPT might offer help. Additionally, offering explanations for the prohibition of Chat GPT in many countries and educational institutions. The discussion has focused on how AI affects the socio-economic gap in the education sector.

Preface

OVERVIEW

In the contemporary environment of technological advancement, where artificial intelligence continually reshapes industries, the service sector stands as a domain ripe for transformation. The advent of OpenAI models, particularly ChatGPT, has revolutionized how businesses engage with their customers. *Revolutionizing the Service Industry with OpenAI Models* comprehensively explores this paradigm shift, delving into various facets of how ChatGPT is reshaping service delivery across diverse sectors.

This book, *Revolutionizing the Service Industry with OpenAI Models*, explores the transformative potential of OpenAI models within various service industry sectors. By examining these models' theoretical foundations, practical applications, and real-world implications, this book aims to provide insights, strategies, and guidance for businesses and professionals seeking to leverage AI to enhance their services, improve customer experiences, and drive innovation. The importance of understanding and harnessing the capabilities of OpenAI models in the service industry cannot be overstated. As consumer preferences evolve and competition intensifies, businesses face increasing pressure to deliver personalized, efficient, high-quality services. OpenAI models offer a unique opportunity to meet these demands by automating tasks, analyzing vast amounts of data, and generating valuable real-time insights. By embracing AI-driven solutions, organizations can gain a competitive edge, unlock new revenue streams, and create lasting value for their customers and stakeholders.

This book covers various topics related to applying OpenAI models in the service industry. From customer service and marketing to logistics and supply chain management, each chapter explores specific use cases, challenges, and opportunities for integrating AI into different aspects of service delivery. Additionally, this book addresses ethical considerations, regulatory frameworks, and best practices for responsible AI implementation, ensuring readers can navigate the complex landscape of AI-powered services with confidence and integrity. At a theoretical level, adopting OpenAI models in the service industry has profound implications for our understanding of human-computer interaction, decision-making processes, and organizational dynamics. By analyzing AI's underlying algorithms, architectures, and principles, researchers can gain valuable insights into how machines learn, adapt, and perform tasks traditionally reserved for human intelligence. Moreover, integrating AI into service workflows challenges conventional notions of work, expertise, and value creation, prompting scholars to rethink existing paradigms and explore new conceptual frameworks for studying the intersection of technology and service delivery.

On a practical level, implementing OpenAI models in the service industry has far-reaching implications for businesses, employees, and consumers. AI-driven solutions offer businesses opportunities to streamline operations, reduce costs, and enhance productivity across various functions, from customer support and sales to data analysis and predictive maintenance. However, the successful deployment of AI also requires careful planning, investment in talent, and ongoing monitoring to mitigate risks and ensure alignment with organizational goals. For employees, integrating AI into service workflows raises questions about job displacement, retraining, and the future of work in an increasingly automated world. By addressing these concerns proactively and fostering a culture of learning and adaptation, businesses can empower their workforce to embrace AI as a complement rather than a replacement for human expertise. Finally, for consumers, the widespread adoption of AI-powered services presents opportunities and challenges regarding convenience, personalization, and privacy. As AI becomes more prevalent in everyday interactions, consumers must remain vigilant about data security, algorithmic bias, and the ethical implications of AI-driven decision-making, advocating for transparency, accountability, and fairness in service delivery.

ORGANIZATION OF THE BOOK

The book is organized into ten chapters. A brief description of each of the chapters follows:

Chapter 1: Investigating the Service Quality of Chatbots on Telecom Service Providers' Websites and Apps

Chapter 1 embarks on a meticulous investigation into the service quality of chatbots deployed on telecom service providers' websites and apps. As organizations increasingly leverage AI-powered chatbots to enhance customer interactions, understanding the efficacy of these systems is paramount. Through empirical analysis and insightful discourse, this chapter sheds light on the nuances of chatbot performance and its implications for the telecom industry.

Chapter 2: Innovations with ChatGPT in the Tourism Industry: Current Challenges and Opportunities

In Chapter 2, the focus shifts to the tourism industry, where ChatGPT is heralding a new era of innovation. Integrating AI-driven chatbots presents challenges and opportunities for tourism that are inherently reliant on effective communication and personalized experiences. This chapter navigates through the current landscape, offering strategic insights into how stakeholders can harness the power of ChatGPT to redefine customer engagement in the tourism sector.

Chapter 3: Data Privacy and Security Safeguarding Customer Information in ChatGPT Systems

As the adoption of AI-driven conversational agents proliferates, Chapter 3 addresses a critical concern: data privacy and security. Safeguarding customer information in ChatGPT systems is not just a regulatory obligation but a moral imperative. This chapter unpacks the intricacies of data protection within AI frameworks, providing invaluable guidance for businesses striving to maintain trust and integrity in their operations.

Chapter 4: Artificial Intelligence Supported Travel Agencies: Analysis of ChatGPT Usage and Future Perspectives

Chapter 4 ventures into artificial intelligence-supported travel agencies, where the integration of ChatGPT is reshaping traditional paradigms. By analyzing the usage patterns and future trajectories of ChatGPT in this domain, this chapter offers a roadmap for travel agencies to navigate the evolving landscape and stay ahead of the curve in delivering personalized, seamless experiences to their clientele.

Chapter 5: Consumers' Drivers of Generative Pre-Trained Transformer (GPT) Conversational Bot Adoption: GPT Adoption

Consumer behavior lies at the heart of Chapter 5, which explores the drivers of generative pre-trained transformer (GPT) conversational bot adoption. Understanding what motivates users to embrace AI-powered chatbots is fundamental to optimizing their utility and effectiveness. Through empirical research and theoretical frameworks, this chapter elucidates the factors shaping consumer perceptions and adoption patterns, paving the way for enhanced user experiences.

Chapter 6: Exploring the Transformative Role of ChatGPT in Marketing: Opportunities, Challenges, and Future Directions

Chapter 6 delves into the transformative role of ChatGPT in marketing, elucidating a myriad of opportunities, challenges, and future directions. As businesses increasingly rely on AI-driven chatbots to drive customer engagement and brand loyalty, navigating the intersection of technology and marketing becomes imperative. This chapter offers strategic insights for leveraging ChatGPT to unlock new avenues of growth and innovation in marketing strategies.

Chapter 7: Case Studies and ChatGPT: Enhancing Tourism Education

The integration of ChatGPT in education is the focal point of Chapter 7, where case studies showcase its potential to enhance tourism education. From simulating real-world scenarios to facilitating interactive learning experiences, ChatGPT emerges as a versatile tool for educators and learners. Through a series of illuminating case studies, this chapter underscores the transformative impact of AI in shaping the future of education.

Chapter 8: Examining the Task: Technology Fit of ChatGPT for Health Care Services

In Chapter 8, the spotlight shifts to the healthcare sector, where the task-technology fit of ChatGPT is examined in detail. As healthcare providers strive to optimize patient care and streamline administrative processes, the role of AI-driven chatbots becomes increasingly pivotal. This chapter evaluates the efficacy of ChatGPT in addressing the unique challenges of healthcare service delivery, offering valuable insights for practitioners and policymakers alike.

Chapter 9: Successful Footprints of ChatGPT Deployments in the Education Sector: Pros Outweigh Cons by Embracing Ethics and Etiquette

Chapter 9 focuses on the successful deployments of ChatGPT in the education sector, where the pros outweigh the cons through a conscientious embrace of ethics and etiquette. As educators grapple with the complexities of integrating AI into pedagogical practices, maintaining ethical standards and fostering respectful interactions are paramount. This chapter elucidates best practices and ethical considerations for harnessing ChatGPT's potential to drive positive educational outcomes.

Chapter 10: Building Trust and Credibility: Ethical Use of AI in the Service Industry

Chapter 10 endeavors to clarify the ethical obligations associated with the implementation of AI technologies in the service sector. By exploring various ethical aspects such as transparency, fairness, privacy, and accountability, this research presents a thorough framework for building trust and credibility in AI-powered service solutions. The chapter provides practical advice for stakeholders aiming to address the ethical challenges of AI integration.

"Revolutionizing the Service Industry with OpenAI Models" is a seminal work that navigates the evolving landscape of AI-driven service delivery with scholarly rigor and practical wisdom. From telecom to tourism, healthcare to education, the transformative impact of ChatGPT reverberates across sectors, promising to redefine customer engagement and organizational efficiency. As we embark on this journey of exploration and innovation, may this book serve as a guiding beacon, illuminating pathways to a future where human ingenuity and artificial intelligence converge to create unparalleled value for society.

Mahmut Demir
Isparta University of Applied Sciences, Turkey

Ali Dalgıç
Isparta University of Applied Sciences, Turkey

Chapter 1
Investigating the Service Quality of Chatbots on Telecom Service Providers' Websites and Apps

Eli Fianu
https://orcid.org/0000-0003-2308-6831
Ghana Communication Technology University, Ghana

Ernest Kwame Affum
https://orcid.org/0000-0001-6724-6580
University of Mines and Technology, Ghana

Fred Amankwah-Sarfo
https://orcid.org/0000-0001-7872-4082
Ghana Communication Technology University, Ghana

William Leslie Brown-Acquaye
https://orcid.org/0000-0001-9679-5976
Ghana Communication Technology University, Ghana

ABSTRACT

The study sought to investigate the service quality of chatbots on telecom service providers' websites and apps. The research model was based on an integration of the expectation confirmation model of IS, the E-S-Qual model, and the technology anxiety construct. The study used a quantitative research design. Data were collected from 263 chatbot users; however, after data cleaning, 255 responses were retained. Data analysis was done using structural equation modelling. The results show significant

DOI: 10.4018/979-8-3693-1239-1.ch001

relationships between confirmation and perceived usefulness, as well as confirmation and satisfaction. Additionally, efficiency and privacy constructs of the E-S-Qual model have significant effects on satisfaction. Post-use confirmation, efficiency, and privacy have the most significant impacts on chatbot usage satisfaction of customers on telecom service providers' websites and apps. Technology anxiety could not significantly mediate the relationship between the E-S-Qual model constructs and post-use confirmation.

INTRODUCTION

Advancements in artificial intelligence (AI) have created significant interest in chatbot (Chhabria, 2022). A chatbot can be described as software that interacts with people using AI (Albayrak et al., 2018). The Chatbot has emerged as an effective tool to address the user queries in an automated, most appropriate and accurate way (Kumar et al., 2022). Technologies that connect customers with a company are characterized by their ability to serve the personalized needs of customers (Venkatesan, 2017; Heavin and Power, 2018). Moreover, these chatbots to interact with humans through text or voice messages Alan (Ramaditiya et al., 2021), answer customers' questions Alan (Kohli et al., 2018), and stimulate interactions with humans (Banu & Patil, 2020). a recent surge in interest in human-chatbot relationships in academia, industry, and public sectors (Aoki, 2020; Barnett et al., 2021). Chatbots have gained popularity in various fields (Akhtar and Neidhardt, 2019; Liu, Li and Xiang, 2022). They help to automate customer service, reduce response time, and provide personalized recommendations (Bhardwaz & Kumar, 2023).

Prior research has investigated how various communication aspects of AI chatbots, including empathy, assertiveness, and customizing content, affect how believable and trustworthy users find them. For example, a study by Lee & Chan (2023) established credibility in AI Chatbots importance of customization, communication competency and user satisfaction. Also, in education studies have been conducted on use of AI chatbots in the context of self-directed learning (Esiyok et al., 2024). This study found that individuals' comfort with technology (ICT self-efficacy) only predicts how easy they find chatbots use. Further, Joshi (2024) studied the role of AI-powered chatbots in project stakeholder engagement as critical aspect of successful project management. The study identified that chatbots enhance communication by offering stakeholders immediate, personalized responses, thereby reducing response times, and improve the efficiency of information exchange.

Jin and Youn (2023) examined the associations among AI-powered chatbots' anthropomorphism (human-likeness, animacy, and intelligence), social presence, imagery processing, psychological ownership, and continuance intention in the context of Human-AI-Interaction. Their results from a path analysis using LISREL 8.54 showed that consumers' perceived human-likeness of AI-powered chatbots is a positive predictor of social presence and imagery processing. The empirical findings entail practical implications for AI-powered chatbot developers and managerial implications for commercial brands such that (1) increasing anthropomorphism of chatbots and inducing the sense of being co-present with the chatbots are important factors AI-chatbot designers and developers need to consider and (2) inducing vivid visualization of the products endorsed by the chatbots is an important feature to understand.

Kumar et al. (2022) on providing customer and public administration-based services using chatbots. Their paper categorized chatbot services into customer and public administration-based services to understand the possibility of improvement and implementation. They discovered the chatbot as a customer assistant ordering food, making appointments, booking flights, and is becoming a part of day-to-day life. The authors averred that public administration services-based chatbots are helpful in resolving the queries of citizens and assist them in availing the needful government services without the involvement of administrative staff. They further stated that with the advancement of AI technology and language processing techniques, possibility it is possible to develop a more accurate, multi-lingual, efficient, and auto-learning chatbot to provide customer and public administration services.

Ganesa, Sanjana and Mane (2020) studied the behavioural intention of telecom customers to use AI-Chatbots using UTAUT2 model with the trust construct. Their study showed that chatbots contribute significantly in terms of entertainment in e-commerce (see Shawar & Atwell, 2007), relationship management (see Saad & Abida, 2016), obtaining assertive information on what customers want (see Veiga et al., 2017), value creation of customers (see Riikkinen et al., 2018) and as a tool to collaborate with customers (see Bolton et al., 2018).

In the telecom industry, customer satisfaction and loyalty is an important process (Adl & Elfergany, 2020). Customer service chatbots are an automatic question-and-answer system based on knowledge management and natural language processing (Liu et al., 2022). This study aims to understand customer interactions with chatbots on telecom service providers' websites and apps from the perspective of the E-S-Qual and expectation-confirmation models.

In line with the E-S-Qual model proposed by Parasuraman et al. (2005), the key dimensions of e-service quality include efficiency, reliability, fulfillment, privacy, responsiveness, compensation, and contact. Prior empirical studies have found that higher perceptions of e-service quality positively influence intentions to use online payment methods and e-commerce platforms (Salma et al., 2024). The rigorous development of ES-QUAL resulted in its widespread adoption in academic literature (Saibaba, 2024). This survey was developed and evaluated based on four primary constructs: efficiency, system availability, fulfillment, and privacy. However, a fifth dimension of empathy can be added to assess website's ability to understand and respond to user needs and emotions in a supportive and personalized manner. This dimension is relevant for chatbot interactions in telecommunication context.

BACKGROUND

The telecommunications industry is rapidly evolving, driven by advancements in technology and an ever-increasing demand for seamless customer service (Dixit, 2022; Stocker & Knieps, 2021). In this dynamic landscape, chatbots are emerging as a promising tool for telecom service providers (TSPs) to enhance customer interactions and improve operational efficiency (Misargopoulos et al., 2022). Chatbots offer 24/7 availability, immediate responses, and the potential for personalized interactions, making them a valuable asset for customer service and self-service solutions (Stoilova, 2021; Jenneboer et al., 2022). However, while chatbots hold immense potential, their effectiveness hinges on their ability to provide a positive and user-centric experience (Ramos et al., 2024; Wang et al., 2022). Early adopters of chatbots in various industries have encountered challenges related to user acceptance, limited capabilities, and lack of personalization (Alsharhan et al., 2023). To ensure successful implementation and maximize the benefits of chatbots, a deeper understanding of user interactions and preferences is crucial.

Moreover, the telecommunications industry has witnessed a paradigm shift with a growing emphasis on digital transformation and customer-centric approaches (Sheth et al., 2023; Al et al., 2022; Mahmoud & Ismail, 2020). As part of this evolution, chatbots have emerged as powerful tools for facilitating customer interactions on service providers' websites (Kumar et al., 2022; Gizelis et al., 2023). In the rapidly evolving landscape of telecommunications, the integration of artificial intelligence, particularly chatbots, has become increasingly prevalent on service providers' websites (Paliwal et al., 2020). Chatbots play a pivotal role in enhancing customer interactions, offering real-time assistance, and streamlining user experiences (Engineering et al., 2021; Aishwarya Gupta et al., 2020). Understanding how customers engage with these chatbots is essential for optimizing their effectiveness in delivering seamless and personalized user experiences (Adam & Adam, 2021; Patel & Trivedi, 2020). Therefore, this research paper aims to provide a comprehensive user-centric analysis of customer interactions with chatbots on telecom service providers' websites, exploring the factors influencing user satisfaction, challenges faced, and opportunities for improvement.

MAIN FOCUS OF THE CHAPTER

The purpose of the research is threefold. First, this study attempts to identify quality dimensions of chatbot services perceived by users (i.e., efficiency, service availability, and privacy), which have rarely been yet to be examined in the context based on IS literature. Second, drawing on the extended post-acceptance model of IS continuance (i.e., the extended expectation-confirmation model), we examine how these quality dimensions of chatbot services influence user confirmation and satisfaction, leading to use continuance intention. Third, we will examine how technology anxiety moderates the relationships between chatbot quality dimensions and post-use confirmation to find out whether technology anxiety may lead to a stronger or weaker relationship, which can inform us whether users consider chatbot services as human-like agents or technology-enabled services. This research would contribute to the body of knowledge on human-computer interactions with AI-driven services and the IS continuance model in the context of chatbot services of telecom service providers. Practically, the results of this study can provide quality assurance specialists, e-service providers, and chatbot developers with guidelines to better understand chatbot users in enhancing their service adoption in the telecom sector.

Theoretical Foundation

The Expectation-Confirmation Model of Information Systems

The Expectation-Confirmation Model (ECM) is a framework for assessing the continuance use of information systems (Lai et al., 2016). In information systems and technologies, ECM is considered one of the notable theories that explain users' post-adoption behavior (Park, 2020a). Bhattacherjee (2001) initially developed the ECM by integrating expectation–confirmation theory (ECT) (Oliver, 1980) and TAM (Davis, 1989). ECM was developed and employed to explain how users continually update their expectations upon gaining new information about their own experiences and others' (Bhattacherjee, 2001). The model suggests three primary factors determining an individual's continued usage of an information system (IS): satisfaction with the IS, confirmation of their initial expectations, and post-adoption perceptions of usefulness (Persada et al., 2021).

ECM is a proven success model to explain users' intention to continue using IS both in the marketing and information technology (IT) literature (Ashfaq et al., 2019; Gupta et al., 2020; Park, 2020b; Joo et al., 2017). ECM has been applied by many scholars to understand users' repurchase intention in several fields, ranging from IT usage (Bhattacherjee, 2001) to mobile application use (Tam, Santos, & Oliveira, 2018), and most recently, mobile advertising (Lu, Wu, & Hsiao, 2019). A recent meta-analysis conducted by Ambalov (2018) based on 51 ECM studies shows that ECM is appropriate to study users' satisfaction and continuance intention (CI). The Expectation-Confirmation Model (ECM) has found widespread application across various fields, including IT usage (Bhattacherjee, 2001), the use of mobile application (Tam et al., 2020), and mobile advertising (Lu et al., 2019). Ashfaq et al. (2020) proposed an analytical framework by combining the expectation-confirmation model (ECM), information system success (ISS) model, TAM, and the need for interaction with a service employee (NFI-SE). Examining data gathered from real chatbot users, their analysis unveils a positive impact of information quality (IQ) and service quality (SQ) on consumer satisfaction. Furthermore, perceived enjoyment (PE), perceived usefulness (PU), and perceived ease of use (PEOU) emerge as significant predictors of continuance intention (CI). The need for human interaction moderates the influence of PEOU and PU on satisfaction.

The E-S-Qual Model

The E-S-Qual Model, developed by Parasuraman, Zeithaml, and Malhotra (2005) is a framework for evaluating the quality of e-commerce websites (Kang et al., 2016). It is based on the concept of service quality, which is the overall perception of how well a service meets the needs and expectations of customers. Parasuraman, Zeithaml, & Malhotra (2005) studied the dimensions of E-S-QUAL model and designed its scale. Jalilvand & Samiei (2012) investigated the impact of Electronic Word of Mouth (EWOM) on brand image and purchase intention. Ahmed et al. (2020) discovered ES-QUAL model's effectiveness on customer satisfaction. The concept of E-S- QUAL has attracted interest among e-commerce vendors to make accurate assessment of the quality provided to customers (Marimon et al., 2009). However, several authors have noted that there are few reports of practitioners having applied the model (Ingle & Connolly, 2006; Kim et al., 2006; (Boshoff, 2007). The E-S-Qual Model has been widely used by researchers and practitioners to assess the quality of e-commerce websites. It has been found to be a valid and reliable measure of e-commerce website quality, and it has been shown to be positively related to customer satisfaction, loyalty, and repurchase intention.

The dimensions of the E-S Qual model are efficiency, privacy, and system availability. Efficiency refers to the extent to which an information system enhances the productivity and performance of users in carrying out their tasks. In the context of the E-S Qual model, efficiency is a crucial dimension that assesses how well the system contributes to the effectiveness and timeliness of operations. A system is considered efficient if it helps users achieve their goals with minimal effort, time, and resources. This dimension focuses on the optimization of processes and workflows, emphasizing the system's ability to streamline tasks and improve overall operational efficiency.

Privacy is a dimension that addresses the protection and management of sensitive information within the information system. It evaluates the system's capability to safeguard user data, maintain confidentiality, and adhere to privacy regulations and policies. In the E-S Qual model, privacy is crucial for building trust among users and ensuring the secure handling of personal and confidential information. Systems that prioritize and effectively implement privacy measures contribute to user confidence and satisfaction, fostering a positive perception of the information system.

System availability is the dimension that assesses the reliability and accessibility of the information system. It evaluates the extent to which the system is consistently operational and accessible to users when needed. In the E-S Qual model, high system availability is essential for minimizing disruptions to user activities. A system with good availability ensures that users can access the required information and functionalities without encountering significant downtime or disruptions. Reliability and accessibility contribute to user satisfaction and the overall success of the information system.

Hypothesis Development

Perceived Usefulness

Perceived usefulness is the degree to which an individual believes that using a particular system will enhance their performance of a specific task. The expectation-confirmation model of IS proposes a positive relationship between perceived usefulness and user satisfaction. The relationship between perceived usefulness and chatbot user satisfaction has been a subject of interest in recent research. Nguyen et al. (2021) demonstrated that satisfaction, perceived usefulness, and trust are significant determinants of chatbot users' continuance intentions, shedding light on the role of trust in strengthening users' willingness to continue using chatbots (Nguyen et al., 2021). Additionally, Lubbe & Ngoma (2021) found that the perceived usefulness of chatbots influences customer experience, affecting user satisfaction (Lubbe & Ngoma, 2021). Chagas et al. (2023) also reported very good scores for chatbot usefulness, ease of use, and user satisfaction, indicating a positive relationship between perceived usefulness and user satisfaction. Ren et al. (2022) emphasized that satisfaction is a crucial usability characteristic used to identify how satisfied users are during the interaction with chatbots (Ren et al., 2022).

Based on the reviewed studies and the expectation-confirmation model of IS, the following hypotheses are proposed:

H1: on the perceived usefulness of ChatBot has a significant influence on customer satisfaction.

H2: The ChatBot's perceived usefulness significantly influences the continued usage of the telecom service providers' website or app.

Confirmation

Confirmation occurs when the perceived performance matches or exceeds the initial expectations. If the actual performance meets or surpasses the expectations, it leads to confirmation. The expectation-confirmation model of IS proposes a positive relationship between post-use confirmation (confirmation) and perceived usefulness. It further offers a positive relationship between post-use confirmation (confirmation) and user satisfaction.

The relationship between post-use confirmation, perceived usefulness, and user satisfaction in using chatbots has been a subject of interest in recent research. Studies have shown that post-use confirmation, perceived usefulness, and user satisfaction are interconnected in chatbot interactions. For instance, Park et al. (2022) proposed a serial mediation model, indicating that user emotional disclosure intention and perceived intimacy with a chatbot serially mediate the relationship between chatbot emotional disclosure and user satisfaction, suggesting that post-use confirmation, as reflected in emotional disclosure intention and perceived intimacy, plays a role in shaping user satisfaction with chatbot interactions. Moreover, Zhu et al. (2021) highlighted that user satisfaction is correlated with user experience, as it can be considered a post-experience evaluation, implying that the confirmation of the usefulness of chatbots during and after the interaction contributes to user satisfaction. Additionally, Hsiao & Chen (2021) found that satisfaction significantly directly affects users' intention, indicating the importance of post-use confirmation and satisfaction in influencing users' continuance intention to use chatbots.

Based on the reviewed studies and the expectation-confirmation model of IS, the following hypotheses are proposed:

H3: Post-use confirmation significantly influences on perceived usefulness of the ChatBot.

H4: Post-use confirmation has a significant influence on customer satisfaction.

Technology Anxiety

The relationship between technology anxiety, efficiency, and post-use confirmation in of chatbots is an area of interest. Lin et al., 2021). suggested that technology anxiety may have a positive moderating role in the relationships between chatbot service quality dimensions and users' post-use confirmation, indicating a potential mediating role of technology anxiety (Lin et al., 2021). Furthermore, Park et al. (2022) proposed a serial mediation model, indicating that user emotional disclosure intention and perceived intimacy with a chatbot serially mediate the relationship between chatbot emotional disclosure and user satisfaction, suggesting that technology anxiety may play a role in shaping user satisfaction with chatbot interactions (Park et al., 2022).

The chatbot service quality dimensions include efficiency, privacy, and system availability. The following hypotheses are thus proposed:

H5A: Technology anxiety will mediate the efficiency dimension of the ES model and post-use confirmation.

H5B: Technology anxiety will mediate the privacy dimension of the ES model and post-use confirmation.

H5C: Technology anxiety will mediate the system availability dimension of the ES-model and post-use confirmation.

Efficiency

The efficiency of company websites and customer satisfaction is supported by the E-S-Qual model. The E-S-Qual model supports the positive relationship between company website efficiency and customer satisfaction. Several studies have highlighted the positive impact of chatbots on customer satisfaction through improved efficiency. For instance, research has shown that chatbots can provide efficient alternative solutions compared with traditional customer service, reducing human chat agents and empowering the ability to respond to various customer needs (Sanny et al., 2020). Additionally, using chatbots has been associated with increased customer satisfaction, as they provide personalized experiences, convenience, reduced customer service times, increased information, and improved productivity (Lubbe & Ngoma, 2021). Efficiency in customer service is closely linked to customer satisfaction, and chatbots play a significant role in this relationship. Studies have indicated that chatbots can assist brands in managing customer relationships, allowing for more efficient use of customer time, and providing a better understanding of product performance (Sands et al., 2020). Moreover, the implementation of chatbots for handling customer inquiries has led to increased efficiency and customer satisfaction in various industries, such as logistics and industrial systems engineering (Hosameldeen et al., 2023).

Based on the reviewed studies and the E-S-Qual model, the following hypotheses are proposed:

H6A: The efficiency dimension of the ES model has a significant influence on customer satisfaction.

Privacy

The E-S-Qual model supports the positive relationship between privacy on company websites and customer satisfaction. The relationship between privacy and customer satisfaction in using chatbots has been extensively studied. Privacy concerns have been identified as a significant factor influencing customer satisfaction in chatbot interactions (Eren, 2021). While chatbots offer convenience and benefits, concerns about privacy regarding the product, technological infrastructure, and security structure may hinder customer satisfaction (Eren, 2021). Additionally, the assurance and reliability of chatbots positively impact customer satisfaction, indicating the importance of addressing privacy-related concerns to enhance customer satisfaction (Yun & Park, 2022). Furthermore, the perceived privacy risk has been found to have a direct and negative effect on customers' intention to use banking chatbots, highlighting the pivotal role of privacy in shaping customer attitudes and satisfaction (Alt et al., 2021). Additionally, trust in chatbots has been positively correlated with satisfaction, emphasizing the importance of privacy and security in fostering trust and ultimately enhancing customer satisfaction (Pesonen, 2021).

Based on the literature, and the E-S-Qual model, the following hypotheses are proposed:

H6B: The privacy dimension of the ES-Model significantly influences customer satisfaction.

System Availability

The model. The E-S-Qual model supports the positive relationship between system availability of company websites and customer satisfaction. Research has shown that the usability and responsiveness of chatbots significantly impact customer satisfaction (Chen et al., 2021). Additionally, the availability of chatbot services has been linked to technological satisfaction, with a significant and positive relationship between self-service technology experience and satisfaction in chatbot interactions (Lubbe & Ngoma, 2021). Moreover, the quality of the chatbot-customer relationship is associated with the performance levels of system quality and experience with chatbots, which can be improved to enhance customer satisfaction (Magno & Dossena, 2022). The assurance and reliability of chatbots have also been identified as factors that positively impact customer satisfaction, emphasizing the importance of system availability in fostering trust and satisfaction.

Based on the reviewed studies and the E-S-Qual model, the following hypotheses are proposed:

H6C: The system availability dimension of the ES model has a significant influence on customer satisfaction.

Satisfaction

The expectation-confirmation model of IS proposes a positive relationship between user satisfaction and usage continuance. Studies have consistently demonstrated a strong positive relationship between user satisfaction and the intention to continue using chatbots. For instance, (Bhattacherjee, 2001) found that users' continuance intention is determined by their satisfaction with information system (IS) use and the perceived usefulness of continued IS use (Bhattacherjee, 2001). Similarly, Zhu et al. (2022) emphasized the importance of user satisfaction in influencing continuance intention in the context of mental health chatbots during the COVID-19 pandemic (Zhu et al., 2022). Furthermore, Lee (2022) revealed that a consumer's parasocial relationship with an AI shopping chatbot ultimately increases continuance usage intentions through perceived communication quality and satisfaction (Lee, 2022).

Moreover, the impact of user satisfaction on continuance intention has been explored in various domains beyond chatbots. For instance, Hsu et al. (2015) highlighted the critical role of satisfaction as a factor related to behaviors such as continuance intention in the context of app usage (Hsu et al., 2015). Additionally, Deng et al. (2010) emphasized the positive relationship between user satisfaction and continual usage intention of information technology (IT) (Deng et al., 2010).

Based on the reviewed studies and the expectation-confirmation model of IS, the following hypotheses are proposed:

H7: Customer satisfaction has a significant influence on the continuance usage intention of the telecom service providers' websites or apps.

The Proposed Research Model

The proposed research model extends the expectation-confirmation model with the E-S-Qual model and the technology anxiety construct. The E-S-Qual model will capture the quality dimensions of the ChatBot. The model is shown in Figure 1.

Figure 1. Proposed research model

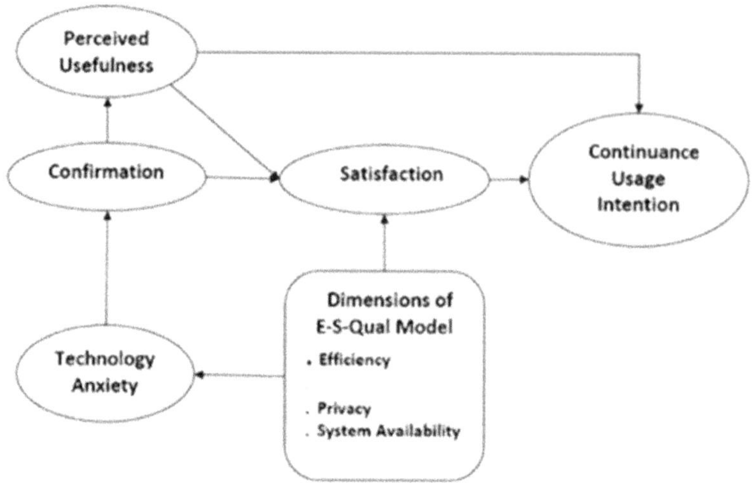

Methodology

Research Design

The study uses a quantitative research design. The quantitative research design is chosen because the researchers want to statistically test the influence of independent latent constructs on mediating latent constructs and dependent latent constructs via path analysis.

Population

The population for the study comprises customers of telecom service providers who have used ChatBots on the service providers' websites or apps.

Sampling

A purposive sampling method was used. Customers who had used chatbots on their telecom service providers' websites or apps were selected. The Cochran (1963) formula for calculating the sample size for an unknown population (large populations) was used. The formula is shown below:

$$n_0 = \frac{Z^2 pq}{e^2}$$

Where:

n_0 = sample size
Z = the Z score. A z-score describes the position of a raw score in terms of its distance from the mean when measured in standard deviation units.
p = the estimated proportion of an attribute present in the population. This is also known as the prevalence rate.
q = 1-p
e = margin of error

A 95% confidence interval is chosen; thus, the margin of error is 0.05. The Z-score at 95% is 1.96. Based on a pilot study, a value of 0.2 was chosen for p.

From equation (1) $n_0 = \frac{3.8416 * 0.2 * 0.6}{0.0025}$

n_0= 246

The minimum sample size is therefore 246.

Data Collection

The survey instrument was developed from the research model. The instrument had two main parts. The first part comprised questions on the demographic details of respondents. The second part comprised 5-point Likert scale questions based on the constructs in the model. Measurement items for the constructs were derived from Bhattacherjee (2001), Parasuraman (2005), and Lopez-Bonilla and Lopez Bonilla (2012). The instrument was constructed using Google Forms, and the link was shared with respondents who had used chatbots on their telecom service providers' websites or apps. Data were collected from two hundred and sixty-three (263) respondents.

Data Analysis and Results

Data analysis was done using Confirmatory Factor Analysis (CFA) and structural equation modelling (SEM) technique via JASP 0.18.1.0. SEM is appropriate for the non-parametric modeling of complex cause-effect relationships between latent variables (Hair et al., 2012). The two-step approach to PLS-SEM proposed by Chin (1998) is used. The measurement model (outer model) was initially assessed, followed by the assessment of the structural model (inner model). Data cleaning was done before PLS-SEM. The data was checked for missing values and outliers using SPSS v23; two hundred and fifty-five (255) responses were retained after data cleaning.

Table 1 shows the reliability and validity of the constructs. The reliability of a measurement model refers to its consistency and stability in measuring constructs. Looking at Cronbach's alpha and McDonald's Omega, which assess internal consistency, most constructs in the table demonstrate strong reliability. Constructs such as Perceived Usefulness, Confirmation, Satisfaction, Efficiency, Privacy, and Usage Intention exhibit excellent reliability, with Cronbach's alpha and McDonald's Omega values consistently above 0.8, indicating high internal consistency among the items measuring these constructs. Technology Anxiety and System Availability show slightly lower but still acceptable levels of reliability.

Moving on to the validity assessment using the Average Variance Extracted (AVE), this metric evaluates the amount of variance captured by the construct about the variance due to measurement error. Constructs with AVE values above 0.5 generally have adequate convergent validity. In this analysis, most constructs, including Perceived Usefulness, Confirmation, Satisfaction, Efficiency, Privacy, and Usage Intention, show satisfactory validity with AVE values well above 0.5, indicating that a substantial portion of the variance is explained by the constructs rather than measurement error.

Table 1. Construct validity and reliability

Construct	Cronbach's Alpha	McDonald's Omega	Average Variance Extracted (AVE)
Perceived Usefulness	0.942	0.943	0.807
Confirmation	0.896	0.903	0.75
Satisfaction	0.894	0.89	0.735
Technology Anxiety	0.873	0.802	0.573
Efficiency	0.916	0.917	0.693
System Availability	0.776	0.792	0.551
Privacy	0.845	0.85	0.652
Usage Intention	0.944	0.945	0.852

The measurement model was also assessed using the heterotrait-monotrait ratio of correlations ($HTMT^{0.90}$). The heterotrait-monotrait ratio of correlations ($HTMT^{0.90}$) measures discriminant validity. If the HTMT value is below 0.90, discriminant validity has been established between two constructs (Hair et al., 2014). Table 2 shows that all the constructs exhibit discriminant validity.

Table 2. Heterotrait-monotrait ratio of correlations (HTMT)

	Perceived Usefulness	Confirmation	Satisfaction	Technology Anxiety	Efficiency	System Availability	Privacy	Usage Intention
Perceived Usefulness	1							
Confirmation	0.687	1						
Satisfaction	0.568	0.828	1					
Technology Anxiety	0.115	0.043	0.062	1				
Efficiency	0.418	0.671	0.687	0.107	1			
System Availability	0.215	0.435	0.508	0.111	0.642	1		
Privacy	0.288	0.476	0.518	0	0.449	0.584	1	
Usage Intention	0.438	0.599	0.7	0.15	0.673	0.415	0.46	1

A bootstrapping procedure was used to assess the structural model to determine the significance of each estimated path. Bootstrapping is the process of drawing many re-samples with replacements from the original sample and then estimating the model parameters for each bootstrap re-sample. The results of the bootstrapping procedure are shown in Table 3.

Firstly, Hypothesis 1 proposed a path from Perceived Usefulness to User Satisfaction, with a path coefficient of 0.066 and a p-value of 0.204, indicating that this relationship was not supported by the data. Similarly, Hypothesis 2 suggested a link between Perceived Usefulness and Intention to Use, but the path coefficient of 0.005 and a high p-value of 0.938 indicated no supported relationship between these constructs. However, Hypothesis 3, which proposed a path from Post-use Confirmation to Perceived Usefulness with a strong path coefficient of 0.672 and a significant p-value of 0.000, was supported by the data. This pattern continued with Hypothesis 4, where Post-use Confirmation was connected to User Satisfaction with a path coefficient of 0.456 and a significant p-value of 0.000, supporting the relationship. Moving on to the indirect effects in Hypotheses 5a, 5b, and 5c, the paths

Table 3. Hypothesis testing results

Hypothesis	Hypothesized Path	Path Coefficient	P-Values	Result
H1	Perceived Usefulness -> Satisfaction	0.066	0.204	Rejected
H2	Perceived Usefulness -> Intention to Use	0.005	0.938	Rejected
H3	Confirmation -> Perceived Usefulness	0.672	0.000	Accepted
H4	Confirmation -> Satisfaction	0.456	0.000	Accepted
H5a	Efficiency -> Tech Anxiety -> Confirmation (Indirect Effect)	-0.086	0.50	Rejected
H5b	Privacy -> Tech Anxiety -> Confirmation (Indirect Effect)	0.004	0.48	Rejected
H5c	System Availability -> Tech Anxiety -> Confirmation (Indirect Effect)	0.063	0.652	Rejected
H6a	Efficiency -> Satisfaction	0.272	0.000	Accepted
H6b	Privacy -> Satisfaction	0.127	0.000	Accepted
H6c	System Availability -> Satisfaction	0.037	0.655	Rejected
H7	Satisfaction -> Intention to Use	0.841	0.000	Accepted
R^2 (Satisfaction) = 0.661 R^2 (Perceived Usefulness) = 0.805 R^2 (Confirmation) = 0.750 SRMR = 0.176				

from Efficiency, Privacy, and System Availability to Post-use Confirmation via Technology Anxiety did not show significant relationships, as evidenced by their path coefficients and p-values, indicating these indirect effects were not supported. In contrast, Hypotheses 6a and 6b showed supported relationships between Efficiency and Privacy, respectively, with User Satisfaction, while Hypothesis 6c did not find a significant link between System Availability and User Satisfaction. Finally, Hypothesis 7 found strong support for the relationship between User Satisfaction and Intention to Use, with a path coefficient of 0.841 and a significant p-value of 0.000. Overall, the analysis reveals mixed results, with some hypotheses supported by the data while others did not find empirical support based on the path coefficients and associated p-values.

Positive path coefficients, such as those found in the connections from Perceived Usefulness to User Satisfaction and Intention to Use, suggest a generally positive association, albeit quite weak in magnitude, indicating that higher perceived usefulness relates marginally to increased satisfaction and intention to use. Conversely, more substantial positive coefficients, like those observed from Post-use Confirmation to Perceived Usefulness and User Satisfaction, indicate strong relationships, implying that greater post-use confirmation significantly contributes to higher perceived usefulness and satisfaction.

In contrast, negative coefficients, as seen in the indirect effects of Efficiency and Technology Anxiety on Confirmation, imply a weak negative relationship, although this relationship lacks practical significance within the model. Similarly, small positive coefficients in indirect paths, like Privacy and System Availability through Technology Anxiety to Post-use Confirmation, suggest minimal, practically insignificant positive relationships in these contexts.

Regarding direct relationships, moderate positive coefficients, such as Efficiency and Privacy to User Satisfaction, indicate moderately strong associations, suggesting that higher efficiency and considerations for privacy moderately contribute to increased user satisfaction. However, smaller coefficients, like System Availability to User Satisfaction, imply a weak relationship, potentially lacking practical importance.

The model highlights robust positive relationships, notably between User Satisfaction and Intention to Use, indicating that higher user satisfaction strongly predicts increased intention to use.

The proposed model explained 64.8% of the variance in User Satisfaction, 44.2% of the variance in Perceived Usefulness, and 46.8% of the variance in Intention to Use. The R square values are shown in Table 3. The standardized root mean square residual (SRMR) was used to assess model fit. Hu & Bentler (1999) proposed that models that have SRMR values less than 0.08 have a good model fit. Table 3 shows SRMR value of 0.176 which implies the model does not have a good fit; however, lack of a good fit does not imply a bad model because of the model possesses good internal consistency, validity (convergent and discriminant), and reliability.

DISCUSSION

The results show significant relationships for confirmation and perceived usefulness, as well as confirmation and satisfaction. Additionally, efficiency and privacy constructs of the E-S-Qual model have significant effects on satisfaction. These findings are consistent with Zhu et al. (2022), Hsiao & Chen (2021), Sanny et al. (2020), Lubbe & Ngoma (2021), and Eren (2021). Post-use confirmation, efficiency, and privacy have the most significant impacts on chatbot usage satisfaction of customers on telecom service providers' websites and apps.

The expectation-confirmation model (Bhattacherjee, 2001) had no construct that predicted post-use confirmation. In the current study, items used to measure post-use confirmation comprised user experience with the chatbot, service level provided by the chatbot, and confirmation of expectations. One can conveniently conclude that user experience and quality of service are key determinants of post-use confirmation. Positive user experience and quality of service provided by the chatbot will positively impact post-use confirmation, and vice versa. Positive user experience and quality of service will thus lead to positive user satisfaction, and vice versa.

The positive and significant impacts of efficiency and privacy on user satisfaction is as expected. Measures of efficiency include ease of getting information, ease of navigation, ease of performing transactions, and simplicity. Measures of privacy include protection of browsing behaviour and protection of personal and financial data. These measures are therefore critical in determining the satisfaction of customers that use the chatbot(s). One would have expected a significant positive relationship between system availability and user satisfaction; however, that was not the case. System availability is one of the service quality constructs and its effect on user satisfaction may be overshadowed by other quality constructs (Al-Okaily et al., 2021). Similarly, the impact of perceived usefulness on user satisfaction and usage continuance may be masked by post-use confirmation and the quality constructs, thus its insignificant impact. Al-Maskari & Sanderson (2010) emphasized that user satisfaction is a subjective variable influenced by several factors such as system effectiveness, user effectiveness, user effort, and user characteristics and expectations, suggesting that the complexity of user satisfaction may diminish the direct effect of perceived usefulness.

While the direct effects of the E-S-Qual constructs on post-use confirmation were not measured, technology anxiety could not significantly mediate the relationship between the E-S-Qual model constructs and post-use confirmation. Technology anxiety expresses inertia to the use of technology. The following question may somewhat express the essence of the mediating role of technology anxiety in the research model: would a user who exhibits technology anxiety have positive post-use confirmation if the efficiency, privacy, and system availability of the system (chatbot) is positive? The results of the study show that the mediating role of technology anxiety could not be established.

The significant positive relationship between user satisfaction and usage continuance supports the expectation-confirmation model of IS and provides support for several studies on the use of chatbots, such as Zhu et al. (2022), Lee (2022), and Deng et al. (2010).

SOLUTIONS AND RECOMMENDATIONS

Post-use confirmation, efficiency, and privacy have the most significant impacts on chatbot usage satisfaction of customers on telecom service providers' websites and apps. User experience and quality of service are key determinants of post-use confirmation. Positive user experience and quality of service provided by the chatbot will positively impact post-use confirmation, and vice versa. Positive user experience and quality of service will thus lead to positive user satisfaction, and vice versa.

Telecom service providers must ensure the chatbots on their websites and apps have very good service quality and deliver excellent user experience. The key things to note while developing and deploying chatbots are as follows: ease of getting information, ease of navigation, ease of performing transactions, simplicity, protection of browsing behaviour and protection of personal and financial data.

Future research should investigate the direct effects of the E-S-Qual constructs on post-use confirmation.

FUTURE RESEARCH DIRECTIONS

Similar research can be conducted in other sectors such as finance, insurance, and e-commerce.

REFERENCES

Adl, A., & Elfergany, A. K. (2020). Tracking How a Change in a Telecom Service Affects Its Customers Using Sentiment Analysis and Personality Insight. *International Journal of Service Science, Management, Engineering, and Technology, 11*(3), 33–46. doi:10.4018/IJSSMET.2020070103

Ahmed, R. R., Romeika, G., Kauliene, R., Streimikis, J., & Dapkus, R. (2020). ES-QUAL model and customer satisfaction in online banking: Evidence from multivariate analysis techniques. *Oeconomia Copernicana, 11*(1), 59–93. doi:10.24136/oc.2020.003

Akhtar, M., & Neidhardt, J. (2019). The Potential of Chatbots : Analysis of Chatbot Conversations. *2019 IEEE 21st Conference on Business Informatics (CBI), 1*, 397–404. 10.1109/CBI.2019.00052

Al-Maskari, A., & Sanderson, M. (2010). A review of factors influencing user satisfaction in information retrieval. *Journal of the American Society for Information Science and Technology, 61*(5), 859–868. doi:10.1002/asi.21300

Al-Okaily, A., Al-Okaily, M., Ai Ping, T., Al-Mawali, H., & Zaidan, H. (2021). An empirical investigation of enterprise system user satisfaction antecedents in Jordanian commercial banks. *Cogent Business & Management, 8*(1), 1918847. Advance online publication. doi:10.1080/23311975.2021.1918847

Albayrak, N., Özdemir, A., & Zeydan, E. (2018). An Overview of Artificial Intelligence Based Chatbots and An Example Chatbot Application. *2018 26th Signal Processing and Communications Applications Conference (SIU)*, 1–4.

Alt, M.-A., Vizeli, I., & Săplăcan, Z. (2021). Banking with a Chatbot – A Study on Technology Acceptance. *Studia Universitatis Babes-Bolyai Oeconomica*, *66*(1), 13–35. doi:10.2478/subboec-2021-0002

Aoki, N. (2020). An experimental study of public trust in AI chatbots in the public sector. *Government Information Quarterly*, *37*(4), 101490. doi:10.1016/j.giq.2020.101490

Ashfaq, M., Yun, J., Waheed, A., Khan, M. S., & Farrukh, M. (2019). *Customers' Expectation, Satisfaction, and Repurchase Intention of Used Products Online: Empirical Evidence From China*. doi:10.1177/2158244019846212

Ashfaq, M., Yun, J., Yu, S., & Maria, S. (2020). I, Chatbot : Modeling the Determinants of Users ' Satisfaction and Continuance Intention of AI-Powered Service Agents. *Telematics and Informatics*, *101473*, 101473. Advance online publication. doi:10.1016/j.tele.2020.101473

Banu, S., & Patil, S. D. (2020). An intelligent web app chatbot. *Proceedings of the International Conference on Smart Technologies in Computing, Electrical and Electronics, ICSTCEE 2020*, 309–315. 10.1109/ICSTCEE49637.2020.9276948

Barnett, A., Savic, M., Pienaar, K., Carter, A., Warren, N., Sandral, E., Manning, V., & Lubman, D. I. (2021). International Journal of Drug Policy Enacting ' more-than-human ' care : Clients ' and counsellors ' views on the multiple affordances of chatbots in alcohol and other drug counselling. *The International Journal on Drug Policy*, *94*, 102910. doi:10.1016/j.drugpo.2020.102910 PMID:33059955

Ben Saad, S., & Abida, F. C. (2016). Social Interactivity and Its Impact on a User ' s Approach Behavior in Commercial Web Sites : A Study Case of Virtual Agent Presence. *Journal of Marketing Management*, *4*(2), 63–80. doi:10.15640/jmm.v4n2a6

Bhardwaz, S., & Kumar, J. (2023). An Extensive Comparative Analysis of Chatbot Technologies - ChatGPT, Google BARD and Microsoft Bing. *2023 2nd International Conference on Applied Artificial Intelligence and Computing (ICAAIC)*, 673–679. 10.1109/ICAAIC56838.2023.10140214

Bhattacherjee, A. (2001). Understanding information systems continuance: An expectation-confirmation model. *Management Information Systems Quarterly*, *25*(3), 351–370. doi:10.2307/3250921

Bolton, R. N., McColl-Kennedy, J. R., Cheung, L., Gallan, A., Orsingher, C., Witell, L., & Zaki, M. (2018). Customer experience challenges: bringing together digital, physical and social realms. In Journal of Service Management (Vol. 29, Issue 5). doi:10.1108/JOSM-04-2018-0113

Boshoff, C. (2007). A psychometric assessment of e-s-qual : A scale to measure electronic service quality. *Journal of Electronic Commerce Research, 8*(1), 101–114.

Chen, J.-S., Le, T.-T.-Y., & Florence, D. (2021). Usability and responsiveness of artificial intelligence chatbot on online customer experience in e-retailing. *International Journal of Retail & Distribution Management, 49*(11), 1512–1531. doi:10.1108/IJRDM-08-2020-0312

Chhabria, K. (2022). Evolving Journey of Chatbots : Insights into Business Decisions. *2022 International Interdisciplinary Humanitarian Conference for Sustainability (IIHC)*, 102–107. 10.1109/IIHC55949.2022.10060780

Chin, W. W. (1998). The partial least squares approach to structural equation modeling. *Modern Methods for Business Research, 295*(2), 295–336.

Cochran, W. G. (1963). *Sampling Techniques* (2nd ed.). John Wiley & Sons.

Cordero, J., Barba-Guaman, L., & Guamán, F. (2022). *Use of chatbots for customer service in MSMEs*. Applied Computing and Informatics., doi:10.1108/ACI-06-2022-0148

Davis, F. D. (1989). Perceived usefulness, perceived ease of use, and user acceptance of information technology. *Management Information Systems Quarterly, 13*(3), 319–340. doi:10.2307/249008

Deng, L., Turner, D. E., Gehling, R., & Prince, B. (2010). User experience, satisfaction, and continual usage intention of IT. *European Journal of Information Systems, 19*(1), 60–75. doi:10.1057/ejis.2009.50

Eren, B. A. (2021). Determinants of customer satisfaction in chatbot use: Evidence from a banking application in Turkey. *International Journal of Bank Marketing, 39*(2), 294–311. doi:10.1108/IJBM-02-2020-0056

Ganesa, P., Sanjana, J., & Mane, A. S. (2020). Behavioural Intention of AI-Chatbots by Telecom Customers – UTAUT2 Perspective with Trust. *04th International Conference on Marketing. Technology in Society, 2020*, 1–2.

Gupta, A., Yousaf, A., & Mishra, A. (2020). How pre-adoption expectancies shape post-adoption continuance intentions: An extended expectation-confirmation model. *International Journal of Information Management*, *52*, 102094. doi:10.1016/j.ijinfomgt.2020.102094

Hair, J. F., Black, W. C., Babin, B. J., & Anderson, R. E. (2014). *Multivariate data analysis* (7th ed.). Pearson Education International.

Hair, J. F., Sarstedt, M., Pieper, T. M., & Ringle, C. M. (2012). The Use of Partial Least Squares Structural Equation Modeling in Strategic Management Research : A Review of Past Practices and Recommendations for Future Applications. *Long Range Planning*, *45*(5–6), 320–340. doi:10.1016/j.lrp.2012.09.008

Heavin, C., & Power, D. J. (2018). Challenges for digital transformation – towards a conceptual decision support guide for managers. *Journal of Decision Systems*, *0125*(sup1), 1–8. doi:10.1080/12460125.2018.1468697

HosameldeenO.AbousamraN. K.Al-AqrabiH.EmbarakO.DurraniU. (2023). *Improving the Accuracy of Customer Service Seq2Seq Chatbots Through Dataset Pruning*. doi:10.20944/preprints202303.0070.v1

Hsiao, K.-L., & Chen, C.-C. (2022). What drives continuance intention to use a food-ordering chatbot? An examination of trust and satisfaction. *Library Hi Tech*, *40*(4), 929–946. doi:10.1108/LHT-08-2021-0274

Hsu, J. S.-C., Lin, T.-C., Fu, T.-W., & Hung, Y.-W. (2015). The effect of unexpected features on app users' continuance intention. *Electronic Commerce Research and Applications*, *14*(6), 418–430. doi:10.1016/j.elerap.2015.06.003

Hu, L., & Bentler, P. M. (1999). Cutoff criteria for fit indexes in covariance structure analysis: Conventional criteria versus new alternatives. *Structural Equation Modeling*, *6*(1), 1–55. doi:10.1080/10705519909540118

Ingle, S., & Connolly, R. (2006). Methodological and Research Issues Using ES-QUAL to Measure Online Service Quality in Irish SMEs. *Irish Journal of Management*, *27*(2).

Jalilvand, M. R., & Samiei, N. (2012). The effect of electronic word of mouth on brand image and purchase intention An empirical study in the automobile. *Marketing Intelligence & Planning*, *30*(4), 460–476. doi:10.1108/02634501211231946

Jin, S. V., & Youn, S. (2023). Social Presence and Imagery Processing as Predictors of Chatbot Continuance Intention in Human-AI-Interaction Social Presence and Imagery Processing as Predictors of Chatbot Continuance. *International Journal of Human-Computer Interaction*, *39*(9), 1874–1886. doi:10.1080/10447318.2022.2129277

Joo, Y. J., Park, S., & Shin, E. K. (2017). Students' expectation, satisfaction, and continuance intention to use digital textbooks. *Computers in Human Behavior*, *69*, 83–90. doi:10.1016/j.chb.2016.12.025

Kang, D., Jang, W., & Park, Y. (2016). Evaluation of e-commerce websites using fuzzy hierarchical TOPSIS based on ES-QUAL. *Applied Soft Computing*, *42*, 53–65. doi:10.1016/j.asoc.2016.01.017

Kim, M., Kim, J., & Lennon, S. J. (2006). Online service attributes available on apparel retail web sites : An E-S-QUAL approach. *Managing Service Quality*, *16*(1), 51–77. doi:10.1108/09604520610639964

Kohli, B., Choudhury, T., Sharma, S., & Kumar, P. (2018). A Platform for Human-Chatbot Interaction Using Python. *2018 Second International Conference on Green Computing and Internet of Things (ICGCIoT)*, 439–444. 10.1109/ICGCIoT.2018.8753031

Kumar, K., Nikhil, N., Singh, K., & Shivshanker, V. (2022). A survey on providing customer and public administration based services using AI : chatbot. In *Multimedia Tools and Applications*. Springer US. doi:10.1007/s11042-021-11458-y

Lai, H., Chen, C., & Chang, Y. (2016). Expectation-Confirmation Model of Information System Continuance : A Meta-Analysis. *World Academy of Science. Engineering and Technology International Journal of Educational and Pedagogical Sciences*, *10*(7), 2325–2330.

Lee, M., & Park, J. (2022). Do parasocial relationships and the quality of communication with AI shopping chatbots determine middle-aged women consumers' continuance usage intentions? *Journal of Consumer Behaviour*, *21*(4), 842–854. doi:10.1002/cb.2043

Li, L., Lee, K. Y., Emokpae, E., & Yang, S.-B. (2021). What makes you continuously use chatbot services? Evidence from chinese online travel agencies. *Electronic Markets*, *31*(3), 575–599. doi:10.1007/s12525-020-00454-z PMID:35603227

Liu, Y., Li, X., & Xiang, Z. (2022). The Effect of Chatbot-customer Interaction on Consumer Brand Advocacy: Exploring the Role of Chatbots. *ICEIEC 2022 - Proceedings of 2022 IEEE 12th International Conference on Electronics Information and Emergency Communication*, 185–190. 10.1109/ICEIEC54567.2022.9835050

Lu, C.-C., Wu, L., & Hsiao, W.-H. (2019). Developing customer product loyalty through mobile advertising: Affective and cognitive perspectives. *International Journal of Information Management*, *47*, 101–111. doi:10.1016/j.ijinfomgt.2018.12.020

Lubbe, I., & Ngoma, N. (2021). Useful chatbot experience provides technological satisfaction: An emerging market perspective. *South African Journal of Information Management*, *23*(1). Advance online publication. doi:10.4102/sajim.v23i1.1299

Magno, F., & Dossena, G. (2023). The effects of chatbots' attributes on customer relationships with brands: PLS-SEM and importance–performance map analysis. *The TQM Journal*, *35*(5), 1156–1169. doi:10.1108/TQM-02-2022-0080

Marimon, F., Vidgen, R., Barnes, S., & Cristobal, E. (2009). Purchasing behaviour in an online supermarket The applicability of E-S-QUAL. *International Journal of Market Research*, *1*(January), 111–129.

Murtarelli, G., Collina, C., & Romenti, S. (2023). "Hi! How can I help you today?": Investigating the quality of chatbots–millennials relationship within the fashion industry. *The TQM Journal*, *35*(3), 719–733. doi:10.1108/TQM-01-2022-0010

Nguyen, D. M., Chiu, Y.-T. H., & Le, H. D. (2021). Determinants of Continuance Intention towards Banks' Chatbot Services in Vietnam: A Necessity for Sustainable Development. *Sustainability (Basel)*, *13*(14), 7625. doi:10.3390/su13147625

Oliver, R. L. (1980). A cognitive model of the antecedents and consequences of satisfaction decisions. *JMR, Journal of Marketing Research*, *17*(4), 460–469. doi:10.1177/002224378001700405

Parasuraman, A., Zeithaml, V. A., & Malhotra, A. (2005). ES-QUAL: A multiple-item scale for assessing electronic service quality. *Journal of Service Research*, *7*(3), 213–233. doi:10.1177/1094670504271156

Park, E. (2020a). Telematics and Informatics User acceptance of smart wearable devices: An expectation-confirmation model approach. *Telematics and Informatics*, *47*. doi:10.1016/j.tele.2019.101318

Park, E. (2020b). User acceptance of smart wearable devices: An expectation-confirmation model approach. *Telematics and Informatics*, *47*, 101318. doi:10.1016/j.tele.2019.101318

Park, G., Chung, J., & Lee, S. (2023). Effect of AI chatbot emotional disclosure on user satisfaction and reuse intention for mental health counseling: A serial mediation model. *Current Psychology (New Brunswick, N.J.)*, *42*(32), 28663–28673. doi:10.1007/s12144-022-03932-z PMID:36406852

Persada, S. F., Miraja, B. A., Nadlifatin, R., Belgiawan, P. F., Redi, A. A. N. P., & Lin, S. (2021). Determinants of Students ' Intention to Continue Using Online Private Tutoring : An Expectation - Confirmation Model. *Technology. Knowledge and Learning*. Advance online publication. doi:10.1007/s10758-021-09548-9

Pesonen, J. A. (2021). 'Are You OK?' Students' Trust in a Chatbot Providing Support Opportunities. doi:10.1007/978-3-030-77943-6_13

Ramaditiya, A., Rahmatia, S., Munawar, A., & Samijayani, O. N. (2021). Implementation chatbot whatsapp using python programming for broadcast and reply message automatically. *Proceeding - 2021 International Symposium on Electronics and Smart Devices: Intelligent Systems for Present and Future Challenges, ISESD 2021*, 1–4. 10.1109/ISESD53023.2021.9501523

Riikkinen, M., Saarijärvi, H., & Sarlin, P. (2018). *Using artificial intelligence to create value in insurance in insurance*. doi:10.1108/IJBM-01-2017-0015

Sands, S., Ferraro, C., Campbell, C., & Tsao, H.-Y. (2021). Managing the human–chatbot divide: How service scripts influence service experience. *Journal of Service Management*, *32*(2), 246–264. doi:10.1108/JOSM-06-2019-0203

Sanny, L., Susastra, A. C., Roberts, C., & Yusramdaleni, R. (2020). The analysis of customer satisfaction factors which influence chatbot acceptance in Indonesia. *Management Science Letters*, 1225–1232. doi:10.5267/j.msl.2019.11.036

Shawar, B. A., & Atwell, E. (2007). Different measurements metrics to evaluate a chatbot system. *Bridging the Gap: Academic and Industrial Research in Dialog Technologies Workshop Proceedings,* 89–96.

Tam, C., Santos, D., & Oliveira, T. (2020). Exploring the influential factors of continuance intention to use mobile Apps: Extending the expectation confirmation model. *Information Systems Frontiers*, *22*(1), 243–257. doi:10.1007/s10796-018-9864-5

Veiga, C., Santos, M. C., Águas, P., & Santos, J. A. C. (2017). Are millennials transforming global tourism? Challenges for destinations and companies. *Worldwide Hospitality and Tourism Themes*, *9*(6), 603–616. doi:10.1108/WHATT-09-2017-0047

Venkatesan, R. (2017). Executing on a customer engagement strategy. *Journal of the Academy of Marketing Science*, *45*(3), 289–293. doi:10.1007/s11747-016-0513-6

Wang, C., Harris, J., & Patterson, P. (2013). The Roles of Habit, Self-Efficacy, and Satisfaction in Driving Continued Use of Self-Service Technologies. *Journal of Service Research*, *16*(3), 400–414. doi:10.1177/1094670512473200

Yun, J., & Park, J. (2022). The Effects of Chatbot Service Recovery With Emotion Words on Customer Satisfaction, Repurchase Intention, and Positive Word-Of-Mouth. *Frontiers in Psychology*, *13*, 922503. Advance online publication. doi:10.3389/fpsyg.2022.922503 PMID:35712132

Zhu, Y., Janssen, M., Wang, R., & Liu, Y. (2022). It Is Me, Chatbot: Working to Address the COVID-19 Outbreak-Related Mental Health Issues in China. User Experience, Satisfaction, and Influencing Factors. *International Journal of Human-Computer Interaction*, *38*(12), 1182–1194. doi:10.1080/10447318.2021.1988236

Zhu, Y., Wang, R., & Pu, C. (2022). "I am chatbot, your virtual mental health adviser." What drives citizens' satisfaction and continuance intention toward mental health chatbots during the COVID-19 pandemic? An empirical study in China. *Digital Health*, *8*. doi:10.1177/20552076221090031 PMID:35381977

ADDITIONAL READING

Abdulquadri, A., Mogaji, E., Kieu, T. A., & Nguyen, N. P. (2020). Digital transformation in financial services provision: A Nigerian perspective to the adoption of chatbot. *Journal of Enterprising Communities: People and Places in the Global Economy*, *15*(2), 258–281. doi:10.1108/JEC-06-2020-0126

Chintkuntlawar, A. A., Shahare, R. S., & Pathan, A. H. (2020). Artificial Intelligence Chatbot Messenger. *International Journal of Research in Engineering. Science and Management*, *3*(3), 3–6.

Toupin, S., & Laval, U. (2024). Civil Society Chatbots: A Plurality of Conceptual Approaches. *International Journal of Communication*, *18*, 947–966.

KEY TERMS AND DEFINITIONS

Artificial Intelligence (AI): The simulation of human intelligence in machines that are programmed to think and learn like humans (Dwivedi et al., 2019; Fjelland,

2020; Gkinko, 2022; Kasneci et al., 2023). It involves the development of algorithms and computational models that enable computers to perform tasks that typically require human intelligence, such as problem-solving, pattern recognition, speech recognition, decision-making, and language understanding (Chan, 2023; Sarker et al., 2021).

Chatbot: Computer program designed to simulate conversation with human users through text or voice interaction (Adamopoulou & Moussiades, 2020; Følstad et al., 2021)

Confirmatory Factor Analysis (CFA): A statistical technique used in research to test whether a pre-defined model of latent variables and observed variables fits the collected data (Marsh et al., 2020). It helps confirm if the relationships expected between different groups of variables actually exist.

Customer Service Chatbots: Specific type of chatbot designed to interact with customers through text or voice, providing automated support and assistance (Sheehan et al., 2020; Nicolescu & Tudorache, 2022). They are becoming increasingly popular tools for businesses to improve customer service efficiency, availability, and personalization.

Dialogue Management: A component of spoken dialogue systems and chatbots, responsible for guiding the conversation and determining the system's responses (Carfora et al., 2020). It essentially acts as the brain behind the conversation, controlling the flow, understanding the user's intent, and generating appropriate responses (Reimann et al., 2023).

E-S-Qual Model: Evaluates the service quality of chatbots based on efficiency, fulfillment, system availability, and privacy (potentially including empathy).

Empathy: The ability of the chatbot to understand and respond to user emotions in a supportive manner.

Ethical Considerations: Bias, transparency, and responsible use of chatbots in the telecommunication industry.

Machine Learning (ML): A field in computer science that focuses on developing algorithms that can learn and improve from data without being explicitly programmed (Mahesh, 2020 ; Bertolini et al., 2021). The aim is to create intelligent machines that can learn from experience and make predictions or decisions.

Natural Language Processing (NLP): Enables chatbots to understand and respond to user queries in natural language (Chowdhary & Chowdhary, 2020; Khurana et al., 2023).

Service Quality Constructs: Fundamental building blocks used to assess and understand the perceived quality of a service(Nunkoo et al., 2020; Lin et al., 2021) . They represent specific aspects of the service experience that customers evaluate when forming their overall impression. By identifying and measuring these constructs, organizations can gain valuable insights into how they can improve their service offerings and deliver greater satisfaction to their customers.

User Experience (UX): A broad term that encompasses all aspects of a user's interaction with a product, service, or system (Luther & Tiberius, 2020). It focuses on how users feel while interacting with the chatbot, aiming for a smooth and satisfying experience (Alomari et al., 2020).

User Interface (UI): The visual and interactive elements that users directly engage with when using a digital product or service (Alomari et al., 2020). It's essentially the "look and feel" that enables users to control, navigate, and interact with the system. Defines the way users interact with the chatbot, including text, voice, or graphical interfaces.

Chapter 2
Innovations With ChatGPT in the Tourism Industry:
Current Challenges and Opportunities

Şirvan Şen Demir
Süleyman Demirel University, Turkey

ABSTRACT

This study explains the pros and cons of using ChatGPT in the tourism industry. Data obtained from interviews with professionals and consumers in the tourism industry have revealed that ChatGPT should not be evaluated solely from one aspect. Although using ChatGPT in the tourism industry offers significant advantages such as personalized holiday and travel recommendations, instant language translation, and the ability to provide 24/7 customer support, significantly enhancing the user experience, providing cultural information, increasing customer satisfaction by assisting in travel planning, etc., it also leads to potential disadvantages such as real-time and limitations in current data, inaccuracies in some cases and lack of a human touch to ensure the processing of sensitive information, ethical and security concerns, etc. As a result, the findings were compared and discussed with the results of the studies in the literature.

DOI: 10.4018/979-8-3693-1239-1.ch002

INTRODUCTION

With the OpenAI research laboratory established in 2015 (Brockman et al., 2016), developments in artificial intelligence technology have accelerated, and many machine-learning products, including DALL-E and ChatGPT, have been made available to the public (Devlin et al.,2018). ChatGPT, a chatbot application based on Open AI's work on language processing technology, is a product of the GPT model series. It is formed from the expression word chat, which refers to the chat robot function, and the abbreviations of the GPT (Generative Pre-Trained Transformer) (Open AI, 2023; Sohail et al., 2023).

Open AI introduced the first GPT series with GPT-1 in 2018 to develop a language model that can be trained on large amounts of text data and used effectively in natural language processing tasks (OpenAI, 2023). In 2019, it developed GPT-2, which is very successful in text generation, classification, and other natural language processing tasks (Radford, 2019). This model laid the foundations of ChatGPT. The model is trained on large amounts of text data, allowing users to answer text-based questions and create a conversational model that can interact with people in natural language. The next version of ChatGPT is GPT-3, a larger model trained with more data than GPT-2. ChatGPT can better understand, produce text, and perform a wide range of natural language processing tasks in this model. Large language models like ChatGPT are complex AI systems trained on large data sets and continually improved. This highly advanced chatbot can handle various text-based requests, from answering simple questions to performing highly complex tasks (Liu et al., 2021).

ChatGPT, a large language model, can be trained on large data sets such as books, web pages, articles, text documents, chat records, and similar content, producing responses that are almost in line with natural human language (Lund & Wang, 2023). ChatGPT is used in many academic and scientific fields for many different purposes, from writing literature, creating content, and computer coding to getting medical diagnosis advice (Sohail et al., 2023). This study investigates how ChatGPT can be used in the tourism industry. In the following sections of the study, the opportunities created by ChatGPT and the risks and concerns it poses are discussed.

BACKGROUND

Artificial Intelligence in the Tourism Industry

The tourism industry is inherently an information-rich valley, with large amounts of data and interaction with internal and external stakeholders. This wealth becomes more effective daily with the developing technology and innovations in the digital age. Artificial intelligence (AI) technologies, one of the most prominent examples of this, have been applied to various aspects of the tourism industry, including management, customer service, marketing, and personalization, and the integration of these technologies into the goods and services has received significant attention in recent years (Demir & Demir, 2023a). So, as a conversational AI model, ChatGPT has excellent potential to improve customer interactions, deliver personalized recommendations (Gursoy et al., 2023; Kumar et al., 2023), and automate routine tasks. Integrating ChatGPT, a powerful natural language processing model (OpenAI, 2023), into the tourism industry has opened new ways to improve consumer experiences, streamline operations, and provide valuable information. The integration of artificial intelligence, especially conversational AI, has significantly transformed various sectors of the global economy, including the tourism industry.

AI has emerged as a transformative force in the tourism industry. It has been pivotal in product development, enriching the traveler's experience, optimizing operational efficiency, and overcoming emerging challenges (Demir & Demir, 2023b). While tour operators and travel agencies are using AI to predict consumer behavior (like flight and hotel cancellations), many businesses, such as booking platforms like Airbnb (ABNB 6.18%), are also using ChatGPT to provide better, more personalized recommendations to travelers (Bowman, 2023). Unsurprisingly, ChatGPT has developed a new service perspective in artificial intelligence and changed how people access information (Dalgıç, 2023; Dwivedi et al., 2023). Such AI assistants can now be used through social media sites such as Facebook Messenger, Skype, and WhatsApp, as well as an application in their own right.

PROS OF USING CHATGPT IN THE TOURISM INDUSTRY

ChatGPT can provide tourism businesses with great ease with its ability to provide 24-hour customer support through websites and messaging platforms. This availability can increase the satisfaction (Mondal et al., 2023) and loyalty of internal and external stakeholders (Vorobeva et al., 2023) and tourists by ensuring they can answer their questions and get help whenever they want. ChatGPT operates 24/7, providing users access to support whenever they want, regardless of time zone or travel schedule, eliminating the frustration of waiting for a human representative (Demir & Demir, 2023; Gursoy et al., 2023). So much so that ChatGPT can effectively answer general and simple questions without human intervention, such as directions, opening hours, or available information about attractions. In case of emergencies or urgent problems, ChatGPT can provide instant guidance, such as contacting local authorities, providing medical assistance information or crisis management instructions, and ensuring the safety and well-being of tourists. Moreover, it can do this by having the ability to communicate in multiple languages (Dwivedi et al., 2023; Gursoy et al., 2023).

ChatGPT's multi-language support feature offers tourism businesses the ability to overcome language barriers, provide excellent customer service, and enter new markets. This can lead to increased bookings, customer satisfaction, and overall growth in the tourism industry. The opportunity that ChatGPT provides users to interact with chatbots or virtual assistants in their preferred language (Dwivedi et al., 2023; Gursoy et al., 2023) also makes significant contributions to establishing communication with businesses and other people (Demir & Demir, 2023a). This support creates the opportunity to go beyond language translation, strengthening communication by providing information about local customs, traditions, and cultural nuances to help tourists understand and respect the local culture (Ali, 2023; Demir & Demir, 2023b).

By analyzing consumer preferences and past interactions, ChatGPT can improve individuals' travel experience and increase cross-selling opportunities by providing personalized recommendations for travel (e.g., destination options), accommodation (e.g., hotel options), events (e.g., festivals, sports, arts, etc.), and dining options. This can encourage travelers to spend more on their trips, leading to increased income, and can also help them find affordable options that fit their financial constraints. Personalized recommendations can lead to more diverse and memorable travel experiences by introducing travelers to lesser-known, niche, or off-the-beaten-track attractions and activities that align with their interests (Bowman, 2023; Gursoy et al., 2023). ChatGPT significantly increases customer satisfaction, higher revenues, and loyalty (Vorobeva et al., 2023) by providing personalized recommendations. Moreover, tourism businesses can leverage data and insights to enhance their offerings and marketing strategies.

ChatGPT's information retrieval feature (Al Shboul et al., 2023; Shin & Kang, 2023) offers significant opportunities in the tourism industry by providing travelers with quick and accurate access to information. This feature empowers tourists to easily access essential details about their destination, such as local attractions, restaurants, transportation options, and cultural knowledge (Demir & Demir, 2023b). It saves travelers time and effort and ensures they have up-to-date information, which is vital for making informed decisions during their trip (Ali, 2023; Gursoy et al., 2023). Whether they seek real-time updates on events or require assistance in customizing their itineraries to match their preferences, information retrieval enhances the overall travel experience by putting valuable knowledge at their fingertips. Moreover, travelers can benefit from language assistance, translations, and communication support, fostering inclusivity and facilitating seamless interactions with locals (Dwivedi et al., 2023; Qureshi et al., 2023). Information retrieval can offer interactive maps, navigation services, and even virtual tours, enabling travelers to explore and navigate their destinations efficiently. For tourism businesses, the data gathered on travelers' preferences and information requests can be invaluable, leading to improved customer service, targeted marketing, and data-driven decisions that enhance the industry's competitiveness and sustainability (Ivanov & Soliman, 2023; Pricope Vancia et al., 2023). ChatGPT's information retrieval feature (Demir & Demir, 2023a) not only enriches the travel experience for tourists but also offers tourism businesses opportunities to provide better services and gather essential insights.

ChatGPT's data analytics feature offers valuable opportunities in the tourism industry by providing a robust platform for collecting, processing, and deriving insights from the vast amount of data generated in the sector (Demir & Demir, 2023a; Shin & Kang, 2023). Tourism businesses can harness this feature to enhance various aspects of their operations. For instance, they can better understand consumer preferences, travel patterns, and market trends. By analyzing data on the types of destinations, accommodations, and activities that attract travelers, businesses can tailor their offerings to meet these demands better, ultimately leading to increased customer satisfaction and loyalty (Ali et al., 2023; Vorobeva et al., 2023). Furthermore, data analytics enables tourism businesses to optimize pricing strategies, promotional efforts, and resource allocation (Demir et al., 2022). By identifying peak travel seasons, popular tourist routes, and emerging markets, tourism businesses can make informed decisions regarding pricing adjustments, marketing campaigns, and where to invest in infrastructure development. This data-driven approach helps maximize revenue and fosters sustainable tourism practices by reducing the environmental impact of over-tourism and better managing resources (Demir et al., 2022; Yaşar et al., 2023). ChatGPT's data analytics feature allows tourism businesses to make informed, strategic decisions that drive growth, improve consumer experiences, and contribute to the industry's long-term sustainability (Carvalho & Ivanov, 2023; Pricope Vancia et al., 2023).

ChatGPT's streamlining operations (Guo et al., 2023; Huseynov, 2023) feature presents valuable opportunities in the tourism industry by optimizing and automating various aspects of tourism businesses' operations. This automation can significantly enhance efficiency, reduce operational costs (Egbemhenghe et al., 2023), and improve service delivery. For example, in the booking and reservation process, automation can simplify and expedite the procedures, making it easier for consumers to plan and book their trips. This not only results in a seamless and convenient experience for travelers but also allows tourism businesses to handle a higher volume of reservations, increasing revenue potential (Demir et al., 2021). Automation can improve inventory management for accommodations, tour operators, and transportation services. It can help businesses keep track of availability, allocate resources efficiently, and avoid overbooking or underutilizing assets. As a result, tourism businesses can enhance customer satisfaction, reduce the workload on their staff, and allocate human resources to more complex and value-added tasks (Guo et al., 2023; Huseynov, 2023). ChatGPT's streamlining operations feature allows tourism businesses to operate more efficiently, increase their capacity to serve customers, and provide a more streamlined and responsive service, ultimately improving profitability and customer satisfaction (Mondal et al., 2023).

ChatGPT's human-AI collaboration (Fui-Hoon Nah et al., 2023) feature can significantly enhance the tourism industry by providing a powerful tool for travelers and service providers. Travelers can benefit from personalized recommendations and information through natural language interactions with AI, making trip planning more efficient and enjoyable (Demir & Demir, 2023a). They can ask about destinations, accommodations, and local attractions and receive real-time translations or navigation assistance. The AI can generate custom itineraries, considering individual preferences and constraints, such as budget, travel dates, and dietary restrictions (Dwivedi et al., 2023). This not only simplifies the planning process but also helps tourists discover hidden gems and experiences they might have otherwise missed. For service providers in the tourism industry, ChatGPT's human-AI collaboration feature can be used to streamline customer support and engagement (Zhou et al., 2023). Travel agencies, hotels, and airlines can employ AI to handle routine inquiries, freeing up human agents to focus on more complex or specialized tasks. This results in cost savings (Egbemhenghe et al., 2023) and improved service quality. Overall, the human-AI collaboration feature empowers the tourism industry to provide more personalized, efficient, and accessible services, ultimately enhancing the overall travel experience for tourists and businesses.

ChatGPT's content generation (Demir & Demir, 2023b; Fui-Hoon Nah et al., 2023) feature holds excellent potential for the tourism industry by revolutionizing how travel-related content is created and distributed. This technology can generate high-quality, informative, and engaging content at scale, enabling travel agencies, websites, and platforms to develop vast tourist resources (Demir et al., 2021). For instance, ChatGPT can automatically generate travel guides, blog posts, and social media content, saving time and effort that would otherwise be spent on manual content creation (Demir & Günaydın, 2023). This results in more comprehensive and up-to-date travel information for tourists, helping them make informed trip decisions. This fosters inclusivity and opens up new opportunities for the tourism industry to tap into international markets and attract a broader range of tourists (Dogru et al., 2023). ChatGPT's content generation feature is a game-changer for the tourism industry, allowing businesses to create and distribute compelling travel content efficiently and effectively, ultimately enhancing the traveler's experience.

ChatGPT's integration with emerging technologies offers exciting prospects for the tourism industry (Demir & Demir, 2023a). One prominent opportunity lies in incorporating augmented reality (AR) and virtual reality (VR) into the traveler's experience (Chaturvedi et al., 2023; Ivanov & Soliman, 2023). ChatGPT can provide real-time information, guidance, and narration as tourists explore destinations through AR or VR applications. For example, tourists wearing AR glasses can receive historical facts, local insights, and navigation assistance in their field of view, enhancing their understanding of the place they're visiting. This immersive and informative experience adds a new dimension to travel, making it more engaging and educational. ChatGPT's integration with the Internet of Things (IoT) enables innovative tourism solutions. Hotels, airports, and tourist attractions can implement IoT devices to collect and transmit data, which ChatGPT can analyze and provide real-time insights to travelers. For instance, a tourist could inquire about the least crowded time to visit a famous museum, and ChatGPT could access IoT data to provide a personalized recommendation. This integration enhances the tourist experience by optimizing travel schedules, reducing waiting times, and ensuring a smoother and more enjoyable trip (Chaturvedi et al., 2023; Ivanov & Soliman, 2023).

ChatGPT's cost savings feature presents many opportunities (Egbemhenghe et al., 2023) for the tourism industry, primarily by streamlining operations and enhancing efficiency. Customer support and service are significant areas where cost savings can be realized. ChatGPT can handle many consumer inquiries and requests, providing prompt and accurate responses 24/7 (Fusté-Forné & Orea-Giner, 2023; Paul et al., 2023). This reduces the need for a large customer support team, resulting in significant labor cost savings (Burger et al., 2023) for travel agencies, hotels, airlines, and other tourism-related businesses. AI can handle routine tasks such as booking confirmations, reservation modifications, and answering frequently asked questions, leaving human agents to focus on more complex and specialized customer interactions (Mich & Garigliano, 2023). Another cost-saving opportunity lies in personalized marketing and recommendations (Egbemhenghe et al., 2023). ChatGPT can analyze customer data to offer tailored travel suggestions and promotions (Ivanov & Soliman, 2023). This targeted approach enhances the consumer experience and optimizes marketing budgets by ensuring that advertisements and promotions reach the most receptive audience (De Bock et al., 2023). Tourism businesses can allocate their resources more efficiently, achieving a higher return on investment.

ChatGPT's feedback collection (Elmohandes & Marghany, 2024) feature can significantly enhance the tourism industry by revolutionizing how businesses gather and utilize consumer insights by seamlessly integrating feedback collection (Jusman et al., 2023). Within their digital platforms and chatbot interactions, tourism businesses can engage with travelers during their journeys, ensuring their experiences are well-documented and issues are addressed promptly. This real-time feedback mechanism allows companies to gauge customer satisfaction (Mondal et al., 2023) and pinpoint areas for improvement, ultimately leading to more responsive and consumer-centric services. The collected feedback can be processed and analyzed by ChatGPT to identify trends and patterns (Jusman et al., 2023). For instance, AI can recognize common concerns, emerging preferences, or suggestions, allowing tourism businesses to adapt their offerings and strategies to align with consumer expectations. This helps businesses stay competitive (Ausat et al., 2023) and agile in a dynamic industry and fosters customer loyalty and positive word-of-mouth marketing.

CONS OF USING CHATGPT IN THE TOURISM INDUSTRY

While ChatGPT brings numerous benefits and opportunities to the tourism industry, it is essential to acknowledge the potential drawbacks and concerns associated with its use (Demir & Demir, 2023a; Dwivedi et al., 2023; Gursoy et al., 2023). Integrating AI-driven chatbots and content-generation tools in the tourism industry can transform the traveler's experience, making it more personalized and efficient. However, it raises concerns about data privacy and security (Mehrolia et al., 2023), as travelers may share personal information and preferences when interacting with these AI systems. Ensuring this data is protected and used responsibly is paramount, as any data breaches or misuse could erode trust and deter tourists from using AI-driven services (Hassani & Silva, 2023). The ethical and privacy concerns underline the importance of robust data protection measures, transparency in AI usage (Alawida et al., 2023; Huseynov, 2023), and ongoing vigilance to ensure that ChatGPT and similar technologies uphold the highest ethical standards in the tourism industry.

In the tourism industry, inaccuracies in the information provided by ChatGPT (Kim et al., 2023) can pose significant challenges. For instance, ChatGPT may sometimes rely on outdated data (Sudirjo et al., 2023) or miss recent developments, potentially leading travelers to choose destinations, accommodations, or activities incorrectly (Demir & Demir, 2023a). In addition, ChatGPT's responses are generated based on patterns in text data, and it may inadvertently provide misleading information due to the inherent limitations of its data. Therefore, while ChatGPT can offer valuable insights (George & George, 2023; Korzynski et al., 2023), managers, professionals, employees, travelers, and stakeholders need to verify information from reliable sources and exercise caution when making tourism services decisions based solely on its responses (Demir & Demir, 2023a).

Addressing bias in ChatGPT's responses is an ongoing challenge, and it requires careful consideration and continuous improvement in the model's developing and filtering processes (Dwivedi et al., 2023). ChatGPT's responses are generated based on a wide range of internet text data, and this data may contain biases present in the sources it was developed (Fusté-Forné & Orea-Giner, 2023; Paul et al., 2023). This means that the information provided by ChatGPT can sometimes reflect stereotypes, cultural biases, or prejudices in the data. For example, it may inadvertently promote specific destinations, cultures, or types of travel over others, reinforcing pre-existing biases and influencing travelers' decisions in ways that may not align with their preferences and values (Demir & Demir, 2023a). This can result in an unfair representation of various regions and communities, potentially hindering diversity and inclusivity within the tourism industry.

ChatGPT's limited tourism industry knowledge (Alawida et al., 2023; Skavronskaya et al., 2023) is a noteworthy constraint. The model's current data extends approximately one and a half years, meaning it may need more information about recent developments, new destinations, travel restrictions, and emerging trends in the tourism industry. To overcome this, businesses and end-users should complement ChatGPT's responses (Paul et al., 2023) with real-time information from reputable sources and consult tourism experts or official websites for the most current and reliable details about their desired tourism services. This limitation underscores the importance of using ChatGPT (Frąckiewicz, 2023; Jarrahi et al., 2023) as a supplementary tool in tourism services and activities rather than as the sole source of guidance (Demir & Demir, 2023b).

The reduced human touch of ChatGPT in the tourism industry is a double-edged sword (Elmohandes & Marghany, 2024). While ChatGPT can provide instant responses (Fusté-Forné & Orea-Giner, 2023) and recommendations, they need the genuine human touch (Akter et al., 2023; Frąckiewicz, 2023) that tourism professionals and travelers often seek when planning their tourism activities and services. Tourism businesses with emotional intelligence can offer personalized advice, empathy, and a deeper understanding of individual preferences, helping users make decisions that align with their needs and desires (Demir & Demir, 2023a). The absence of human interaction (Chaturvedi et al., 2023; Iskender, 2023; Muñoz & Chen, 2023) can be particularly noticeable when dealing with complex holiday itineraries, intricate cultural considerations, or sensitive travel issues, where human expertise, experience, and emotional intelligence can play a crucial role in providing a well-rounded and personalized travel and holiday experience.

METHODOLOGY

Research Design

This study employs a qualitative approach to explore the challenges and opportunities associated with integrating ChatGPT in the tourism industry. Qualitative research is well-suited for gaining in-depth insights into complex, multifaceted phenomena, such as using artificial intelligence in the tourism industry. Engaging with qualitative methods, it is aimed to uncover the diverse perspectives, experiences, and perceptions of various stakeholders within the industry. Qualitative research offers the opportunity to understand and explain events and phenomena more deeply. Researchers can gain a more detailed understanding by closely examining participants' experiences, feelings, thoughts, and perspectives. An ideal method for addressing complex issues and contexts, qualitative research can help develop new theories and test existing ideas by allowing participants to express their own experiences and perspectives. For these reasons, the qualitative research method was used in this study.

Sample And Data Collection

In qualitative research methods, sample selection and data collection processes may differ depending on the research question, objectives, and design. Since this research focuses on ChatGPT's tourism industry, managers of tourism businesses that use artificial intelligence were included when determining the sample. In other words, the purposeful sampling technique was adopted because ChatGPT is a current issue, the population is unknown, the research involves a specific situation, and the desire to focus directly on a particular topic (Demir & Demir, 2023a). The primary condition for participants to be included in this sample is that they know ChatGPT. Data was collected by conducting in-depth online interviews with participants using semi-structured questionnaires. During the data collection process, participants were allowed to share their opinions in addition to the two main research questions. Each meeting lasted approximately 30 minutes via the Zoom application.

Data Analysis

This study used thematic analysis, a qualitative research method that systematically examines text data. Thematic analysis is used to identify patterns, themes, and meanings found in texts. This method helps the researcher understand and interpret data authentically. In thematic analysis, codes are created and classified as similar or related. After categorizing the codes, themes or main patterns are identified. Afterward, the themes that are determined are interpreted according to the research questions and purposes.

Demographic Information of Participants

Participants consist of managers of accommodation, travel, food, and beverage businesses operating in the tourism industry and consumers who benefit from these services. All participants have used any artificial intelligence application, and approximately 75% have experienced ChatGPT. While the average age of participants in managerial positions is 39, the average age in consumer positions is 24. 80% of the participants are university graduates.

RESULTS

The research has two main questions for tourism professionals and consumers in the tourism industry. First, what are the positive outcomes of ChatGPT as an artificial intelligence application in the tourism industry? Secondly, what are the negative consequences of ChatGPT as an artificial intelligence application in the tourism industry? The same questions were asked of consumers, who were asked to evaluate from the consumer's perspective.

Pros of ChatGPT for Businesses and Consumers in the Tourism Industry

While the participants, who were professional tourism managers, evaluated the positive results of ChatGPT within the framework of the sectors in which their businesses operate, consumers expressed a general opinion regarding the tourism services they experienced. The positive effects of ChatGPT reflect the issues expressed by participants that it offers transformative potential for the tourism industry by improving consumer experiences (P1), offering automated marketing solutions (P5), improving data analysis (P6), and increasing scalability (P11). P4 and P9 argue that tourism businesses should continue to invest in AI technologies to maximize the benefits of ChatGPT.

The use of ChatGPT in the tourism industry is evaluated differently by participants. For example, P2 explained that ChatGPT *"could be useful for tourism businesses that do not have social media staff to analyze social media posts."* On the other hand, P7 emphasizes that tourism-related businesses need to define their individual goals better to unlock the potential benefits of ChatGPT. It is possible to summarize the opinions of some other participants on this subject as follows: ChatGPT has the potential to reduce the management and marketing costs of businesses in the tourism industry (P12). At the same time, dealing with many issues can reduce the customer service department's workload and allow them to focus on more complex tasks that require human involvement (P9). As a result, ChatGPT can automate other tasks and provide service anytime (P6). P14 supports this with a statement, *"Customers have the perception that they are valued, and being able to receive support without waiting helps them feel appreciated"* (P16).

ChatGPT can be an essential tool in tourism businesses' data collection and analysis process. ChatGPT can also produce customer communication materials such as SMS texts, emails, social media messages, etc. (P3). On this issue, the views of travel agency managers were more descriptive than those of other tourism business managers. For example, P15 supported his statement that "ChatGPT stores all the chats we have, and we can use them again later," P24, a customer participant, supported his argument with the statement, *"I can access my conversations with chatbot later."* On the other hand, P7, as a hotel manager, evaluated it from a different perspective with the statement, *"ChatGPT is very important for Search Engine Optimization (SEO) effectiveness."* It should be noticed that when used carefully, ChatGPT can help improve search rankings by helping to create high-quality content.

ChatGPT can create significant opportunities because businesses in the tourism industry have consumers worldwide (P8). This also provides considerable convenience for consumers and removes the obstacles that individuals may encounter in communicating with each other and tourism businesses (P13). Therefore, ChatGPT can be extremely useful in tourism as it can communicate freely in many languages (P17). ChatGPT facilitates on-site communication despite a language barrier between customers and staff, providing more significant customer, employee, and manager satisfaction.

Individual consumers have shown that they agree that ChatGPT offers many advantages. For example, according to P19, ChatGPT can provide a positive experience for individuals as it can produce persuasive and personal answers to their questions. Likewise, P22 stated, "Consumers can start a conversation to ask questions about holidays and travel, get information, compare options, and make reservations." P25 claims that ChatGPT's comprehensive language analysis capabilities provide the opportunity to look at consumers' wants, preferences, holiday and travel history and use these as the basis for personalized recommendations. P18 and P21 commented similarly that ChatGPT provides significant convenience for trips and holidays. P20 commented, *"ChatGPT can suggest alternative destinations and routes, provide information about local weather conditions, and provide important information about visa requirements, travel and health restrictions."*

CONS OF CHATGPT FOR BUSINESSES AND CONSUMERS IN THE TOURISM INDUSTRY

Despite the many advantages of using ChatGPT in the tourism industry, there are also some disadvantages. These serious issues need to be considered for tourism businesses and consumers. While explaining the weaknesses of ChatGPT, participants relate it to the problems they have experienced. Therefore, participants can use ChatGPT for different purposes and evaluate the results according to their experiential satisfaction levels.

Both participant P2 and consumer-participant P20 felt that ChatGPT could be challenging to program to understand complex queries. For this reason, he claims that it will inevitably cause ChatGPT to have some disadvantages. Similarly, P7 suggests that tourism businesses should be aware of the potential drawbacks of using ChatGPT, such as difficulty understanding complex queries and lack of empathy. Participants P3, P7, and P21 emphasized that ChatGPT technology is still in its early stages and that there may be limitations in the types of queries and information the chatbot can understand and provide. In line with this view, P8, P13, and P19 argue that if ChatGPT is not appropriately designed, it may not correctly understand the query of managers and consumers and may cause frustration. P5 and P23 think that since ChatGPT is a language model based on the data on which it is trained if the data is biased, the chatbot may also reflect this bias and lead to wrong recommendations.

Participants generally agreed that no human behavior should be expected from ChatGPT. While predicting this, they explained it based on some concerns about AI. For example, some participants' explanations on this subject are as follows: P1 *"I think ChatGPT may not have a full understanding of every consumer's tourism or holiday query,"* P6 *"ChatGPT's lack of empathy may lead individuals to feel as if they are interacting with a machine,"* P18 *"ChatGPT may create technical errors that can negatively affect the consumer experience,"* P25 *"ChatGPT may not be able to perform complex tasks due to its limited functionality"* and P11 *"Although ChatGPT has the potential to provide valuable information and predictions, its accuracy may be limited by the accuracy of the data."*

Almost all participants think that ethical concerns regarding ChatGPT may pose serious problems. They claim that ChatGPT could be used to create text that could be misleading, biased, or used for malicious purposes, raising ethical concerns about advertising, reviews, and news about businesses in the tourism industry. P23's comments on this issue should be addressed: *"Tourism businesses can ensure the ethical use of ChatGPT by regularly reviewing their interactions with all stakeholders, especially customers. By setting guidelines and standards, business managers can ensure that ChatGPT is not used in a way that could lead to discrimination in business, violate personal data or privacy laws".*

DISCUSSION AND CONCLUSIONS

ChatGPT technology has ushered in a new era of innovation and efficiency in the tourism industry. This powerful AI-driven tool has brought about many positive effects for businesses and consumers, reshaping how they interact and engage with tourism-related services. This advanced AI-powered tool has revolutionized how tourism-related information is disseminated, customer service is provided, and enhanced holiday and travel experiences (Chaturvedi et al., 2023; Ivanov & Soliman, 2023; Yaşar et al., 2023). It is possible to evaluate the positive impacts of ChatGPT on businesses and consumers in the tourism industry under four main headings, in parallel with the study of Demir and Demir (2023a).

First, ChatGPT has revolutionized customer service in the tourism industry by providing businesses with a 24/7 virtual assistant capable of handling various consumer inquiries (Gursoy et al., 2023). This has significantly improved response times, increasing customer satisfaction and loyalty (Skavronskaya et al., 2023). ChatGPT has dramatically enhanced customer engagement and support in the tourism industry. Businesses can deploy chatbots and virtual assistants powered by ChatGPT to respond instantly to consumer inquiries, increasing efficiency and improving customer satisfaction (Mich & Garigliano, 2023; Mondal et al., 2023). These AI-driven systems are available around the clock, allowing travelers to obtain information and assistance anytime, which is especially valuable for international tourists in different time zones.

Second, businesses in the tourism industry have experienced significant cost savings (Egbemhenghe et al., 2023) and operational efficiency gains through ChatGPT. Chatbots and virtual assistants powered by ChatGPT can handle routine tasks like booking confirmations, ticket reservations, and FAQs, reducing manual intervention and staffing costs (Demir & Demir, 2023b). This provides various recommendations, allowing staff to focus on more complex and value-added tasks (Yaşar et al., 2023). This leads to improved profitability for tourism businesses while ensuring that customers receive quick and accurate responses (George & George, 2023; Korzynski et al., 2023).

Third, ChatGPT collects and analyzes a wealth of data from customer interactions, providing valuable insights for businesses (Fusté-Forné & Orea-Giner, 2023; Paul et al., 2023). These insights help understand consumer behavior, preferences, and pain points, allowing companies to refine their marketing strategies, improve services, and make data-driven decisions for future business development (Demir et al., 2022). This personalization enhances the consumer experience, increasing sales and consumer retention (Demir & Demir, 2023b). Fourth, ChatGPT has broken down language barriers (Dwivedi et al., 2023) for both businesses and consumers. ChatGPT offers multilingual support for international travelers, breaking language barriers (Gursoy et al., 2023). This not only caters to a broader consumer base but also makes foreign travelers feel more welcome and comfortable (Demir & Demir, 2023a).

ChatGPT positively affects consumers (Paul et al., 2023) and tourism businesses. First, ChatGPT's ability to analyze vast amounts of data and understand consumer preferences allows it to provide highly personalized recommendations and itinerary planning services (Ivanov & Soliman, 2023; Yaşar et al., 2023). Tourism businesses can utilize this technology to offer tailored travel suggestions (Demir & Demir,

2023a), hotel and restaurant recommendations (Dalgıç, 2023), and activity options based on individual preferences, creating a more customized and memorable travel experience for consumers (Gursoy et al., 2023; Kumar et al., 2023). Consumers can receive personalized travel recommendations that match their interests, preferences, and budget. ChatGPT's ability to understand user data ensures that every trip is tailored to individual needs (Demir & Demir, 2023b).

Second, consumers benefit from quick and accurate responses (Fusté-Forné & Orea-Giner, 2023; Paul et al., 2023) to their travel-related questions, whether it's about destinations, accommodations, or activities. This empowers them to make well-informed decisions in real time. Third, ChatGPT offers the convenience of accessing tourism and travel information and services through various platforms, such as websites, mobile apps, and messaging services. This flexibility aligns with the digital preferences of modern travelers. Finally, ChatGPT streamlines the booking process, saving consumers time and effort. Travelers can easily make reservations, get directions, and plan itineraries, reducing the stress associated with travel planning (Mich & Garigliano, 2023).

Although the integration of ChatGPT in the tourism industry has undoubtedly brought about several advantages (Demir & Demir, 2023a), such as enhanced customer service, efficient booking processes, and personalized recommendations, it is crucial to acknowledge that this technological advancement also comes with its set of negative consequences on businesses and consumers. One of the significant effects of ChatGPT in the tourism industry is the reduction in human interaction. While ChatGPT and other AI-powered chatbots can handle routine queries, they need more empathy, nuanced understanding, and cultural awareness that human agents bring to customer interactions (Fui-Hoon Nah et al., 2023). This can lead to customer dissatisfaction (Mondal et al., 2023), especially in cases where customers seek a more personalized experience (Gursoy et al., 2023) or emotional interaction (Muñoz & Chen, 2023).

Second, using AI chatbots involves collecting and storing vast amounts of customer data, including personal information and preferences (Harahap et al., 2023). This raises concerns about data privacy and the potential for data breaches or misuse, which can harm a business's reputation and erode consumer trust (Iskender, 2023). Businesses in the tourism industry must be vigilant in safeguarding consumer information to avoid privacy breaches, which can result in legal consequences and damage to their reputation. Third, businesses in the tourism industry must invest heavily in technology infrastructure (Demir et al., 2023), including AI development and maintenance. This can strain financial resources, especially for smaller enterprises, leading to a digital divide where larger companies with more significant resources can exploit AI capabilities more effectively. Fourth, while ChatGPT has made significant advancements in understanding and generating human-like text

(Chen et al., 2023; Iskender, 2023), it still needs help to grasp the full context of a conversation. An over-reliance on AI chatbots can decrease emphasis on employee training and development (Elmohandes & Marghany, 2024). Businesses may need to pay more attention to the importance of a skilled and knowledgeable workforce, leading to potential issues in handling complex or unique consumer requests.

ChatGPT undoubtedly has disadvantages not only for tourism businesses but also has negative effects on consumers (Demir & Demir, 2023a). For example, consumers may find ChatGPT interactions frustrating, especially when dealing with complex issues or seeking unique recommendations. The lack of human intuition, misunderstandings or misinterpretations of their queries, and the inability to provide nuanced responses can result in dissatisfaction. ChatGPT often needs help to provide highly personalized recommendations (Kumar et al., 2023), as they rely on historical data and predefined algorithms. Consumers seeking tailored travel experiences may need help finding the level of personalization they desire, impacting their overall satisfaction (Mondal et al., 2023).

As chatbots become more prevalent in the tourism industry, consumers may question the authenticity of online reviews (Akakpo, 2023) and recommendations, suspecting that AI rather than genuine travelers generate them. The convenience of ChatGPT can lead to an overreliance on technology, with consumers potentially missing out on authentic, off-the-beaten-path experiences by relying solely on chatbot recommendations. On the other hand, not all consumers have access to or are comfortable using AI chatbots, which can create a digital divide (Chen et al., 2023; Dwivedi et al., 2023). Older generations or individuals with limited access to technology may feel excluded and underserved in the tourism industry.

Tourism businesses will inevitably accept wider technology adoption and run their operations with creative and innovative ideas (Demir & Demir, 2023b). The future of tourism will significantly depend on digital and technological discoveries such as using chatbots for reservations, mobility models to manage visitor flow, augmented, virtual, and mixed realities, artificial intelligence, IoT, 5G, service robots, and gamification methods for HR (Demir & Demir, 2023a). Adopting ChatGPT and AI chatbots in the tourism industry offers numerous benefits, such as mentioned above, but it also presents a set of negative effects for businesses and consumers. Striking a balance between technology and human interaction, addressing data privacy concerns, and investing in employee training is essential for businesses to mitigate these negative impacts. For consumers, it is vital to manage expectations, advocate for data protection, and encourage businesses to maintain a human touch in customer service to ensure a more satisfying and trustworthy travel experience. The tourism industry should be cautious about embracing AI at the expense of the unique qualities that make travel and hospitality a truly human experience. As technology advances, addressing these challenges and refining the use of AI in the tourism industry will be crucial for businesses and consumers. It is essential to adapt and evolve while keeping human interaction and personalization at the forefront of the consumer experience in the tourism industry.

REFERENCES

Akakpo, M. G. (2023). Skilled for the Future: Information Literacy for AI Use by University Students in Africa and the Role of Librarians. *Internet Reference Services Quarterly*, 1–8.

Akter, S., Hossain, M. A., Sajib, S., Sultana, S., Rahman, M., Vrontis, D., & McCarthy, G. (2023). A framework for AI-powered service innovation capability: Review and agenda for future research. *Technovation*, *125*, 1–17. doi:10.1016/j.technovation.2023.102768

Al Shboul, M. K. I., Alwreikat, A., & Alotaibi, F. A. (2023). Investigating the Use of ChatGpt as a Novel Method for Seeking Health Information: A Qualitative Approach. *Science & Technology Libraries*, 1–10. doi:10.1080/0194262X.2023.2250835

Alawida, M., Mejri, S., Mehmood, A., Chikhaoui, B., & Isaac Abiodun, O. (2023). A Comprehensive Study of ChatGPT: Advancements, Limitations, and Ethical Considerations in Natural Language Processing and Cybersecurity. *Information (Basel)*, *14*(8), 462. Advance online publication. doi:10.3390/info14080462

Ali, F. (2023). Let the devil speak for itself: Should ChatGPT be allowed or banned in hospitality and tourism schools? *Journal of Global Hospitality and Tourism*, *2*(1), 1–6. doi:10.5038/2771-5957.2.1.1016

Ali, F., Yasar, B., Ali, L., & Dogan, S. (2023). Antecedents and consequences of travelers' trust towards personalized travel recommendations offered by ChatGPT. *International Journal of Hospitality Management*, *114*, 1–9. doi:10.1016/j.ijhm.2023.103588

Ausat, A. M. A., Azzaakiyyah, H. K., Permana, R. M., Riady, Y., & Suherlan, S. (2023). The Role of ChatGPT in Enabling MSMEs to Compete in the Digital Age. *Innovative: Journal Of Social Science Research*, *3*(2), 622–631.

Bowman, J. (2023). *How AI Is Being Used in the Travel Industry*. https://www.fool.com/investing/stock-market/market-sectors/information-technology

Burger, B., Kanbach, D. K., Kraus, S., Breier, M., & Corvello, V. (2023). On the use of AI-based tools like ChatGPT to support management research. *European Journal of Innovation Management*, *26*(7), 233–241. doi:10.1108/EJIM-02-2023-0156

Carvalho, I., & Ivanov, S. (2023). ChatGPT for tourism: Applications, benefits, and risks. *Tourism Review*, 1–14. doi:10.1108/TR-02-2023-0088

Chaturvedi, R., Verma, S., Das, R., & Dwivedi, Y. K. (2023). Social companionship with artificial intelligence: Recent trends and future avenues. *Technological Forecasting and Social Change*, *193*, 1–20. doi:10.1016/j.techfore.2023.122634

Chen, S., Zhang, K., Li, X., Ye, H., Lin, K. J., & Law, R. (2023). ChatGPT: Cross-cultural tourism research imperative. *Journal of Economics and Management*, *45*(1), 137–146. doi:10.22367/jem.2023.45.07

Dalgıç, A. (2023). Restoran İşletmelerine Yapılan Olumsuz Yorumları ChatGPT Değerlendirebilir Mi? TripAdvisor'da Bir Uygulama. *İşletme Araştırmaları Dergisi*, *15*(4), 3069-3080.

De Bock, K. W., Coussement, K., De Caigny, A., Slowiński, R., Baesens, B., Boute, R. N., ... Weber, R. (2023). Explainable AI for Operational Research: A defining framework, methods, applications, and a research agenda. *European Journal of Operational Research*, 1–24. doi:10.1016/j.ejor.2023.09.026

Demir, M., & Demir, Ş. Ş. (2023b). Is ChatGPT the right technology for service individualization and value co-creation? Evidence from the travel industry. *Journal of Travel & Tourism Marketing*, *40*(5), 383–398. doi:10.1080/10548408.2023.2255884

Demir, M., Demir, Ş. Ş., Dalgıç, A., & Ergen, F. D. (2021). Impact of COVID-19 pandemic on the tourism industry: An evaluation from the hotel managers' perspective. *Journal of Tourism Theory and Research*, *7*(1), 44–57. doi:10.24288/jttr.857610

Demir, M., Demir, Ş. Ş., & Yaşar, E. (2022). Big data and innovative organizational performance: Evidence from a moderated-mediated model. *Creativity and Innovation Management*, *31*(4), 696–709. doi:10.1111/caim.12525

Demir, M., & Günaydın, Y. (2023). A digital job application reference: How do social media posts affect the recruitment process? *Employee Relations*, *45*(2), 457–477. doi:10.1108/ER-05-2022-0232

Demir, M., Yaşar, E., & Demir, Ş. Ş. (2023). Digital transformation and human resources planning: The mediating role of innovation. *Journal of Hospitality and Tourism Technology*, *14*(1), 21–36. doi:10.1108/JHTT-04-2021-0105

Demir, Ş. Ş., & Demir, M. (2023a). Professionals' perspectives on ChatGPT in the tourism industry: Does it inspire awe or concern? *Journal of Tourism Theory and Research*, *9*(2), 61–77. doi:10.24288/jttr.1313481

Dogru, T., Line, N., Mody, M., Hanks, L., Abbott, J. A., Acikgoz, F., Assaf, A., Bakir, S., Berbekova, A., Bilgihan, A., Dalton, A., Erkmen, E., Geronasso, M., Gomez, D., Graves, S., Iskender, A., Ivanov, S., Kizildag, M., Lee, M., ... Zhang, T. (2023). Generative Artificial Intelligence in the Hospitality and Tourism Industry: Developing a Framework for Future Research. *Journal of Hospitality & Tourism Research (Washington, D.C.)*, 1–19. doi:10.1177/10963480231188663

Dwivedi, Y. K., Kshetri, N., Hughes, L., Slade, E. L., Jeyaraj, A., Kar, A. K., Baabdullah, A. M., Koohang, A., Raghavan, V., Ahuja, M., Albanna, H., Albashrawi, M. A., Al-Busaidi, A. S., Balakrishnan, J., Barlette, Y., Basu, S., Bose, I., Brooks, L., Buhalis, D., ... Wright, R. (2023). "So what if ChatGPT wrote it?" Multidisciplinary perspectives on opportunities, challenges, and implications of generative conversational AI for research, practice, and policy. *International Journal of Information Management*, *71*, 1–63. doi:10.1016/j.ijinfomgt.2023.102642

Egbemhenghe, A., Ojeyemi, T., Iwuozor, K. O., Emenike, E. C., Ogunsanya, T. I., Anidiobi, S. U., & Adeniyi, A. G. (2023). Revolutionizing Water Treatment, Conservation, and Management: Harnessing the Power of AI-Driven ChatGPT Solutions. *Environmental Challenges*, *13*, 100782. Advance online publication. doi:10.1016/j.envc.2023.100782

Elmohandes, N., & Marghany, M. (2024). Effective or ineffective? Using ChatGPT for staffing in the hospitality industry. *European Journal of Tourism Research*, *36*, 3617–3627. doi:10.54055/ejtr.v36i.3286

Frąckiewicz, M. (2023). *Chat GPT-4 in Travel and Tourism: Enhancing Experiences with AI.* https://ts2.space/en/chat-gpt-4-in-travel-and-tourism-enhancing-experiences-with-ai/#:~:text=Overall%2C%20AI%2Dpowered%20chat%20GPT,and%20automate%20customer%20support%20tasks

Fui-Hoon Nah, F., Zheng, R., Cai, J., Siau, K., & Chen, L. (2023). Generative AI and ChatGPT: Applications, challenges, and AI-human collaboration. *Journal of Information Technology Case and Application Research*, *25*(3), 277–304. doi:10.1080/15228053.2023.2233814

Fusté-Forné, F., & Orea-Giner, A. (2023). Gastronomy in tourism management and marketing: An interview with ChatGPT. *ROBONOMICS: The Journal of the Automated Economy*, *4*, 1–13.

George, A. S., & George, A. H. (2023). A review of ChatGPT AI's impact on several business sectors. *Partners Universal International Innovation Journal*, *1*(1), 9–23.

Guo, Y. M., Ng, W. L., Hao, F., Zhang, C., Liu, S. X., & Aman, A. M. (2023). Trust in Virtual Interaction: The Role of Avatars in Sustainable Customer Relationships. *Sustainability (Basel)*, *15*(18), 1–11. doi:10.3390/su151814026

GuptaB.MuftiT.SohailS. S.MadsenD. Ø. (2023). *ChatGPT: A Brief Narrative Review*. Preprints.org. doi:10.20944/preprints202304.0158.v1

Gursoy, D., Li, Y., & Song, H. (2023). ChatGPT and the hospitality and tourism industry: An overview of current trends and future research directions. *Journal of Hospitality Marketing & Management*, *32*(5), 1–14. doi:10.1080/19368623.2023.2211993

Harahap, M. A. K., Ausat, A. M. A., Rachman, A., Riady, Y., & Azzaakiyyah, H. K. (2023). Overview of ChatGPT Technology and its Potential in Improving Tourism Information Services. *Jurnal Minfo Polgan*, *12*(2), 424–431. doi:10.33395/jmp.v12i1.12416

Hassani, H., & Silva, E. S. (2023). The role of ChatGPT in data science: How ai-assisted conversational interfaces are revolutionizing the field. *Big Data and Cognitive Computing*, *7*(2), 1–16. doi:10.3390/bdcc7020062

Huseynov, F. (2023). Chatbots in digital marketing: Enhanced customer experience and reduced customer service costs. In *Contemporary Approaches of Digital Marketing and the Role of Machine Intelligence* (pp. 46–72). IGI Global. doi:10.4018/978-1-6684-7735-9.ch003

Iskender, A. (2023). Holy or unholy? Interview with open AI's ChatGPT. *European Journal of Tourism Research*, *34*, 3414–3414. doi:10.54055/ejtr.v34i.3169

Ivanov, S., & Soliman, M. (2023). Game of algorithms: ChatGPT implications for the future of tourism education and research. *Journal of Tourism Futures*, 1-8. doi:10.1108/JTF-02-2023-0038

Jarrahi, M. H., Kenyon, S., Brown, A., Donahue, C., & Wicher, C. (2023). Artificial intelligence: A strategy to harness its power through organizational learning. *The Journal of Business Strategy*, *44*(3), 126–135. doi:10.1108/JBS-11-2021-0182

Jusman, I. A., Ausat, A. M. A., & Sumarna, A. (2023). Application of ChatGPT in Business Management and Strategic Decision Making. *Jurnal Minfo Polgan*, *12*(2), 1688–1697. doi:10.33395/jmp.v12i2.12956

Kim, J. H., Kim, J., Kim, S., & Hailu, T. B. (2023). Effects of AI ChatGPT on travelers' travel decision-making. *Tourism Review*. Advance online publication. doi:10.1108/TR-07-2023-0489

Korzynski, P., Mazurek, G., Altmann, A., Ejdys, J., Kazlauskaite, R., Paliszkiewicz, J., Wach, K., & Ziemba, E. (2023). Generative artificial intelligence as a new context for management theories: analysis of ChatGPT. *Central European Management Journal*, 1-11. doi:10.1108/CEMJ-02-2023-0091

Kumar, A., Gupta, N., & Bapat, G. (2023). Who is making the decisions? How retail managers can use the power of ChatGPT. *The Journal of Business Strategy*, 1–9. doi:10.1108/JBS-04-2023-0067

Liu, X., Zheng, Y., Du, Z., Ding, M., Qian, Y., Yang, Z., & Tang, J. (2021). GPT understands, too. arXiv. *arXiv preprint arXiv:2103.10385*.

Lund, B. D., & Wang, T. (2023). Chatting about ChatGPT: How may AI and GPT impact academia and libraries? *Library Hi Tech News*, *40*(3), 26–29. doi:10.1108/LHTN-01-2023-0009

Mehrolia, S., Alagarsamy, S., Moorthy, V., & Jeevananda, S. (2023). Will Users Continue Using Banking Chatbots? The Moderating Role of Perceived Risk. *FIIB Business Review*, 1-19. doi:10.1177/23197145231169900

Mich, L., & Garigliano, R. (2023). ChatGPT for e-Tourism: A technological perspective. *Information Technology & Tourism*, *25*(1), 1–12. doi:10.1007/s40558-023-00248-x

Mondal, S., Das, S., & Vrana, V. G. (2023). How to bell the cat? A theoretical review of generative artificial intelligence towards digital disruption in all walks of life. *Technologies*, *11*(2), 1–17. doi:10.3390/technologies11020044

Muñoz, K. E., & Chen, L. H. (2023). Can dating app users' self-disclosure foster travel intentions? An appnography approach. *Journal of Hospitality and Tourism Management*, *55*, 493–501. doi:10.1016/j.jhtm.2023.05.020

OpenA. I. (2023). *ChatGPT*. https://openai.com

Paul, J., Ueno, A., & Dennis, C. (2023). ChatGPT and consumers: Benefits, pitfalls and future research Agenda. *International Journal of Consumer Studies*, *47*(4), 1–13. doi:10.1111/ijcs.12928

Pricope Vancia, A. P., Băltescu, C. A., Brătucu, G., Tecău, A. S., Chițu, I. B., & Duguleană, L. (2023). Examining the Disruptive Potential of Generation Z Tourists on the Travel Industry in the Digital Age. *Sustainability (Basel)*, *15*(11), 1–19. doi:10.3390/su15118756

Qureshi, R., Shaughnessy, D., Gill, K. A., Robinson, K. A., Li, T., & Agai, E. (2023). Are ChatGPT and large language models "the answer" to bringing us closer to systematic review automation? *Systematic Reviews, 12*(1), 1–4. doi:10.1186/s13643-023-02243-z PMID:37120563

Radford, A., Narasimhan, K., Salimans, T., & Sutskever, I. (2018). *Improving language understanding by generative pre-training*. https://www.mikecaptain.com/resources/pdf/GPT-1.pdf

Radford, A., Wu, J., Child, R., Luan, D., Amodei, D., & Sutskever, I. (2019). Language models are unsupervised multitask learners. *OpenAI Blog, 1*(8), 9.

Shin, H., & Kang, J. (2023). Bridging the gap of bibliometric analysis: The evolution, current state, and future directions of tourism research using ChatGPT. *Journal of Hospitality and Tourism Management, 57*, 40–47. doi:10.1016/j.jhtm.2023.09.001

Skavronskaya, L., Hadinejad, A., & Cotterell, D. (2023). Reversing the threat of artificial intelligence to opportunity: A discussion of ChatGPT in tourism education. *Journal of Teaching in Travel & Tourism, 23*(2), 253–258. doi:10.1080/15313220.2023.2196658

Sohail, S. S., Farhat, F., Himeur, Y., Nadeem, M., Madsen, D. Ø., Singh, Y., Atalla, S., & Mansoor, W. (2023). Decoding ChatGPT: A taxonomy of existing research, current challenges, and possible future directions. *Journal of King Saud University. Computer and Information Sciences, 35*(8), 1–23. doi:10.1016/j.jksuci.2023.101675

Sudirjo, F., Diawati, P., Riady, Y., Ausat, A. M. A., & Suherlan, S. (2023). The Role of ChatGPT in Enhancing the Information Search and Decision-Making Process of Travellers. *Jurnal Minfo Polgan, 12*(2), 500–507. doi:10.33395/jmp.v12i1.12443

Vorobeva, D., Costa Pinto, D., António, N., & Mattila, A. S. (2023). The augmentation effect of artificial intelligence: Can AI framing shape customer acceptance of AI-based services? *Current Issues in Tourism*, 1–21. doi:10.1080/13683500.2023.2214353

Yaşar, E., Demir, M., & Taşdemir, T. (2023). Embedded big data in packaged foods: Examining consumer sentiment during the purchasing process post-COVID-19. *British Food Journal, 125*(10), 1–17. doi:10.1108/BFJ-12-2022-1124

Zhou, W., Zhang, C., Wu, L., & Shashidhar, M. (2023). ChatGPT and marketing: Analyzing public discourse in early Twitter posts. *Journal of Marketing Analytics*, 1-14.

ADDITIONAL READING

Christensen, J., Hansen, J. M., & Wilson, P. (2024). Understanding the role and impact of Generative Artificial Intelligence (AI) hallucination within consumers' tourism decision-making processes. *Current Issues in Tourism*, 1–16. doi:10.1080/13683500.2023.2300032

Demir, M., & Demir, Ş. Ş. (2023). Reflection of artificial intelligence applications on students' critical and analytical abilities. *Scientific Collection. InterConf*, (184), 459–467.

Demir, Ş. Ş., & Demir, M. (2022). Evaluation of digital tour guide technology and applications by professional tourist guides. *Scientific Collection. InterConf*, (135), 51–61.

Francis, R. S., Anantharajah, S., Sengupta, S., & Singh, A. (2024). Leveraging ChatGPT and Digital Marketing for Enhanced Customer Engagement in the Hotel Industry. In *Leveraging ChatGPT and Artificial Intelligence for Effective Customer Engagement* (pp. 55–68). IGI Global. doi:10.4018/979-8-3693-0815-8.ch004

Singh, V., & Singh, A. (2024). Revolutionizing the Hospitality Industry: How chatGPT Empowers Future Hoteliers. In Leveraging ChatGPT and Artificial Intelligence for Effective Customer Engagement (pp. 192-203). IGI Global.

Solomovich, L., & Abraham, V. (2024). Exploring the influence of ChatGPT on tourism behavior using the technology acceptance model. *Tourism Review*. Advance online publication. doi:10.1108/TR-10-2023-0697

KEY TERMS AND DEFINITIONS

AI Planning: Involves developing algorithms that enable machines to plan and make decisions in complex, dynamic environments.

AI Technologies: Encompass various techniques and approaches, such as machine learning, deep learning, natural language processing, computer vision, robotics, expert systems, and reinforcement learning.

Artificial Intelligence (AI): Is the simulation of human intelligence in machines programmed to think, learn, and perform tasks that typically require human intelligence (Demir & Demir, 2023a).

ChatGPT: A chatbot application based on Open AI's work on language processing technology, is a product of the GPT model series.

GPT: Is the abbreviation for Generative Pre-Trained Transformer.

Chapter 3
Data Privacy and Security Safeguarding Customer Information in ChatGPT Systems

Wasswa Shafik
https://orcid.org/0000-0002-9320-3186
Dig Connectivity Research Laboratory, Kampala, Uganda & School of Digital Science, Universiti Brunei Darussalam, Brunei

ABSTRACT

This research focuses on data privacy and security in ChatGPT systems, which have gained popularity in various industries. It aims to identify potential risks and propose effective strategies to ensure data privacy and security, fostering user trust. The chapter explores privacy-preserving techniques like differential privacy, federated learning (FL), secure multi-party computation, and homomorphic encryption to mitigate risks. Compliance with data protection regulations, for example, CCPA and GDPR, is essential for ensuring data privacy. Implementing a secure infrastructure with encryption, data access controls, and regular security audits strengthens the overall security posture. User awareness and consent are also crucial, with transparent data collection and usage policies, informed consent, and opt-out mechanisms. A well-structured incident response plan, communication strategies, and learning from security breaches enhance system resilience. The chapter presents case studies and best practices for secure ChatGPT systems, drawing insights from past privacy failures.

DOI: 10.4018/979-8-3693-1239-1.ch003

INTRODUCTION

Chatbot systems are computer programs designed to engage in interactive conversations with users, typically using natural language processing (NLP) techniques (Gabbiadini et al., 2023). They have gained significant popularity across various industries due to their versatility and ability to respond instantly to user queries and requests. These conversational AI and ML technologies aim to simulate human-like conversations, offering users a seamless and personalized experience (McGee, 2023; Shafik, 2024a).

The concept of chatbots dates to the mid-20th century, with early attempts to create conversational programs like ELIZA in the 1960s. Over the years, AI, machine learning, and NLP advancements have revolutionized chatbot capabilities, enabling more sophisticated interactions and natural language understanding (Dida et al., 2023). Rule-based chatbots follow pre-defined rules and scripted responses to specific keywords or patterns in user input. On the other hand, AI-driven chatbots utilize machine learning algorithms and NLP models to understand and respond to user queries dynamically (Haman & Školník, 2023).

Chatbot systems, particularly those employing advanced NLP capabilities, have seen a remarkable surge in adoption across diverse industries. Among these, ChatGPT systems have garnered significant attention for their versatility in engaging customers and users in interactive conversations (Cotton et al., 2023). These conversational AI technologies have been deployed for customer support, virtual assistants, and personalized recommendations, enabling seamless and efficient interactions. However, this increasing reliance on chatbots to handle customer interactions has brought to the forefront a critical concern: data privacy and security (Polonsky & Rotman, 2023).

In the context of ChatGPT systems, safeguarding sensitive customer information has become an imperative task. As these systems interact with users and process their queries, they collect and store substantial amounts of personal data (Liu et al., 2023; Shafik, 2024b). Ensuring the protection of this data from unauthorized access, misuse, or breaches has become a significant challenge for organizations utilizing these technologies. The potential risks of mishandling customer data can have severe consequences, such as damage to user trust, regulatory non-compliance, and reputational harm (Sakirin & Ben Said, 2023; Jun et al., 2021).

Figure 1. ChatGPT application

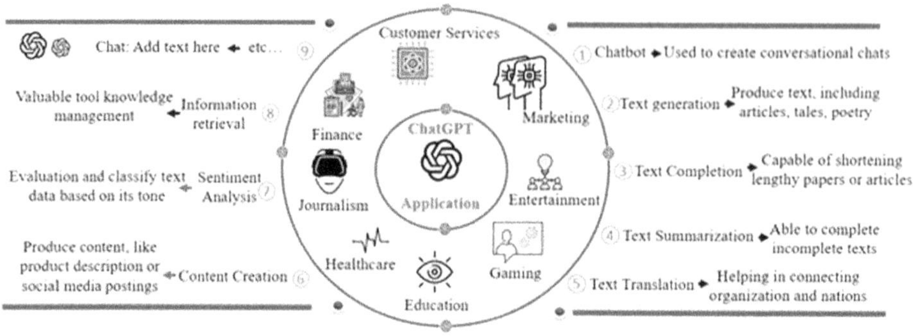

Chatbot systems find applications in various domains, including customer support, virtual assistants, e-commerce, healthcare, finance, and entertainment, as demonstrated in Figure 1. They can efficiently handle repetitive tasks, provide instant information, and streamline customer interactions, enhancing user engagement and overall user experience (Nastasi et al., 2023). Despite their benefits, chatbots face several challenges. Understanding complex user queries, maintaining context across conversations, and ensuring response accuracy remain ongoing research areas. Privacy and security concerns are also critical, mainly when dealing with sensitive user information (Mattas, 2023).

Safeguarding customer information refers to implementing measures and strategies to protect customers' or users' sensitive and confidential data from unauthorized access, use, disclosure, alteration, or destruction. The goal of safeguarding customer information is to ensure the privacy, security, and integrity of personal and financial data entrusted to an organization by its customers (Chinonso et al., 2023). This includes names, addresses, contact details, payment information, passwords, and any other data that can be used to identify or link to specific individuals.

Safeguarding customer information involves adopting a range of technical, organizational, and administrative controls to prevent data breaches, cyberattacks, and privacy violations. Organizations typically employ encryption, access controls, firewalls, intrusion detection systems, regular security audits, employee training, and data protection policies to safeguard customer information (Shue et al., 2023). Compliance with relevant data protection regulations and industry standards is also vital to ensuring customer data's proper handling and protection. By safeguarding customer information, organizations demonstrate their commitment to maintaining user trust, respecting privacy rights, and upholding ethical data practices (Antaki et al., 2023).

MAIN FOCUS OF THE CHAPTER

The contributions of the chapter are listed below:

- The chapter thoroughly investigates data privacy and security concerns in ChatGPT systems, covering data collection, unauthorized access, breaches, user profiling, and potential data misuse.
- Highlights advanced privacy-preserving methods like differential privacy, federated learning (FL), SMPC, and homomorphic encryption for safeguarding customer data while maintaining AI model efficacy.
- Emphasizes adhering to data protection regulations, focusing on CCPA, GDPR, and other pertinent laws to ensure legal compliance.
- Advocates for encryption, data access controls, and regular security audits to enhance the overall security of ChatGPT systems.
- The chapter highlights the importance of transparent data policies, informed consent, and user opt-out mechanisms to empower users and build trust.
- The chapter presents real-world examples of secure ChatGPT implementations, offering insights from past failures and successful privacy-conscious approaches.
- The chapter concludes with a roadmap outlining future research areas and development needs in data privacy and security for ChatGPT systems.

DATA PRIVACY RISKS IN ChatGPT SYSTEMS

Data privacy risks in ChatGPT systems are critical due to the extensive collection and processing of user data during interactions. As conversational AI technologies, such as ChatGPT, become more prevalent in various applications, understanding, and addressing these risks is essential to safeguard sensitive customer information. The following are vital data privacy risks associated with ChatGPT systems, as illustrated in Figure 2.

Figure 2. Top data privacy risks

Data Collection and Storage

ChatGPT systems need to collect and store user data to generate contextually relevant responses. However, this data may include personally identifiable information (PII) or sensitive details that, if mishandled or accessed by unauthorized parties, can lead to privacy breaches and potential misuse (Zielinski et al., 2023). Unauthorized Access: Inadequate access controls and security measures may expose user data to unauthorized access by hackers or malicious actors. Unauthorized access can result in identity theft, financial fraud, or other privacy violations (Biswas, 2023).

Data Breaches

ChatGPT systems possess extensive databases that store substantial quantities of user data, rendering them susceptible to future data breaches. An effective breach can reveal confidential data, causing harm to the organization's brand and undermining user confidence. Profiling users and retaining their data: AI-powered chatbots such as ChatGPT have the potential to unintentionally generate user profiles by utilizing data gathered during interactions (Adetayo, 2023). Extended data retention can result in the collection of personal information, giving rise to concerns over user privacy and data security.

Misuse of Customer Information

When data from ChatGPT systems are misused or shared with third parties without proper consent, users' privacy may be compromised. This misuse can lead to targeted advertising, spamming, or other unwarranted invasions of user privacy. Contextual Inference: Advanced AI models like ChatGPT can generate responses based on learned patterns from user interactions (Nisar & Aslam, 2023). While this enhances conversational fluency, it may inadvertently reveal private information that users did not explicitly disclose. Users interacting with chatbots may not be fully aware of the extent of data collection, storage, and usage. The lack of transparency in data practices can lead to a loss of user trust and hinder informed decision-making regarding data sharing (Magazine & 2023, 2023).

Lack of Transparency

The deprivation of transparency leaves users unaware of the methods and purposes behind the collection and utilization of personal data, ultimately eroding confidence. Lacking an understanding of decision-making processes, individuals may raise concerns about the ethical management of their personal information. Furthermore, a lack of openness impedes accountability, making it difficult to identify and correct biases or security flaws. To tackle this problem, companies must make a collective endeavor to convey their procedures transparently, fostering a better-informed and trusted bond between users and the technology responsible for handling their data.

CUSTOMER DATA COLLECTION AND STORAGE

Customer data collection and storage pose significant data privacy risks in ChatGPT systems. As conversational AI technologies interact with users, they naturally gather vast amounts of data, including user queries, responses, and contextual information. While data collection is crucial for improving AI model performance and providing personalized experiences, it raises concerns about user privacy (Analytica, 2023). Organizations must be transparent with users about the data types being collected, the purposes of data usage, and the retention period. Implementing clear data handling policies and obtaining informed consent from users is essential to ensure ethical data practices and maintain user trust (Giunti et al., 2023).

Figure 3. ChatGPT resilience and trust (c, confidentiality; i, integrity; a, availability; p, privacy; s, safety; r, reliability)

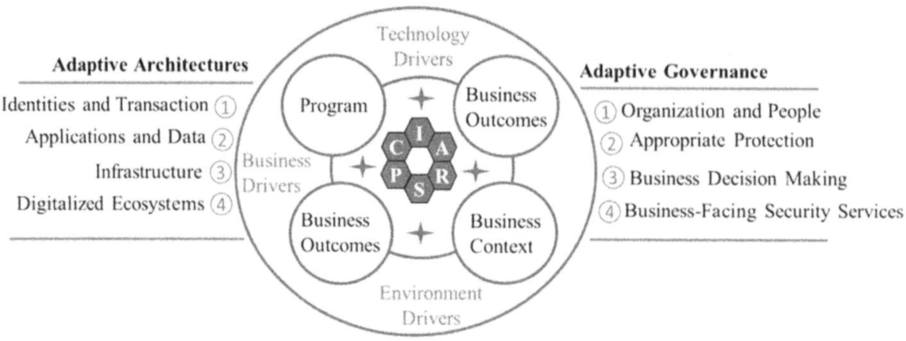

Securing the storage of customer data is equally critical. ChatGPT systems often store user data in databases or cloud servers, making them potential cyberattack targets; some ChatGPT is demonstrated in Figure 3. Organizations should employ robust encryption mechanisms, access controls, and regular security audits to protect user data from unauthorized access and data breaches (Gunawan, 2023). Additionally, the principle of data minimization should be upheld, ensuring that only necessary data is stored, reducing the potential impact of a security breach. By adopting privacy-preserving techniques and adhering to data protection regulations, organizations can balance collecting valuable data to improve AI capabilities and safeguard user privacy in ChatGPT systems (Perkins, 2023).

RISKS OF UNAUTHORIZED ACCESS AND DATA BREACHES

The risks of unauthorized access and data breaches present significant data privacy and security concerns in ChatGPT systems. As conversational AI technologies, such as ChatGPT, interact with users and store their data, they become potential targets for malicious actors seeking to exploit vulnerabilities and gain unauthorized access to sensitive information (Gregorcic & Pendrill, 2023). Unauthorized access to a ChatGPT system can occur through various means, such as exploiting software vulnerabilities, weak authentication mechanisms, or insider threats. If successful, malicious individuals may gain access to user data, including personally identifiable information (PII) and other sensitive details. This unauthorized access can lead to identity theft, financial fraud, or other forms of privacy violations, causing severe harm to affected users and damaging the reputation of the organization deploying the system (HS Kumar, 2023).

Data breaches in ChatGPT systems can have devastating consequences. A data breach occurs when cybercriminals or unauthorized entities access the system's database or storage, allowing them to extract, copy, or manipulate sensitive user data. Breached data may include chat logs, user profiles, or other personal information, which can be exploited for criminal purposes, sold on the dark web, or used in targeted phishing attacks (Mijwil et al., 2023). The aftermath of a data breach can be costly for organizations, resulting in legal penalties, financial losses, and erosion of customer trust.

Organizations must implement robust security measures to mitigate the risks of unauthorized access and data breaches. These include regular security assessments, encryption of stored data, multifactor authentication for system access, and continuous monitoring of suspicious activities (Halloran et al., 2023). Employing advanced cybersecurity protocols and ensuring that personnel has limited access to sensitive data can minimize the likelihood of unauthorized access. Additionally, having a well-structured incident response plan can help organizations swiftly respond to potential data breaches and mitigate the impact on users and the organization's reputation (Alshurafat, 2023). By proactively addressing these risks, organizations can better protect user data and maintain a privacy-conscious and secure ChatGPT system.

THE CHALLENGE OF USER PROFILING AND DATA RETENTION

The challenge of user profiling and data retention in ChatGPT systems raises significant data privacy and ethical considerations. As conversational AI technologies interact with users, they gather valuable data to personalize responses and enhance user experiences (Shaji George et al., 2023). However, accumulating user data over time may inadvertently lead to the creation of detailed user profiles, potentially containing sensitive information. User profiling involves analyzing user interactions, preferences, and behavior patterns to create a comprehensive profile of an individual (AlAfnan et al., 2023). While this can improve the accuracy and relevance of AI-generated responses, it raises concerns about user privacy. Detailed user profiles can expose personal attributes, beliefs, and potential vulnerabilities, leading to privacy breaches and unauthorized access if not adequately protected (Grünebaum et al., 2023).

Data retention is another critical aspect related to user profiling. The more extended data is retained within ChatGPT systems, the greater the potential risk of misuse or unintended exposure. Prolonged data retention increases the likelihood of the system holding outdated or irrelevant information, making it vulnerable to exploitation in the event of a security breach or unauthorized access (Ahn, 2023). Addressing the challenge of user profiling and data retention requires a balanced approach that respects user privacy while maintaining the effectiveness of the AI system. Organizations should prioritize data minimization, only collecting and retaining data necessary for the immediate purpose of the conversation. Implementing data anonymization or aggregation techniques can also help mitigate the risks associated with detailed user profiling (Fido & Wallace, 2023). Transparent data retention policies, informed consent from users, and clear guidelines for data deletion are essential to foster a privacy-conscious environment and establish trust with users.

POTENTIAL MISUSE OF CUSTOMER INFORMATION

The potential misuse of customer information in ChatGPT systems poses a significant data privacy risk that demands vigilant attention. As conversational AI technologies interact with users, they often collect sensitive data, including personally identifiable information (PII) and other private details (Yusuf, 2023). Suppose this information falls into the wrong hands or is misused. In that case, it can have severe consequences for individuals and organizations, such as identity theft, financial fraud, or targeted advertising based on user interactions. Organizations must prioritize data privacy and security by implementing robust measures like access controls, encryption, and data anonymization techniques to combat this risk (Gao et al., 2023). Transparent data handling policies and obtaining informed consent from users are essential to establishing trust and maintaining privacy.

Moreover, a breach of customer information can lead to significant reputational damage for organizations, resulting in diminished customer trust and loyalty. To mitigate this risk, organizations should conduct regular security audits, monitor suspicious activities, and have a swift incident response plan to address any potential misuse of customer data promptly (Castro Nascimento & Pimentel, 2023). By proactively safeguarding customer information and adhering to ethical data practices, organizations can create a safe and secure environment for users interacting with ChatGPT systems, protecting their privacy and fostering a privacy-conscious culture.

PRIVACY-PRESERVING TECHNIQUES FOR CHATGPT

Privacy-preserving techniques are crucial in safeguarding customer data and maintaining data privacy in ChatGPT systems. These techniques aim to protect sensitive information while ensuring the AI model remains effective and provides accurate responses. Some of the key privacy-preserving techniques suitable for ChatGPT systems include.

DIFFERENTIAL PRIVACY

Differential privacy is a rigorous privacy concept that protects individual user information during data processing. In the context of ChatGPT systems, noise is deliberately added to the data during the training phase before it is used to train the AI model. This noise obscures specific individual contributions, making it challenging for an adversary to determine whether a particular data point was used in the training set (Ali et al., 2023). By providing privacy guarantees, differential privacy prevents the AI model from memorizing specific user interactions while still being able to learn from the overall dataset's statistical patterns. This technique ensures that user data remains secure, even during a security breach or unauthorized access to the trained model (Sinha et al., 2023).

FEDERATED LEARNING (FL)

FL is a decentralized approach to model training that allows AI models to be trained across multiple devices or servers without sharing raw user data centrally. In ChatGPT systems, each user's device or server locally trains a personalized version of the AI model using the user's interactions (Gabbiadini et al., 2023). Only the model updates (not the raw data) are sent to a central server, where they are aggregated to create a global model. This process keeps individual user data on the user's device, reducing the risk of data exposure and enhancing privacy (McGee, 2023). FL allows the AI model to learn from diverse user interactions without transferring sensitive data to a central repository, making it suitable for privacy-conscious applications.

SECURE MULTI-PARTY COMPUTATION (SMPC)

SMPC is a cryptographic technique that allows multiple parties to collaboratively perform computations on encrypted data without revealing the underlying data to each other. In the context of ChatGPT systems, SMPC enables secure model training using encrypted user data (Dida et al., 2023). Each party encrypts its data, and then computations are performed on the encrypted data without decrypting it. This ensures that no party has access to sensitive user information while still being able to train the AI model effectively (Haman & Školník, 2023). SMPC is particularly valuable in scenarios where multiple entities need to collaborate on AI model training without compromising the privacy of their respective datasets.

HOMOMORPHIC ENCRYPTION

Homomorphic encryption is a cryptographic technique that allows data to be encrypted so that it can still be used for computations. In the context of ChatGPT systems, homomorphic encryption enables the AI model to process encrypted user data without decrypting it, preserving the privacy of user interactions (Cotton et al., 2023). The model can perform operations on encrypted data and generate encrypted responses, which the receiving party then decrypts. This ensures the data remains confidential throughout the process, even during computations (Regalia, 2023). While homomorphic encryption can be computationally intensive, it provides a robust privacy solution for AI systems that require secure data processing.

ANONYMIZATION DATA AND AGGREGATION

Data aggregation involves combining user data at a higher level, such as grouping data based on common attributes or trends. Aggregating data obscures individual user details, and the AI model learns from general patterns rather than specific user interactions (Shah, 2023). Anonymization involves removing or encrypting personally identifiable information from the data, further protecting individual privacy (Eke, 2023). These techniques allow the AI model to provide personalized responses without accessing granular user data, enhancing privacy while maintaining utility.

MODEL DISTILLATION

Model distillation is a technique that involves training a smaller and less resource-intensive model (student) to mimic the behavior of a larger, more complex model (teacher). In the context of ChatGPT systems, a larger pre-trained AI model serves as the teacher model (Gabbiadini et al., 2023). The student model is trained on encrypted or aggregated data, minimizing the risk of memorizing specific user interactions. The student model aims to replicate the teacher model's responses, achieving similar performance with reduced computational requirements (McGee, 2023). Model distillation helps protect individual user data while providing accurate responses from a smaller, more privacy-conscious AI model.

COMPLIANCE WITH DATA PROTECTION REGULATIONS

By employing these privacy-preserving techniques, organizations can ensure that ChatGPT systems respect user privacy, comply with data protection regulations, and foster a responsible and ethical approach to AI deployment. These techniques balance data privacy and AI model performance, enabling secure and privacy-conscious interactions with users.

GENERAL DATA PROTECTION REGULATION (GDPR) COMPLIANCE

Compliance with the General Data Protection Regulation (GDPR) is of utmost importance for organizations operating ChatGPT systems, especially when processing the personal data of individuals residing in the European Union (EU) (Gabbiadini et al., 2023; McGee, 2023). The GDPR is a comprehensive data protection regulation that came into effect on May 25, 2018, with the primary aim of safeguarding EU residents' privacy rights and personal data. Non-compliance with GDPR can lead to significant fines and reputational damage for organizations, making it crucial to understand and adhere to its key principles (Dida et al., 2023).

Organizations must have a lawful basis for processing personal data in ChatGPT systems. This may include obtaining explicit user consent, fulfilling contractual obligations, complying with legal requirements, protecting vital interests, performing tasks in the public interest, or pursuing legitimate interests, provided they do not override the rights and freedoms of the individual (Haman & Školník, 2023). Organizations must be transparent with users about the data processing activities in ChatGPT systems. This involves providing clear and concise information on data collection, purposes of processing, data retention periods, and users' rights regarding their data. Privacy policies and notices should be easily accessible and written in plain language (Regalia, 2023).

GDPR grants users several rights concerning their data, such as access, rectification, erase, restrict processing, data portability, and object to processing. Organizations must facilitate the exercise of these rights and respond to user requests promptly and competently (Eke, 2023). Organizations must implement appropriate technical and organizational measures to ensure the security and confidentiality of personal data in ChatGPT systems. This includes encryption, access controls, regular security assessments, and incident response procedures to mitigate data breaches (Regalia, 2023).

Data Minimization and Purpose Limitation: Organizations should practice data minimization, ensuring that only necessary and relevant data is collected for the specific purposes disclosed to users. Data should not be retained for longer than required for its intended use. Cross-Border Data Transfers: If personal data is transferred to countries outside the EU, organizations must ensure adequate safeguards, such as using standard contractual clauses or other approved transfer mechanisms, are in place (Polonsky & Rotman, 2023).

Data Protection Impact Assessment (DPIA): In some instances, organizations may need to conduct a DPIA to assess the potential impact of data processing activities on user privacy. This is particularly relevant when deploying new technologies or processing sensitive data. By complying with GDPR requirements, organizations can build user trust, demonstrate commitment to data privacy, and mitigate the risk of regulatory penalties (Liu et al., 2023). GDPR compliance not only protects the privacy rights of users but also fosters a privacy-conscious culture in ChatGPT systems and throughout the organization.

CALIFORNIA CONSUMER PRIVACY ACT (CCPA) COMPLIANCE

The CCPA is a comprehensive privacy law that grants California residents specific rights and control over their personal information. Organizations that collect or process the personal data of California residents must comply with the CCPA's stringent requirements (Sakirin & Ben Said, 2023). In the context of ChatGPT systems, organizations need to ensure that they are transparent about data collection practices and provide clear notice to users about the types of data being collected and the purposes for which it will be used. Additionally, users must be allowed to opt out of the sale of their personal information, and organizations must respect these preferences. Implementing robust security measures to protect user data and promptly responding to user requests for data access or deletion are essential components of CCPA compliance (Benoit, 2023). Organizations must also refrain from discriminating against users who exercise their privacy rights under the CCPA.

OTHER RELEVANT DATA PROTECTION LAWS AND FRAMEWORKS

Apart from GDPR, several other data protection laws and frameworks exist worldwide, each with its requirements and principles. Organizations operating ChatGPT systems must know and comply with these laws, especially when interacting with users from different locations. Some of the other relevant data protection laws and frameworks include:

Personal Data Protection Act (PDPA) – Singapore

PDPA of Singapore is a comprehensive data protection law enacted in 2012 to regulate the collection, use, and disclosure of personal data by organizations. The PDPA aims to protect individuals' privacy rights while allowing organizations to collect and use personal data for legitimate purposes. Under the PDPA, organizations must obtain individuals' consent before collecting and processing their data and limit the data's use to specified purposes. Individuals have the right to access their data and request corrections if necessary (Sakirin & Ben Said, 2023). Organizations are also accountable for ensuring the security and protection of the personal data they handle. To comply with the PDPA, organizations must appoint a Data Protection Officer and implement policies and practices to safeguard personal data (Bishop, 2023). Non-compliance with the PDPA can lead to fines and penalties, making it crucial for businesses and entities operating in Singapore to adhere to the law's provisions and maintain strict data protection measures to respect individuals' privacy rights (Bommineni et al., 2023; Shafik, 2023).

Personal Information Protection and Electronic Documents Act (PIPEDA) – Canada

Enacted in 2000, PIPEDA applies to organizations engaged in commercial activities and aims to safeguard individuals' privacy rights while facilitating the flow of personal information in the digital economy. PIPEDA requires organizations to obtain informed consent before collecting, using, or disclosing personal information and limits the purposes for which the information can be used. Individuals have the right to access their personal information held by organizations and to challenge its accuracy (Gabbiadini et al., 2023). PIPEDA also mandates organizations to implement appropriate security safeguards to protect personal information from unauthorized access, disclosure, or misuse. With the ever-evolving technological landscape, PIPEDA plays a crucial role in ensuring that Canadian organizations uphold strong privacy standards and maintain individuals' trust and confidence in handling their personal information (McGee, 2023).

Health Insurance Portability and Accountability Act (HIPAA) – United States

HIPAA is a critical healthcare data privacy and security law in the United States that was enacted in 1996. HIPAA's primary objective is to protect the privacy and security of individuals' health information while ensuring its portability and improving the efficiency of the healthcare system (Dida et al., 2023). HIPAA applies to covered entities, including healthcare providers, health plans, healthcare clearinghouses, and their business associates who handle PHI. The law sets standards for using and disclosing PHI, requiring organizations to obtain individuals' authorization before using or disclosing their health information for purposes other than treatment, payment, or healthcare operations (Haman & Školník, 2023). HIPAA mandates covered entities to implement administrative, physical, and technical safeguards to protect PHI from unauthorized access, use, or disclosure. Compliance with HIPAA is of utmost importance for healthcare organizations to uphold patient confidentiality, maintain the integrity of health data, and foster public trust in the healthcare system's ability to safeguard sensitive health information (Cotton et al., 2023).

Privacy Act – Australia

The Privacy Act is a comprehensive data protection law in Australia that governs the handling of personal information by government agencies and private sector organizations. Enacted in 1988 and amended in 2014, the Privacy Act aims to protect individuals' privacy rights while promoting transparency and accountability in handling personal data (Eke, 2023). The law sets out specific privacy principles that organizations must follow, such as collecting and storing personal information only for lawful purposes, providing individuals with access to their information, and ensuring the security and confidentiality of the data. The Privacy Act also includes provisions for cross-border data transfers and the handling of sensitive information (Sakirin & Ben Said, 2023). Organizations that breach the Privacy Act may face penalties and fines, emphasizing the importance of compliance with the law to protect the privacy and rights of individuals in Australia.

Data Protection Directive – EU Member States

The Data Protection Directive, officially known as Directive 95/46/EC, was a significant data protection regulation in the European Union (EU) that aimed to harmonize data protection laws among EU member states. Adopted in 1995, the directive provided a framework for protecting individuals' data within the EU (Bommineni et al., 2023). It laid down principles and rules governing the processing of personal data, such as the requirement for informed consent, purpose limitation, data accuracy, and security measures. The Data Protection Directive also established individuals' rights to access their data and request its correction or deletion. Furthermore, the directive prohibited the transfer of personal data to countries outside the EU that did not ensure adequate data protection (Mattas, 2023). While the Data Protection Directive played a crucial role in shaping data protection practices across the EU, it was superseded by the GDPR in 2018, providing a more modern and robust framework for data protection within the EU (Chinonso et al., 2023).

Personal Information Protection Act (PIPA) – Japan

PIPA is a fundamental data protection law in Japan that regulates the handling of personal information by businesses and organizations. Enacted in 2003 and amended in 2015, PIPA aims to protect the privacy rights of individuals while promoting the appropriate use of personal data (Dida et al., 2023). The law defines personal information broadly and requires organizations to obtain consent from individuals before collecting, using, or disclosing their data. PIPA also outlines specific principles for adequately handling personal information, including the purpose limitation, data accuracy, security safeguards, and the prohibition of providing personal data to third parties without consent (Haman & Školník, 2023). Additionally, PIPA sets forth individuals' rights to access and request the correction or deletion of their personal information. Compliance with PIPA is crucial for businesses and organizations operating in Japan to protect personal data and build trust with their customers or users (Haman & Školník, 2023).

Personal Data Protection Bill – India

India is implementing a comprehensive data protection law known as the Personal Data Protection Bill to regulate the processing of personal data in the country. Organizations must stay up-to-date with the data protection laws and frameworks relevant to their operations and user demographics (Cotton et al., 2023). Compliance with these laws ensures that ChatGPT systems are designed and operated with user privacy in mind, regardless of the jurisdiction in which users reside. Adhering to these data protection regulations fosters a culture of responsible data handling and establishes trust with users by demonstrating a commitment to protecting their personal information (Eke, 2023).

IMPLEMENTING SECURE INFRASTRUCTURE

Implementing a secure infrastructure is crucial for ensuring the privacy and security of user data in ChatGPT systems. A secure infrastructure involves a combination of technical measures, policies, and best practices to protect data from unauthorized access, breaches, and misuse.

Data Encryption and Access Controls

Employ robust encryption techniques, such as Advanced Encryption Standard (AES) or Rivest-Shamir-Adleman (RSA), to protect sensitive data. Encrypt user interactions, personal information, and any other data transmitted between the user and the ChatGPT system (Gabbiadini et al., 2023). Furthermore, ensure that data stored in databases or cloud repositories is encrypted to prevent unauthorized access to the data. Implement fine-grained access controls to restrict data access to only authorized personnel. Use role-based access control (RBAC) to assign specific privileges based on job roles and responsibilities (Dida et al., 2023; McGee, 2023). Apply the principle of least privilege, granting only the minimum necessary access to perform tasks.

Secure Data Storage and Secure APIS

Choose reliable and secure cloud providers or data centers with robust security protocols. Regularly audit access to stored data and employ encryption and access controls to protect data at rest (Dida et al., 2023). Implement data segmentation to separate different data types and limit access to specific databases. Ensure secure API endpoints if the ChatGPT system exposes APIs for integration with other applications. Employ secure authentication mechanisms, for instance, Open Authorization (OAuth), and enforce authorization checks to verify the legitimacy of API requests (Haman & Školník, 2023). Implement rate limiting and input validation to prevent potential API attacks, such as injection or data manipulation.

Security Audits and Incident Response Plan

Conduct regular security audits and vulnerability assessments to identify potential weaknesses in the system. Engage third-party security experts to perform penetration testing to simulate real-world attacks and evaluate the system's resilience against security threats (Cotton et al., 2023). Address identified vulnerabilities promptly. Similarly, develop a detailed incident response plan that outlines the steps to be taken in case of a security breach or data incident. The plan should include clear roles and responsibilities, communication protocols, and containment, mitigation, and recovery steps (Eke, 2023; Lieberman, 2023). Regularly test and update the incident response plan to ensure its effectiveness.

Employee Training, Regular Updates, and Patching

Train all personnel operating the ChatGPT system on data security best practices. Educate employees about social engineering threats, such as phishing, and how to identify and report potential security incidents (Polonsky & Rotman, 2023). Foster a culture of security awareness throughout the organization. Keep all software, applications, and operating systems updated with the latest security patches and updates. Regularly review and update the system's dependencies to ensure that potential vulnerabilities are addressed promptly (Liu et al., 2023).

User Authentication and Data Backups

Enforce strong user authentication mechanisms, such as multi-factor authentication (MFA), to ensure that only authorized users can access the ChatGPT system. Use secure password policies and encourage the use of strong and unique passwords. Regularly back up all data to a secure and separate location. Maintain a data backup and recovery plan to ensure data availability during data loss, system failures, or security incidents. Organizations can establish a robust and secure infrastructure for their ChatGPT systems by meticulously implementing these security measures (Benoit, 2023). Prioritizing data privacy and security safeguards user data and fosters trust among users, demonstrating a commitment to ethical and responsible AI deployment.

User Awareness and Consent

User awareness and obtaining informed consent are critical components of data privacy in ChatGPT systems. Users must know how the AI system collects, processes, and uses their data (Bishop, 2023). Implementing transparent data collection and usage policies and providing informed consent and opt-out mechanisms helps foster trust and empowers users to make informed decisions about their data.

TRANSPARENT DATA COLLECTION AND USAGE POLICIES

Transparent data collection and usage policies are essential for building trust and promoting user awareness in ChatGPT systems. To achieve transparency, organizations should provide clear and easily accessible information about the data collection practices and the purpose of processing user data (Nastasi et al., 2023). The policies should explain the collected data types, such as user interactions, device information, IP addresses, and any other relevant data points. Additionally, organizations should disclose how long the data will be retained and whether it will be shared with third parties. The policies should use plain language, avoiding complex legal jargon, to ensure that users can easily understand how their data will be used (Bommineni et al., 2023). Providing examples of data usage scenarios can further clarify the purpose of data collection. Transparency extends beyond the initial user interaction; organizations should inform users about any data collection or usage policy changes and seek renewed consent if required.

INFORMED CONSENT AND OPT-OUT MECHANISMS

Obtaining informed consent is a fundamental principle of data privacy, and it is especially crucial for ChatGPT systems that process user data. Informed consent means that users are fully aware of the data practices and explicitly agree to the terms (Mattas, 2023). Organizations should present the data collection and usage policies to users in a conspicuous manner, ensuring that consent is not buried within lengthy terms and conditions. For consent to be valid, it must be freely given, specific, informed, and unambiguous. Users should actively opt-in to data collection; pre-ticked boxes or assumed consent are not compliant with data protection regulations. Organizations must provide a precise mechanism for users to indicate their consent, such as through checkboxes or explicit statements (Shue et al., 2023).

Additionally, organizations should offer users the ability to exercise their right to withdraw consent at any time. Users should have access to simple and easily accessible opt-out mechanisms that allow them to revoke their consent and have their data deleted or anonymized promptly. Organizations must respect users' decisions to opt out and refrain from penalizing them or providing inferior services based on their privacy choices (Macey-Dare, 2023). Organizations should regularly review and update their data collection and usage policies to ensure ongoing compliance, seeking user feedback and adjusting the policies as needed. Engaging users in the consent process and promoting transparency instills confidence in users, emphasizing that their privacy is respected and protected in the ChatGPT system (Antaki et al., 2023). By prioritizing user awareness and consent, organizations demonstrate their commitment to responsible data practices and ethical AI deployment.

HANDLING SECURITY INCIDENTS AND BREACHES

Handling security incidents and breaches in ChatGPT systems requires a comprehensive and well-structured incident response plan. The following are some of the detailed step-by-step processes for effectively managing security incidents.

INCIDENT DETECTION AND REPORTING

Implement robust monitoring tools and security systems to detect potential security incidents in real-time. These tools can include intrusion detection systems (IDS), security event logging, and anomaly detection mechanisms (Gabbiadini et al., 2023). Review system logs and network traffic regularly to identify suspicious activities or abnormal patterns. Encourage all users, employees, and stakeholders to report any security concerns or unusual behavior they observe promptly (McGee, 2023).

INCIDENT RESPONSE TEAM

Form a dedicated incident response team composed of cybersecurity experts, information technology personnel, legal advisors, communication specialists, and relevant stakeholders (Gabbiadini et al., 2023). Define clear roles and responsibilities for each team member and the authority to make crucial decisions during the incident response process (Dida et al., 2023). Ensure that the team is well-trained and prepared to handle various security incidents effectively.

INCIDENT CLASSIFICATION AND ASSESSMENT

Classify the detected incident based on its severity and impact on the ChatGPT system and user data. Conduct a thorough assessment to understand the incident's scope, nature, and extent (Haman & Školník, 2023). This assessment is crucial for developing an appropriate response strategy tailored to the incident.

INCIDENT CONTAINMENT

Take immediate action to contain the incident and prevent further damage. This may involve isolating affected parts of the system, disconnecting compromised devices or networks, or deactivating compromised user accounts (Cotton et al., 2023). The goal is to limit the spread of the incident and minimize its impact on the overall system.

MITIGATION AND RECOVERY

Once the incident is contained, focus on mitigating its effects and restoring the ChatGPT system to regular operation. This may include applying security patches, updating software, changing passwords, or restoring data from clean backups (Regalia, 2023). Prioritize critical functions and services to ensure minimal disruption to users.

COMMUNICATION AND NOTIFICATION

Transparently communicate with all relevant stakeholders about the incident. This includes users, customers, employees, regulatory authorities, and other affected parties (Eke, 2023). Provide clear and timely updates throughout the incident response process, sharing the nature of the incident, containment measures taken, progress in recovery efforts, and future action plans.

FORENSIC INVESTIGATION

Conduct a thorough forensic investigation to determine the incident's root cause and identify any exploited vulnerabilities. Preserve evidence to support legal or regulatory actions (Polonsky & Rotman, 2023). The investigation helps prevent similar incidents in the future and ensures that the ChatGPT system becomes more resilient against potential threats.

LEARNING AND IMPROVEMENT

Perform a comprehensive post-incident review to analyze the incident response process, identify strengths and weaknesses, and draw lessons for improvement. Update incident response procedures, security policies, and preventive measures based on the insights gained from the incident (Liu et al., 2023). Share these learnings with the incident response team and the organization to enhance cybersecurity awareness.

REPORTING AND COMPLIANCE

If applicable, adhere to legal and regulatory requirements for reporting security incidents and data breaches. Maintain detailed records of the incident response process, actions taken, and stakeholder communication. These records may be required for audits, investigations, or regulatory compliance (Benoit, 2023). By following this detailed incident response process, organizations can effectively manage security incidents and breaches, minimize their impact, protect user data, and demonstrate a commitment to maintaining a secure and privacy-conscious ChatGPT system.

CASE STUDIES AND BEST PRACTICES

Successful implementations of secure ChatGPT systems showcase how organizations can safeguard user data and ensure privacy in their AI applications. The following are some examples of practices and case studies that demonstrate the successful implementation of secure ChatGPT systems.

SUCCESSFUL IMPLEMENTATIONS OF SECURE CHATGPT SYSTEMS

Successful implementations of secure ChatGPT systems prioritize user privacy, comply with data protection regulations, and employ privacy-preserving techniques to protect user data throughout the system's lifecycle (Gabbiadini et al., 2023). By adopting these practices, organizations can create a safe and trustworthy environment for users to interact with AI technology.

End-to-End Encryption and Federated Learning for User Privacy

A ChatGPT system implemented end-to-end encryption, ensuring user interactions and data remained encrypted throughout the communication. This approach protected user privacy, as the data was only accessible by the intended recipients, making it impossible for the service provider or any other intermediary to access the user's conversations (McGee, 2023). The system also provided transparent data collection and usage policies, giving users complete control over their data and fostering trust in the service. Another successful implementation involved using FL to train the ChatGPT model. This approach allowed the AI model to be trained on decentralized data sources without centralizing or exposing individual user data (Dida et al., 2023). User interactions were processed locally on their devices, and only aggregated model updates were sent to the central server. This ensured user data privacy while benefiting from diverse user interactions' collective intelligence (Haman & Školník, 2023).

CCPA, GDPR Compliance, and Differential Privacy for Enhanced Data Security

A ChatGPT system achieved compliance with data protection regulations, such as GDPR and CCPA. The system integrated robust consent mechanisms, enabling users to provide informed consent for data processing. Users were presented with transparent and user-friendly options to opt out of data collection or revoke consent at any time (Cotton et al., 2023). The system also implemented data retention policies, ensuring that user data was stored only for the necessary duration and promptly deleted upon request. A ChatGPT system employed differential privacy to protect user data during model training. By adding carefully calibrated noise to the training data, the system ensured that individual user interactions remained indistinguishable, safeguarding against the risk of re-identification (Regalia, 2023). This approach assured users that their interactions contributed to model training without compromising their privacy.

Proactive Incident Response and User-Focused Security Education

A secure ChatGPT system demonstrated a proactive incident response strategy. The system had a dedicated incident response team trained to handle potential security breaches. Regular security audits and vulnerability assessments were conducted to identify and address potential weaknesses (Lieberman, 2023). The team also conducted tabletop exercises to simulate various security incidents and test the efficacy of their response plan. An exemplary implementation emphasized user-focused security education. The ChatGPT system gave users clear guidelines on secure usage and potential risks. Users were educated on recognizing phishing attempts, protecting sensitive information, and reporting suspicious activities (Polonsky & Rotman, 2023). Regular security awareness campaigns increased user vigilance and contributed to a safer user experience.

Continuous Improvement and Feedback

A successful, secure ChatGPT system established a culture of continuous improvement. User feedback and suggestions were actively sought to enhance security features and user privacy. The system regularly updated its security protocols and measures based on the latest cybersecurity best practices and evolving threats (Shah, 2023; Alnssyan et al., 2023). These successful implementations exemplify the importance of a holistic approach to data privacy and security in ChatGPT systems. By integrating privacy-preserving techniques, complying with data protection regulations, engaging users, and maintaining proactive incident response capabilities, organizations can build secure and trustworthy ChatGPT systems that prioritize user privacy and data security (Liu et al., 2023).

LESSONS LEARNED FROM PRIVACY FAILURES IN CHATBOT DEPLOYMENTS

Insights learned from successful implementations of secure ChatGPT systems provide valuable insights for organizations seeking to enhance data privacy and security in their AI applications.

Privacy by Design, User Awareness, and Consent

Incorporate privacy considerations from the very beginning of the ChatGPT system development process. Design the system with privacy as a core principle, integrating privacy-preserving techniques and data protection measures from the outset. This proactive approach ensures that user privacy is prioritized throughout the system's lifecycle. Transparently inform users about data collection and usage policies and obtain informed consent for data processing. Prioritize user awareness through clear and accessible privacy policies and terms of service. Empower users to make informed decisions about their data and provide simple opt-out mechanisms to respect user privacy preferences.

Compliance With Data Protection Regulations

Organizations must adhere to relevant laws and frameworks, like the GDPR, CCPA, and other applicable regional data protection laws. Compliance entails implementing measures to ensure the lawful and ethical handling of customer data, obtaining informed consent for data processing, and providing transparent data collection and usage policies. Organizations must also establish processes for data subject access requests and breach notifications, as required by the regulations. Regular reviews and updates to data protection practices are essential to comply with evolving legal requirements. By complying with data protection regulations, organizations demonstrate their commitment to protecting customer privacy and upholding ethical data management practices in ChatGPT systems.

Secure Infrastructure and Incident Response

Establish a robust and secure infrastructure with encryption, access controls, and regular security audits. Develop a comprehensive incident response plan to quickly detect, contain, and recover from security incidents. Regularly test the incident response procedures through simulations and tabletop exercises.

Data Minimization, User Education, and Engagement

Implement data minimization principles to collect and retain only necessary user data. Utilize anonymization techniques to reduce the risk of re-identification and protect user identities. Promote user education on data privacy and security best practices. Engage users through security awareness campaigns, guiding, recognizing, and reporting security threats. Encourage users to actively participate in providing feedback to improve the system's security measures. Building and maintaining user trust is essential for the success of any ChatGPT system. Organizations can foster user trust by prioritizing data privacy and security, leading to increased user engagement and loyalty. By applying these lessons, organizations can create a secure and privacy-conscious environment for their ChatGPT systems, ensuring AI technology's responsible and ethical use while safeguarding user data and privacy.

Collaboration, Transparency, and Continuous Improvement

Foster a culture of collaboration and transparency within the organization and with users. Engage in open communication about security practices, incident response, and privacy policies. Build trust with users by demonstrating a commitment to transparency and user-centric security measures. Continuously monitor and assess the security posture of the ChatGPT system. Regularly update security protocols, data protection measures, and privacy policies based on the latest industry standards and emerging threats. Ensure that the deployment of ChatGPT systems adheres to ethical principles and respects user rights. Strive for responsible and fair use of AI technology, avoiding any potential misuse of user data.

SOLUTIONS AND RECOMMENDATIONS

To enhance data privacy and security in ChatGPT systems, enterprises should implement a comprehensive and multifaceted strategy. Implementing strong encryption methods for data during transmission and storage guarantees the confidentiality of consumer information. Enforcing stringent access restrictions and authentication systems limits unwanted access while conducting frequent security audits and updates strengthens the system against emerging threats. Therefore, the following suggestions could be proposed for data privacy and security in ChatGPT systems:

- Employ robust encryption to protect client data both during transmission and while stored, preventing illegal access. Enforce access restrictions and authentication techniques to limit system entrance, guaranteeing that only authorized workers can retrieve sensitive data.

- Perform routine security audits and vulnerability assessments to detect and rectify any potential vulnerabilities in the system. Deliver extensive user education and training on optimal security protocols to empower users in identifying and minimizing potential security risks.
- Incorporate privacy by design concepts into the development process by integrating data protection measures at the fundamental level of the system's architecture. Perform privacy impact evaluations to detect and alleviate any privacy hazards, guaranteeing a proactive and privacy-aware strategy.
- Ensure that your staff is well-informed and adheres to data protection standards, adapting your processes to meet legal obligations. Effectively and openly engage with clients about the utilization and safeguarding of data, cultivating confidence and showcasing a dedication to ethical data management.
- Direct attention towards doing research and development activities aimed at improving comprehensibility, clarity, and reduction of bias in language models. This guarantees that these models adhere to ethical norms, meet user expectations, and contribute to a more responsible and safer AI ecosystem.
- Create and uphold a thorough incident response plan to effectively handle and minimize the consequences of security issues. Provide a clear and concise outline of the necessary actions to be implemented in the case of a data security breach, facilitating a prompt and efficient reaction to mitigate any harm.
- Investigate progress in multi-modal language models that possess the ability to comprehend and produce material across several modalities, including text, pictures, and audio. Explore novel frameworks and instructional approaches to develop AI systems that are adaptable and perceptive, enhancing the functionalities of ChatGPT while prioritizing the safeguarding of data privacy and security.

FUTURE RESEARCH DIRECTIONS

An area of concentration involves improving the comprehensibility and clarity of models such as ChatGPT. Researchers aim to devise techniques that offer consumers a more lucid comprehension of model judgments, thereby cultivating trust and comprehension. This entails exploring methods for producing more comprehensible outputs and creating tools to visually represent and clarify the inner mechanisms of intricate language models. In addition, further studies will probably investigate enhancing the process of fine-tuning to increase the adaptability of models to individual user requirements while reducing biases. The imperative objective is to comprehend and alleviate biases in language models to guarantee equitable and comprehensive artificial intelligence (Zhao et al., 2022). The researchers will examine approaches to remove bias from training data, assess the performance of models across various user demographics, and incorporate strategies that prioritize ethical issues during the creation and implementation of these systems.

There is an increasing fascination with multi-modal language models that possess the ability to comprehend and produce content encompassing various modalities, incorporating text, graphics, and maybe audio. The incorporation of various forms of data into language models poses fresh difficulties and prospects, compelling researchers to investigate inventive structures and training approaches for AI systems that are more adaptable and sensitive to context. The future research directions emphasize the dedication to enhancing language models by prioritizing transparency, fairness, and wider usability in many domains and user scenarios.

CONCLUSION

The convergence of data privacy, security, and transparency in technology is crucial for cultivating a reliable and morally upright digital environment. The importance of strong encryption, access controls, and ongoing research to improve interpretability is evident as technologies like ChatGPT continue to influence human-machine interactions. The harmonious interaction among regulatory compliance, privacy by design, and proactive user education establishes the basis for conscientious management of data. An important obstacle is the widespread absence of transparency, which can undermine consumer confidence and hinder accountability. To effectively traverse these intricacies, firms must give priority to transparent communication regarding data practices. Maintaining a harmonious equilibrium between innovation and openness guarantees the ongoing development of sophisticated technologies while also demonstrating a dedicated effort to safeguarding user interests. This, in turn, sets the stage for a future where state-of-the-art AI is synonymous with transparency, security, and ethical management of data.

The effective deployment of secure ChatGPT systems showcases the utmost significance of data privacy and security in the swiftly advancing realm of AI technology. Organizations can establish user trust and confidence by using privacy-preserving procedures and strong data protection protections right from the beginning of the system's development, following a privacy-by-design strategy. Transparent policies about data collection and usage, along with procedures for informed consent and opting out, empower users to make well-informed choices about their data. This reinforces the ideals of user autonomy and control. Adhering to data protection regulations guarantees adherence to the law and demonstrates the organization's dedication to protecting user privacy and rights. Furthermore, establishing a robust architecture that incorporates encryption, access controls, and proactive incident response capabilities strengthens the system's ability to withstand future threats, hence improving data security. The successful implementation of these studies demonstrates the importance of ongoing enhancement, user instruction, and ethical deployment of AI. This underscores the necessity of a cooperative and open approach to safeguarding data privacy and security. As AI technology progresses, placing importance on data privacy and security will continue to be crucial in building user confidence, encouraging responsible AI usage, and designing a future where ChatGPT systems empower users while protecting their sensitive information.

ABBREVIATION

AES Advanced Encryption Standard
AI Artificial Intelligence
API Application Programming Interface
APPs Australian Privacy Principles
CCPA California Consumer Privacy Act
CIA Confidentiality, Integrity, and Availability
DPIA Data Protection Impact Assessment
ELIZA Excellence in Learning and Intelligent Systems
GDPR General Data Protection Regulation
HIPAA Health Insurance Portability and Accountability Act
IDS Intrusion Detection Systems
MFA Multi-Factor Authentication
ML Machine Learning
NLP Natural Language Processing
PDPA Personal Data Protection Act
PII Personally Identifiable Information
PIPA Personal Information Protection Act
PIPEDA Personal Information Protection and Electronic Documents Act
RBAC Role-Based Access Control
RSA Rivest-Shamir-Adleman
SMPC Secure Multi-Party Computation

REFERENCES

Adetayo, A. J. (2023). Artificial intelligence chatbots in academic libraries: The rise of ChatGPT. *Library Hi Tech News*, *40*(3), 18–21. Advance online publication. doi:10.1108/LHTN-01-2023-0007

Ahn, C. (2023). Exploring ChatGPT for information of cardiopulmonary resuscitation. *Resuscitation*, *185*, 109729. Advance online publication. doi:10.1016/j.resuscitation.2023.109729 PMID:36773836

AlAfnan, Dishari, Jovic, & Lomidze. (2023). ChatGPT as an Educational Tool: Opportunities, Challenges, and Recommendations for Communication, Business Writing, and Composition Courses. *Journal of Artificial Intelligence and Technology*. doi:10.37965/jait.2023.0184

Ali, J. K. M., Shamsan, M. A. A., Hezam, T. A., & Mohammed, A. A. Q. (2023). Impact of ChatGPT on Learning Motivation. *Journal of English Studies in Arabia Felix*, *2*(1), 41–49. Advance online publication. doi:10.56540/jesaf.v2i1.51

Alnssyan, B., Ahmad, Z., Malela-Majika, J. C., Seong, J. T., & Shafik, W. (2023). On the identifiability and statistical features of a new distributional approach with reliability applications. *AIP Advances*, *13*(12), 125211. Advance online publication. doi:10.1063/5.0178555

Alshurafat, H. (2023). The Usefulness and Challenges of Chatbots for Accounting Professionals: Application On ChatGPT. SSRN *Electronic Journal*. doi:10.2139/ssrn.4345921

Analytica, O. (2023). *ChatGPT dramatically fuels corporate interest in AI*. Emerald Expert Briefings. doi:10.1108/OXAN-ES275852

AntakiF.ToumaS.MiladD.El-KhouryJ.DuvalR. (2023). Evaluating the Performance of ChatGPT in Ophthalmology: An Analysis of its Successes and Shortcomings. MedRxiv. doi:10.1101/2023.01.22.23284882

BenoitJ. R. A. (2023). ChatGPT for Clinical Vignette Generation, Revision, and Evaluation. MedRxiv. doi:10.1101/2023.02.04.23285478

Bishop, L. (2023). Can ChatGPT "Think Like a Lawyer?" A Socratic Dialogue. SSRN *Electronic Journal*. doi:10.2139/ssrn.4338995

Biswas, S. (2023). ChatGPT and the Future of Medical Writing. *Radiology*, *307*(2), e223312. Advance online publication. doi:10.1148/radiol.223312 PMID:36728748

BommineniV. L.BhagwagarS. Z.BalcarcelD. & ... (2023). Performance of ChatGPT on the MCAT: The Road to Personalized and Equitable Premedical Learning. MedRxiv. doi:10.1101/2023.03.05.23286533

Castro Nascimento, C. M., & Pimentel, A. S. (2023). Do Large Language Models Understand Chemistry? A Conversation with ChatGPT. *Journal of Chemical Information and Modeling*, *63*(6), 1649–1655. Advance online publication. doi:10.1021/acs.jcim.3c00285 PMID:36926868

Chinonso, O. E., Theresa, A. M.-E., & Aduke, T. C. (2023). ChatGPT for Teaching, Learning and Research: Prospects and Challenges. *Global Academic Journal of Humanities and Social Sciences*, *5*(02), 33–40. Advance online publication. doi:10.36348/gajhss.2023.v05i02.001

Cotton, D. R. E., Cotton, P. A., & Shipway, J. R. (2023). Chatting and cheating: Ensuring academic integrity in the era of ChatGPT. *Innovations in Education and Teaching International*. Advance online publication. doi:10.1080/14703297.2023.2190148

Dida, H. A., Chakravarthy, D., & Rabbi, F. (2023). *ChatGPT and Big Data: Enhancing Text-to-Speech Conversion*. Mesopotamian Journal of Big Data. doi:10.58496/MJBD/2023/005

Eke, D. O. (2023). ChatGPT and the rise of generative AI: Threat to academic integrity? *Journal of Responsible Technology*, *13*, 100060. Advance online publication. doi:10.1016/j.jrt.2023.100060

Fido, D., & Wallace, L. (2023). *The Unique Role of ChatGPT in Closing the Awarding Gap*. The Interdisciplinary Journal of Student Success.

Gabbiadini, A., Dimitri, O., Baldissarri, C., & Manfredi, A. (2023). Does ChatGPT Pose a Threat to Human Identity? SSRN *Electronic Journal*. doi:10.2139/ssrn.4377900

Gao, Y., Tong, W., Wu, E. Q., Chen, W., Zhu, G. Y., & Wang, F. Y. (2023). Chat with ChatGPT on Interactive Engines for Intelligent Driving. *IEEE Transactions on Intelligent Vehicles*, *8*(3), 2034–2036. Advance online publication. doi:10.1109/TIV.2023.3252571

Giunti, M., Garavaglia, F. G., Giuntini, R., Pinna, S., & Sergioli, G. (2023). Chatgpt Prospective Student at Medical School. SSRN *Electronic Journal*. doi:10.2139/ssrn.4378743

Gregorcic, B., & Pendrill, A. M. (2023). ChatGPT and the frustrated Socrates. *Physics Education*, *58*(3), 035021. Advance online publication. doi:10.1088/1361-6552/acc299

Grünebaum, A., Chervenak, J., Pollet, S. L., Katz, A., & Chervenak, F. A. (2023). The Exciting Potential for ChatGPT in Obstetrics and Gynecology. *American Journal of Obstetrics and Gynecology*, *228*(6), 696–705. Advance online publication. doi:10.1016/j.ajog.2023.03.009 PMID:36924907

Gunawan, J. (2023). Exploring the future of nursing: Insights from the ChatGPT model. *Belitung Nursing Journal*, *9*(1), 1–5. Advance online publication. doi:10.33546/bnj.2551 PMID:37469634

Halloran, L. J. S., Mhanna, S., & Brunner, P. (2023). AI tools such as ChatGPT will disrupt hydrology, too. *Hydrological Processes*, *37*(3), e14843. Advance online publication. doi:10.1002/hyp.14843

Haman, M., & Školník, M. (2023). Using ChatGPT to conduct a literature review. *Accountability in Research*, 1–3. Advance online publication. doi:10.1080/08989621.2023.2185514 PMID:36879536

Jun, Y., Craig, A., Shafik, W., & Sharif, L. (2021). Artificial intelligence application in cybersecurity and cyberdefense. *Wireless Communications and Mobile Computing*, *2021*, 1–10. doi:10.1155/2021/3329581

Kumar, H. S. (2023). Analysis of ChatGPT Tool to Assess the Potential of its Utility for Academic Writing in Biomedical Domain. *Biology, Engineering. Medicine and Science Reports*, *9*(1), 24–30. Advance online publication. doi:10.5530/bems.9.1.5

Lieberman, M. (2023). What Is ChatGPT and How Is It Used in Education? *Education Week*, *42*(18). https://www. edweek. org/technology/what-is-chatgpt-and-how-is-it-used-in-education/2023/01

LiuS.WrightA. P.PattersonB. L.WandererJ. P.TurerR. W.NelsonS. D.McCoyA. B.SittigD. F.WrightA. (2023). *Assessing the Value of ChatGPT for Clinical Decision Support Optimization*. doi:10.1101/2023.02.21.23286254

Macey-Dare, R. (2023). ChatGPT & Generative AI Systems as Quasi-Expert Legal Advice Lawyers - Case Study Considering Potential Appeal Against Conviction of Tom Hayes. SSRN *Electronic Journal*. doi:10.2139/ssrn.4342686

Magazine, B. A.-C. D. (2023). Why ChatGPT is such a big deal for education. *Scholarspace.Jccc.Edu*.

Mattas, P. S. (2023). ChatGPT: A Study of AI Language Processing and its Implications. *International Journal of Research Publication and Reviews*, *04*(02), 435–440. Advance online publication. doi:10.55248/gengpi.2023.4218

McGee, R. W. (2023). Capitalism, Socialism and ChatGPT. SSRN *Electronic Journal*. doi:10.2139/ssrn.4369953

Mijwil, M., Aljanabi, M., & Ali, A. H. (2023). *ChatGPT: Exploring the Role of Cybersecurity in the Protection of Medical Information*. Mesopotamian Journal of Cyber Security. doi:10.58496/MJCS/2023/004

NastasiA. J.CourtrightK. R.HalpernS. D.WeissmanG. E. (2023). Does ChatGPT Provide Appropriate and Equitable Medical Advice? A Vignette-Based, Clinical Evaluation Across Care Contexts. MedRxiv. doi:10.1101/2023.02.25.23286451

Nisar, S., & Aslam, M. S. (2023). Is ChatGPT a Good Tool for T&CM Students in Studying Pharmacology? SSRN *Electronic Journal*. doi:10.2139/ssrn.4324310

Perkins, M. (2023). Academic Integrity considerations of AI Large Language Models in the post-pandemic era: ChatGPT and beyond. *Journal of University Teaching & Learning Practice*, *20*(2). Advance online publication. doi:10.53761/1.20.02.07

Polonsky, M., & Rotman, J. (2023). Should Artificial Intelligent (AI) Agents be Your Co-author? Arguments in favour, informed by ChatGPT. SSRN *Electronic Journal*. doi:10.2139/ssrn.4349524

Regalia, J. (2023). ChatGPT and Legal Writing: The Perfect Union? SSRN *Electronic Journal*. doi:10.2139/ssrn.4371460

Sakirin, T., & Ben Said, R. (2023). *User preferences for ChatGPT-powered conversational interfaces versus traditional methods*. Mesopotamian Journal of Computer Science. doi:10.58496/MJCSC/2023/006

Shafik, W. (2023). A Comprehensive Cybersecurity Framework for Present and Future Global Information Technology Organizations. In *Effective Cybersecurity Operations for Enterprise-Wide Systems* (pp. 56–79). IGI Global. doi:10.4018/978-1-6684-9018-1.ch002

Shafik, W. (2024a). Introduction to ChatGPT. In *Advanced Applications of Generative AI and Natural Language Processing Models* (pp. 1–25). IGI Global. doi:10.4018/979-8-3693-0502-7.ch001

Shafik, W. (2024b). Predicting Future Cybercrime Trends in the Metaverse Era. In *Forecasting Cyber Crimes in the Age of the Metaverse* (pp. 78–113). IGI Global. doi:10.4018/979-8-3693-0220-0.ch005

Shah, C. (2023). The Rise of AI Chat Agents and the Discourse with Dilettantes. SSRN *Electronic Journal*. doi:10.2139/ssrn.4327315

Shaji George, A., Hovan George, A., & Martin, A. (2023). A Review of ChatGPT AI's Impact on Several Business Sectors. *Partners Universal International Innovation Journal, 1*(1).

ShueE.LiuL.LiB.FengZ.LiX.HuG. (2023). Empowering Beginners in Bioinformatics with ChatGPT. BioRxiv. doi:10.1101/2023.03.07.531414

Sinha, R. K., Deb Roy, A., Kumar, N., & Mondal, H. (2023). Applicability of ChatGPT in Assisting to Solve Higher Order Problems in Pathology. *Cureus*. Advance online publication. doi:10.7759/cureus.35237 PMID:36968864

Yusuf, S. (2023). ChatGPT, the Blade in Scientific Writing. *Indonesian Contemporary Nursing Journal*. https://orcid.org/0000-0002-5993-9325

Zhao, L., Zhu, D., Shafik, W., Matinkhah, S. M., Ahmad, Z., Sharif, L., & Craig, A. (2022). Artificial intelligence analysis in cyber domain: A review. *International Journal of Distributed Sensor Networks, 18*(4), 15501329221084882. doi:10.1177/15501329221084882

Zielinski, C., Winker, M., Aggarwal, R., Ferris, L., Heinemann, M., Lapeña, Jr, J. F., Pai, S., Ing, E., & Citrome, L. (2023). Chatbots, ChatGPT, and Scholarly Manuscripts: WAME Recommendations on ChatGPT and Chatbots in Relation to Scholarly Publications. *Open Access Macedonian Journal of Medical Sciences, 11*(A). doi:10.3889/oamjms.2023.11502

ADDITIONAL READING

Babu, C. S., & Akshara, P. M. (2024). Revolutionizing Conversational AI: Unleashing the Power of ChatGPT-Based Applications in Generative AI and Natural Language Processing. In Advanced Applications of Generative AI and Natural Language Processing Models (pp. 228-248). IGI Global.

Bapat, G., Mahindru, R., Kumar, A., Rroy, A. D., Bhoyar, S., & Vaz, S. (2024). Leveraging ChatGPT for Empowering MSMEs: A Paradigm Shift in Problem Solving. *Engineering Proceedings*, *59*(1), 197.

Bhayana, R. (2024). Chatbots and Large Language Models in Radiology: A Practical Primer for Clinical and Research Applications. *Radiology*, *310*(1), e232756. doi:10.1148/radiol.232756 PMID:38226883

Bouteraa, M., Chekima, B., Thurasamy, R., Bin-Nashwan, S. A., Al-Daihani, M., Baddou, A., Sadallah, M., & Ansar, R. (2024). Open Innovation in the Financial Sector: A Mixed-Methods Approach to Assess Bankers' Willingness to Embrace Open-AI ChatGPT. *Journal of Open Innovation*, *10*(1), 100216. doi:10.1016/j.joitmc.2024.100216

Coello, C. E. A., Alimam, M. N., & Kouatly, R. (2024). Effectiveness of ChatGPT in Coding: A Comparative Analysis of Popular Large Language Models. *Digital*, *4*(1), 114–125. doi:10.3390/digital4010005

Dwivedi, Y. K., Pandey, N., Currie, W., & Micu, A. (2024). Leveraging ChatGPT and other generative artificial intelligence (AI)-based applications in the hospitality and tourism industry: Practices, challenges and research agenda. *International Journal of Contemporary Hospitality Management*, *36*(1), 1–12. doi:10.1108/IJCHM-05-2023-0686

Kondurkar, I., Raj, A., & Lakshmi, D. (2024). Modern Applications with a Focus on Training ChatGPT and GPT Models: Exploring Generative AI and NLP. In *Advanced Applications of Generative AI and Natural Language Processing Models* (pp. 186–227). IGI Global.

Tyagi, A. K. (2024). Transformative Effects of ChatGPT on the Modern Era of Education and Society: From Society's and Industry's Perspectives. In *Machine Learning Algorithms Using Scikit and TensorFlow Environments* (pp. 374–387). IGI Global.

Zhang, H., & Shao, H. (2024). Exploring the Latest Applications of OpenAI and ChatGPT: An In-Depth Survey. *CMES-Computer Modeling in Engineering & Sciences, 138*(3).

Zhao, J., & Wang, X. (2024). Unleashing efficiency and insights: Exploring the potential applications and challenges of ChatGPT in accounting. *Journal of Corporate Accounting & Finance*, *35*(1), 269–276. doi:10.1002/jcaf.22663

KEY TERMS AND DEFINITIONS

ChatGPT Systems: Is an artificial intelligence developed by OpenAI, which is an advanced language model based on the GPT-3.5 architecture, capable of generating human-like text responses and understanding a wide array of natural language inputs.

Customer Information: Pertains to the data and particulars concerning individuals or entities that participate in transactions, interactions, or associations with a business or service provider. This data may encompass personal particulars, such as names, contact details, and purchase records.

Data Privacy: Can be defined as the safeguarding of individuals' personal information and the conscientious management of data to guarantee confidentiality, integrity, and security. Data privacy encompasses the regulation and management of the collection, utilization, dissemination, and retention of personal information by both entities and individuals.

Data Security: Embraces the strategies and procedures put in place to safeguard digital data from unauthorized entry, disclosure, modification, destruction, and other types of data breaches or cyber risks.

OpenAI: Is an AI research facility and corporation dedicated to promoting the development of digital intelligence in a secure and advantageous manner. The company was established in December 2015 by Elon Musk, Sam Altman, Greg Brockman, Ilya Sutskever, John Schulman, and Wojciech Zaremba, among other individuals. The objective of OpenAI is to guarantee that artificial general intelligence (AGI) is advantageous for the entirety of humanity.

Chapter 4
Artificial Intelligence-Supported Travel Agencies:
Analysis of ChatGPT Usage and Future Perspectives

Emre Yaşar
Isparta University of Applied Sciences, Turkey

Eda Yayla
Nevşehir Hacı Bektaş Veli University, Turkey

Nesrin Aydın Alakuş
https://orcid.org/0000-0001-7263-4457
Süleyman Demirel University, Turkey

ABSTRACT

This research aims to determine the use of ChatGPT in travel agencies. Another aim is to make inferences about the potential effects and use of ChatGPT in the future. The potential of ChatGPT to offer convenience and time-saving benefits to travel agencies is highlighted, particularly in the context of tour preparation and content generation. Integrating ChatGPT into the workflow of travel agencies is seen as a means to enhance customer satisfaction. ChatGPT will likely have a positive impact on customer satisfaction. The ability to swiftly and effectively access information, along with the potential to deliver more in-depth and precise data to customers, is identified as key contributors to increased satisfaction. It is thought that ChatGPT can encourage customers to create their own travel plans by providing more information on their travels and may lead them to travel without an agent.

DOI: 10.4018/979-8-3693-1239-1.ch004

INTRODUCTION

Artificial intelligence applications, or chatbots, are used in various ways in different sectors (Ali, 2023). ChatGPT, one of these applications, is positioned ahead of previous artificial intelligence applications with its impact (Ray, 2023). The fact that it fulfills various task definitions with mutual conversation differentiates ChatGPT from other artificial intelligence-supported applications (Chen et al., 2023). For this reason, ChatGPT is known as the application that has been popular and has attracted attention in artificial intelligence for the last two years. (Mich & Garigliano, 2023). ChatGPT is a chat agent functional language model developed under the direction of OPENAI (OpenAI, 2023).

ChatGPT offers customized suggestions for customers' preferences in different sectors and assists marketing efforts by concluding their preferences (Paul et al., 2023). ChatGPT can be utilized to develop new products and processes (Carvalho & Ivanov, 2023). ChatGPT is a tool that can creatively solve problems in individuals' daily lives (Korzynski et al., 2023). The fact that these positive contributions are realized at any time of the day in line with the wishes of individuals and the availability of a free version makes ChatGPT even more preferable (Chui et al., 2022; Keiper, 2023). The use of ChatGPT in various business, education, and management areas is increasing due to its contribution and ease of use (Kasneci et al., 2023). The tourism sector is suitable for ChatGPT (Dwivedi et al., 2023a).

Artificial intelligence (applications such as ChatGPT) is an essential resource in realizing the digital transformation of the tourism sector (Demir & Demir, 2015). Although artificial intelligence-supported ChatGPT is in its infancy in the tourism sector (Dwivedi et al., 2023b), significant advantages can be achieved in the tourism sector using ChatGPT (Wong et al., 2023). The main contributions of ChatGPT to the tourism sector are expressed in terms of destinations, businesses, and tourists (Gursoy et al., 2023). Some of the prominent contributions of ChatGPT are identifying new market areas for destinations and creating promotional activities for emerging destinations (Mich & Garigliano, 2023), providing support to the management and human resources of hotels (Carvalho & Ivanov, 2023), and providing travel and activity suggestions based on tourists' wishes (Fusté-Forné & Orea-Giner, 2023).

It is seen that ChatGPT is effective in providing services in the tourism sector in a more efficient and personalized manner to the wishes of the customers (Demir & Demir, 2023a). Additionally, ChatGPT is an invaluable resource for tourism businesses to draw conclusions about current and future trends and develop strategies. Travel agencies are part of these businesses. However, research on the use and effects of ChatGPT in travel agencies is limited (Demir & Demir, 2023b).

With the digital transformation process, the widespread use of artificial intelligence applications such as ChatGPT represents a critical development area for travel agencies and other businesses in the tourism sector. For this reason, it is necessary to examine the use and areas of ChatGPT in travel agencies' current activities and make inferences for the future. Within the scope of this information, this research aims to determine the use of ChatGPT in travel agencies, perceived advantages and disadvantages, and essential impressions. In addition, another aim is to make inferences about the potential effects and use of ChatGPT in the future.

BACKGROUND

ChatGPT and Tourism

Stakeholders in the tourism sector, including entities such as travel agencies, hotels, destination management, and tourists, can leverage ChatGPT for various purposes (Demir & Demir, 2023a). The application of ChatGPT facilitates the innovation process within tourism businesses (Ali et al., 2023). contribute artificial intelligence tools, such as ChatGPT, contributes to an enhanced understanding of customer preferences, streamlined reservation processes, and comprehensive management of customer complaints (Demir et al., 2022). Moreover, ChatGPT proves to be a valuable asset in recruiting human resources for businesses (Carvalho & Ivanov, 2023). The integration of ChatGPT in business decision-making processes is advantageous (Ivanov, 2022). Its efficiency extends to analyzing customer preferences and identifying trends, making it a recommended tool (Harahap et al., 2023).

Destination management can effectively employ ChatGPT in promotional activities (Soliman & Al Balushi, 2023). This includes the creation of advertising texts and visuals for destination promotion, as well as tracking tourist preferences. Additionally, extracting keywords from tourist comments makes it feasible to discern both positive and negative aspects throughout the destination (Carvalho & Ivanov, 2023).

Tourists can derive substantial benefits from ChatGPT throughout the entire travel process from pre-travel arrangements to during and after their travel. ChatGPT simplifies trip planning for tourists by offering a cost-effective alternative, eliminating the necessity for a travel agency or intermediary. Furthermore, ChatGPT excels at generating fitting and logical recommendations through extensive research within its broad knowledge base (Dwivedi et al., 2023a). Before embarking on their travels, tourists utilize ChatGPT to craft personalized travel plans tailored to their preferences (Sudirjo et al., 2023). Within the realm of travel planning, ChatGPT meticulously outlines programs encompassing accommodations, sightseeing destinations, restaurants, and entertainment centers, all designed to align with the individual desires of the tourists (Carvalho & Ivanov, 2023). This personalized travel plan serves as a reflection of the specific wishes of the tourists (Iskender, 2023).

A significant advantage offered by ChatGPT prior to travel is its ability to shield tourists from unnecessary information. By furnishing essential information and suggestions in line with tourists' preferences while filtering out extraneous details, ChatGPT ensures that travelers remain focused on pertinent information, ultimately saving them valuable time (Wong et al., 2023).

While traveling, tourists can utilize ChatGPT to adapt their travel plans in real-time, catering to instant requests and seeking alternative suggestions (Ali et al., 2023). In the event of any disruptions, ChatGPT remains accessible throughout the day, offering solutions and facilitating adjustments as required (Chatterjee & Dethlefs, 2023). ChatGPT not only aids in logistical adjustments but also serves as an educational tool, allowing tourists to immerse themselves in different cultures and engage with diverse people during their travels (Wong et al., 2023).

Post-travel, ChatGPT continues to be a valuable asset by assisting tourists creatively and enthusiastically in sharing their experiences (Gursoy et al., 2023). It can help users craft engaging narratives and designs, enhancing the storytelling aspect of their travel adventures. Additionally, ChatGPT and similar artificial intelligence tools can be employed to create visually appealing pictures and videos that tourists are likely to share on social media platforms, further enriching the post-travel narrative (Cao et al., 2023).

ChatGPT and Travel Agencies

Artificial intelligence technologies such as ChatGPT are transforming many industries and providing businesses with opportunities to optimize processes, improve decision-making, enhance customer experiences, and innovate in ways that were not previously possible (Demir & Demir, 2023a). ChatGPT and chatbots respond to customer requests and needs and frequently asked questions. In 2016, for example, Kayak was used as a travel planning robot on Facebook Messenger. The chatbot assists users with flight, hotel, and rental car requests and provides personalized travel recommendations based on user preferences (Loureiro et al., 2022). Another example is Expedia. Announcing via tweet that it will add a beta ChatGPT interface to its app, Expedia creates a system that allows users to plan their vacations by presenting their preferences, length of stay, and budget to the chatbot and some natural language responses that offer hotel or activity recommendations (Barr, 2023).

In addition, Matador Network's ChatGPT-powered travel assistant GuideGeek offers travel tips and live flight and vacation rental data, all accessible via WhatsApp. As the examples show, ChatGPT can bring many benefits to travel agencies. Based on this, the advantages of ChatGPT for travel agencies can be listed as follows;

- Travel agencies use ChatGPT in a supply-driven manner, and consumers in a demand-driven manner. ChatGPT can save time and cost for travel agencies by automating goods and services queries in routine tasks such as flight and hotel bookings (George & George, 2023).
- It can increase productivity and efficiency by further facilitating customer service in in-office and out-of-office operations in travel agencies (Carvalho & Ivanov, 2023).
- It can create customized flight forecasts, pricing optimization, destination preferences, activities, accommodation options, optimized travel plans with efficient routes, menu planning, and alternative holiday preferences according to the tastes and needs of the consumer (Demir & Demir, 2023a).
- With data collection and analysis capabilities, ChatGPT can create personalized recommendations based on consumers' previous travels (Demir & Demir, 2023b).

On the other hand, businesses need to use ChatGPT correctly integrate it into their operational processes and continuously evaluate and improve its performance. In addition to the benefits that ChatGPT will provide to the tourism sector and, subsequently, to travel agencies, there are also unresolved question marks. ChatGPT has shortcomings regarding reality-based information (Zhuo et al., 2023). For this reason, ChatGPT users need to check the accuracy of the data obtained. In addition, ChatGPT has a human fluency in data transfer but does not have a human's reasoning ability. Therefore, there may be difficulties in generating answers to complex and abstract questions and understanding the context and consequences of text input (OpenAI, 2023).

ChatGPT can pose a significant threat to cybersecurity as it has the potential to significantly increase the creation and distribution of content such as spam, misinformation, phishing, and malware (Karanjai, 2022). Therefore, complete reliance on ChatGPT without human control and expertise can lead to significant inaccuracies and content falsification (Carvalho & Ivanov, 2023). From this perspective, the hesitations about ChatGPT can be listed as follows;

- There is no mechanism to indicate the need for more accuracy of an answer provided by ChatGPT (Chui et al., 2022), and it cannot ask clarifying questions about ambiguous prompts (OpenAI, 2023).
- Although it has an extensive database on specific topics, it may provide limited data on understanding and responding to the nuances of particular languages, user experiences, and cultural differences (Demir & Demir, 2023a).
- The use of ChatGPT to solve customer problems reduces staff-customer interaction and may deprive customers of personal contact, empathy, and

authentic experience (Iskender, 2023). As a result, the social value of travel experiences may decrease, and consumers may become lonely (Tussyadiah, 2020).

- ChatGPT's predefined algorithms and rules may lead to the standardization of services in travel agencies and hinder staff creativity (Demir & Demir, 2023b).
- Using ChatGPT may cause data privacy and security risks in terms of sharing customers' data with third parties with travel agencies.
- Users involved in third-age tourism with less experience with ChatGPT may have problems with access and use. This may lead to inequalities in travel experiences.

MAIN FOCUS OF THE CHAPTER

Research Method

This research adopted a qualitative research method to obtain comprehensive information about ChatGPT from the perspective of travel agency employees. Qualitative research is chosen for its ability to delve deeply into individuals' thoughts on a subject (Creswell, 2013). In this research, semi-structured interview technique, which is a qualitative research method, was used to learn the opinions of travel agency employees about ChatGPT. This technique allows the researcher to begin with predefined questions and adapt the interview structure based on the participant's responses (Brinkmann, 2014). To facilitate this, an interview form was developed, comprising five demographic questions and 11 questions aimed at understanding the opinions of travel agency employees about ChatGPT. These questions were inspired by the work of Demir and Demir (2023a, 2023b). The initial three questions aim to ascertain general impressions and thoughts of employees regarding ChatGPT. Following these, five questions (4-8) were crafted to identify the possible effects of ChatGPT on the operational aspects of travel agencies. Lastly, three questions (9-11) were formulated to discern the possible effects of ChatGPT on travel agency customers. The questions in the interview form are as follows:

1. As you began using ChatGPT, what were your initial impressions?
2. Were there any security and privacy concerns that you encountered while utilizing ChatGPT?
3. In your perspective, what are the advantages and disadvantages associated with ChatGPT?

4. How would you assess the role of employing artificial intelligence applications, such as ChatGPT, in the travel industry?
5. Do you anticipate that ChatGPT will impact your daily workflow and activities in your current role?
6. From your viewpoint, how might the utilization of ChatGPT influence the business model of travel agencies?
7. In your opinion, could travel agencies incorporating ChatGPT make a substantial difference in the sector?
8. What recommendations would you offer to enhance the effective utilization of ChatGPT and similar technologies by travel agencies in the future?
9. Do you believe that ChatGPT and other artificial intelligence applications can have an impact on or differentiate customer satisfaction?
10. How do you envision AI tools, like ChatGPT, shaping customer demands within the travel industry?
11. In your perspective, how might the integration of ChatGPT affect customers' plans for travel?

Sample and Data Collection

The study employed purposive sampling, which involves selecting participants based on specific criteria aligned with the study's objectives (Bernard, 2017). In this case, the participants chosen for the study were employees of a travel agency operating in Antalya with nationwide activities, and a key criterion was that these employees had utilized ChatGPT at least once in their professional duties. Employees who had not utilized ChatGPT were excluded from the study. A total of 7 travel agency employees meeting these criteria were interviewed.

Instead, interviews can continue until data saturation is reached, indicating that ample information has been gathered (Miles & Huberman, 1994). Marshall (1996) emphasizes that interviews should conclude when responses from participants become repetitive. Creswell (2013) suggests that a range of 5 to 25 participants is typically sufficient for interviews. Following this guidance, the interviews for this study were concluded with a total of 7 participants.

The interviews took place between September 25, 2023, and November 22, 2023, at times convenient for the participants and the researcher. On average, each interview lasted for approximately 58 minutes. Before the commencement of the interviews, participants were briefed about the research topic. Voluntary participation and consent for recording were obtained from each participant. After the conclusion of the interviews, the recordings underwent transcription, and both the tapes and transcripts underwent a thorough review.

The collected records were subjected to thematic analysis, a method where researchers identify themes and codes based on the relevant literature. In this study, themes and codes were determined following the approach outlined by Braun and Clarke (2006). The analysis involved several steps, including recognizing the data, creating preliminary codes to reveal content, identifying frequently recurring themes, conducting a thorough check of the themes, defining and naming the themes, finalizing the analysis, and preparing the report, as per the methodology outlined by Braun and Clarke (2006).

Controlling and analyzing the data was a collaborative effort involving three authors. Two academics with expertise in the research subject conducted the final verification. Demographic characteristics of the participants are shown in Table 1.

Table 1. Demographic characteristics of the participants

Participant	Gender	Age	Education	Working Time	Interview Time
P1	Female	26	Master's Degree	2 years	61 minutes
P2	Male	21	Bachelor's	3 years	67 minutes
P3	Female	26	Master's Degree	3 years	48 minutes
P4	Male	27	Bachelor's	6 years	54 minutes
P5	Male	24	Bachelor's	2 years	38 minutes
P6	Male	27	Master's Degree	4 years	78 minutes
P7	Female	27	Bachelor's	5 years	57 minutes

Results

After analyzing participants' responses, three main themes emerged in the research. These themes include general ideas on ChatGPT, the potential effects of ChatGPT on travel agencies, and the potential effects of ChatGPT on customers. The main theme of general ideas about ChatGPT encompasses participants' overall perceptions of ChatGPT usage processes and their thoughts regarding the advantages or disadvantages of ChatGPT. Sub-themes and codes related to the main theme of general ideas about ChatGPT are detailed in Table 2.

Table 2. General ideas about ChatGPT

Main Theme	Sub Themes	Sub Codes	
		Positive Views	**Negative Views**
General Ideas About ChatGPT	ChatGPT First Use Impressions	Being simple and effective	Responses are not original
		Being fast	Repeated responses
		Producing human-like responses	Responses addressed to the general public
	ChatGPT Privacy and Security Perceptions	No privacy and security problems	Perception of insecurity due to the information requested for membership
	ChatGPT Advantages and Disadvantages	Being fast	The need to verify information
		Providing direct access to information	Repetitive responses
		Presenting information in summary form	Presenting outdated and incomplete information
		Time saving	Failure to understand and respond

When the participants' responses indicating their thoughts when they used ChatGPT for the first time are evaluated, it is a common opinion that ChatGPT is simple, effective, and fast. For example, P1 said, *"I think it is simple and useful. It is a fast program that will not take up one's time.''* P7 said, *"I think it has a simple screen and is straightforward to use. You need to write clearly what you want.''* Participants shared positive experiences of ChatGPT's comprehensive, human-like answers that exceeded their expectations. In this regard, P2 said, *"It was an application that exceeded my expectations. I found it strange because I did not expect it to give such detailed and human answers."* It is understood that the participants saw ChatGPT as a simple and effective application during their first use of ChatGPT. It was also reported that ChatGPT produced answers quickly and was as comprehensive as human answers.

In their first use of ChatGPT, participants expressed their hesitations about the reliability and authenticity of the answers. P3 stated, *"I was a bit hesitant because I was not sure that the idea, the answers given to me, were authentic.''* The lack of personalization, especially the lack of user-specific general recommendations, stands out among the areas for improvement. P4 said, *"I didn't like that it summarized the information and presented it to me as a summary; I expected it to be a more personalized application. When I ask for advice, it gives general answers and does not give personalized information.''* Participants who think ChatGPT will be helpful in various sectors have become aware of content repetition and poor quality over time.

P6 said, *"The fact that it does not give personalized answers turned into repetitive content after a while. I realized that the content became poor quality over time.''* It was also stated that more accessible access to language options should be provided. After the first use, the participants generally stated that they preferred ChatGPT because they found it helpful but that specific improvements should be made.

According to the participants' views on privacy and security on ChatGPT, some stated that they did not experience any privacy and security problems on ChatGPT. P5 stated, *"No, I haven't. I can say that sharing this kind of information has become almost natural.''* Participants point out that basic information, such as e-mail and phone number, is requested even when signing up for any site or game. P4 said, *"No, I haven't. When I register for a game, it asks for the same information requested from me, so I haven't experienced any security concerns.''* Therefore, they do not hesitate to share their personal information while becoming a ChatGPT member and trust ChatGPT.

Some participants said they were worried and anxious about disseminating their personal information. These participants stated that they were surprised to be asked for a phone number at the ChatGPT membership creation stage and that they thought an e-mail address would be sufficient. P1 explained, *"I was uneasy about being asked for my number while registering.''* Participants expressed concerns about the security of their phone numbers in connection with disseminating their information or irrelevant advertisements. P2 said, *"I was worried, especially after it became widespread. Because everyone quickly accesses the information I accessed, and the information given to me was given to other people in the same way, causing us to be in a position of repeating each other.''* At this point, it is seen that the participants' concerns about privacy and security are focused on the request for phone information at the login stage and the sharing of information after ChatGPT became popular.

According to participants' responses, ChatGPT's advantages are diverse. Participants highlighted the most crucial advantage of ChatGPT, which is its efficiency. Time-conscious individuals expressed that ChatGPT enables them to access information directly and efficiently. P1 stated, *"It is nice to access information directly without wasting time. For example, if I type 'places to visit in Antalya' in Google, it suggests multiple sites, and I must examine them individually. Still, thanks to ChatGPT, I can access all this information quickly and on a single page with the collected data."* Another significant advantage participants emphasize in terms of time-saving is ChatGPT expediting the research process. Participants noted that they could accomplish tasks that would have taken hours of research and information gathering in just a few minutes using ChatGPT. P2 mentioned, *"Sometimes my customers ask me questions about places I have never heard of before, and I can quickly learn about the destinations in that region through the application instead of flipping through pages one by one.*" This feature is especially advantageous for professionals who respond rapidly and accurately to customer inquiries.

Another advantage of ChatGPT is its ability to summarize information. Participants noted that ChatGPT's capacity to condense data makes intricate information more understandable, enabling them to concentrate on essential information without being burdened by unnecessary details. P4 stated, *"It provides convenience; that is, it puts all the data in front of us in summary form."* ChatGPT generally facilitates the swift completion of tasks, saving time and enhancing individuals' productivity, especially in time-sensitive situations.

Participants focus on several potential disadvantages related to ChatGPT. First, the information provided by the application should always be confirmed. Because the application responds by collecting data from the internet, there may be things that could be improved. P6 stated, *"It brings us the first information it finds online, not the current information. I can say that the biggest disadvantage is wrong information. For this reason, it is necessary to use it by confirming it.''* Participants also stated that ChatGPT tends to give the same information to everyone and offers repeated answers after a certain point. P2 stated, *"I can say that it repeats itself after a certain point. You need to ask for detailed information; otherwise, it can give superficial or irrelevant answers.''* The concern that unless detailed information is requested, superficial answers may be received, and the application may repeat itself has come to the forefront.

Participants criticized ChatGPT for its tendency to reference information from the internet instead of creating original ideas in response to questions. They pointed out difficulties in language editing and cited this as a disadvantage. They stated that ChatGPT sometimes needs to guide users as intended and may need to understand certain Turkish expressions. P7 expressed, *''To prevent it from being misunderstood and bringing up irrelevant items; we must write exactly what we want to ask or research in detail. Furthermore, the information given is not always accurate and current. When I sought information about a location, it provided me with information that was 2-3 years old.''* Participants emphasized that the application is lacking, particularly in topics with current content, and stressed the importance of verifying the accuracy of the information provided.

The main theme of the potential effects of ChatGPT on travel agencies explains the effects of ChatGPT on travel agencies and determines the effects of ChatGPT in the future. The sub-themes and codes related to the main theme are shown in Table 3.

Table 3. Potential effects of ChatGPT on travel agencies

<table>
<tr><th rowspan="2">Main Theme</th><th rowspan="2">Sub Themes</th><th colspan="2">Sub Codes</th></tr>
<tr><th>Positive Views</th><th>Negative Views</th></tr>
<tr><td rowspan="16">Potential Effects of ChatGPT on Travel Agencies</td><td rowspan="3">Role in the Travel Industry</td><td>Providing convenience</td><td>Sector structure is not yet appropriate</td></tr>
<tr><td>Time saving</td><td rowspan="2">The possibility of unemployment of employees</td></tr>
<tr><td>Facilitating access to information</td></tr>
<tr><td rowspan="2">Effect on Business Activities</td><td>Getting the job done in a short period of time</td><td rowspan="2">There are currently no negative effects</td></tr>
<tr><td>Accelerating information access</td></tr>
<tr><td rowspan="4">Effect on Business Model</td><td>Increasing digitalization</td><td rowspan="4">Reduced number of employees</td></tr>
<tr><td>Preparation of different tours and activities</td></tr>
<tr><td>Establishment of new departments</td></tr>
<tr><td>Making things practical</td></tr>
<tr><td rowspan="3">The Difference It Creates in Agencies</td><td>Competitive Advantage</td><td rowspan="3">It does not make a difference</td></tr>
<tr><td>Customer Satisfaction</td></tr>
<tr><td>Fast service delivery</td></tr>
<tr><td rowspan="3">Recommendations for Travel Agencies</td><td>Training managers and personnel for ChatGPT-like applications</td><td rowspan="3">There are no negative suggestions or opinions.</td></tr>
<tr><td>The individuals to be employed must be knowledgeable about artificial intelligence applications</td></tr>
<tr><td>Establishing a department for ChatGPT and other artificial intelligence applications</td></tr>
</table>

Participants see the impact of ChatGPT on the travel industry as both positive and negative. With ChatGPT's expansion, customers will have more information about local destinations, and activities will become more diverse. P2 said, *''If it is more widely known, everyone can use it to learn more about the Antalya region and participate in more cultural activities.''* At this moment, ChatGPT needs to provide more detailed and personalized information. ChatGPT has the potential to provide convenience and save time for agencies, not just customers. P3 stated, *''It plays a crucial role in the travel industry by making things easier to do or to be done. Agency employees can save time.''*

Participants expressing reservations about ChatGPT's role in the travel industry view it as a helpful tool but emphasize the continued necessity of the human element in an industry that serves many people. P5 emphasized, *"A human element is needed for service in our industry. You need a smiling face and sincerity, which artificial intelligence alone cannot provide."* The frequent use of ChatGPT raises concerns about potential staff reductions in travel agencies and shifts in the workforce. P4 stated, *"Although it is good for people to prepare and go on tours on their own, it may lead to a reduction in staff in travel agencies."* Some argue that ChatGPT cannot directly contribute to traditional travel agency patterns. Nevertheless, as digitalization progresses and the travel industry further embraces this change, the impact of ChatGPT may intensify over time. P1 expressed, *"I don't think it will directly contribute to the travel industry in the first place because travel agencies have a regular pattern. As time passes and the tourism industry adapts more to digitalization, it might."*

The effects of ChatGPT on daily work activities differ among participants. Some participants stated that ChatGPT does not affect their work activities. P5 said, *"It does not affect, but from a future perspective, it may affect. Because, as I mentioned before, the human factor is significant for our sector.''* P1 said, *''Such applications are only tools. With these tools, we can access information quickly and save time.''* On the other hand, P7 thinks that ChatGPT does not affect their business at the moment but will affect it in the future with its increased use. She predicts that artificial intelligence applications such as travel assistants will become more common and facilitate customer communication. P7 said, *''It will affect in the future, but it does not affect today. As its use becomes more widespread, I am sure that we will be intertwined with ChatGPT or other artificial intelligence applications.''*

Some respondents explained that ChatGPT has positively impacted their business activities. It is argued that ChatGPT saves time by providing data quickly. P6 said, *''Yes, it does. I need to write text while doing digital marketing. But when I do it through ChatGPT, I can prepare it faster. These speeds up my work, and I can work more because it saves time.''* P4 said, *''It affects my work positively. Because it saves me time because it quickly filters the data and presents it in front of me."* Some participants stated that ChatGPT does not have a severe impact on their daily work activities at the moment but that its impact will increase shortly. P3 said, *"Its contribution to my workflow may be to save time for the future.''*

Participants stress the importance of digitalization for travel agencies in the context of ChatGPT and its potential effects on their business models. Travel agencies must keep up with digitalization and stay current, according to the statement at this point. In particular, it is noted that agencies should adapt to recent technological innovations by abandoning traditionalism and be able to use applications such as ChatGPT actively. P2 said, *"Agencies need to get out of tradition and keep up to date.''* P5, who thinks digitalization is an inevitable part of business life in general, states that using such artificial intelligence applications by travel agencies can enable them to get ahead of other agencies. P5 said, *"Digitalization is an inevitable part of our age. If an agency uses this kind of artificial intelligence application, it will put it ahead of other travel agencies.''*

P6, who thinks that ChatGPT has the potential to change agencies' business models, states that not digitizing agencies' business may have negative consequences. However, noting that ChatGPT does not provide up-to-date information, he suggests that a new unit may need to be established to filter the data. P6 explained, *"Utilizing artificial intelligence will save time and reduce the number of people doing that job.''* P3 stated that the number of employees in tour planning jobs in travel agencies can be reduced. P3 said, *"The number of people working in tour planning in agencies can be reduced. The workforce can be reduced. Different rotations and activities can be created. Practicality emerges with digitalization. It can attract people's attention more and increase sales.''* On the other hand, P7 stated that a department or section should be established to use ChatGPT more effectively in travel agencies. P7 said, *"First, a department/division must be established. Because there may be inaccuracies in the information and a team should keep the information flow under control to detect and correct these inaccuracies.''* Having a team to detect and correct inaccuracies in the information stands out as an essential step for using ChatGPT effectively.

The majority of participants believe that travel agencies incorporating ChatGPT into their business activities will achieve greater success in the sector, gaining a competitive edge. P2 highlights, *"If they can directly transfer the information from ChatGPT after analyzing it, agencies can be more successful in their business and benefit more from time. If the transfer of the information received from ChatGPT can be done properly, other travel agencies can be ahead of other travel agencies."* The direct transfer of information from ChatGPT is seen as a key factor contributing to success.

Moreover, participants stress that ChatGPT can confer advantages to travel agencies by saving time and enhancing customer satisfaction. P4 emphasizes the value of time, stating, *"Since people's time is valuable, using such artificial intelligence will put us ahead of other companies. Time is important, and this means that we value your time."* Additionally, P5 believes that ChatGPT can distinguish travel agencies from others, saying, *"It will be ahead of other agencies. If the agency uses an artificial intelligence application such as ChatGPT, it allows the guest to access information faster."* Fast information access is considered a means to promptly respond to customers, ultimately boosting sales.

P3, who thinks ChatGPT will not make a big difference in economic conditions, argues that more than artificial intelligence is required in tour arrangement processes requiring expertise and regional knowledge. However, he states that it has the potential to create a new trend and that agencies can gain a competitive advantage with the right marketing strategies. P3 says, *"I don't think it will make much difference in economic conditions because it is a matter of debate how efficient the tours organized by artificial intelligence will be compared to those organized by people who have known this business for years. The person who organizes the tour is usually the person who knows that region. Since artificial intelligence is web-based, it may not have up-to-date information that is not uploaded to the web.''* P6, on the other hand, thinks that ChatGPT will not make a big difference in this period and states that artificial intelligence can only provide preliminary information in the travel industry. P6 says, *"I don't think it will make a difference in this period. It can only help for preliminary information in the travel industry.''*

It is stated that for ChatGPT to be implemented successfully, managers should first know this issue. P1 says, *"First, managers need to know this subject. As they improve themselves, the staff will also improve.''* The importance of providing regular training to managers and staff is emphasized. P4 states, *"In this process, existing staff can be trained on the effective use of such applications.''* P3 points out that agencies should train their staff by hiring people who are competent in the subject to keep up with the developing age. P3 says, *"They need to train their staff by hiring people with good command of this subject.''* P2 states that agencies should be integrated into digital applications, and ChatGPT should be adopted in all areas. P2 says, *"They should be integrated into such digital applications.''*

P6 states that in order to use artificial intelligence applications, data should be filtered in advance and information pollution should be eliminated. He also states that travel agencies have important responsibilities in this regard and that it is necessary to create a new unit with personnel who have knowledge in this field. P6 said, *"A new unit should be established with personnel who have knowledge in the field of artificial intelligence''*. P7, a participant who thinks that the establishment of an artificial intelligence or technology department is important, states that this department should follow and develop applications that are made suitable for travel agencies. P7 said, *"An artificial intelligence or technology department can be established. A department that follows such applications closely and works to make them suitable for the agency.''*

The main theme of the potential effects of ChatGPT on customers refers to how ChatGPT can change customers' expectations and preferences. The sub-themes and codes related to the main theme are shown in Table 4.

Table 4. Potential effects of ChatGPT on customers

Main Theme	Sub Themes	Sub Codes	
		Positive Views	**Negative Views**
Potential Effects of ChatGPT on Customers	Customer Satisfaction	It will positively affect customer satisfaction as it provides information quickly and in the desired manner.	If the information is missing or incorrect, it will negatively affect customer satisfaction.
	Customer Requests	There may be an increase in demand for different destinations	Demand for travel agencies may decrease
		Instant demands of customers at destinations may increase	
	Customers' Travel Plans	Travel agencies continue to be preferred	Individual travel increases

Participants have a common opinion that ChatGPT will positively affect customer satisfaction. P2 said, *"ChatGPT can provide deeper information and give the desired information more clearly and quickly, that is, being able to access information faster positively affects customer satisfaction.''* The fact that the customer can access the information they want more effectively and quickly creates a positive experience. P7 stated, *"It will affect customer satisfaction, and customer satisfaction is already being achieved with applications such as small-scale travel assistants.''* It can be stated that diversification and personalization of artificial intelligence applications in the future may increase satisfaction. P3 states that agencies should use ChatGPT as a marketing tool. P3 said, *"If agency employees convey that they are preparing a tour through artificial intelligence, attractiveness can be created. Such a marketing strategy will positively affect customer satisfaction in terms of attractiveness.''*

Participants such as P4 and P6 mentioned that ChatGPT will positively affect customer satisfaction, but if the information is incorrect or incomplete in content, it may cause dissatisfaction. P4 said, *"Not getting clear answers can anger people and lead to dissatisfaction. People like clear answers."* P6 emphasized, *"Since it is web-based, the lack of a filtering system can lead to dissatisfaction if it misleads customers.''*

Participants state that ChatGPT will create a change in customers' demands. It is emphasized that ChatGPT will increase customers' knowledge about the destination, and different destinations will be preferred. P1 stated, *"Seeing different destinations while researching the destination they want to go to may cause them to research other destinations and want to see them. This may lead to an increase in demand for other destination areas.''* There is also a possibility of an increase in customers' spontaneous demand. P3 said, *"It may increase because people can search for every uncomfortable issue through the application. Time perception may come into play.*

It can increase customer demand. When there is a tour that is not organized, it can help to access direct information instantly when the customer wants a tour for a different place.''

P7 states that customers' demand for travel agencies will decrease. It is mentioned that young people, who are transferred as the new generation, conduct research with ChatGPT, and their loyalty to other businesses and individuals decreases. P7 also claims that customers over middle age will continue to demand travel agencies. P7 said, *"It may reduce the demand for agencies unless the agencies sense this early and make a breakthrough. First, middle-aged and older adults, whose vacation culture is established and has become a habit, want to have a human being in front of them. Habits are hard to change. In the new generation, this situation is different.''*

Participants have various opinions about possible customer travel plan changes after ChatGPT. For example, participants such as P1, P2, and P6 state that after ChatGPT, customers can create travel plans without an agency. P6 stated, *"There will be changes in travel preferences. For example, if I go to Mardin, I will look at the Mardin castle from ChatGPT and other web-based applications and go there. The contribution of artificial intelligence in creating travel routes will be very high in the future. Digitalization is inevitable today. I think people's vacation plans have changed a lot. They want to see more places now. Even I use it when I go on vacation.''*

Participants such as P4, P5, and P7 state that travel plans will now be more individualized, but middle-aged customers will still prefer travel agencies. P4 said, *"At the moment, especially the middle age group, comes to us saying that I don't understand technology and want to make reservations and other transactions by meeting face to face or meeting someone. For this reason, there will be no change in people's travel preferences, especially in the middle-aged and elderly segments. I can say that it will be more effective for the new generation.''* P3 states that customers will prefer travel agencies, mainly due to economic conditions, even if they use applications like ChatGPT. P3 said, "*There are factors such as how much it will cost when they go on their tour according to the planning of the artificial intelligence application or calculating what the cost will be when they go with the travel agency.''*

SOLUTIONS AND RECOMMENDATIONS

The first-time participants used ChatGPT, they described ChatGPT as simple to use, effective, and fast. These positive opinions are supported by the participants' mention of the advantages of ChatGPT, such as saving time and providing comprehensive answers. Demir and Demir (2023a) state that if managers adopt ChatGPT, they will quickly obtain various information. Khurana et al. (2023) state that ChatGPT comprehensively provides the requested information to individuals and fulfills this with natural language processing. Harahap et al. (2023) state that natural language processing is the main feature distinguishing ChatGPT from similar applications. With its natural language processing feature, ChatGPT produces responses by making sense of individuals' requests. However, during the initial use process, participants expressed hesitations about the reliability and authenticity of ChatGPT responses. Fusté-Forné and Orea-Giner (2023) mention the possibility of inconsistent information obtained from ChatGPT. Therefore, it is suggested that the information obtained should be checked, and its accuracy should be decided. Mich and Garigliano (2023) think that inaccurate and erroneous data will quickly become widespread in ChatGPT, so this risk should be minimized. At this point, it is suggested that ChatGPT should be more clearly personalized, and answers should be reduced to the specific rather than the general.

There are different opinions among the participants about privacy and security. One group of participants stated that they did not experience any security problems during the ChatGPT membership and usage process and that it was natural to share basic information. However, another group of participants stated that they were concerned about disseminating personal information and wanted more transparency in this regard. The concern about information being shared is especially prominent as ChatGPT has become popular. Soliman and Al Balushi (2023) emphasize that privacy and security issues are important in ChatGPT. According to the authors, inadequate protection of personal information and data in applications such as ChatGPT may lead to misuse of individuals' information. In the event of this situation, the trust in ChatGPT may weaken. Ali (2023) supports the concern about the privacy of personal information in ChatGPT. Helberger and Diakopoulos (2023) point out that there should be legal regulations to protect the privacy and security of personal information in ChatGPT.

One of the notable advantages of ChatGPT is its swift operation, efficient summarization of information, and time-saving capabilities. Keiper (2023) highlights that ChatGPT stands out for its user-friendly interface and rapid performance. Participants in the study emphasized that ChatGPT provides a significant advantage, particularly by delivering prompt and accurate responses to customer inquiries. This sentiment aligns with findings in the relevant literature. According to Demir and Demir (2023b), travel agencies can streamline their services with minimal effort and in less time through ChatGPT. Paul et al. (2023) argue that the integration of ChatGPT is crucial for crafting service content that aligns with customers' specific needs in the tourism sector. Gürsoy et al. (2023) assert that ChatGPT has diversified customer services, increasing personalized service delivery.

Potential disadvantages associated with ChatGPT include the necessity to verify information, the app's inclination to provide repetitive responses, and challenges related to language editing. Participants underscored that the application could be more complete, particularly when addressing subjects with current or trending content, requiring additional efforts to confirm the accuracy of information. Carvalho and Ivanov (2023) posit that ChatGPT relies on a knowledge base for generating responses. In cases where the information within this knowledge base is outdated or incomplete, users may encounter difficulties. Consequently, it becomes imperative to validate the responses obtained from ChatGPT. Reiss (2023) highlights that individuals' trust in ChatGPT diminishes when exposed to inaccurate and incomplete information. Haleem et al. (2022) elucidate that ChatGPT often imparts incomplete information due to inherent limitations. Zhou et al. (2023) assert that ChatGPT exhibits insecurity in delivering precise information.

Participants underscored various impacts of ChatGPT on the travel industry, particularly emphasizing its role in providing customers with more information about local destinations. This aligns with the findings of Carvalho and Ivanov (2023), who suggest that ChatGPT plays a crucial role in offering diverse information about destinations during travelers' planning. The application informs tourists about various aspects of their destination, including recommended places to visit, restaurants, and accommodations. The widespread use of ChatGPT is expected to foster increased customer interest in local destinations and greater participation in cultural activities (Dwivedi et al., 2023b). By avoiding unnecessary and confusing details, ChatGPT efficiently informs customers about their destination, offering valuable insights (Gürsoy et al., 2023). This not only saves customers time but also expedites decision-making processes (Wong et al., 2023). However, participants expressed concerns about ChatGPT's limitations, such as its inability to provide detailed, personalized information and potential timeliness issues. Addressing these concerns could enhance the application's effectiveness and further positively impact the travel industry.

The potential of ChatGPT to offer convenience and time-saving benefits to travel agencies is highlighted, particularly in the context of tour preparation and content generation. Integrating ChatGPT into the workflow of travel agencies is seen as a means to enhance customer satisfaction. Existing literature supports the idea that ChatGPT contributes to quicker service delivery in the travel industry (Carvalho & Ivanov, 2023; Demir & Demir, 2023a, 2023b). The application's ability to swiftly complete tasks is acknowledged as a time and cost-saving advantage for travel agencies (George and George, 2023). The efficiency gains from ChatGPT are expected to streamline customer service processes and boost overall productivity and efficiency in travel agencies (Dwivedi et al., 2023a). However, it is essential to note that, despite these positive contributions, participants and the literature agree on the irreplaceable role of the human factor in the travel industry. There is a consensus that ChatGPT can only partially replace human involvement and expertise. A notable concern raised by participants is the potential impact on employment in travel agencies. With the widespread adoption of ChatGPT, there is apprehension about job displacement for employees in the industry. The development of artificial intelligence tools, including ChatGPT, is perceived as introducing competition to human roles within travel agencies, leading to fears of unemployment among employees. This highlights the need for a balanced approach that leverages the benefits of ChatGPT while preserving the essential role of human professionals in the travel industry.

Participants express diverse opinions regarding the impact of ChatGPT on the business model of travel agencies. One group believes that ChatGPT has the potential to reshape the business model of travel agencies, offering a competitive advantage. These participants highlight the increasing trend of digitalization within travel agencies, emphasizing the creation of new and innovative tours, streamlining processes, and establishing AI-focused departments. They view ChatGPT as a tool that enhances practicality in service delivery. On the other hand, some participants emphasize the enduring importance of the human factor in the travel industry. They believe that ChatGPT's integration into the industry will take time. For effective utilization of ChatGPT, participants suggest that managers must possess adequate knowledge, and staff should undergo regular training to adapt to the ongoing digitalization process. The sentiment is that while artificial intelligence, including ChatGPT, can bring significant benefits, it should complement the human touch rather than replace it entirely. To use artificial intelligence applications effectively, participants argue for the necessity of pre-filtering data and establishing new units or departments. This proactive approach is seen as essential to prevent information pollution and ensure the accuracy and reliability of the information provided by ChatGPT. Overall, participants emphasize a balanced integration of ChatGPT into the existing business models of travel agencies, combining technological advancements with the essential human touch.

The consensus among participants is that ChatGPT will likely positively impact customer satisfaction. The ability to swiftly and effectively access information, along with the potential to deliver more in-depth and precise data to customers, is identified as key contributors to increased satisfaction. Participants also note the positive influence of applications like small-scale travel assistants in enhancing the overall customer experience. Moreover, utilizing ChatGPT as a marketing tool is seen as a strategy to create attractiveness, further enhancing customer satisfaction. However, participants caution against potential risks, particularly the risk of customer dissatisfaction when faced with inaccurate or incomplete information. The importance of providing clear and accurate information is emphasized, and participants stress the need to prevent information pollution. Concerns are raised about ChatGPT's lack of a robust filtering system, which could potentially lead to misinformation and, subsequently, customer dissatisfaction. In summary, while the potential for positive effects on customer satisfaction is recognized, participants underscore the importance of addressing challenges related to information accuracy and completeness.

The participants have different opinions on whether ChatGPT will change customers' demands. Some participants think ChatGPT will increase customers' knowledge about the destination, and the need for various destinations may improve. Other participants stated that there may be an instant increase in customer demands, as customers can quickly research the issues they are uncomfortable with. However, it is noted that the need for travel agencies from new-generation customers may decrease.

Theoretical Implications

As can be seen in the information provided in the literature section, ChatGPT has a number of effects on different stakeholders in the tourism sector. It has been stated that businesses in the tourism sector such as hotels and travel agencies can use ChatGPT to provide better quality service, to analyze customers' preferences, and as an auxiliary resource in human resources and management decisions. However, there needs to be more research on the possible effects of ChatGPT on travel agencies and their customers. This research aims to fill this research gap. This research provides a comprehensive overview of the impressions of ChatGPT from the perspective of travel agency employees and the effects of ChatGPT on travel agencies and customers.

The research explicitly identifies the impacts of ChatGPT on both travel agencies and their customers. The related literature reveals diverse findings, which can be categorized into three main themes. Firstly, travel agency employees express positive sentiments toward using ChatGPT, although concerns exist regarding information accuracy and data privacy. Secondly, ChatGPT is acknowledged for its effectiveness in enhancing the business activities of travel agencies. Lastly, the study suggests that ChatGPT has the potential to alter customers' expectations in the context of travel services.

Practical Implications

This research offers several practical contributions to the field. Firstly, it establishes that ChatGPT plays a crucial role in enabling travel agencies to expedite their business activities efficiently. Secondly, the research identifies that ChatGPT contributes to an increase in digitalization trends within the travel industry, fostering the development of innovative tours and activities. Moreover, ChatGPT prompts travel agencies to contemplate the establishment of new departments dedicated to artificial intelligence. Thirdly, the study highlights a notable interest among travel agency employees in receiving training on artificial intelligence tools, including ChatGPT. Finally, the research indicates discernible changes in customers' travel plans and expectations, with the anticipation that these changes will intensify with the widespread adoption of ChatGPT. These findings provide valuable insights for both travel agencies and industry professionals, offering guidance on leveraging ChatGPT for operational enhancements and strategic planning.

FUTURE RESEARCH DIRECTIONS

This research was conducted with a qualitative research method. Therefore, inferences about the subject align with the interviewees' views. Similar studies can be performed with quantitative research methods in future research. The employees interviewed in this research are located in Antalya destination. The findings of the research can be improved with employees from different destinations. This research was conducted specifically for travel agencies. Similar research can be performed with other businesses in the sector.

CONCLUSION

In a comprehensive evaluation, participants generally expressed positive views on ChatGPT, highlighting its fast operation and efficient information summarization. Nevertheless, specific areas for improvement and the implementation of security measures were identified. While the application impressed users with its rapid performance, concerns regarding security, privacy, the necessity for information verification, and challenges in language editing were acknowledged. Addressing these aspects in future updates could enhance user satisfaction and bolster the overall reliability of ChatGPT. The potential of ChatGPT to offer convenience and time-saving benefits to travel agencies is highlighted, particularly in the context of tour preparation and content generation. Integrating ChatGPT into the workflow of travel agencies is seen as a means to enhance customer satisfaction. ChatGPT can potentially reshape the business model of travel agencies, offering a competitive advantage.

It is thought that ChatGPT can encourage customers to create their own travel plans by providing more information on their travels and may lead them to travel without an agency. Some participants stated that travel plans may become more individualized, but middle-aged and older customers may still prefer travel agencies. Economic conditions may also affect this preference. In conclusion, there are different opinions among the participants about the effects of ChatGPT on customer satisfaction, demands and travel plans. These views suggest that ChatGPT has the potential to create significant change in the travel industry, but more time and adaptation is needed to determine how these changes will take place.

REFERENCES

Ali, F. (2023). Let the devil speak for itself: Should ChatGPT be allowed or banned in hospitality and tourism schools? *Journal of Global Hospitality and Tourism*, *2*(1), 1–6. doi:10.5038/2771-5957.2.1.1016

Ali, F., Yasar, B., Ali, L., & Dogan, S. (2023). Antecedents and consequences of travelers' trust towards personalized travel recommendations offered by ChatGPT. *International Journal of Hospitality Management*, *114*, 103588. doi:10.1016/j.ijhm.2023.103588

Barr, K. (2023). *Expedia Wants You to Trust ChatGPT With Your Travel Plans*. Retrieved from: https://gizmodo.com/expedia-chatgpt-travel-hotels-ai-vrbo-1850302553

Bernard, H. R. (2017). *Research methods in anthropology: Qualitative and quantitative approaches*. Rowman & Littlefield.

Braun, V., & Clarke, V. (2006). Using thematic analysis in psychology. *Qualitative Research in Psychology*, *3*(2), 77–101. doi:10.1191/1478088706qp063oa

Brinkmann, S. (2014). Unstructured and semi-structured interviewing. The Oxford handbook of qualitative research, 2, 277-299.

Cao, Y., Li, S., Liu, Y., Yan, Z., Dai, Y., Yu, P. S., & Sun, L. (2023). A comprehensive survey of ai-generated content (aigc): A history of generative ai from gan to chatgpt. *arXiv preprint arXiv:2303.04226*. https://doi.org//arXiv.2303.04226 doi:10.48550

Carvalho, I., & Ivanov, S. (2023). ChatGPT for tourism: Applications, benefits and risks. *Tourism Review*, 1–14. doi:10.1108/TR-02-2023-0088

Chatterjee, J., & Dethlefs, N. (2023). This new conversational AI model can be your friend, philosopher, and guide... and even your worst enemy. *Patterns (New York, N.Y.)*, *4*(1), 1–3. doi:10.1016/j.patter.2022.100676 PMID:36699746

Chen, S., Zhang, K., Li, X., Ye, H., Lin, K. J., & Law, R. (2023). ChatGPT: Cross-cultural tourism research imperative. *Journal of Economics and Management*, *45*(1), 137–146. doi:10.22367/jem.2023.45.07

Chui, M., Roberts, R., & Yee, L. (2022). *Generative AI is here: How tools like ChatGPT could change your business*. Quantum Black AI by McKinsey.

Creswell, J. W. (2013). *Qualitative inquiry and research design: Choosing among five approaches*. Sage publications.

Demir, M., & Demir, Ş. Ş. (2015). *Otel işletmelerinde yenilik yönetimi: ilkeler ve örnekler*. Detay Yayıncılık.

Demir, M., & Demir, Ş. Ş. (2023b). Is ChatGPT the right technology for service individualization and value co-creation? evidence from the travel industry. *Journal of Travel & Tourism Marketing*, *40*(5), 383–398. doi:10.1080/10548408.2023.2255884

Demir, M., Demir, Ş. Ş., & Yaşar, E. (2022). Big data and innovative organizational performance: Evidence from a moderated mediated model. *Creativity and Innovation Management*, *31*(4), 696–709. doi:10.1111/caim.12525

Demir, Ş. Ş., & Demir, M. (2023a). Professionals' perspectives on ChatGPT in the tourism industry: Does it inspire awe or concern? *Journal of Tourism Theory and Research*, *9*(2), 61–76. doi:10.24288/jttr.1313481

Dwivedi, Y. K., Kshetri, N., Hughes, L., Slade, E. L., Jeyaraj, A., Kar, A. K., Baabdullah, A. M., Koohang, A., Raghavan, V., Ahuja, M., Albanna, H., Albashrawi, M. A., Al-Busaidi, A. S., Balakrishnan, J., Barlette, Y., Basu, S., Bose, I., Brooks, L., Buhalis, D., ... Wright, R. (2023a). "So what if ChatGPT wrote it?" Multidisciplinary perspectives on opportunities, challenges and implications of generative conversational AI for research, practice and policy. *International Journal of Information Management*, *71*, 102642. doi:10.1016/j.ijinfomgt.2023.102642

Dwivedi, Y. K., Pandey, N., Currie, W., & Micu, A. (2023b). Leveraging ChatGPT and other generative artificial intelligence (AI)-based applications in the hospitality and tourism industry: practices, challenges and research agenda. *International Journal of Contemporary Hospitality Management*. doi:10.1108/IJCHM-05-2023-0686

Fusté-Forné, F., & Orea-Giner, A. (2023). Gastronomy in tourism management and marketing: An interview with ChatGPT. ROBONOMICS. *The Journal of the Automated Economy*, *4*, 42–42.

George, A. S., & George, A. H. (2023). A review of ChatGPT AI's impact on several business sectors. *Partners Universal International Innovation Journal*, *1*(1), 9–23. doi:10.5281/zenodo.7644359

Gursoy, D., Li, Y., & Song, H. (2023). ChatGPT and the hospitality and tourism industry: An overview of current trends and future research directions. *Journal of Hospitality Marketing & Management*, *32*(5), 579–592. doi:10.1080/19368623.2023.2211993

Haleem, A., Javaid, M., & Singh, R. P. (2022). An era of ChatGPT as a significant futuristic support tool: A study on features, abilities, and challenges. *Bench Council Transactions on Benchmarks, Standards and Evaluations, 2*(4), 100089. doi:10.1016/j.tbench.2023.100089

Harahap, M. A. K., Ausat, A. M. A., Rachman, A., Riady, Y., & Azzaakiyyah, H. K. (2023). Overview of ChatGPT Technology and its Potential in Improving Tourism Information Services. *Jurnal Minfo Polgan, 12*(2), 424–431. doi:10.33395/jmp.v12i1.12416

Helberger, N., & Diakopoulos, N. (2023). ChatGPT and the AI Act. *Internet Policy Review, 12*(1), 1–6. doi:10.14763/2023.1.1682

Huang, M. H., & Rust, R. T. (2018). Artificial intelligence in service. *Journal of Service Research, 21*(2), 155–172. doi:10.1177/1094670517752459

Iskender, A. (2023). Holy or unholy? Interview with open AI's ChatGPT. *European Journal of Tourism Research, 34*, 3414–3414. doi:10.54055/ejtr.v34i.3169

Ivanov, S. H. (2023). Automated decision-making. *Foresight, 25*(1), 4-19. doi:10.1108/FS-09-2021-0183

Karanjai, R. (2022). Targeted phishing campaigns using large scale language models. *arXiv preprint arXiv:2301.00665*. https://doi.org//arXiv.2301.00665 doi:10.48550

Keiper, M. C. (2023). ChatGPT in practice: Increasing event planning efficiency through artificial intelligence. *Journal of Hospitality, Leisure, Sport and Tourism Education, 33*, 100454. doi:10.1016/j.jhlste.2023.100454

Khurana, D., Koli, A., Khatter, K., & Singh, S. (2023). Natural language processing: State of the art, current trends and challenges. *Multimedia Tools and Applications, 82*(3), 3713–3744. doi:10.1007/s11042-022-13428-4 PMID:35855771

Korzynski, P., Mazurek, G., Altmann, A., Ejdys, J., Kazlauskaite, R., Paliszkiewicz, J., Wach, K., & Ziemba, E. (2023). Generative artificial intelligence as a new context for management theories: Analysis of ChatGPT. *Central European Management Journal, 31*(1), 3–13. doi:10.1108/CEMJ-02-2023-0091

Loureiro, S. M. C., Ali, F., & Ali, M. (2022). Symmetric and asymmetric modeling to understand drivers and consequences of hotel chatbot engagement. *International Journal of Human-Computer Interaction*, 1–13. doi:10.1080/10447318.2022.2124346

Marshall, M. N. (1996). Sampling for qualitative research. *Family Practice, 13*(6), 522–526. doi:10.1093/fampra/13.6.522 PMID:9023528

Mich, L., & Garigliano, R. (2023). ChatGPT for e-Tourism: A technological perspective. *Information Technology & Tourism*, *25*(1), 1–12. doi:10.1007/s40558-023-00248-x

Miles, M. B., & Huberman, A. M. (1994). *Qualitative data analysis: An expanded sourcebook*. Sage.

OpenA. I. (2023). *ChatGPT.* https:// openai.com

Paul, J., Ueno, A., & Dennis, C. (2023). ChatGPT and consumers: Benefits, pitfalls and future research agenda. *International Journal of Consumer Studies*, *47*(4), 1213–1225. doi:10.1111/ijcs.12928

Ray, P. P. (2023). ChatGPT: A comprehensive review on background, applications, key challenges, bias, ethics, limitations and future scope. *Internet of Things and Cyber-Physical Systems*, 121-154. doi:10.1016/j.iotcps.2023.04.003

Reiss, M. V. (2023). Testing the reliability of chatgpt for text annotation and classification: A cautionary remark. *arXiv preprint arXiv:2304.11085*. / arXiv.2304.11085 doi:10.31219/osf.io/rvy5p

Soliman, M., & Al Balushi, M. K. (2023). Unveiling destination evangelism through generative AI tools. *ROBONOMICS: The Journal of the Automated Economy*, *4*(54), 1.

Sudirjo, F., Diawati, P., Riady, Y., Ausat, A. M. A., & Suherlan, S. (2023). The Role of ChatGPT in Enhancing the Information Search and Decision-Making Process of Travellers. *Jurnal Minfo Polgan*, *12*(2), 500–507. doi:10.33395/jmp.v12i1.12443

Tussyadiah, I. (2020). A review of research into automation in tourism: Launching the Annals of Tourism Research Curated Collection on Artificial Intelligence and Robotics in Tourism. *Annals of Tourism Research*, *81*, 102883. doi:10.1016/j.annals.2020.102883

Zhuo, T. Y., Huang, Y., Chen, C., & Xing, Z. (2023). Exploring ai ethics of chatgpt: A diagnostic analysis. *arXiv preprint arXiv:2301.12867*. https://doi.org// arXiv.2301.12867 doi:10.48550

ADDITIONAL READING

Demir, M., & Demir, Ş. Ş. (2023b). Is ChatGPT the right technology for service individualization and value co-creation? evidence from the travel industry. *Journal of Travel & Tourism Marketing*, *40*(5), 383–398. doi:10.1080/10548408.2023.2255884

Demir, Ş. Ş., & Demir, M. (2023a). Professionals' perspectives on ChatGPT in the tourism industry: Does it inspire awe or concern*? Journal of Tourism Theory and Research*, *9*(2), 61–76. doi:10.24288/jttr.1313481

KEY TERMS AND DEFINITIONS

ChatGPT: A chatbot based on artificial intelligence.

Travel Agency: A business that sells its services of different contents to tourists.

Chapter 5
Consumers' Drivers of Generative Pre-Trained Transformer (GPT) Conversational Bot Adoption

Omar H. Fares
https://orcid.org/0000-0003-0950-0661
Toronto Metropolitan University, Canada

Queenie Zhu
Toronto Metropolitan University, Canada

Seung Hwan (Mark) Lee
Toronto Metropolitan University, Canada

Joseph Aversa
Toronto Metropolitan University, Canada

ABSTRACT

This chapter examines the relationship between society and artificial intelligence (AI), emphasizing the factors driving consumer adoption of AI conversational bots. The authors examine how societal norms, past experiences, and trust in technology influence the acceptance and usage of generative-pre trained transformer (GPT) bots. They provide a theoretical framework, integrating key concepts from social influence and technology acceptance theory, to understand the complex dynamics of GPT bot adoption. Conducting a survey, they analyze data from 412 participants in North America to test various hypotheses. The findings broadly support the proposed model, highlighting the significant roles of social norms, word of mouth, and trust in shaping consumer behaviour towards AI conversational bots. However, an intriguing exception is found in the lack of a direct relationship between behavioural intention and actual technology usage, pointing to the need for further investigation into the factors that bridge the gap between the intention to use and the actual use of AI technologies in everyday contexts.

DOI: 10.4018/979-8-3693-1239-1.ch005

INTRODUCTION

The relationship between society and human intellect is intricate and profound, as societal structures and norms are fundamentally shaped by human cognition and decision-making processes. In this context, integrating artificial intelligence (AI) into human cognitive capabilities is a subject of considerable debate and exploration (Russel & Norvig, 2010). While AI presents notable opportunities for augmenting human capabilities, its potential impact on societal progress is complex and multifaceted (Brynjolfsson & McAfee, 2014). The accelerated advancement in Artificial Intelligence (AI) and Natural Language Processing (NLP) technologies have led to the emergence of unique cutting-edge conversational agents such as the Generative Pre-trained Transformer (GPT) (Abdul-Kader, 2021; Kusal et al., 2022; Paul et al., 2023). The GPT is a significant advancement in the natural language processing field, as this technology enables machines to provide humans with a perception of understanding and communicate in a human-like manner (Yenduri, 2023). It gained popularity due to its extensive performance capabilities and practical conversational abilities (Cano, 2023). A recent version of GPT that captured the public's interest is GPT-3. GPT-3 has demonstrated logical and intellectual responses that mimic that of humans, making it a powerful tool for various sectors, formulating ideas for design concepts (Zhu, 2021) and potential implications for healthcare systems (Sezgin, 2022). These advancements represent a profound and transformative trend in integrating complex AI tools into daily consumer experiences, reshaping how consumers interact with technology (Cano, 2023).

A conversational agent is a multimodal system designed to imitate human conversations by employing spoken or written language, typically through internet-based interactions (Adamopoulou & Moussiades, 2020). As such, this technology can accomplish tasks comparable to the work of many human employees, resulting in possible significant cost savings for organizations (Kusal et al., 2022). The significant capabilities of conversational agents have allowed many organizations and businesses to adopt them into practice. Healthcare, customer services, e-commerce, education, media, and manufacturing are just a few examples (Kustal et al., 2022). The chatbot market saw over a 20% compound annual growth rate increase in 2023 and is expected to grow to a market size of 32.4 billion USD by 2032 (DataHorizzon Research, 2023).

While conversational agents such as the SamBot and other retail-service chatbots have been in place for several years (Pradana et al., 2017; Tran et al., 2021), the technology was more limited to specific applications and industries (Fares et al., 2023). However, the landscape changed dramatically with the emergence of ChatGPT at the end of 2022 (Paul et al., 2023). ChatGPT, developed by OpenAI, is a machine-learning system that uses generative AI tools to provide conversational responses to respond to prompts using algorithm generation (van Dis et al., 2023). It quickly gained public popularity due to its ability to generate detailed responses entertainingly and creatively (Thorp, 2023). The model's success can be attributed to its core techniques, encompassing expansive language models and reinforcement learning derived from human feedback (Wu, 2023). This makes it more advanced than existing chatbots, as it has the ability to process and generate natural language more effectively. When asked to define itself, ChatGPT responded:

It is designed to generate human-like text based on the input it receives, making it suitable for various natural language processing tasks, including generating text for conversation, answering questions, providing explanations, and more. ChatGPT is often used for chatbots, virtual assistants, and other text-based applications where human-like language generation is required. It's part of the broader family of GPT (Generative Pre-trained Transformer) models known for their natural language processing capabilities.

This interaction is an illustrative example of AI's role in bridging human cognition and AI. This task, highlighted by ChatGPT's core design to "generate human-like text based on the input it receives," highlights its objective to emulate human language processing. Such an objective is technically significant and aligns with philosophical explorations into how knowledge and understanding are constructed in AI systems (Russel & Norvig, 2016; Tegmark, 2018). From an ontological perspective, AI technologies like ChatGPT represent a distinct form of 'being.' They exist not as entities with consciousness but as advanced software programs, essentially a compilation of algorithms and data processed by computers. This distinction is crucial in understanding AI's nature: it does not learn in the human sense but operates based on pre-defined instructions and information. Also, AI's knowledge acquisition is fundamentally different from human understanding. For AI systems like ChatGPT, knowledge is the encoded information in its programming and training data, accessed and processed to generate responses. This mode of knowing lacks personal experience or interpretation, relying solely on data processing and pattern recognition. Furthermore, ChatGPT's versatility in handling "various natural language processing tasks" is highlighted in this self-reflective exercise. The model demonstrates adaptability and relevance across various applications, from simple conversations to complex explanatory discourses. Moreover, being a part of the "broader family of GPT models," ChatGPT's response to defining itself also reflects the advancements in NLP inherent in its lineage. This introspective look offers a practical example of how these models have evolved in their journey toward understanding and generating human-like language.

The emergence of AI technology and the combination of user-friendly interfaces marks a monumental turning point in the landscape of conversational agents and public perceptions of such technologies. With the introduction of this technology, conversational agents have become more proficient in understanding and responding to human interactions, offering a more efficient user experience. As such, conversational AI has spread across a multitude of sectors, including retail (Kumar et al., 2023), education (Kasneci et al., 2023), healthcare (Sallam, 2023), and entertainment (Haque et al., 2022). The increasing integration of conversational AI in retail, education, healthcare, and entertainment reflects a broader shift in today's digital era (Paul et al., 2023). This shift highlights the evolving dynamics of trust and collaboration between humans and AI, underlining a growing dependence on AI-mediated interactions (Xiong et al., 2023). The widespread acceptance and adoption of technologies like ChatGPT signify deeper societal changes, emphasizing the importance of comprehensive research into the factors influencing their use. In this chapter, we aim to examine the intricacies of GPT conversational bot adoption, examining the interplay of social and individual factors in shaping user acceptance. Our exploration intends to provide valuable insights for policymakers and marketers, aiming to harness these technologies for societal benefit while navigating the complexities of innovation and responsible AI development in the modern era. As we pursue the key aim of this research, it is essential also to recognize the broader societal and cultural context in which these technologies operate. Different cultural backgrounds can significantly influence consumer attitudes and interactions with AI technologies, shaping both their adoption and effectiveness. While this research primarily focuses on the technological and cognitive aspects of AI integration, acknowledging the potential impact of cultural factors is crucial for a comprehensive understanding of how these technologies are received and assimilated across diverse global communities. This recognition paves the way for future explorations into the cultural dimensions of AI adoption, ensuring that the development and deployment of such technologies are sensitive to the varied tapestry of global cultures.

BACKGROUND

Conversational Bots

The development of chatbots focuses on maintaining the human-machine relationship, a concept inspired by the Turing test, originally proposed by Turing (1950). Weizenbaum (1966) created ELIZA, marking the first publicly known chatbot. This natural language communication program was designed to facilitate conversation between humans and machines (Weizenbaum, 1966). Following ELIZA, Colby

(1975) developed PARRY, a chatbot that mimics the behaviour of a paranoid person. Since the inception of ELIZA and PARRY, various chatbots have emerged to assist with tasks. Psyxpert is a system for disease diagnosis support (Overby, 1987), and SESAM-DIABETE aids in diabetic patient education (Levy et al., 1987). In 1995, ALICE (Artificial Linguistic Internet Computer Entity) became the first computer system to use natural language processing to interpret user input (Suta et al., 2020).

A significant advancement in chatbot technology occurred in 2001 with the creation of SmarterChild, a bot that aided in practical daily tasks and information retrieval such as news, weather, and stock prices (Molnár & Szüts, 2018). This capability marked a significant advancement in both machine intelligence and human-computer interaction, enabling access to information systems through conversations with a chatbot (Adamopoulou & Moussiades, 2020).

Artificial Intelligence chatbots have gone one step further in recent years by developing intelligent personal voice assistants built into devices such as smartphones or home speakers. This technology could process voice commands and respond with digital voices, handling everyday tasks such as monitoring calendars, home devices, and emails (Adamopoulou & Moussiades, 2020). More specifically, Siri paved the way for chatbot personal assistants in 2010. Apple developed this smart tool, so iPhone users could voice command inquiries and have conversations with this chatbot (Siri, 2023). Following this innovation, many other big tech companies came out with their own renditions of chatbots. Google Now (Google Now, 2020) was developed in 2012, Microsoft's personal assistant Cortana came out in 2014 (Cortana), and Amazon's Alexa came out in the same year (Digital Trends, 2019). More recently, AI and conversational bots have been used in many industries, ranging from customer service to medical healthcare, and are continuing to make advancements as technology evolves (King, 2023).

Generative Pre-Trained Transformers

Although language generation models have been employed in customer service contexts and conversation simulations for years, recent strides in AI and machine learning have made it possible and accessible to develop context awareness in these bots (Botpress, 2023). More recently, there are Chabot engines that have the capability that appear to comprehend the contexts of human interaction conversations. Generative Pre-Trained Transformers (GPT) is a sophisticated iteration of AI that employs generative models and powerful machine learning (ML) techniques to create conversational interactions (Mercier, 2023). Due to the rapid development of AI and Natural Language Processing (NLP) technologies, generative AI was developed for tasks such as text generation and language understanding (Ray, 2023). Within these models, ChatGPT, an AI model created by OpenAI, has surfaced as a powerful tool with diverse applications across various domains (King, 2023). GPT models are designed to produce natural language text, like sentences, paragraphs, and even entire documents, in a way that is aligned and consistent with the language we know as humans (Ray, 2023). The key feature that defines GPT models is their ability to undergo pre-training on extensive volumes of text data, followed by fine-tuning subsequent downstream tasks like text classification or question answering (Ray, 2023).

The trajectory of generative pre-trained transformers (GPT) represents a significant advancement in natural language processing, beginning with the introduction of GPT-1 in 2018. Ali (2023) noted that GPT-1 was the inaugural model in OpenAI's series of language models employing transformer architecture. This architecture allowed GPT-1 to generate fluent and coherent language responses to given prompts, a substantial leap in AI capabilities at the time. Despite its groundbreaking nature, GPT-1 had 117 million parameters, which, as Ray (2023) points out, was relatively modest compared to its successors. Following GPT-1, GPT-2 was released in 2019, building upon the transformer structure to enhance the generation of human-like text. As Zheng et al. (2021) described, GPT-2 demonstrated improved language generation capabilities. However, Ali (2023) notes that GPT-2 encountered challenges with complex iterations and longer text passages, often struggling to maintain context in such scenarios. The development of GPT-3 in 2020 marked a monumental milestone in the evolution of generative models, as Ray (2023) highlighted. GPT-3 was larger, with an unprecedented 175 billion parameters, and more advanced, capable of producing highly sophisticated and contextually accurate language outputs. This model set a new standard for language generation, significantly expanding the potential applications of AI in various sectors. Most recently, the launch of GPT-4 on March 14, 2023, as announced by OpenAI (2023), represents this series's latest and most advanced iteration. GPT-4 is a large multimodal model, distinct in its ability to process both image and text inputs while producing text and image outputs. This multimodal capacity signifies a substantial evolution in AI language models, allowing for more diverse and complex interactions and applications. The ongoing development of GPT models reflects a continual push towards more sophisticated, versatile, and human-like AI capabilities, shaping the future of natural language processing and AI interaction.

MAIN FOCUS OF THE CHAPTER

We develop a theoretical framework (refer to Figure 1) that examines the interplay of social and individual drivers in affecting adoption behaviour, grounded in well-established concepts of social influence, consumer decision-making, and technology acceptance (Azjen, 1991; Davis, 1985; Dwivdei et al., 2019; Huete-Alcocer, 2017; Venkatesh & Bala, 2008). The social drivers can be broken down into social norms and Word of Mouth (WOM). Individual drivers consist of trust in technology and prior experience. By weaving together these interconnected social and individual elements, the framework offers a nuanced lens through which to explore and understand the multifaceted dynamics of GPT adoption, bridging theoretical insights with practical implications for businesses, developers, and policymakers.

Social and individual drivers affect adoption behaviour and are specifically chosen due to their significant impact on decision-making. Fisher (1992) and Sarkar (2019) highlight the significance of social influence. Specifically, Fisher (1992) focuses on the impacts of perceived visibility in consumption (i.e., social approval from referents) and superorder group influence (i.e., intrinsically valued product benefits) on early adoption behaviour. In addition, Sarkar (2019) highlights the impact of social influence and the importance social signals have on decision-making and adoption patterns. The second element in the adoption behaviour interplay we are examining is the role played by individual drivers. This plays a significant role across various domains, such as mobile data services and car-sharing technology (Choi, 2011; Prieto, 2017). Research in this realm identified both intrinsic and extrinsic factors as motivations to influence adoption behaviour (Choi, 2011). Venkatesh (2001) highlighted the impact of utilitarian, hedonic, and social outcomes and a fear of obsolescence. Evidently, extant research has shined a light on the significance of social and individual drivers in influencing consumer adoption behaviour (e.g., Patil et al., 2017; Talwar et al., 2020; Zerbini et al., 2022).

Figure 1. Theoretical framework

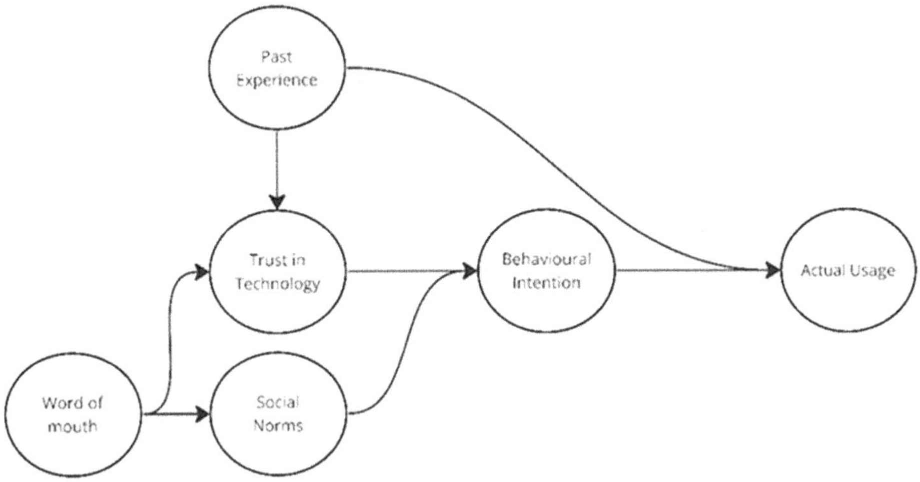

HYPOTHESIS DEVELOPMENT

Social norms are generally thought of as established rules that shape behaviour through the encouragement of conformity (Bicchieri & Mercier, 2014). Generally, norms can be thought of as providing rules and order to a situation that could be deemed ambiguous, uncertain, or even threatening (Raven & Rubin, 1976). They can also be defined as a sort of social behaviour that characterizes a collective sociocultural unit compared to individuals observed as random (Pepitone, 1976). These definitions collectively revolve around the central theme that there is a shared awareness within a certain group regarding preferred and appropriate behaviours. Thus, social norms serve as catalysts for behaviour. These norms inform group members how to feel and behave in a certain situation, exerting social influence on members by identifying what kind of behaviour is appropriate and what is not (Abrams et al., 1990). The Theory of Reasoned Action (TRA) posits that behavioural intention is significantly influenced by an individual's attitude towards the behaviour and subjective norms, including the perceived expectations of significant others (Ajzen, 1991). Therefore, considering the influential role of social norms as outlined in these theories, we hypothesize that:

H1: Social norms will positively influence behavioural intention.

Word of Mouth (WOM) and its impact on consumer behaviour has been pivotal in social sciences and consumer-to-consumer interactions. In the contemporary context, characterized by the proliferation of digital platforms, WOM transcends traditional boundaries, leveraging online networks to amplify its reach and impact (Cheng & Zhou, 2010). The definition of WOM as the exchange of interpersonal information among adopters and potential adopters of a product or service (Maxham, 2001) has expanded to include digital exchanges, making it a dynamic and pervasive force in shaping consumer opinions and behaviours (Cheng and Zhou, 2010). The credibility of WOM in guiding consumer decisions, particularly in the digital context, has been reinforced in recent studies (Donthu et al., 2021). This credibility stems from the authentic and personal nature of the information shared, rendering it more influential than traditional marketing channels (Hung & Li, 2007). Additionally, the social consequences of WOM are more pronounced in the digital sphere, where the gap between the expected and actual impact of shared information can be significant. This discrepancy highlights the complex interplay between individual perceptions and collective dynamics in digital communities (Palmeira et al., 2020). WOM's role in aggregating information and facilitating social learning is particularly critical in online environments. It guides individual consumer choices and contributes to shaping collective understanding and preferences, leading to socially efficient outcomes (Ellison & Fudenberg, 1995). In this digital era, WOM's influence extends beyond mere product preferences to shaping broader social norms within online communities (Donthu et al., 2021). Consequently, this leads us to hypothesize that:

H2: Word of mouth will positively influence social norms.

Recent literature has increasingly emphasized the role of Word of Mouth (WOM) in shaping consumers' trust in technology. Multiple studies have shown that WOM, particularly in digital contexts like social media and online forums, significantly influence consumers' perceptions and trust in new technologies (King et al., 2014; Liu & Lopez, 2016). This influence is attributed to WOM's authentic and personalized nature, which provides potential adopters with real-world insights and experiences related to technological products (Lee et al., 2018). Furthermore, the impact of WOM on trust is not limited to direct product attributes but extends to the broader perception of the technology's reliability, usability, and overall value. This effect is particularly pronounced in the context of emerging technologies, where consumer knowledge is often limited, and trust is a critical factor in adoption decisions (Chen & Xie, 2018; Smith et al., 2012). The role of WOM in disseminating information and shaping perceptions is crucial, as it helps bridge the gap between technological advancements and consumer understanding, thereby fostering a sense of trust and confidence in new technologies. Therefore, we hypothesize that:

H3: Word of mouth will positively influence trust in technology.

Trust plays a pivotal role in shaping consumer perception and influencing technology adoption, acting as a critical factor in consumers' decision-making processes (Wu & Chen, 2005). The integration of trust with prior acceptance research has been extensively researched in consumer acceptance studies (e.g., Park et al., 2019; Talwar et al., 2020), particularly in contexts like online shopping environments. Studies in these settings, such as those by Gefen et al. (2003a), have shown that trust is a robust predictor of behavioural intentions in technology-related scenarios. These findings highlight the importance of trust in the acceptance and successful integration of new technologies in consumer lifestyles. The significance of trust is further highlighted by its role in mitigating concerns such as privacy risks, which are prevalent in the adoption of new technologies (Meyer-Waarden & Cloarec, 2022). Trust alleviates the inherent uncertainty often associated with new technological advancements, enhancing consumer confidence and willingness to engage with new technologies (Hernandez-Ortega, 2011). This aspect is crucial in the context of rapidly evolving technological landscapes, where consumers are frequently confronted with novel products and services. The establishment of trust encourages the initial adoption of these technologies and fosters long-term user engagement and loyalty. Given the essential role of trust in acceptance and its capacity to address key consumer concerns, we hypothesize that:

H4: Trust in technology will positively influence behavioural intentions.

The level of trust in technology and one's prior experience with it are significantly intertwined, playing a crucial role in explaining adoption behaviour (Dutton, 2006). The relationship between prior experience and trust is often directly correlated with levels of certainty and familiarity. Without exposure to the technology, resulting in a lack of prior experience, users tend to exhibit higher levels of reluctance to trust it (Gefen et al., 2003b). This hesitance can stem from a lack of familiarity or understanding of the technology, leading to uncertainty and apprehension. Prior research (e.g., Ling et al., 2010) has indicated that a customer's prior experience is a key determinant of their attitude and behaviour in online settings. This experience informs their perception of the technology, influencing their level of comfort and willingness to engage with it. Moreover, Lee and Turban (2001) found that this level of prior experience also affects trust propensity. As consumers become more familiar with technology through previous interactions, their trust in the technology tends to increase. This accumulated experience can lead to the development of loyalty and trust toward the technology as consumers become more assured of its reliability and usefulness. Based on these insights, it is evident that prior experience plays a fundamental role in fostering trust in technology. Consumers who have positively interacted with technology are more likely to trust and continue using it. Therefore, we propose the following hypothesis:

H5: Prior experience will positively influence trust in technology.

Taylor & Todd (1995) developed a model to investigate the extent to which a user's level of experience influences technology usage. Their inquiry into this relationship is anchored in the broader understanding of behaviour determinants, where prior experience has been recognized as a key factor (Ajzen, 1980; Bagozzi, 1981). These foundational studies in behavioural psychology and consumer behaviour theory underline the significance of past experiences in shaping an individual's future actions. Specifically, Fishbein & Ajzen (1975) have demonstrated that the knowledge gained from prior experience plays a critical role in forming intentions. This connection between past experience and future intention highlights how previous interactions with technology can inform and shape users' attitudes toward its acceptance. The results of Taylor & Todd's (1995) conceptual model further emphasize this relationship, suggesting a stronger correlation between intention and actual behaviour in users with previous experience. This implies that familiarity with a technology developed through past use shapes intention and translates more effectively into actual usage behaviour. Given the prevalent emphasis in existing research on the impact of prior experience on behavioural intentions, we propose the following hypothesis:

H6: Prior experience will positively influence behavioral intention.

Substantial prior research utilizing intention-based models has consistently demonstrated that behavioural intention plays a crucial role in influencing actual technology usage. The Technology Acceptance Model (TAM) Davis (1986) posits a direct and positive relationship between behavioural intention and the actual use of technology. This model suggests that how a user intends to use technology is a strong indicator of how they will actually use it in practice. Furthermore, recent studies by researchers like Vărzaru et al. (2021) and Chao (2019) reinforce this notion, emphasizing that behavioural intention is one of the primary drivers leading an individual towards the actual usage of technology. These studies contribute to a growing body of empirical evidence suggesting that the likelihood of technology adoption and sustained use is significantly influenced by the initial intention to use it. Therefore, we propose the following hypothesis:

H7: Behavioral intention will positively influence actual usage.

Research Methodology

Sample and Procedure

This study employed the Partial Least Squares Structural Equation Modelling (PLS-SEM) approach to explore the multifaceted factors influencing GPT adoption. Recognized for its capability to navigate complex models (Wong, 2019), PLS-SEM is chosen due to its robustness in exploring intricate relationships between variables, which is particularly useful in investigating the nuanced factors that influence the adoption of cutting-edge technologies like GPT. This method's capacity for simultaneously examining multiple causal relationships makes it particularly suitable for our research objectives. The data for this study is collected from 473 participants through Amazon Mechanical Turk (MTurk). Data integrity is ensured by implementing stringent quality checks, such as screening for straight-lining (consistent response patterns) and incomplete responses. After this rigorous validation process, a total of 412 responses are deemed valid and retained for an in-depth analysis. To determine an optimal sample size, we adhered to the guidelines proposed by Memon et al. (2020), employing G*Power software for our calculations. The input parameters were carefully set: an effect size of 0.15 to reflect a medium effect size, an α level of 0.05 for significance, and a power of 0.95 to ensure a high probability of detecting an effect if one exists. Given these parameters and considering five predictors in our model, the required sample size was calculated to be a minimum of 89 participants. Thus, our sample size of 412 offers robust statistical power for our analysis. Regarding the demographics of our participant pool, we observed a balanced gender representation with 204 males, 205 females, and 3 individuals identifying as other. The average age of the participants was 33.4 years, indicating a diverse age distribution ranging from 20 to 69 years, allowing for insights across various life stages.

Furthermore, participants were queried about their specific uses of GPT technology. The results, depicted in Figure 2, reveal several primary use cases. Users display a range of applications, with 'Getting answers to General knowledge questions' being the most common use case among participants, as indicated by 171 instances. This is followed by 'Customer support for business challenges' and 'Personalized assistance for tasks', such as suggesting recipes, both also ranking highly with 131 and 130 instances, respectively. Figure 2 illustrates a descending order of frequency for other uses, including language translation, entertainment, and writing assistance, and down to less frequent uses like legal advice and home decor suggestions. The breadth of applications showcases GPT's versatility and its growing integration into various aspects of daily life.

Figure 2. Usage of GPT

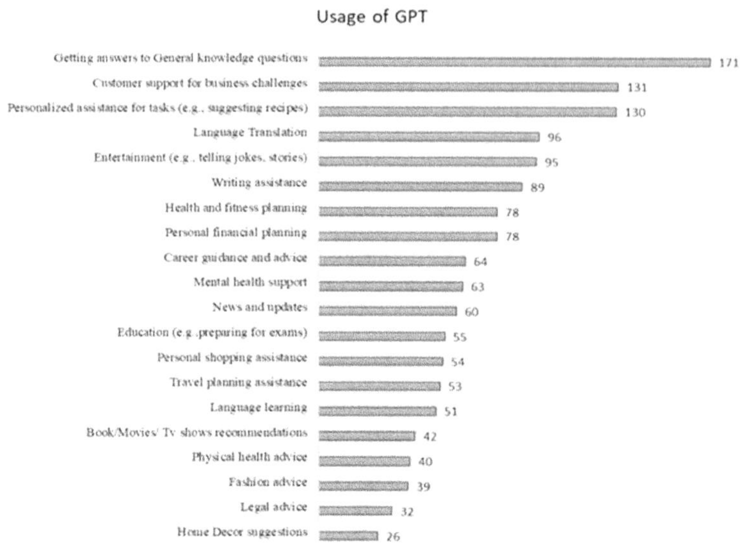

Measurement of Variables

This study employed established scales to measure the variables under examination. The trust-in-technology scale was adapted from Thomson (2006), the word-of-mouth scale drew from Heitmann et al. (2007), and the remaining constructs were derived from the work of Venkatesh and Bala (2008). To address concerns of multicollinearity, Variance Inflation Factor (VIF) values, ranging from 1.000 to 1.677, were computed, indicating that this issue does not pose a threat in the proposed model (Johnston et al., 2018). The internal consistency and reliability of the constructs were thoroughly assessed to ensure the reliability of the findings. Cronbach's alpha values for all constructs surpassed the established threshold of 0.70, as suggested by Hair et al. (2021). This affirms their internal consistency and reassures these constructs' reliability in measuring the intended variables. Furthermore, the reliability of these constructs was reinforced by composite reliability values, all exceeding the recommended threshold of 0.70. The average variance extracted (AVE) values, surpassing the recommended benchmark of 0.6, as also noted by Hair et al. (2021), provide additional assurance of the constructs' robustness and strength in capturing the essence of the variables under study (refer to Table 1). Discriminant validity, crucial for ensuring that constructs are distinct and do not overlap significantly, was rigorously evaluated using the Heterotrait-Monotrait Ratio of Correlations (HTMT) approach. All values falling below the designated threshold of 0.90, as outlined by Henseler et al. (2015), confirm that the constructs possess adequate discriminant validity, an essential aspect of construct validity (refer to Table 2). The model fit assessment involved a thorough and comprehensive examination of various indices through Partial Least Squares Structural Equation Modeling (PLS-SEM) analysis. This included comparing the saturated and estimated models using multiple fit indices. The Standardized Root Mean Square Residual (SRMR) values (0.074 and 0.107), unweighted least squares discrepancy (0.498 and 1.048), geodesic discrepancy (0.249 and 0.288), and chi-square values (681.375 and 725.059) were meticulously considered. The Normed Fit Index (NFI) for the saturated and estimated models, recorded at 0.687 and 0.667, respectively, further contributed to a holistic and rigorous evaluation of model fit, as emphasized in the comprehensive work of Hair et al. (2021). This multifaceted assessment of model fit reinforces the methodological rigour and reliability of the study's findings, ensuring the robustness of the conclusions.

Table 1. Measurement model assessment

	Cronbach's Alpha	Composite Reliability	Average Variance Extracted (AVE)
BI	0.705	0.836	0.63
SN	0.8	0.869	0.625
Trust	0.704	0.871	0.771
WOM	0.751	0.889	0.801

Table 2. Discriminant validity (HTMT)

	BI	EXP	SN	Trust	USAGE	WOM
BI						
EXP	0.602					
SN	0.817	0.607				
Trust	0.869	0.684	0.758			
USAGE	0.128	0.154	0.134	0.171		
WOM	0.673	0.566	0.825	0.62	0.115	

DATA ANALYSIS AND RESULTS

The measurement model includes two assessments of reliability and validity, which were measured by investigating internal consistencies of convergent and discriminant validity (Fornell & Larcker, 1981). Cronbach's reliability, internal consistencies, and composite reliability for each latent factor surpass the suggested threshold of 0.70. After analyzing the results of the PLS-SEM, we found support for all hypotheses except Hypothesis 7. Table 3 shows the statistical breakdown of each hypothesis and its significance. Figure 3 visually illustrates the conceptual framework that connects the variables together with the significant paths leading to overall usage. The loading of all items for each element exceeded the value of 0.7 and was statistically significant (p-value < 0.05). Tables 1 and 2 showcase the results of the measurement model assessment. The Average Variance Extracted (AVE) for all variable values surpasses the recommended benchmark of 0.50 (Fornell & Larcker, 1981).

Table 3. Results of hypothesis testing

Relationships	Original Sample (O)	Sample Mean (M)	Standard Deviation (STDEV)	T Statistics	P-Value	Hypothesis
SN -> BI	0.392	0.397	0.073	5.406	0.000	Supported
WOM -> SN	0.644	0.644	0.049	13.084	0.000	Supported
WOM -> Trust	0.221	0.224	0.06	3.661	0.000	Supported
TiT -> BI	0.39	0.387	0.066	5.931	0.000	Supported
EXP -> TiT	0.469	0.467	0.052	9.017	0.000	Supported
EXP -> USAGE	0.164	0.162	0.049	3.363	0.001	Supported
BI -> USAGE	-0.021	-0.018	0.052	0.41	0.682	Not supported

Figure 3. Hypotheses testing

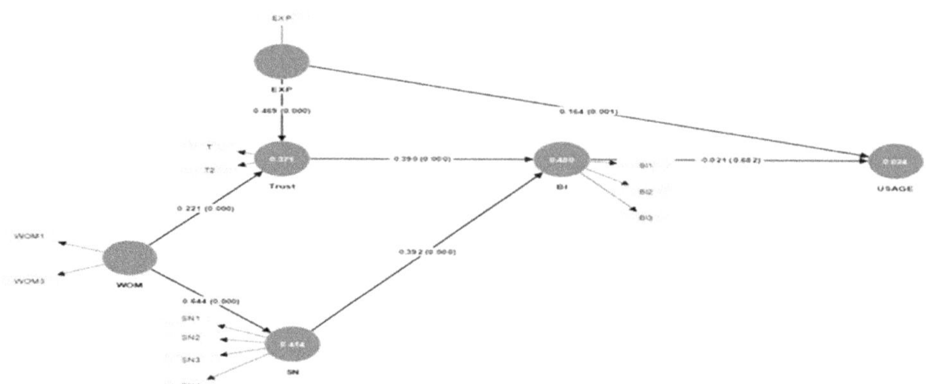

Structural Model

The significance of path coefficients was evaluated through T-tests using the bootstrapping technique, with a significance level set at 5%. Bootstrapping, a nonparametric method, was employed to test coefficients such as path coefficients and outer factor weights by assessing standard errors for estimation. SmartPLS V3.2 was employed to conduct both the inner and outer models, determining the t-value for significance. The threshold values for significance levels of 10%, 5%, and 1% were established at 1.65, 1.96, and 2.58, respectively.

Figure 3 and Table 3 presents our hypotheses testing. H1 suggested that behavioural intention is expected to be positively influenced by social norms. Our results confirmed this hypothesis, indicating a strong positive relationship. This suggests that the prevailing social expectations and standards within a given community or group are likely to play an influential role in shaping and encouraging an individual's inclinations toward certain behaviours. H2 posited that sharing experiences through Word of Mouth (WOM) will positively shape social norms. The results corroborated this hypothesis, reinforcing the role of WOM on social norms. This implies that engaging in conversations and sharing their experiences or opinions with others contributes to the collective construction of accepted behaviours within a community or social group. H3 proposed that sharing WOM will enhance trust in technology, which is ratified in our findings, illustrating a statistically significant positive relationship. The presence of WOM in technology operates as a powerful trust-building mechanism. Individuals sharing their experiences with this product creates an authentic and influential endorsement, garnering trust through this peer influence.

H4 hypothesized that through the positive influence of trust in technology, this effect would extend to shape behavioural intentions. Our results indicated that this effect and relationship is significant, supporting our hypothesis. This highlights the importance of trust in a consumer's behavioural intentions as it serves as a psychological anchor, influencing users to form intentions aligned with their belief in the technology's capabilities. H5 predicted that past encounters and experiences will contribute to a favourable influence on trust in technology. Our results supported this hypothesis. H6 stated that positive past experiences will thus positively shape an individual's intention to use the technology. The familiarity gained through prior experience reduces the uncertainties and perceived risks often associated with new technology; it creates a sense of comfort that positively impacts trust as users are more likely to rely on past encounters as a benchmark for assessing the trustworthiness of future new technologies. Our results indicated that this effect and relationship is significant, supporting our hypothesis. Thus, the influence of prior experience on the intention to use technology is rooted in the notion that individuals tend to draw upon their past interactions to inform future decisions. Moreover, these positive past experiences contribute to a user's perceived competence and ease of use associated with the technology. The more familiar they are with this technology, the more likely they intend to use it in the future. Finally, H7 anticipated that behavioural intention would positively influence the technology's actual usage. Surprisingly, our results did not support this hypothesis. The unexpected result of H7 emphasizes the complexity of transitioning in this tech landscape and necessitates further investigation. Interestingly, prior experience's positive influence on usage adds further complexity, suggesting it may shape actual AI bot usage. These results highlight the multifaceted dynamics of AI adoption and provide actionable insights for businesses and developers, emphasizing the importance of understanding social influences and individual factors and aligning strategies to bridge the intention-adoption gap.

DISCUSSION

In this chapter, we conduct a detailed examination of the factors driving the adoption of GPT conversational bots, focusing on social and individual determinants that shape usage patterns. Our study examines the intersectionality of internal drivers and broader societal values, uncovering the complex and nuanced aspects of GPT adoption among consumers. We highlight the multifaceted nature of technological adoption and emphasize the importance of ethically responsible development in an AI-centric landscape (Atkins et al., 2021; Dennehy et al., 2023; Kooli, 2023). By analyzing the roles of social norms and individual behavioural elements, we illustrate how societal expectations and personal experiences intertwine to influence consumer behaviour toward GPT bots. This analysis contributes significantly to the existing body of knowledge on advanced AI technology adoption and provides strategic management and policymakers with a comprehensive understanding of the dynamic factors that drive consumer engagement and acceptance of these technologies.

Our results indicated the positive, significant correlation that social norms have on behavioural intention. This aligns with existing research that social norms are perceived as established rules that promote conformity (Bichieri & Mercier, 2014; Kaushik et al., 2015) and define collective behaviours within a sociocultural unit (Pepitone, 1976). For instance, Kaushik et al. (2015) found that subjective norms significantly affect behavioural intention toward new technologies including chatbots. As such, these norms collectively shape preferred behaviour, influencing how individuals feel and act in various situations (Abrams et al., 1990). To shape these social norms, we found that WOM has a positive significant impact. This prevalent relationship has been crucial in social sciences and consumer-to-consumer interactions. WOM is a highly credible source of marketing information, and its impact is recognized in existing literature (Amron et al., 2018; Halim et al., 2022; Hung & Li, 2007). For instance, Amron et al. (2018) found that electronic WOM can affect subjective norms in the financial services context. Moreover, our results show that WOM also positively influences trust in technology. This leads to our findings that establishing trust in technology will positively impact behavioural intentions. Aligned with Wu and Chen (2005) and Kaushik et al. (2015), trust is a pivotal factor influencing technology adoption and has been integrated into previous technology acceptance research. Positive past experiences are necessary to build this trust, as indicated by our research findings. This correlation, explained by Dutton (2006), is often associated with certainty levels. Lack of exposure and limited prior experience tend to result in user hesitancy and reduced trust (Gefen et al., 2003b). Positive prior experiences ultimately lead to increased usage intention (Ingebrigtsen et al., 2014). Extant literature has shown that this has been a known determinant of behaviour (e.g., Ajzen, 1980; Bagozzi, 1981) and has been demonstrated to shape intention through acquired knowledge (Fishbein & Ajzen, 1975). Finally, our lack of support for H7 indicates that although the relationship between behavioural intention and actual usage has been heavily researched, the landscape for emerging technology has shifted consumer behaviour significantly. There are added complexities associated with this adoption process.

In addition to the explored social and individual determinants, it is imperative to consider the profound impact of cultural factors on the adoption and effectiveness of GPT conversational bots (Shine et al., 2022). Cultural nuances, ranging from language preferences to societal norms and values, may influence consumer attitudes toward these AI technologies. Different cultural contexts may lead to varied perceptions of and interactions with conversational bots, affecting their acceptance and functional utility. For instance, how trust in technology is established and how social norms influence behavioural intentions can vary greatly across cultures. In some societies, there might be a greater readiness to embrace new technologies like GPT, while in others, traditional values and skepticism towards AI could pose challenges to adoption. Furthermore, linguistic diversity and regional communication styles necessitate a culturally sensitive approach in designing and programming these bots to ensure they resonate with and are accessible to a global audience. Acknowledging and addressing these cultural dimensions is crucial for a more inclusive analysis and vital for the successful global integration of conversational AI technologies.

SOLUTIONS AND RECOMMENDATIONS

We propose a set of solutions and recommendations to enhance the adoption and impact of AI technologies like GPT. Firstly, increasing transparency in AI operations is crucial. Users should be provided with clear information about how AI systems function, particularly in terms of data processing and decision-making algorithms. This step is key to demystifying AI and building user trust. Secondly, integrating ethical AI practices is essential. The focus should be on privacy, security, and bias mitigation within AI development. Ethical considerations need to be a primary focus to ensure responsible usage of AI. Thirdly, adopting a user-centric approach in the design of GPT applications is essential. This involves creating intuitive, user-friendly interfaces and functionalities that meet the target audience's specific needs. Additionally, implementing regular user feedback mechanisms can help continuously refine AI systems.

Fourthly, educational initiatives and public awareness campaigns are necessary to bridge the understanding gap about AI. These should aim to inform the public about the capabilities and limitations of AI, supplemented by specialized training programs in sectors like healthcare and education. Fifthly, collaborating with regulatory bodies to develop standards and regulations for AI development and deployment is needed. Alongside this, strengthening data privacy and security policies is crucial to protect user information and maintain trust in AI. Sixthly, encouraging innovation and research in AI and NLP is vital. This includes fostering partnerships between academia, industry, and government and investing in areas like language understanding and context awareness to propel the field forward. Lastly, ensuring broad accessibility and inclusion in AI development is paramount. AI technologies should cater to diverse languages and cultural contexts, and their design should be inclusive, making them accessible to individuals with various abilities.

By systematically implementing these strategies, the integration of AI technologies like GPT in society can be optimized, leading to responsible and ethical development, enhanced user engagement, and broader acceptance and application across various sectors.

FUTURE RESEARCH DIRECTIONS

Our research is subject to certain limitations that may be enhanced in future research, primarily stemming from the reliance on survey-based and self-report measures, which may introduce inherent biases in the respondents' responses. Using a sample consisting exclusively of North American respondents sourced from Mturk also poses a limitation, potentially affecting the generalizability of our findings to other cultural and geographic contexts. To address these limitations, future research should adopt a more comprehensive approach by incorporating various methods, both quantitative and qualitative, to investigate consumer GPT adoption. This multi-method approach would provide a more nuanced understanding of the social and individual factors driving GPT adoption. Furthermore, future research endeavours should extend and replicate our studies and explore external factors that could impact ethical and privacy concerns as GPT advances. The landscape of Generative Pre-trained Transformers (GPT) adoption in consumer behaviour should broaden its focus beyond social and individual factors to encompass a holistic understanding. As GPT facilitates personalized content tailored to users, it becomes crucial to investigate the potential ethical implications and privacy concerns associated with this technology.

In addition, our model identified six factors that intertwine and shape actual usage intention. However, future research can contribute to the field by extending this model and identifying additional elements that may influence GPT adoption. By diving deeper into the intricate web of factors influencing consumer behaviour towards GPT, researchers can provide more comprehensive insights and contribute to developing technologies aligned with users' expectations. This holistic approach encourages organizations to consider a wider range of influences on GPT adoption, fostering the creation of technologies that are not only efficient but also ethically and culturally sensitive.

CONCLUSION

To summarize, this chapter comprehensively examined GPT conversational bot adoption drivers, offering a detailed analysis of the interplay between social and individual factors that influence usage patterns. The analysis conducted in this chapter underscores the underexplored yet multifaceted nature of GPT adoption in consumer behaviour. Our findings contribute valuable insights into existing literature on technological innovation adoption and highlight the importance of understanding consumer perceptions in today's AI-dominated landscape. By exploring underlying factors driving consumer adoption, this chapter disentangles the impact of social norms and individual elements on adoption, identifying key application areas where GPT conversational bots find prominent usage. The positive and significant correlation between social norms and behavioural intention aligns with existing research, highlighting the influential role of established rules in promoting conformity within sociocultural units. Word of mouth (WOM) emerges as a powerful influencer of social norms, echoing its recognized impact in consumer-to-consumer interactions and as a credible source of consumer behaviour.

Furthermore, the research establishes that WOM also positively influences trust in technology, a pivotal factor in technology adoption in line with existing literature. The critical role of trust in shaping behavioural intentions is emphasized, emphasizing the necessity of positive past experiences and the associated certainty levels in building user trust. This trust-building process is intricately linked to increased usage intention, aligning with established determinants of behaviour in extant literature. Interestingly, the lack of support for H7 suggests a shifting landscape in consumer behaviour associated with emerging technologies. The complexities inherent in the adoption process for GPT conversational bots signal the need for a nuanced understanding of the evolving dynamics between behavioural intention and actual usage. This research contributes to the current knowledge base and highlights the evolving challenges in the ever-changing landscape of technology adoption. As we navigate this landscape, the insights derived from this study can inform strategic decision-making and contribute to formulating policies in the rapidly advancing era of artificial intelligence.

REFERENCES

Abdul-Kader, S. (2021). Application Of Speech-To-Text synthesizer by using Natural Language Processing (NLP). *Turkish Online Journal of Qualitative Inquiry, 12*(10).

Abrams, D., Wetherell, M., Cochrane, S., Hogg, M. A., & Turner, J. C. (1990). Knowing what to think by knowing who you are: Self-categorization and the nature of norm formation, conformity and group polarization. *British Journal of Social Psychology, 29*(2), 97–119. doi:10.1111/j.2044-8309.1990.tb00892.x PMID:2372667

Adamopoulou, E., & Moussiades, L. (2020). Chatbots: History, technology, and applications. *Machine Learning with Applications, 2*, 100006. doi:10.1016/j.mlwa.2020.100006

Ajzen, I. (1980). Understanding attitudes and predicting social behavior. Academic Press.

Ajzen, I. (1991). The theory of planned behavior. *Organizational Behavior and Human Decision Processes, 50*(2), 179–211. doi:10.1016/0749-5978(91)90020-T

Ali, F. (2023, April 11). *GPT-1 to GPT-4: Each of OpenAI's GPT Models Explained and Compared*. MakeUseOf. Retrieved November 9, 2023, from https://www.makeuseof.com/gpt-models-explained-and-compared/

Apple. (n.d.). *Siri*. Apple. Retrieved November 8, 2023, from https://www.apple.com/ca/siri/

Arndt, J. (1967). Role of product-related conversations in the diffusion of a new product. *JMR, Journal of Marketing Research*, *4*(3), 291–295. doi:10.1177/002224376700400308

Atkins, S., Badrie, I., & van Otterloo, S. (2021). *Applying Ethical AI Frameworks in practice: Evaluating conversational AI chatbot solutions*. Computers and Society Research Journal.

Bagozzi, R. P. (1981). Attitudes, intentions, and behavior: A test of some key hypotheses. *Journal of Personality and Social Psychology*, *41*(4), 607–627. doi:10.1037/0022-3514.41.4.607

Bicchieri, C., & Mercier, H. (2014). Norms and beliefs: How change occurs. *The complexity of social norms*, 37-54.

Brynjolfsson, E., & McAfee, A. (2014). *The second machine age: Work, progress, and prosperity in a time of brilliant technologies*. WW Norton & Company.

Cano, C. A. G., Castillo, V. S., & Gallego, T. A. C. (2023). Unveiling the Thematic Landscape of Generative Pre-trained Transformer (GPT) Through Bibliometric Analysis. *Metaverse Basic and Applied Research*, *2*, 33–33. doi:10.56294/mr202333

Chao, C. M. (2019). Factors determining the behavioral intention to use mobile learning: An application and extension of the UTAUT model. *Frontiers in Psychology*, *10*, 1652. doi:10.3389/fpsyg.2019.01652 PMID:31379679

Chen, Y., & Xie, J. (2008). Online consumer review: Word-of-mouth as a new element of marketing communication mix. *Management Science*, *54*(3), 477–491. doi:10.1287/mnsc.1070.0810

Cheng, X., & Zhou, M. (2010, August). Study on effect of eWOM: A literature review and suggestions for future research. In *2010 International conference on management and service science* (pp. 1-4). IEEE. 10.1109/ICMSS.2010.5576663

Choi, H., Kim, Y., & Kim, J. (2011). Driving factors of post adoption behavior in mobile data services. *Journal of Business Research*, *64*(11), 1212–1217. doi:10.1016/j.jbusres.2011.06.025

Colby, K. M. (2013). *Artificial paranoia: A computer simulation of paranoid processes* (Vol. 49). Elsevier.

Cortana. (n.d.). *Microsoft*. Retrieved November 8, 2023, from https://www.microsoft.com/en-us/cortana

DataHorizzon Research. (2019, March 9). *Chatbot Market Size to Reach USD 32.4 Billion By 2032 CAGR: 21.6%. Report By DataHorizzon Research*. Yahoo!Finance. Retrieved October 29, 2023, from https://finance.yahoo.com/news/chatbot-market-size-reach-usd-235000000.html?guccounter=1

Davis, F. D. (1985). *A technology acceptance model for empirically testing new end-user information systems: Theory and results* [Doctoral dissertation]. Massachusetts Institute of Technology.

Dichter, E. (1966). How word-of-mouth advertising works. *Harvard Business Review*, *44*, 147–166.

Donthu, N., Kumar, S., Pandey, N., Pandey, N., & Mishra, A. (2021). Mapping the electronic word-of-mouth (eWOM) research: A systematic review and bibliometric analysis. *Journal of Business Research*, *135*, 758–773. doi:10.1016/j.jbusres.2021.07.015

Dwivedi, Y. K., Rana, N. P., Jeyaraj, A., Clement, M., & Williams, M. D. (2019). Re-examining the unified theory of acceptance and use of technology (UTAUT): Towards a revised theoretical model. *Information Systems Frontiers*, *21*(3), 719–734. doi:10.1007/s10796-017-9774-y

Ellison, G., & Fudenberg, D. (1995). Word-of-mouth communication and social learning. *The Quarterly Journal of Economics*, *110*(1), 93–125. doi:10.2307/2118512

Fares, O. H., Butt, I., & Lee, S. H. M. (2023). Utilization of artificial intelligence in the banking sector: A systematic literature review. *Journal of Financial Services Marketing*, *28*(4), 835–852.

Fishbein, M., & Ajzen, I. (1977). *Belief, attitude, intention, and behavior: An introduction to theory and research*. Academic Press.

Fisher, R. J., & Price, L. L. (1992). An investigation into the social context of early adoption behavior. *The Journal of Consumer Research*, *19*(3), 477–486. doi:10.1086/209317

Fornell, C., & Larcker, D. F. (1981). Evaluating structural equation models with unobservable variables and measurement error. *JMR, Journal of Marketing Research*, *18*(1), 39–50. doi:10.1177/002224378101800104

Gefen, D., Karahanna, E., & Straub, D. W. (2003a). Trust and TAM in online shopping: An integrated model. *Management Information Systems Quarterly*, *27*(1), 51–90. doi:10.2307/30036519

Gefen, D., Karahanna, E., & Straub, D. W. (2003b). Inexperience and experience with online stores: The importance of TAM and trust. *IEEE Transactions on Engineering Management, 50*(3), 307–321. doi:10.1109/TEM.2003.817277

Google Now. (2020). https://www.google.co.uk/landing/now/

Hair, J. Jr, Hair, J. F. Jr, Hult, G. T. M., Ringle, C. M., & Sarstedt, M. (2021). *A primer on partial least squares structural equation modeling (PLS-SEM)*. Sage Publications. doi:10.1007/978-3-030-80519-7

Haque, M. U., Dharmadasa, I., Sworna, Z. T., Rajapakse, R. N., & Ahmad, H. (2022). "I think this is the most disruptive technology": Exploring Sentiments of ChatGPT Early Adopters using Twitter Data. *arXiv preprint arXiv:2212.05856*.

Heitmann, M., Donald, R. L., & Andreas, H. (2007). Choice Goal Attainment and Decision and Consumption Satisfaction. *JMR, Journal of Marketing Research, 44*(2), 234–250. doi:10.1509/jmkr.44.2.234

Henseler, J., Ringle, C. M., & Sarstedt, M. (2015). A new criterion for assessing discriminant validity in variance-based structural equation modeling. *Journal of the Academy of Marketing Science, 43*(1), 115–135. doi:10.1007/s11747-014-0403-8

Hernandez-Ortega, B. (2011). The role of post-use trust in the acceptance of a technology: Drivers and consequences. *Technovation, 31*(10-11), 523–538. doi:10.1016/j.technovation.2011.07.001

How GPT will change the way we interact with Chatbots. (n.d.). Botpress Blog. https://botpress.com/blog/how-gpt-will-change-the-way-we-interact-with-chatbots

Huete-Alcocer, N. (2017). A literature review of word of mouth and electronic word of mouth: Implications for consumer behavior. *Frontiers in Psychology, 8*, 1256. doi:10.3389/fpsyg.2017.01256 PMID:28790950

Hung, K. H., & Li, S. Y. (2007). The influence of eWOM on virtual consumer communities: Social capital, consumer learning, and behavioral outcomes. *Journal of Advertising Research, 47*(4), 485–495. doi:10.2501/S002184990707050X

Jansson, J., Pettersson, T., Mannberg, A., Brännlund, R., & Lindgren, U. (2017). Adoption of alternative fuel vehicles: Influence from neighbors, family and coworkers. *Transportation Research Part D, Transport and Environment, 54*, 61–73. doi:10.1016/j.trd.2017.04.012

Johnston, R., Jones, K., & Manley, D. (2018). Confounding and collinearity in regression analysis: A cautionary tale and an alternative procedure, illustrated by studies of British voting behaviour. *Quality & Quantity*, *52*(4), 1957–1976. doi:10.1007/s11135-017-0584-6 PMID:29937587

Kasneci, E., Seßler, K., Küchemann, S., Bannert, M., Dementieva, D., Fischer, F., Gasser, U., Groh, G., Günnemann, S., Hüllermeier, E., Krusche, S., Kutyniok, G., Michaeli, T., Nerdel, C., Pfeffer, J., Poquet, O., Sailer, M., Schmidt, A., Seidel, T., ... Kasneci, G. (2023). ChatGPT for good? On opportunities and challenges of large language models for education. *Learning and Individual Differences*, *103*, 102274. doi:10.1016/j.lindif.2023.102274

King, M. R., & Chat, G. P. T. (2023). A conversation on artificial intelligence, chatbots, and plagiarism in higher education. *Cellular and Molecular Bioengineering*, *16*(1), 1–2. doi:10.1007/s12195-022-00754-8 PMID:36660590

King, R. A., Racherla, P., & Bush, V. D. (2014). What we know and don't know about online word-of-mouth: A review and synthesis of the literature. *Journal of Interactive Marketing*, *28*(3), 167–183. doi:10.1016/j.intmar.2014.02.001

Kusal, S., Patil, S., Choudrie, J., Kotecha, K., Mishra, S., & Abraham, A. (2022). AI-based Conversational Agents: A Scoping Review from Technologies to Future Directions. *IEEE Access : Practical Innovations, Open Solutions*, *10*, 92337–92356. doi:10.1109/ACCESS.2022.3201144

Lee, D., Hosanagar, K., & Nair, H. S. (2018). Advertising content and consumer engagement on social media: Evidence from Facebook. *Management Science*, *64*(11), 5105–5131. doi:10.1287/mnsc.2017.2902

Lee, M. K., & Turban, E. (2001). A trust model for consumer internet shopping. *International Journal of Electronic Commerce*, *6*(1), 75–91. doi:10.1080/10864415.2001.11044227

Lee, S., & Kim, B. G. (2009). Factors affecting the usage of intranet: A confirmatory study. *Computers in Human Behavior*, *25*(1), 191–201. doi:10.1016/j.chb.2008.08.007

Lee, W., Xiong, L., & Hu, C. (2012). The effect of Facebook users' arousal and valence on intention to go to the festival: Applying an extension of the technology acceptance model. *International Journal of Hospitality Management*, *31*(3), 819–827. doi:10.1016/j.ijhm.2011.09.018

Levy, M., Ferrand, P., & Chirat, V. (1989). SESAM-DIABETE, an expert system for insulin-requiring diabetic patient education. *Computers and Biomedical Research, an International Journal*, *22*(5), 442–453. doi:10.1016/0010-4809(89)90037-2 PMID:2776447

Ling, K. C., Chai, L. T., & Piew, T. H. (2010). The effects of shopping orientations, online trust and prior online purchase experience toward customers' online purchase intention. *International Business Research*, *3*(3), 63. doi:10.5539/ibr.v3n3p63

Liu, Y., & Lopez, R. A. (2016). The impact of social media conversations on consumer brand choices. *Marketing Letters*, *27*(1), 1–13. doi:10.1007/s11002-014-9321-2

Maxham, J. G. III. (2001). Service recovery's influence on consumer satisfaction, positive word-of-mouth, and purchase intentions. *Journal of Business Research*, *54*(1), 11–24. doi:10.1016/S0148-2963(00)00114-4

Mercier, M. (2023, February 15). *How GPT Will Change The Way We Interact With Chatbots*. Botpress. Retrieved November 9, 2023, from https://botpress.com/blog/how-gpt-will-change-the-way-we-interact-with-chatbots

Meyer-Waarden, L., & Cloarec, J. (2022). "Baby, you can drive my car": Psychological antecedents that drive consumers' adoption of AI-powered autonomous vehicles. *Technovation*, *109*, 102348. doi:10.1016/j.technovation.2021.102348

Molnár, G., & Szüts, Z. (2018, September). The role of chatbots in formal education. In *2018 IEEE 16th International Symposium on Intelligent Systems and Informatics (SISY)* (pp. 197-202). IEEE. 10.1109/SISY.2018.8524609

Open, A. I. (2023, March 14). *GPT*-4. OpenAI. Retrieved November 9, 2023, from https://openai.com/research/gpt-4

Overby, M. A. (1987). Psyxpert: An expert system prototype for aiding psychiatrists in the diagnosis of psychotic disorders. *Computers in Biology and Medicine*, *17*(6), 383–393. doi:10.1016/0010-4825(87)90056-4 PMID:3319379

Palmeira, M., Spassova, G., & Quoidbach, J. (2020). You're not yelping your case: The unexpected social consequences of word of mouth. *European Journal of Marketing*, *54*(2), 419–447. doi:10.1108/EJM-08-2018-0551

Park, J., Amendah, E., Lee, Y., & Hyun, H. (2019). M-payment service: Interplay of perceived risk, benefit, and trust in service adoption. *Human Factors and Ergonomics in Manufacturing*, *29*(1), 31–43. doi:10.1002/hfm.20750

Parry, M. E., Kawakami, T., & Kishiya, K. (2012). The effect of personal and virtual word-of-mouth on technology acceptance. *Journal of Product Innovation Management*, *29*(6), 952–966. doi:10.1111/j.1540-5885.2012.00972.x

Patil, P. P., Dwivedi, Y. K., & Rana, N. P. (2017). Digital payments adoption: an analysis of literature. *Digital Nations–Smart Cities, Innovation, and Sustainability: 16th IFIP WG 6.11 Conference on E-Business, E-Services, and E-Society, I3E 2017, Delhi, India, November 21–23, 2017 Proceedings*, *16*, 61–70.

Paul, J., Ueno, A., & Dennis, C. (2023). ChatGPT and consumers: Benefits, Pitfalls and Future Research Agenda. *International Journal of Consumer Studies*, *47*(4), 1213–1225. doi:10.1111/ijcs.12928

Pepitone, A. (1976). Toward a normative and comparative biocultural social psychology. *Journal of Personality and Social Psychology*, *34*(4), 641–653. doi:10.1037/0022-3514.34.4.641

Pradana, A., Sing, G. O., & Kumar, Y. J. (2017). SamBot-intelligent conversational bot for interactive marketing with consumer-centric approach. *International Journal of Computer Information Systems and Industrial Management Applications, 6*(2014), 265-275.

Prieto, M., Baltas, G., & Stan, V. (2017). Car sharing adoption intention in urban areas: What are the key sociodemographic drivers? *Transportation Research Part A, Policy and Practice*, *101*, 218–227. doi:10.1016/j.tra.2017.05.012

Raven, B. H., & Rubin, J. Z. (1976). *Social psychology: People in groups*. Academic Press.

Ray, P. P. (2023). ChatGPT: A comprehensive review on background, applications, key challenges, bias, ethics, limitations and future scope. *Internet of Things and Cyber-Physical Systems*.

Rimal, R. N., & Real, K. (2005). How behaviors are influenced by perceived norms: A test of the theory of normative social behavior. *Communication Research*, *32*(3), 389–414. doi:10.1177/0093650205275385

Russell, S. J., & Norvig, P. (2010). Artificial intelligence a modern approach. Academic Press.

Sallam, M. (2023, March). ChatGPT utility in healthcare education, research, and practice: systematic review on the promising perspectives and valid concerns. In Healthcare (Vol. 11, No. 6, p. 887). MDPI. doi:10.3390/healthcare11060887

Sánchez-Prieto, J. C., Olmos-Migueláñez, S., & García-Peñalvo, F. J. (2017). MLearning and pre-service teachers: An assessment of the behavioral intention using an expanded TAM model. *Computers in Human Behavior*, *72*, 644–654. doi:10.1016/j.chb.2016.09.061

Sarkar, S., Aleali, A., Shakarian, P., Armenta, M., Sanchez, D., & Lakkaraju, K. (2019, August). Impact of social influence on adoption behavior: An online controlled experimental evaluation. In *Proceedings of the 2019 IEEE/ACM International Conference on Advances in Social Networks Analysis and Mining* (pp. 226-233). 10.1145/3341161.3342882

Sezgin, E., Sirrianni, J., & Linwood, S. L. (2022). Operationalizing and implementing pretrained, large artificial intelligence linguistic models in the US health care system: Outlook of generative pretrained transformer 3 (GPT-3) as a service model. *JMIR Medical Informatics*, *10*(2), e32875. doi:10.2196/32875 PMID:35142635

Shin, D., Chotiyaputta, V., & Zaid, B. (2022). The effects of cultural dimensions on algorithmic news: How do cultural value orientations affect how people perceive algorithms? *Computers in Human Behavior*, *126*, 107007. doi:10.1016/j.chb.2021.107007

Smith, A. N., Fischer, E., & Yongjian, C. (2012). How does brand-related user-generated content differ across YouTube, Facebook, and Twitter? *Journal of Interactive Marketing*, *26*(2), 102–113. doi:10.1016/j.intmar.2012.01.002

Suta, P., Lan, X., Wu, B., Mongkolnam, P., & Chan, J. H. (2020). An overview of machine learning in chatbots. *International Journal of Mechanical Engineering and Robotics Research*, *9*(4), 502–510. doi:10.18178/ijmerr.9.4.502-510

Talwar, S., Dhir, A., Khalil, A., Mohan, G., & Islam, A. N. (2020). Point of adoption and beyond. Initial trust and mobile-payment continuation intention. *Journal of Retailing and Consumer Services*, *55*, 102086. doi:10.1016/j.jretconser.2020.102086

Talwar, S., Talwar, M., Kaur, P., & Dhir, A. (2020). Consumers' resistance to digital innovations: A systematic review and framework development. *Australasian Marketing Journal*, *28*(4), 286–299. doi:10.1016/j.ausmj.2020.06.014

Taylor, S., & Todd, P. (1995). Assessing IT usage: The role of prior experience. *Management Information Systems Quarterly*, *19*(4), 561–570. doi:10.2307/249633

Tegmark, M. (2018). *Life 3.0: Being human in the age of artificial intelligence*. Vintage.

Thomson, M. (2006). Human Brands: Investigating Antecedents to Consumers' Strong Attachments to Celebrities. *Journal of Marketing*, *70*(3), 104–119. doi:10.1509/jmkg.70.3.104

Thorp, H. H. (2023). ChatGPT is fun, but not an author. *Science*, *379*(6630), 313–313. doi:10.1126/science.adg7879 PMID:36701446

Tran, A. D., Pallant, J. I., & Johnson, L. W. (2021). Exploring the impact of chatbots on consumer sentiment and expectations in retail. *Journal of Retailing and Consumer Services*, *63*, 102718. doi:10.1016/j.jretconser.2021.102718

Turing, A. (1950). Computing machinery and intelligence. *Mind*, *59*(236), 433–460. doi:10.1093/mind/LIX.236.433

Van Dis, E. A., Bollen, J., Zuidema, W., van Rooij, R., & Bockting, C. L. (2023). ChatGPT: Five priorities for research. *Nature*, *614*(7947), 224–226. doi:10.1038/d41586-023-00288-7 PMID:36737653

Vărzaru, A. A., Bocean, C. G., Rotea, C. C., & Budică-Iacob, A. F. (2021). Assessing antecedents of behavioral intention to use mobile technologies in e-commerce. *Electronics (Basel)*, *10*(18), 2231. doi:10.3390/electronics10182231

Venkatesh, V., & Bala, H. (2008). Technology acceptance model 3 and a research agenda on interventions. *Decision Sciences*, *39*(2), 273–315. doi:10.1111/j.1540-5915.2008.00192.x

Venkatesh, V., & Brown, S. A. (2001). A longitudinal investigation of personal computers in homes: Adoption determinants and emerging challenges. *Management Information Systems Quarterly*, *25*(1), 71–102. doi:10.2307/3250959

Weizenbaum, J. (1966). ELIZA—A computer program for the study of natural language communication between man and machine. *Communications of the ACM*, *9*(1), 36–45. doi:10.1145/365153.365168

What exactly is alexa? where does she come from? and how does she work? (2019). Digital Trends website: https://www.digitaltrends.com/home/what-is-amazonsalexa-and-what-can-it-do/

Wong, K. K. K. (2019). *Mastering partial least squares structural equation modeling (PLS-Sem) with Smartpls in 38 Hours*. IUniverse.

Wu, C. S., Cheng, F. F., Yen, D. C., & Huang, Y. W. (2011). User acceptance of wireless technology in organizations: A comparison of alternative models. *Computer Standards & Interfaces*, *33*(1), 50–58. doi:10.1016/j.csi.2010.03.002

Wu, T., He, S., Liu, J., Sun, S., Liu, K., Han, Q. L., & Tang, Y. (2023). A brief overview of ChatGPT: The history, status quo and potential future development. *IEEE/CAA Journal of Automatica Sinica, 10*(5), 1122-1136.

Xiong, W., Wang, C., & Ma, L. (2023). Partner or subordinate? Sequential risky decision-making behaviors under human-machine collaboration contexts. *Computers in Human Behavior, 139*, 107556. doi:10.1016/j.chb.2022.107556

Yenduri, G., Ramalingam, M., Chemmalar Selvi, G., Supriya, Y., Srivastava, G., Maddikunta, P. K. R., ... Athanasios, V. (n.d.). *GPT (Generative Pre-trained Transformer)–A Comprehensive Review on Enabling Technologies, Potential Applications, Emerging Challenges, and Future Directions*. Academic Press.

Zerbini, C., Bijmolt, T. H., Maestripieri, S., & Luceri, B. (2022). Drivers of consumer adoption of e-Commerce: A meta-analysis. *International Journal of Research in Marketing, 39*(4), 1186–1208. doi:10.1016/j.ijresmar.2022.04.003

Zheng, X., Zhang, C., & Woodland, P. C. (2021, December). Adapting GPT, GPT-2 and BERT language models for speech recognition. In *2021 IEEE Automatic Speech Recognition and Understanding Workshop (ASRU)* (pp. 162-168). IEEE. 10.1109/ASRU51503.2021.9688232

Zhu, Q., & Luo, J. (2022). Generative pre-trained transformer for design concept generation: an exploration. *Proceedings of the design society, 2*, 1825-1834. 10.1017/pds.2022.185

ADDITIONAL READING

Dwivedi, Y. K., Pandey, N., Currie, W., & Micu, A. (2024). Leveraging ChatGPT and other generative artificial intelligence (AI)-based applications in the hospitality and tourism industry: Practices, challenges and research agenda. *International Journal of Contemporary Hospitality Management, 36*(1), 1–12. doi:10.1108/IJCHM-05-2023-0686

Gill, S. S., Xu, M., Patros, P., Wu, H., Kaur, R., Kaur, K., . . . Buyya, R. (2024). Transformative effects of ChatGPT on modern education: Emerging Era of AI Chatbots. Internet of Things and Cyber-Physical Systems, 4, 19-23. doi:10.1016/j.iotcps.2023.06.002

Lian, Y., Tang, H., Xiang, M., & Dong, X. (2024). Public attitudes and sentiments toward ChatGPT in China: A text mining analysis based on social media. *Technology in Society, 76*, 102442. doi:10.1016/j.techsoc.2023.102442

Niu, B., & Mvondo, G. F. N. (2024). I Am ChatGPT, the ultimate AI Chatbot! Investigating the determinants of users' loyalty and ethical usage concerns of ChatGPT. *Journal of Retailing and Consumer Services*, *76*, 103562. doi:10.1016/j.jretconser.2023.103562

Oehler, A., & Horn, M. (2024). Does ChatGPT provide better advice than robo-advisors? *Finance Research Letters*, *60*, 104898. doi:10.1016/j.frl.2023.104898

Polyportis, A., & Pahos, N. (2024). Navigating the perils of artificial intelligence: A focused review on ChatGPT and responsible research and innovation. *Humanities & Social Sciences Communications*, *11*(1), 1–10. doi:10.1057/s41599-023-02464-6

Rejeb, A., Rejeb, K., Appolloni, A., Treiblmaier, H., & Iranmanesh, M. (2024). Exploring the impact of ChatGPT on education: A web mining and machine learning approach. *International Journal of Management Education*, *22*(1), 100932. doi:10.1016/j.ijme.2024.100932

Rice, S., Crouse, S. R., Winter, S. R., & Rice, C. (2024). The advantages and limitations of using ChatGPT to enhance technological research. *Technology in Society*, *76*, 102426. doi:10.1016/j.techsoc.2023.102426

Stahl, B. C., & Eke, D. (2024). The ethics of ChatGPT–Exploring the ethical issues of an emerging technology. *International Journal of Information Management*, *74*, 102700. doi:10.1016/j.ijinfomgt.2023.102700

KEY TERMS AND DEFINITIONS

Artificial Intelligence (AI): The simulation of human intelligence in machines, characterized by the capability of performing tasks that typically require human cognition (Russel & Norvig, 2010; Brynjolfsson & McAfee, 2014).

Behavioural Intention: An individual's perceived likelihood or propensity to engage in a particular behaviour. It is influenced by the individual's attitude towards the behaviour and subjective norms, including the perceived expectations of significant others. (Ajzen, 1991).

Chatbot: A specific type of conversational agent that interacts with users primarily through text. It includes retail-service chatbots like SamBot, used for various industry applications (Pradana et al., 2017; Tran et al., 2021).

ChatGPT: A machine-learning system developed by OpenAI, using generative AI tools to provide conversational responses. It is part of the broader family of GPT models, known for their natural language processing capabilities (van Dis et al., 2023).

Conversational Agent: A multimodal system designed to imitate human conversations by employing spoken or written language, typically through internet-based interactions. These agents can perform tasks comparable to many human employees (Adamopoulou & Moussiades, 2020).

Generative Pre-Trained Transformer (GPT): A significant advancement in the natural language processing field, which enables machines to provide humans with a perception of understanding and communicate in a human-like manner. GPT models are pre-trained on extensive text data and fine-tuned for specific tasks (Yenduri, 2023).

Natural Language Processing (NLP): A domain of AI that deals with the interaction between computers and human language. It involves the development of algorithms that enable machines to interact, interpret, and generate human-like language (Abdul-Kader, 2021).

Social Norms: Established rules that shape behaviour through the encouragement of conformity. They inform group members how to feel and behave in certain situations, exerting social influence on members (Bicchieri & Mercier, 2014; Raven & Rubin, 1976).

Technology Acceptance Model (TAM): A theoretical model that predicts and explains how users accept and use a technology. The core premise of TAM is that the perceived usefulness and perceived ease of use of technology are primary factors influencing a user's decision to adopt and use that technology. (Davis, 1986).

Trust in Technology: The degree of confidence and reliability placed in technology by users. It influences the adoption and usage of technological products and is shaped by WOM and prior experiences (King et al., 2014; Liu & Lopez, 2016).

Word of Mouth (WOM): The exchange of interpersonal information among adopters and potential adopters of a product or service. In the digital context, WOM leverages online networks to amplify its reach and impact (Cheng & Zhou, 2010; Maxham, 2001).

Chapter 6
Exploring the Transformative Role of ChatGPT in Marketing:
Opportunities, Challenges, and Future Directions

Michael Boadi Nyamekye
University of Professional Studies, Accra, Ghana

Emmanuel Arthur
Department of Business Studies, Lancaster University, Ghana

George Cudjoe Agbemabiese
University of Professional Studies, Accra, Ghana

Gloria Ama Konadu Sraha
Department of Business Studies, Lancaster University, Ghana

Mahmoud Abdulai Mahmoud
Business School, University of Ghana, Ghana

Fidelis Quansah
University of Professional Studies, Accra, Ghana

Patrick Amfo Anim
https://orcid.org/0000-0002-4384-2772
Department of Business Studies, Lancaster University, Ghana

ABSTRACT

Artificial intelligence (AI) and technology's possibilities and influence on marketing are crucial and well-known. ChatGPT is a new AI-powered technology that has caused a worldwide boom since its release, with substantial ramifications for all business practises. While acknowledging the growing body of work on ChatGPT, this study attempts to contribute to the ongoing debate by identifying the numerous prospects for employing ChatGPT as an enabler in marketing research and practise.

DOI: 10.4018/979-8-3693-1239-1.ch006

It also highlights the difficulties associated with employing ChatGPT in marketing research. The chapter also discusses the potential for incorporating ChatGPT into other disciplines of marketing, including consumer behaviour, advertising, branding, and sales, as well as the practical consequences for managers. Finally, the chapter recognises the need for more study to better understand the scope of ChatGPT and offers a future research strategy. The chapter concludes by emphasising the significance of incorporating ChatGPT into marketing research and practises with human interaction.

INTRODUCTION

The landscape of human-machine interaction has evolved significantly with technological advancements such as machine usage and machine-to-machine interaction. A notable shift has occurred towards conversational interactions between humans and machines. OpenAI's ChatGPT, a natural language processing model, stands out as a groundbreaking technology in this paradigm, enabling seamless and natural conversations between humans and machines (Ooi et al., 2023). Developed by a research company co-founded by visionaries like Elon Musk, Sam Altman, Greg Brockman, Ilya Sutskever, and John Schulman, ChatGPT harnesses the power of deep learning algorithms trained on extensive datasets comprising billions of web pages and papers. This training enables ChatGPT to generate text responses that closely mimic human-like conversation patterns (Fui-Hoon, 2023). ChatGPT represents a significant advancement in the realm of artificial intelligence language models. Its remarkable capabilities in producing human-like responses to text-based prompts have garnered widespread attention from various sectors, including academia, marketing, and industry (Dwivedi et al., 2023). The potential applications of ChatGPT are vast, but its utilization also raises concerns about potential misuse, prompting a closer examination of its implications.

Other language models like Google's Bard and Meta's LLaMA have also evolved to compete in the market, indicating the transformative potential of these models across various sectors. The development of language models like ChatGPT has roots dating back more than 20 years, with early attempts emerging as far back as the 1960s. However, recent advancements in deep learning AI, increased computational power provided by graphics processing units (GPUs), and the availability of extensive datasets have significantly enhanced the capabilities and feasibility of these models (Kung et al., 2022). ChatGPT, built on the transformer architecture and trained on millions of conversations from diverse sources, represents a leap forward in natural language processing (Bahrini et al., 2023).

During the pandemic, applications such as ChatGPT revolutionized consumer behavior by providing instant answers to user queries, akin to Yahoo and Google search engines. As an AI natural language processing model, ChatGPT employs generative AI techniques to generate algorithm-generated responses to user prompts, enhancing customer service effectiveness and marketing power (Paul et al., 2023). ChatGPT offers distinct advantages over previous AI tools, with significant application potential in marketing research, services marketing, customer service, creative writing, education, finance, health, and entertainment (Rivas & Zhao, 2023). The vast database it operates on is poised to bring about major changes in marketing and other fields. Understanding the potential applications of ChatGPT in marketing, its opportunities, risk, challenges and future prospects is crucial in leveraging its capabilities to build stronger customer relationships, increase market influence, and achieve financial success (Saqib, 2021; Haleem et al., 2022).

BACKGROUND OF THE STUDY

One exemplary model in this realm of AI system is OpenAI's ChatGPT, based on the Generative Pre-trained Transformer (GPT) architecture. ChatGPT's robust text generation capabilities have found applications in linguistic transformation, text summarization, and natural-sounding conversation generation. What sets ChatGPT apart is its adaptability; it can be trained for various tasks, including language recognition, question answering, and paragraph completion, making it invaluable for chatbot development and other interactive applications (Javaid et al., 2023; Dwivedi et al., 2023). ChatGPT's significance in advancing scientific research is rooted in its role as a linguistic model, distinct from Generative Adversarial Network (GAN) models. While GANs are predominantly used for tasks like image generation, ChatGPT is tailored to NLP tasks, contributing to text generation, translation, and data analysis. Its genesis lies within the field of NLP, a subfield of AI dedicated to teaching computers to understand and generate human language (Godwin-Jones, 2019). The motivation behind creating ChatGPT was to establish a versatile AI language model capable of contributing to various tasks, bridging the gap between human-generated and machine-generated content in language understanding and text generation. This evolution underscores ChatGPT's significance in the ongoing AI and NLP revolution.

ChatGPT has quickly gained popularity after its original release in November 2022, drawing a large user base. It had over 100 million users as of January 2023, making it the consumer application with the quickest growth (Attaran, 2023). ChatGPT has demonstrated extraordinary adaptability and usefulness across a wide range of sectors, from information technology to healthcare. Furthermore, it is shown to be useful in marketing research (Dwivedi et al., 2023). The market research industry is now investigating the ramifications of ChatGPT. It is critical to recognise ChatGPT's enormous marketing potential since it provides a myriad of applications such as content creation, keyword research, customer support, language translation, and text summary. Marketers all across the world have used ChatGPT to develop captivating content, sustain consumer interactions, and modify brand advertising strategies (Ooi et al., 2023). ChatGPT can help marketers and researchers perform more effective global commercial operations, revolutionising the landscape of marketing research and practise. ChatGPT has the potential to improve marketing in a variety of ways, such as improved research outputs and practical applications. ChatGPT works with marketers on everything from market research to content creation (Rivas & Zhao, 2023). ChatGPT may be used by marketing researchers to automate tasks ranging from researching consumer behaviour to enhancing advertising and branding endeavours. However, because AI is still a relatively young issue, particularly in business study and practise, much remains to be uncovered.

This chapter represents a significant contribution to the ongoing theoretical discourse by acknowledging the groundbreaking research conducted by Dwivedi et al. (2023). Drawing insights from experts across various domains, with a specific focus on the services sector, the chapter employs an editorial and opinion-based approach to catalyze future research and theoretical exploration. In doing so, it serves a dual purpose: offering valuable guidance to managers contemplating the integration of ChatGPT into their marketing strategies, while also increasing awareness about the potential and challenges of using this technology within the evolving realm of marketing research and practices. The chapter delves into the development of AI language models and explores ChatGPT's applications in marketing, shedding light on both the opportunities and difficulties associated with its implementation. By critically examining the applications of ChatGPT in marketing research, the chapter highlights key insights and challenges, paving the way for further exploration in this field. Moreover, the chapter concludes with valuable solutions and recommendations aimed at addressing these challenges and maximizing the potential of ChatGPT in marketing practices.

MAIN FOCUS OF THE CHAPTER

Development of AI-Language Models

The introduction of ChatGPT by OpenAI on November 30, 2022, sparked widespread interest among academics, researchers, and the general public, eager to explore its potential applications (Grassini, 2023). While ChatGPT represents a significant advancement in natural language processing (NLP) models, its development is rooted in the history of language processing models, dating back to the 1960s with the creation of ELIZA by Joseph Weizenbaum, followed by ALICE developed by Richard Wallace in the 1990s (Ciesla, 2024). These early models laid the foundation for subsequent advancements, including Cleverbot by Rollo Carpenter and OpenAI's Generative Pre-Trained Transformer (GPT) language model series, culminating in the release of GPT-3 in 2020 (Saka et al., 2023). The evolution of language models has been marked by significant milestones, with each iteration introducing enhancements in terms of model size, capabilities, and performance. GPT-3, with its 175 billion parameters, demonstrated exceptional proficiency across various language tasks, setting a new standard in natural language understanding and generation (Iskender, 2023).

The introduction of ChatGPT-3 further expanded the capabilities of the GPT series, particularly in the realm of social media tasks, enabling seamless interaction with users through natural language inputs (Aljanabi et al., 2023). This feature has been particularly beneficial for marketers, eliminating the need for specific keywords or phrases and allowing for intuitive content creation processes (Aljanabi et al., 2023). The rapid adoption of ChatGPT was evidenced by its reported user base of over 100 million within just two months of its launch, prompting the release of ChatGPT-4 in March 2023 (George et al., 2023). Additionally, Microsoft's release of Visual ChatGPT further augmented ChatGPT's functionality by enabling the exchange of images within chat dialogs (Fraiwan & Khasawneh, 2023). As these technologies continue to evolve, driven by differentiation and the addition of new features, they hold the potential to bring about significant transformations in various sectors, particularly in digital marketing. The widespread use of natural language models like ChatGPT introduces new dynamics in supply and demand, offering advantages such as automatic access to data, streamlined processes, and cost-effectiveness (Fraiwan & Khasawneh, 2023). The development of natural language models like ChatGPT and their applications in sectors such as marketing are intertwined, with each influencing the other in a mutually reinforcing cycle. As these models become increasingly sophisticated, their impact on digital development and marketing strategies is poised to become even more pronounced, shaping the future of human-computer interaction and information access.

Opportunities in Using ChatGPT Applications in Marketing

Voice assistants like Amazon Alexa and Siri, alongside Smart Home technologies, have garnered widespread popularity as AI tools. Extensive academic research has delved into the impacts of artificial intelligence (AI) on various stakeholders. The advent of ChatGPT has sparked significant interest and anticipation within the marketing community, capturing the attention of both practitioners and academics alike (Rivas & Zhao, 2023). Marketing, as a multifaceted process, encompasses strategic development, implementation, and management of various endeavours aimed at creating, communicating, and distributing value to consumers (Varadarajan, 2010). While meeting the organization's commercial objectives, marketing primarily seeks to fulfil customers' needs and desires (Sutrisno et al., 2023). It encompasses a range of strategic activities, including market research, segmentation, pricing strategy development, product development, distribution channel implementation, and promotion (Rathore, 2023). Recent technological innovations have significantly impacted the implementation and planning of these strategies. ChatGPT, a natural language processing model, has emerged as a transformative tool in the marketing landscape, offering novel applications that are reshaping traditional marketing practices.

The integration of artificial intelligence, big data analytics, Internet of Things (IoT), and blockchain has the potential to revolutionize marketing and shape its future trajectory (Rivas & Zhao, 2023). Academic literature has explored numerous applications of ChatGPT across various domains, including management, e-commerce, supply chain management, marketing, real estate, business analytics, human resources, accounting, finance, retail, and insurance (Bahrini et al., 2023). In marketing and sales activities, businesses leverage ChatGPT as a virtual assistant for personalized marketing, preparation of technical sales content such as text and images, and managing social media interactions. Marketers utilize ChatGPT for tasks such as creating user guides, analyzing consumer feedback, and enhancing sales force effectiveness (Dwivedi et al., 2023).

Furthermore, ChatGPT plays a supportive role in creating assistants suitable for various business functions, from personalized marketing to retail activities. It assists in interpreting the fundamental components of marketing (Mutoffar et al., 2023) as discussed below.

Market Research: ChatGPT can assist service firms in conducting market research by analysing customer interactions and feedback. For example, in the banking sector, ChatGPT can analyse customer inquiries and complaints to identify emerging trends and preferences, allowing banks to tailor their services accordingly. Similarly, in the insurance industry, ChatGPT can analyse customer queries to understand their insurance needs and preferences, helping insurance companies develop customized insurance products. In healthcare, ChatGPT can analyse patient feedback and inquiries to identify areas for improvement in healthcare services and develop targeted marketing strategies to attract more patients.

Market Segmentation: ChatGPT can help service firms segment their markets based on geographic, demographic, psychographic, or behavioural features. For instance, in the transportation sector, ChatGPT can analyse customer data to identify different customer segments based on factors such as travel preferences, frequency of travel, and preferred destinations. This segmentation can help transportation companies tailor their services to meet the specific needs of different customer segments, such as offering personalized travel packages or discounts for frequent travellers (Demir & Demir, 2023).

Product Development: ChatGPT can support product development by analysing customer feedback and preferences to identify potential product features and improvements. For example, in the hospitality industry, ChatGPT can analyse guest feedback to identify common complaints or suggestions for improvement in hotel amenities and services. This information can then be used to inform the development of new hotel features or services that better meet customer needs and preferences.

Pricing: ChatGPT can assist service firms in pricing their products or services by analysing market demand, competitor pricing strategies, and customer preferences. For example, in the retail sector, ChatGPT can analyse pricing data from competitors and customer feedback to determine the optimal pricing strategy for a new product. Similarly, in the healthcare industry, ChatGPT can analyse patient feedback and inquiries to determine the willingness to pay for different healthcare services and treatments, helping healthcare providers set competitive prices.

Distribution: ChatGPT can support distribution by analysing customer data to identify optimal distribution routes and channels. For example, in the retail sector, ChatGPT can analyse customer data to identify the most popular shopping channels and locations, helping retailers optimize their distribution network. Similarly, in the transportation industry, ChatGPT can analyse travel patterns and customer preferences to identify optimal routes (Dalgıç & Birdir, 2017) and schedules for transporting goods or passengers.

Promotion: ChatGPT can assist service firms in promotional activities by analysing customer data to identify effective marketing techniques and channels. For example, in the hospitality industry, ChatGPT can analyse guest feedback and inquiries to identify the most effective advertising channels and messaging for promoting hotel services and amenities (Gursoy et al., 2023). Similarly, in the banking sector, ChatGPT can analyse customer data to identify the most effective marketing channels and strategies for promoting new banking products or services.

In marketing practices, ChatGPT facilitates the generation of product descriptions, customer feedback analysis, and creation of social media content. It enhances Chatbot customer interactions and offers tailored recommendations based on customer preferences. However, given the expansive capabilities of ChatGPT, defining its precise role and potential applications in marketing remains challenging. Academics and marketing practitioners alike utilize this technology for recommendations and to streamline their work processes, yet the full extent of its applications is yet to be fully explored (Fraiwan & Khasawneh, 2023). Table 1 presents various marketing applications described by Fraiwan and Khasawneh (2023), shedding light on the diverse ways in which ChatGPT can be utilized in the marketing sector.

Table 1. Applying ChatGPT in marketing

Marketing Application	Explanation
Customer service	ChatGPT provides personalized assistance for customers by responding to inquiries about goods and services, making suggestions based on client preferences, and aiding in resolving client problems and grievances.
Sales	ChatGPT enhances sales efforts by providing personalized product recommendations and suggesting add-ons or upgrades based on customer data and natural language descriptions. It assists throughout the sales process, contributing to upselling and cross-selling efforts.
Lead Generation	ChatGPT contributes to lead generation by analyzing customer data and creating natural language descriptions of new clients. Additionally, it aids in qualifying leads by examining consumer feedback and identifying potential prospects.
Content Creation	ChatGPT supports content creation for marketing campaigns by brainstorming ideas for social media posts, email marketing strategies, and blog posts. Additionally, it leverages natural language descriptions of marketing objectives to generate attention-grabbing headlines, compelling product descriptions, and effective promotional messages.
Personalization	By analyzing customer data and creating individualized product and service recommendations, ChatGPT assists in customizing marketing campaigns. Moreover, it utilizes natural language descriptions of customer demographics and preferences to customize marketing messages to specific customer segments.
Market Research	ChatGPT facilitates market research by creating surveys, analyzing customer feedback, and uncovering patterns and valuable information through the evaluation of natural language descriptions related to research objectives.

Source: Fraiwan & Khasawneh, 2023

The range of marketing applications enabled by ChatGPT is indeed extensive. ChatGPT's assistance in various marketing practices and activities may exhibit diverse and distinct functionalities. However, comprehensively addressing all these capabilities presents a challenge due to the boundless nature of AI-supported language models. Therefore, in this section, we will explore some specific applications of ChatGPT based on insights from academic literature.

Customer Service and ChatGPT

Service corporations, unlike traditional manufacturing-centric organizations, primarily deal with perishable and intangible products that are produced, presented, and consumed in a single instance or a series of closely related episodes (Koc et al., 2003). In such contexts, customer expectations play a crucial role, and service providers must meet or exceed these expectations to ensure customer satisfaction. ChatGPT can play a significant role in assisting service corporations by providing personalized recommendations and support to customers (Ray, 2023). By analyzing user behavior and preference data, ChatGPT can offer specialized recommendations that enhance the overall customer experience. This includes answering inquiries about goods and services, providing tailored recommendations based on customer preferences, and addressing customer challenges and complaints (Fraiwan & Khasawneh, 2023). The capabilities of ChatGPT in customer service are diverse and adaptable. For example, it can serve as a virtual customer support agent in contact centres, offering quick and accurate solutions to customer queries while reducing the need for human intervention and associated expenses (Rivas & Zhao, 2023). Additionally, ChatGPT can analyse real-time data from various sources to identify user behaviour patterns, which can be invaluable in the development of new products that align with customer preferences and needs. Research suggests that ChatGPT has the potential to significantly contribute to customer service and improve the effectiveness of operations for small and medium-sized enterprises (SMEs) (Subagja et al., 2023). However, SMEs must consider various factors, including client context, staff training, and data privacy and security, when implementing ChatGPT to ensure its successful integration and maximize its benefits. Over time, as SMEs gain a better understanding of consumer preferences and behaviors through ChatGPT, they can enhance customer satisfaction and drive business growth.

Sales and ChatGPT

Although ChatGPT primarily functions as a language model, it does not directly engage in sales activities like other areas. Businesses cannot use this technology to interact with consumers or conduct sales transactions. However, it can offer valuable suggestions and analyze data gathered during the sales process, making it a crucial tool for enhancing sales effectiveness and efficiency. By providing personalized guidance to sales professionals on product positioning, objection handling, and closing deals, ChatGPT contributes to sales enablement. Leveraging data on client behavior and preferences, ChatGPT equips sales representatives with the necessary resources to achieve higher success rates in closing deals (Ray, 2023). Moreover, ChatGPT can also facilitate sales analysis. According to Suárez et al. (2024), the seven steps for utilizing ChatGPT to uncover and analyze sales insights are as follows:

- **Gather Pertinent Sales Data:** Collect the relevant sales data for analysis.
- **Prepare the Data:** Clean and organize the data for analysis.
- **Define Analysis Goals:** Clearly articulate the objectives of the sales analysis.

- **Interact with ChatGPT:** Engage with ChatGPT by asking questions related to the sales analytics goals.
- **Analyze Responses:** Examine the responses generated by ChatGPT to gain insights into the sales data.
- **Visualize Data:** Present the analyzed data using charts, graphs, or dashboards for clear and informative visualization.
- **Continuous Improvement:** Continuously refine queries and analysis based on the knowledge gained from previous interactions with ChatGPT.

As evident, ChatGPT offers various benefits in the sales domain, ranging from providing suggestions to conducting sales analysis. It's important to note that the utility of ChatGPT extends beyond these functions. Businesses and marketers should explore all potential applications of ChatGPT, both before, during, and after the sales process, to maximize its capabilities and enhance their sales strategies.

ChatGPT and Lead Generation

Lead generation, when facilitated by ChatGPT, operates within a consumer context that closely resembles lean manufacturing principles. Analogous to the conversion rates in production line applications, ChatGPT can significantly impact consumer conversion rates by offering tailored recommendations to potential customers. These recommendations, derived from technology-driven insights, provide several benefits to businesses and marketers by aiding in the identification of new customer groups or the creation of new product lines. By leveraging ChatGPT's capabilities, businesses can effectively reduce errors and streamline circulation, akin to lean manufacturing principles. Existing literature indicates that ChatGPT plays a pivotal role in lead generation by supporting elements such as creating potential customers and enhancing customer conversion rates. According to Ayoola et al. (2023), ChatGPT facilitates the creation of consumer leads through the analysis of data on consumer behavior and preferences. Similarly, Ray (2023) emphasizes that ChatGPT's language model assists businesses in generating leads and subsequently boosting customer conversion rates by offering specific recommendations about goods or services.

Content Creation and ChatGPT

Social media, as defined by Baruah et al. (2024), is an interface facilitating interactive dialogues among various verbal and written communication elements. This system, particularly highlighted with the emergence of Web 2.0, encompasses diverse platforms such as social networking sites, virtual worlds, microblogging sites, blogs, and wikis (Haile, 2024). Users of social networks are broadly categorized into two groups: content creators and curators, as delineated by Larkin et al. (2023). Content creators are those who share self-generated content on social platforms, while curators are individuals who redistribute existing knowledge within their social networks. Businesses often find themselves participating in both roles, either by disseminating information produced by others or by generating content related to their own activities. However, the need for content creation extends beyond social networks and encompasses various areas within business operations. Artificial intelligence (AI) applications have brought about notable changes in marketing activities, contributing to improved operational quality and faster production (Cannas et al., 2023). Notably, AI algorithms capable of generating new content and supporting marketing activities have demonstrated potential in enhancing the performance of marketing content while reducing transaction costs (Peres et al., 2023). Furthermore, these AI-driven processes have been observed to streamline qualitative processes, resulting in more efficient outputs (John et al., 2023). Amidst these advancements, ChatGPT stands out as a pivotal tool in content production, offering a range of features such as providing suggestions to users, delving into details, and efficiently preparing content according to desired specifications. Its ability to produce positions ChatGPT content swiftly and effectively as a valuable resource for marketing practitioners across various business activities and social networking platforms.

ChatGPT and Personalization

AI holds significant potential in revolutionizing e-commerce by enhancing product recommendations and customer satisfaction. AI-enabled chatbots, for instance, can streamline customer service by addressing frequently asked questions, thereby reducing the burden on customer service representatives. This automation not only improves efficiency but also contributes to higher customer satisfaction levels (Singh, 2023). Moreover, AI-driven search algorithms play a crucial role in directing customers to the right products swiftly, thereby enhancing the accuracy and relevance of product recommendations. Personalization algorithms further augment the customer experience by predicting user behavior and offering tailored pricing strategies. These algorithms also facilitate personalized product recommendations, enabling businesses to effectively market their products and services (Singh, 2023).

The trend of personalization in marketing is on the rise, driven by modern marketing practices. Direct marketers have long employed personalization techniques, and now, mass marketers are increasingly adopting personalized marketing strategies. For instance, campaigns like Adidas' personalized TV commercials, which incorporate the viewer's name, illustrate the growing emphasis on personalized marketing across various sectors (Hashem, 2023).

As businesses aim to enhance efficiency while aligning with their objectives, the integration of AI technologies like ChatGPT into marketing applications becomes inevitable. ChatGPT, with its multifaceted capabilities, has the potential to democratize marketing by assisting startups, small companies, influencers, nonprofits, and various other entities in personalized communication and application development (Peres et al., 2023). However, the effectiveness of new approaches to marketing content development using ChatGPT must be rigorously evaluated across different contexts. Despite the anticipated benefits of one-to-one marketing and customer relationship management, marketers must strive to meet client expectations while avoiding spam responses (Roman & Hernstein, 2004). Furthermore, advancements in information and communication technologies have opened up new avenues for customer data collection, analysis, and personalization. Technologies like ChatGPT play a pivotal role in providing and producing information swiftly and efficiently, thereby revolutionizing marketing activities by enabling seamless personalization at scale (Bansal et al., 2024).

Market Research and ChatGPT

Market research serves as a vital method for delving into and addressing issues related to human behaviour. Market researchers employ a diverse arsenal of methods, including exploratory, descriptive, and experimental techniques, to categorize behaviour at its most fundamental level. A crucial task for market researchers is to explore the tactical and strategic options available to managers and provide recommendations, as understanding behaviour often leads to requests for explanations. The primary responsibility of the market research function in an organization is to provide trustworthy information that aids managers in making better decisions (Yoshikuni et al., 2023). Responses generated by ChatGPT can play a significant role in marketing research activities. ChatGPT responses can be utilized to create personalized and compelling advertisements, conduct market research to gain deeper insights into customer behaviour, and develop social media content that is more relevant to users (Paul et al., 2023). However, effective market research involves the integration of various technological elements, from data mining to ChatGPT, across different stages of the process. These elements are utilized for tasks such as gathering market data, identifying consumer trends, and analysing customer feedback. ChatGPT has received overwhelmingly positive reviews, with users praising its advanced capabilities and user-friendly interface. With its conversational style and broad range of topics, ChatGPT has shown promise in revolutionizing human interaction with technology. As businesses increasingly leverage ChatGPT for market research applications, its features are expected to serve as an exceptional tool for obtaining valuable insights and enhancing decision-making processes (Haleem et al., 2022).

ChatGPT and Consumers

ChatGPT, powered by natural language processing (NLP) and machine learning algorithms, is a transformative tool poised to revolutionize digital marketing. This technology enables the creation of conversational AI chatbots capable of understanding client needs, autonomously solving their problems, and facilitating purchases (Huseynov, 2023). Kshetri et al. (2023) extensively explored the integration of artificial intelligence in marketing, particularly focusing on the use of chatbots and language models to enhance customer experience and relationship management systems. Through ChatGPT, consumers gain access to an empowering platform offering a diverse range of insights across various categories. For example, when tourist users inquire about "places to visit" ChatGPT not only highlights well-known tourist attractions but also introduces new and intriguing destinations nearby. Visitors can explore information on local cuisines, specialty restaurants, optimal visiting times, and typical price ranges, all thanks to ChatGPT's capabilities (Dwivedi et al., 2023). These recommendations and analytics extend to multiple domains, showcasing ChatGPT's potential to deliver significant benefits to consumers. ChatGPT emerges as a vital support element for businesses in providing tailored suggestions to consumers and enhancing the overall consumer experience. The benefits of using ChatGPT for consumers, as outlined by Paul et al. (2023), include:

- **Increased Consumer Engagement**: Supported by chatbots and conversation agents, ChatGPT offers a more engaging and interactive experience compared to traditional communication methods.
- **Enhanced Customer Service**: ChatGPT-powered chatbots respond promptly to customer queries, delivering efficient solutions faster than traditional customer service channels.
- **Shopping and Personalization**: Anthropomorphic chatbots foster trust and enhance shopping satisfaction by analysing consumer behaviour and preferences to provide personalized marketing messages, shopping tips, and product recommendations.
- **Social Interaction**: ChatGPT facilitates socialization through technological channels, offering welfare benefits to consumers and alleviating stress and loneliness for some users.
- **Social Communication and Interaction Application**: Particularly useful for individuals with social communication disorders, ChatGPT provides a low-impact environment to establish communication and foster trust.
- **Cost Effectiveness**: ChatGPT-powered chatbots deliver cost-effective customer support by handling multiple interactions simultaneously without human intervention, thus improving productivity and service quality.

- **Insight into Consumer Behaviour**: ChatGPT analyses consumer preferences, emotions, behaviours, and opinions, providing valuable insights for businesses to understand and cater to consumer needs effectively.
- **Improved Marketing Campaigns**: By crafting compelling marketing messages tailored to consumer preferences, ChatGPT enhances engagement and conversion rates, ultimately leading to more effective marketing campaigns.

CHALLENGES OF USING CHATGPT IN MARKETING

ChatGPT, a powerful tool in marketing research and applications, is not without its challenges. Ray (2023) highlights several limitations, including biases in data, difficulty in distinguishing outdated or incomplete information, and challenges related to ethical reasoning, contextual aptitude, visual content creation, and conversational linking. While ChatGPT presents tremendous opportunities, it also poses drawbacks for marketing research. Academics and researchers utilize ChatGPT at various stages of research to improve and expedite their work. However, Jain et al. (2023) emphasizes the necessity of acknowledging and overcoming the limitations of ChatGPT. For instance, in the services sector, a hotel chain might employ ChatGPT to analyse customer reviews and feedback to improve service quality and personalize guest experiences. However, the challenge arises when ChatGPT's analysis fails to accurately interpret nuanced customer sentiments, leading to misguided service improvements or recommendations. One significant challenge is the potential for ChatGPT to produce misleading or inaccurate information due to biases in the training data. This can inadvertently affect the direction of scientific research, leading to overconfidence and reducing researchers' ability to problem-solve independently (Ray, 2023). Furthermore, ChatGPT's access to large datasets raises data protection and privacy concerns, highlighting the need for robust safeguards (Ray, 2023). For example, in the healthcare sector, a medical institution might use ChatGPT to analyse patient feedback from online surveys. However, if ChatGPT fails to protect patient privacy adequately, it could result in breaches of confidentiality and trust. Despite these challenges, ChatGPT holds promise for bibliometric analysis, aiding in data collection, cleaning, visualization, analysis, and interpretation (Kirtania, 2023; Rakap, 2023). However, researchers may encounter challenges such as limited content knowledge, biases, interpretation issues, and ethical considerations. For instance, a marketing research firm might utilize ChatGPT to analyse social media data to understand consumer sentiment towards a new product launch. However, if ChatGPT lacks context-specific knowledge or fails to identify subtle nuances in language, it could lead to inaccurate conclusions and flawed marketing strategies. Moreover, the need for domain knowledge and human interaction presents a significant hurdle. ChatGPT, as a general-purpose model, lacks expertise in the marketing discipline and cannot accurately replicate human reactions and interactions, especially in consumer-focused research (Jain et al., 2023). Ensuring control over data quality and accuracy is essential, as ChatGPT's output may be affected by incomplete, inaccurate, or biased data. For example, a retail company might utilize ChatGPT to generate product recommendations for online shoppers. However, if ChatGPT's training data is biased towards certain products or demographics, it could result in recommendations that do not align with customer preferences, leading to lost sales opportunities. Additionally, ChatGPT's complexity makes it challenging to explain and interpret its outputs, and its potential to generate harmful content like fake news or hate speech is a concern (Ray, 2023). Moreover, ChatGPT may provide biased responses influenced by linguistic and cultural factors, impacting the reliability of its text generation capabilities (Ray, 2023). For instance, a financial institution might use ChatGPT to generate customer service responses on their website. However, if ChatGPT inadvertently generates responses that contain offensive language or misinformation, it could damage the institution's reputation and customer trust.

SOLUTIONS

Bias Mitigation and Data Quality Control

One of the primary challenges with using ChatGPT in marketing research is the potential for biases in the training data to influence the model's outputs. To mitigate this challenge, organizations must implement robust mechanisms to identify and rectify biases in the data used to train ChatGPT. This includes conducting thorough data audits, incorporating diverse perspectives into training datasets, and regularly updating datasets to ensure representativeness. Additionally, organizations can explore techniques such as adversarial training to expose ChatGPT to diverse viewpoints and reduce algorithmic biases.

Ethical Guidelines and Privacy Protection

Protecting user privacy and adhering to ethical guidelines are paramount when using ChatGPT in marketing research. Organizations must develop comprehensive ethical guidelines that outline the responsible use of ChatGPT and ensure compliance with data protection regulations, such as the General Data Protection Regulation (GDPR). This involves implementing privacy-preserving measures, such as data anonymization and encryption, and establishing transparent consent mechanisms for data collection and processing. Clear disclosures regarding the use of ChatGPT-generated insights should also be provided to users to uphold transparency and trust.

Domain Expertise and Human Oversight

Integrating domain-specific expertise into the training and evaluation of ChatGPT models is essential to enhance their contextual understanding and accuracy in marketing applications. Collaboration between AI experts, marketers, and domain specialists is crucial to ensure comprehensive interpretation of results and validation of ChatGPT-generated outputs. Human oversight and intervention mechanisms should be implemented to validate ChatGPT-generated outputs, especially in complex and sensitive domains such as healthcare and consumer behaviour research.

Interpretability and Explainability

Improving the interpretability and explainability of ChatGPT-generated outputs is crucial for stakeholders to understand the reasoning behind the model's decisions. Techniques such as attention mechanisms, feature attribution, and model introspection can provide insights into the decision-making process of ChatGPT. Transparent documentation of model architectures, training methodologies, and decision criteria facilitates stakeholder understanding and trust in ChatGPT-generated outputs.

Continuous Monitoring and Evaluation

Establishing ongoing monitoring and evaluation protocols is essential to assess the performance and impact of ChatGPT in marketing research applications. Regular audits of ChatGPT-generated outputs for biases, inaccuracies, and ethical implications enable organizations to identify areas for improvement and refine ChatGPT models iteratively. Soliciting feedback from stakeholders and end-users is also valuable for continuous improvement and ensuring alignment with organizational goals.

Education and Training

Providing comprehensive education and training programs for researchers, marketers, and other stakeholders involved in using ChatGPT in marketing research is crucial for responsible AI deployment (Rahman & Watanobe, 2023). These programs should offer guidance on best practices, ethical considerations, and risk mitigation strategies to empower users in navigating the complexities of ChatGPT-enabled marketing applications. Fostering a culture of continuous learning and knowledge sharing promotes responsible AI usage and enhances decision-making processes.

RECOMMENDATIONS

Researchers should conduct rigorous validation studies to assess the accuracy, reliability, and ethical implications of ChatGPT-generated outputs in marketing research (Yu, 2023). This involves collaborating across disciplines, including AI experts, marketers, domain specialists, and ethicists, to ensure a comprehensive understanding and responsible use of ChatGPT. Transparent publication of methodologies detailing training data, model architectures, and evaluation criteria promotes transparency, reproducibility, and trust in research findings. Policy makers play a crucial role in developing comprehensive ethical guidelines and regulations governing the use of AI, including ChatGPT, in marketing research. Supporting data governance policies and frameworks, such as data anonymization, encryption, and consent mechanisms, safeguards user privacy and mitigates risks associated with data misuse. Additionally, allocating resources to support education and training initiatives raises awareness about ethical considerations and best practices in AI-enabled marketing research. Marketers should prioritize data quality and integrity when leveraging ChatGPT for marketing research. Conducting data audits, validating insights through human oversight, and addressing biases in training data enhance the accuracy and reliability of ChatGPT-generated outputs. Enhancing interpretability by implementing techniques to explain model outputs and adhering to ethical standards, including obtaining informed consent for data collection and processing, respects user privacy and avoids unethical practices in AI-enabled marketing campaigns. Practitioners must establish protocols for continuous monitoring and evaluation of ChatGPT-generated outputs in marketing applications. Regular audits assess performance, identify biases, and address any ethical implications. Incorporating human oversight and intervention mechanisms validates ChatGPT-generated insights, ensuring accuracy, relevance, and ethical integrity in marketing strategies. Staying informed about the latest developments, best practices, and ethical considerations in AI-enabled marketing research through ongoing education and training enhances expertise in leveraging ChatGPT effectively while upholding ethical standards and responsible AI usage.

FUTURE RESEARCH DIRECTIONS

One promising future research direction in the field of ChatGPT applications in marketing is the exploration of personalized and context-aware conversational AI solutions. As technology advances, there is a growing need for AI models like ChatGPT to not only understand user queries but also adapt their responses based on individual preferences, behaviours, and situational contexts. Future research could focus on developing and refining ChatGPT models capable of providing personalized recommendations, tailored marketing messages, and real-time assistance to users in various marketing scenarios. Moreover, investigating the integration of contextual cues, such as location, time of day, user sentiment, and browsing history, into ChatGPT-based marketing interactions could enhance the relevance and effectiveness of AI-driven marketing campaigns. This could involve leveraging techniques from natural language processing, machine learning, and contextual computing to enable ChatGPT to generate more contextually relevant and personalized responses. Additionally, exploring the ethical implications and user perceptions of personalized conversational AI in marketing contexts is crucial. Future research could examine user attitudes towards personalized marketing interactions facilitated by ChatGPT, as well as the impact of privacy concerns, data transparency, and trust-building strategies on user acceptance and engagement.

CONCLUSION

ChatGPT has unquestionably had a significant impact on marketing research, providing researchers with new ways to improve the efficacy, accuracy, and inventiveness of their work. While ChatGPT has several limits, the benefits of this powerful technology exceed the negatives. We may expect more exciting breakthroughs in the following years as academics investigate ChatGPT's potential in marketing research, providing an opportunity to utilize it in numerous marketing disciplines for enhanced research and market outcomes. It is important to note that constraints such as errors, reliance on obsolete data, and ethical problems continue to exist. Furthermore, as platforms grow, AI and human input cohabitation will become increasingly important. ChatGPT, on the other hand, has shown how AI can be harnessed effectively in various applications, including sales, customer service, search, marketing, content generation, and knowledge bases. ChatGPT as a powerful illustration of the immense potential that can be unlocked through the synergy of AI and technology. This chapter attempts to synthesize the benefits and disadvantages of utilizing ChatGPT in marketing endeavours within various industries with specific focus to the services sector. When considering the numerous options provided by ChatGPT, it is utilised with caution, much like human involvement. It is also vital for the user to recognize and comprehend the benefits and drawbacks of ChatGPT as a facilitator in research and practice. Finally, this chapter highlights the need for more research in ChatGPT as a marketing research guide. It gives a thorough overview of how ChatGPT might assist academics, marketers and policy makers in various marketing sectors. These findings will be helpful to both marketers and scholars.

REFERENCES

Aljanabi, M. (2023). ChatGPT: Future directions and open possibilities. *Mesopotamian Journal of Cybersecurity, 2023*, 16-17.

Attaran, M. (2023). The impact of 5G on the evolution of intelligent automation and industry digitization. *Journal of Ambient Intelligence and Humanized Computing, 14*(5), 5977–5993. doi:10.1007/s12652-020-02521-x PMID:33643481

Ayoola, O. O., Alenoghena, R., & Adeniji, S. (2023). ChatGPT impacts on access-efficiency, employment, education and ethics: The socio-economics of an AI language model. *BizEcons Quarterly, 16*, 1–17.

Bahrini, A., Khamoshifar, M., Abbasimehr, H., Riggs, R. J., Esmaeili, M., Majdabadkohne, R. M., & Pasehvar, M. (2023, April). ChatGPT: Applications, opportunities, and threats. In *2023 Systems and Information Engineering Design Symposium (SIEDS)* (pp. 274-279). IEEE. 10.1109/SIEDS58326.2023.10137850

Bansal, G., Chamola, V., Hussain, A., Guizani, M., & Niyato, D. (2024). Transforming Conversations with AI—A Comprehensive Study of ChatGPT. *Cognitive Computation*, 1–24. doi:10.1007/s12559-023-10236-2

Baruah, H., Singh, S. R., & Sarmah, P. (2024). *Transliteration Characteristics in Romanized Assamese Language Social Media Text and Machine Transliteration*. ACM Transactions on Asian and Low-Resource Language Information Processing. doi:10.1145/3639565

Cannas, V. G., Ciano, M. P., Saltalamacchia, M., & Secchi, R. (2023). Artificial intelligence in supply chain and operations management: A multiple case study research. *International Journal of Production Research*, 1–28.

Ciesla, R. (2024). *The Book of Chatbots: From ELIZA to ChatGPT*. Springer Nature. doi:10.1007/978-3-031-51004-5

Dwivedi, Y. K., Kshetri, N., Hughes, L., Slade, E. L., Jeyaraj, A., Kar, A. K., Baabdullah, A. M., Koohang, A., Raghavan, V., Ahuja, M., Albanna, H., Albashrawi, M. A., Al-Busaidi, A. S., Balakrishnan, J., Barlette, Y., Basu, S., Bose, I., Brooks, L., Buhalis, D., ... Wright, R. (2023). "So what if ChatGPT wrote it?" Multidisciplinary perspectives on opportunities, challenges and implications of generative conversational AI for research, practice and policy. *International Journal of Information Management, 71*, 102642. doi:10.1016/j.ijinfomgt.2023.102642

Fraiwan, M., & Khasawneh, N. (2023). A Review of ChatGPT Applications in Education, Marketing, Software Engineering, and Healthcare: Benefits, Drawbacks, and Research Directions. *arXiv preprint arXiv:2305.00237.*

Fui-Hoon Nah, F., Zheng, R., Cai, J., Siau, K., & Chen, L. (2023). Generative AI and ChatGPT: Applications, challenges, and AI-human collaboration. *Journal of Information Technology Case and Application Research*, *25*(3), 277–304. doi:10.1080/15228053.2023.2233814

Godwin-Jones, R. (2019). In a world of SMART technology, why learn another language? *Journal of Educational Technology & Society*, *22*(2), 4–13.

Grassini, S. (2023). Shaping the future of education: Exploring the potential and consequences of AI and ChatGPT in educational settings. *Education Sciences*, *13*(7), 692. doi:10.3390/educsci13070692

Haile, T. T. (2024). Web's Progression: Moving from Passive Content Consumption to Active Content Creation and Content Validation. *International Journal of Business and Management*, *18*(6), 135–135. doi:10.5539/ijbm.v18n6p135

Haleem, A., Javaid, M., & Singh, R. P. (2022). An era of ChatGPT as a significant futuristic support tool: A study on features, abilities, and challenges. *Bench Council Transactions on Benchmarks, Standards and Evaluations,* *2*(4), 100089.

Hashem, T. N. (2023). Can Aggressive Marketing Cause an Ethical Dilemma? *International Journal (Toronto, Ont.)*, *10*(4), 1216–1229.

Huseynov, F. (2023). Chatbots in digital marketing: Enhanced customer experience and reduced customer service costs. In *Contemporary Approaches of Digital Marketing and the Role of Machine Intelligence* (pp. 46–72). IGI Global. doi:10.4018/978-1-6684-7735-9.ch003

Jain, V., Rai, H., Subash, P., & Mogaji, E. (2023). The Prospects and Challenges of ChatGPT on Marketing Research and Practices. *Emmanuel, The Prospects and Challenges of ChatGPT on Marketing Research and Practices.*

Javaid, M., Haleem, A., & Singh, R. P. (2023). ChatGPT for healthcare services: An emerging stage for an innovative perspective. *BenchCouncil Transactions on Benchmarks. Standards and Evaluations*, *3*(1), 100105.

John, M. M., Olsson, H. H., & Bosch, J. (2023). Towards an AI-driven business development framework: A multi-case study. *Journal of Software (Malden, MA)*, *35*(6), e2432. doi:10.1002/smr.2432

KirtaniaD. K. (2023). OpenAI ChatGPT for Library and Information Science (LIS) Professionals. *Available at* SSRN 4404903. doi:10.2139/ssrn.4404903

Koc, E., Hatipoglu, S., Kivrak, O., Celik, C., & Koc, K. (2023). Houston, we have a problem!: The use of ChatGPT in responding to customer complaints. *Technology in Society*, *74*, 102333. doi:10.1016/j.techsoc.2023.102333

Kshetri, N., Dwivedi, Y. K., Davenport, T. H., & Panteli, N. (2023). Generative artificial intelligence in marketing: Applications, opportunities, challenges, and research agenda. *International Journal of Information Management*, 102716.

Kung, T. H., Cheatham, M., Medenilla, A., Sillos, C., De Leon, L., Elepaño, C., Madriaga, M., Aggabao, R., Diaz-Candido, G., Maningo, J., & Tseng, V. (2023). Performance of ChatGPT on USMLE: Potential for AI-assisted medical education using large language models. *PLOS Digital Health*, *2*(2), e0000198. doi:10.1371/journal.pdig.0000198 PMID:36812645

Larkin, J., Ballatore, A., & Mityurova, E. (2023). Museums, COVID-19 and the pivot to social media. *Curator (New York, N.Y.)*, *66*(4), 629–646. doi:10.1111/cura.12558

Mutoffar, M. M., Kuswayati, S., Anggraeny, F. T., & Sumarni, T. (2023). Exploring the Potential of ChatGPT in Improving Online Marketing and Promotion of MSMEs. *Jurnal Minfo Polgan*, *12*(2), 480–489. doi:10.33395/jmp.v12i1.12440

Paul, J., Ueno, A., & Dennis, C. (2023). ChatGPT and consumers: Benefits, pitfalls and future research agenda. *International Journal of Consumer Studies*, *47*(4), 1213–1225. doi:10.1111/ijcs.12928

Peres, R., Schreier, M., Schweidel, D. A., & Sorescu, A. (2023). Blockchain meets marketing: Opportunities, threats, and avenues for future research. *International Journal of Research in Marketing*, *40*(1), 1–11. doi:10.1016/j.ijresmar.2022.08.001

Rathore, B. (2023). Digital Transformation 4.0: A Case Study of LK Bennett from Marketing Perspectives. *International Journal of Enhanced Research in Management & Computer Applications*, *10*(11), 45–54.

Ray, P. P. (2023). AI in Sensor Research: A Reality Check and the Underestimated Potential of ChatGPT. *ACS Sensors*, *8*(4), 1371–1372. doi:10.1021/acssensors.3c01045 PMID:37318550

Rivas, P., & Zhao, L. (2023). Marketing with chatgpt: Navigating the ethical terrain of gpt-based chatbot technology. *AI*, *4*(2), 375–384. doi:10.3390/ai4020019

Saka, A., Taiwo, R., Saka, N., Salami, B. A., Ajayi, S., Akande, K., & Kazemi, H. (2023). GPT models in construction industry: Opportunities, limitations, and a use case validation. *Developments in the Built Environment*, 100300.

Saqib, N. (2020). Positioning–a literature review. *PSU Research Review*, *5*(2), 141–169. doi:10.1108/PRR-06-2019-0016

Singh, S., Thakur, P., & Singh, S. (2023). How Does the Use of AI in HRM Contribute to Improved Business Performance?: A Systematic Review. *Advances in Human Resources Management and Organizational Development*, *5*(0), 131–139. doi:10.4018/978-1-6684-6745-9.ch008

Suárez, A., Jiménez, J., de Pedro, M. L., Andreu-Vázquez, C., García, V. D. F., Sánchez, M. G., & Freire, Y. (2024). Beyond the Scalpel: Assessing ChatGPT's potential as an auxiliary intelligent virtual assistant in oral surgery. *Computational and Structural Biotechnology Journal*, *24*, 46–52. doi:10.1016/j.csbj.2023.11.058 PMID:38162955

Subagja, A. D., Ausat, A. M. A., Sari, A. R., Wanof, M. I., & Suherlan, S. (2023). Improving Customer Service Quality in MSMEs through the Use of ChatGPT. *Jurnal Minfo Polgan*, *12*(2), 380–386. doi:10.33395/jmp.v12i1.12407

Sutrisno, S., Ausat, A. M. A., Permana, B., & Harahap, M. A. K. (2023). Do Information Technology and Human Resources Create Business Performance: A Review. *International Journal of Professional Business Review: Int. J. Prof. Bus. Rev.*, *8*(8), 14.

Varadarajan, R. (2010). Strategic marketing and marketing strategy: Domain, definition, fundamental issues and foundational premises. *Journal of the Academy of Marketing Science*, *38*(2), 119–140. doi:10.1007/s11747-009-0176-7

Yoshikuni, A. C., Dwivedi, R., Dultra-de-Lima, R. G., Parisi, C., & Oyadomari, J. C. T. (2023). Role of Emerging Technologies in Accounting Information Systems for Achieving Strategic Flexibility through Decision-Making Performance: An Exploratory Study Based on North American and South American Firms. *Global Journal of Flexible Systems Management*, 1-20.

ADDITIONAL READING

Dalgıç, A., & Birdir, K. (2017). Otel işletmeciliğinde yeni trendler. In Y. Akgündüz (Ed.), *Otel İşletmeciliği* (pp. 311–328). Paradigma Akademi.

Demir, M., & Demir, Ş. Ş. (2023). Is ChatGPT the right technology for service individualization and value co-creation? evidence from the travel industry. *Journal of Travel & Tourism Marketing*, *40*(5), 383–398. doi:10.1080/10548408.2023.2255884

Gursoy, D., Li, Y., & Song, H. (2023). ChatGPT and the hospitality and tourism industry: An overview of current trends and future research directions. *Journal of Hospitality Marketing & Management*, *32*(5), 579–592. doi:10.1080/19368623.2023.2211993

Iskender, A. (2023). Holy or unholy? Interview with open AI's ChatGPT. *European Journal of Tourism Research*, *34*, 3414–3414. doi:10.54055/ejtr.v34i.3169

Ooi, K. B., Tan, G. W. H., Al-Emran, M., Al-Sharafi, M. A., Capatina, A., Chakraborty, A., Dwivedi, Y. K., Huang, T.-L., Kar, A. K., Lee, V.-H., Loh, X.-M., Micu, A., Mikalef, P., Mogaji, E., Pandey, N., Raman, R., Rana, N. P., Sarker, P., Sharma, A., ... Wong, L. W. (2023). The potential of Generative Artificial Intelligence across disciplines: Perspectives and future directions. *Journal of Computer Information Systems*, 1–32. doi:10.1080/08874417.2023.2261010

Rahman, M. M., & Watanobe, Y. (2023). ChatGPT for education and research: Opportunities, threats, and strategies. *Applied Sciences (Basel, Switzerland)*, *13*(9), 5783. doi:10.3390/app13095783

Rakap, S. (2023). Chatting with GPT: Enhancing Individualized Education Program Goal Development for Novice Special Education Teachers. *Journal of Special Education Technology*, 01626434231211295. doi:10.1177/01626434231211295

Yu, H. (2023). Reflection on whether Chat GPT should be banned by academia from the perspective of education and teaching. *Frontiers in Psychology*, *14*, 1181712. doi:10.3389/fpsyg.2023.1181712 PMID:37325766

KEY TERMS AND DEFINITIONS

Artificial Intelligence (AI): Is a branch of computer science focused on creating systems that can perform tasks requiring human-like intelligence.

Chatbot: Is an advanced computer program specifically designed to initiate and conduct conversations with human users, typically over the internet.

ChatGPT: A prominent example of AI technology, consists of vast data sets that can be analysed computationally to uncover patterns, trends, and associations, particularly in human behaviour and interactions.

Internet of Things (IoT): Refers to a network of interconnected objects, ranging from smartphones and corridor signs to room thermostats, that can communicate and exchange data with each other.

Chapter 7
Case Studies and ChatGPT:
Enhancing Tourism Education

Ayşegül Simge Demircioğlu Dalgıç
Süleyman Demirel University, Turkey

ABSTRACT

In today's world, the presence of artificial intelligence applications is observable in various aspects of life. One of the artificial intelligence-based applications, ChatGPT, has been employed in many fields. Scientific research has delved into the potential applications of ChatGPT in different domains. In the realm of tourism education, research studies focusing on ChatGPT are increasingly emerging. This study investigates the impact of case studies created through ChatGPT on tourism students, in addition to the theoretical knowledge provided in tourism education. Interviews were conducted with 32 tourism students, and the detailed results are presented.

INTRODUCTION

With the advancements in technology, it is observed that people's tools for acquiring information have transformed, making knowledge more easily accessible wherever desired (Çelik, 2023). Recently, the school term has started to be defined as a place where students and teachers come together physically or virtually to perform learning and teaching activities, based on recent studies and events (Timms, 2016). Looking at this definition, it is possible to say that artificial intelligence technologies are now integrated into every aspect of our lives, including education (İşler & Kılıç, 2021). The concept of artificial intelligence was first coined by McCarthy in 1956 (Russell & Norvig, 2010). Artificial intelligence is defined as information

DOI: 10.4018/979-8-3693-1239-1.ch007

processing technologies initially developed by humans to perform tasks that are feasibly achievable by humans (Skilton & Hovsepian, 2017). In 1997, a historic achievement was accomplished when the computer program named “Deep Blue,” developed by IBM, defeated the reigning world chess champion, Garry Kasparov, in a chess match. This event, marking the victory of a computer over a human chess champion, became a symbolic representation of the competition between human intelligence and developed machines. It is widely recognized as a turning point in artificial intelligence (Campbell, 2002). According to Kurzweil’s (1990) definition, artificial intelligence is characterized not only by machines and systems developed to perform tasks using human intelligence but also by the art of developing such machines. Artificial intelligence technologies aim to enable machines developed through these technologies to solve complex problems more akin to human problem-solving (Sridhar, 2018).

OpenAI is a research company aiming to benefit humanity with artificial intelligence without pursuing profit (OpenAI, 2023). GPT-3, a language model, was developed by OpenAI on November 30, 2022 (Tong & Zhang, 2023). This artificial intelligence robot/program, known as ‘ChatGPT,’ gained recognition and usage as it engages in natural conversations with users (Erul & Işın, 2023). ChatGPT is a chatbot application developed based on OpenAI’s GPT technology. It can process a wide range of text-based requests, from basic questions and queries to more complex tasks, providing responses that go beyond mere information retrieval (Lund, 2022). Through a fine-tuning process that incorporates dialogue optimization, ChatGPT is endowed with the ability to respond to requests in a conversational style, similar to human interaction (Health, 2023). ChatGPT is utilized in various sectors, particularly benefiting tourists who utilize sub-sectors such as accommodation, transportation, services, and entertainment, all considered components of tourism. Tourists often resort to artificial intelligence applications to gain different insights and information about where hospitality spirit is more prevalent, where service quality is better, and which places are attractive, all in pursuit of creating unforgettable experiences (Erul & Işın, 2023; Goeldner & Ritchie, 2012). In recent times, advancements in deep machine learning have led to the emergence of platforms capable of generating text that mimics human writing, thinking similarly to humans. Several content writing platforms have AI capabilities, including Rytr, Jasper, ChatGPT, and CopyAI. Currently, the most impressive and captivating among these platforms is ChatGPT. The user-friendly interface of the ChatGPT application has contributed to its rapid growth in a short period (Gleason, 2022).

The groups that adapt most rapidly to technological developments and changes are generally school-aged youths, as they closely follow technology trends, and consequently, individuals in this group are frequent users of artificial intelligence applications. Given ChatGPT’s ability to respond to various topics and assist, it is considered an artificial intelligence application that greatly captures the interest of young individuals (Quadir, 2022). The tourism sector stands out as one of the industries where labor-intensive service provision is essential, underscoring the significance of close relationships between customers and employees. Due to the labor-intensive nature of the tourism sector, a positively correlated relationship exists between the success of businesses operating in the sector and the success, performance, and satisfaction of the workforce. Consequently, owners and managers of businesses in the tourism sector aim to employ qualified personnel within their organizations to enhance their organizational achievements. Simultaneously, improving the quality of tourism education is essential to address the need for more qualified personnel in the industry. Given the rapid development of digital technologies in contemporary times, integrating artificial intelligence technologies into tourism education is believed to be highly significant for cultivating knowledgeable and experienced professionals (Türk & Eren, 2023). The application of artificial intelligence (AI) in education has progressed from the use of computers and related technologies to web-based and online intelligent learning systems. It has further advanced towards developing robots designed to think in a human-like manner and chatbots capable of answering questions asked in a web-based format (Chen et al., 2020).

Users utilize ChatGPT for information retrieval, feedback provision, obtaining knowledge in grammar and language, and generating comparative and innovative ideas. ChatGPT is an application openly accessible to everyone with a free account created on OpenAI. Additionally, it can be accessed by synchronizing with a Google or Microsoft account. Users integrate the program for information gathering, feedback, language proficiency, and the exchange of new ideas. It is available to the public through a freely accessible application and can be accessed by creating an OpenAI account or synchronizing with Google or Microsoft accounts (Erul & Işın, 2023; Swiecki vd., 2022). Artificial intelligence is known to be a product created using human intelligence, and in many aspects, human intelligence is still considered superior to artificial intelligence (Teng, 2019). However, there are distinctions in favor of artificial intelligence concerning accuracy, decision-making, speed, adaptability to change, minimization of energy consumption, functionality, awareness level, and interaction points despite the acknowledgment that human intelligence is the basis for artificial intelligence.

The ChatGPT application goes beyond encouraging students to learn topics related to their interests; it enhances learning experiences (Fırat, 2023). Designed to focus on text generation and language learning skills, ChatGPT can be utilized for various tasks such as translating texts into the desired language, summarizing texts, and implementing question-answer systems. In the educational context, it assists in creating writing topics for students and providing feedback on student writings to benefit their learning (Božić, 2023). It has the potential to ensure the continuity of interaction between students and course materials, helping them stay more connected to their learning experiences and proceed more willingly (Fuchs, 2023). Supportive programs in educational topics contribute to the development of 'student's knowledge base and can enhance not only their self-confidence in educational environments but also their motivation in educational environments (Patil & Abraham, 2010). Thanks to artificial intelligence technologies, educators and teachers can provide more effective and efficient education to their students through personalized and adaptive teaching methods. They can offer specialized support to individual students in specific subjects and leverage the awareness of knowledge gaps to address and rectify deficiencies (Guan, Mou & Jiang, 2020). While the ChatGPT application offers significant and positive contributions for students, it has also been observed that some students resort to using artificial intelligence programs to cheat and plagiarize in completing their assignments. However, it is believed that the abundance of positive contributions may outweigh the negative features, leading to a certain level of tolerance for the drawbacks it brings (Adeshola & Adepoju, 2023). Although there is existing research on ChatGPT in the context of tourism education, no research has been found regarding whether the case studies generated by ChatGPT would impact reinforcing theoretically taught information. Additionally, another aspect to be explored is whether case studies created through ChatGPT would benefit tourism students in addressing challenges they may encounter in their professional lives. This research is important as it fills a gap in the relevant literature and provides different outputs for practitioners.

BACKGROUND

Literature Review

In the literature review conducted, it can be noted that there are studies on ChatGPT and education; however, no research specifically addresses the role of case studies in tourism education. Lo (2023) concluded in their study that the artificial intelligence application ChatGPT facilitates students' ease of accessing information and supports teachers in creating course materials and offering suggestions related to course delivery. Grassini (2023) aimed to contribute to understanding how artificial intelligence technologies, including ChatGPT, have recently changed and improved educational norms. The study found that while some educators praised its positive and supportive impact on the education sector, others raised concerns about its potential to reduce analytical skills, promote laziness, and encourage incorrect behavior.

Sok and Heng (2023) discussed the benefits and risks of using the ChatGPT application in education and research. They identified at least five main advantages:

creating learning assessments, enhancing pedagogical practices, providing personalized virtual teaching, assisting in finding article topics or drafting research article outlines, and facilitating brainstorming by combining ideas. However, they also highlighted risks in academic integrity, unfair learning assessment, the risk of accessing incorrect information, and the potential for excessive dependence on AI-based applications.

Rahman and Watanobe (2023) aimed to determine the general potential opportunities and threats that ChatGPT presents to education from the perspectives of students and educators. Their study identified opportunities such as personalized feedback, accessibility, interactive conversations, providing materials for lesson preparation, evaluating topics desired for research from the application, and finding new ways to teach complex concepts. Alongside these opportunities, the study also identified various threats posed by ChatGPT to the traditional education and research system, including the possibility of students cheating in online exams, generating text that appears human-like, reducing students' critical thinking skills, and challenges in evaluating information produced by ChatGPT.

Rudolph et al. (2023) conducted a study examining artificial intelligence chatbots like ChatGPT in the context of the future of learning, teaching, and assessment in higher education. In their analysis, they positioned ChatGPT within the scope of current research in Artificial Intelligence in Education (AIEd), discussing applications for students, teachers, and the system, and analyzing opportunities and threats. The research findings emphasized the importance of students being knowledgeable about AI applications but suggested that AI should be used merely as a tool in writing skills. They emphasized the need to focus on critical and creative thinking and to verify the accuracy of information independently.

İlaslan's (2023) study, conducted to determine the contributions of using Artificial Intelligence Chat Robots and ChatGPT in nursing education, revealed that the ChatGPT application increased student engagement and knowledge acquisition. The study highlighted several advantages: personalized learning, instant feedback, and simulation scenarios. However, it also identified challenges such as reliability issues, providing accurate information, lack of human interaction, concerns related to privacy and security, inconsistencies, and plagiarism.

In their study conducted to investigate whether the ChatGPT application has a positive impact on the learning and teaching process when implemented for students in the educational environment, Rueda et al. (2023) concluded that the application has a positive effect on students. However, the results also highlighted the importance of teachers receiving proper training to use the application accurately to provide contributions to students in a correct and timely manner. Pradana et al. (2023) deemed it appropriate to evaluate using bibliometric analysis and systematic literature review in their research on how OpenAI ChatGPT is utilized in education.

They examined published articles to observe the most significant contributions of ChatGPT in education, important subtopics, and potential future studies. They revealed an increase in the quantity of articles published on this subject between 2022 and 2023. In İskender's study conducted in 2023, aimed to reveal the effects of ChatGPT on students. He emphasized that students could use ChatGPT to generate new ideas, and the application could have a positive contribution to students. However, in addition to the positive impacts, Ali pointed out the potential risks associated with students developing excessive dependence on ChatGPT, including a decrease in critical thinking, a desire for shortcuts, and the possibility of exacerbating educational inequalities.

MAIN FOCUS OF THE CHAPTER

Case Study

A case study is fundamentally a research method that encourages critical thinking, develops problem-solving skills, and thoroughly examines a specific situation, event, or topic. It is often used to present real-life situations to students, adapting concepts taught in the classroom to narrative scenarios for problem-solving, connecting to course material and raw data, and brainstorming among groups (Al Zuned, 2017; Beckisheva, Gasparyan, & Kovalenko, 2015). Generally, a case study is a narratively presented scenario prepared for classroom use, aiming to provide an opportunity for students to discuss, problem-solve, and generate new ideas based on imaginary scenarios created around real-life situations (Sajjad, 2010). According to Lawrence (1953), a well-crafted case study brings a part/person related to the story to the class to collaborate with the teacher, enhancing the realism of the story and connecting the classroom discussion to real-life situations.

The case study method allows for a more comprehensive view of a process, as it enables in-depth observations covering various aspects, facilitating the examination and correlation of these aspects within the total environment of the process (Gummesson, 1988). The detailed observations in case study methodology allow for the exploration of "how" and "why" questions related to a series of events (Leonard-Barton, 1990). Martinez Casanovas, Ruiz-Munzon, and Buil-Fabrega (2022) concluded in their study that the case study method is an effective learning methodology that promotes sustainable development skills. Furthermore, case studies, along with other methods like discussion, role-playing, problem-based learning, flipped classrooms, and discussions, were found to be more effective in enhancing thinking and active learning, ensuring lasting impacts on learning and student minds (Bassey, 1999; Buil-Fabrega et al., 2019; Meyer, 2001).

Yin (1993) categorizes case studies into exploratory, explanatory, and descriptive. Exploratory case studies involve fieldwork and data collection before defining research questions and hypotheses, serving as preliminary studies for various social research. Explanatory case studies are suitable for causal studies, especially in more complex and multivariate situations, allowing the use of pattern-matching techniques in the analysis. Descriptive case studies require researchers to start with a descriptive theory, creating hypotheses about cause-and-effect relationships. Through case study studies, readers/students can draw lessons from the situation and form opinions on how to adapt what they have learned from the situation to their own lives, school, and institutional events. This is referred to elsewhere as “identifying with the situation inspired by it” (Wals & Alblas, 1997).

RESEARCH METHOD

This research uses the qualitative research method with a case study design. Qualitative research is an approach that endeavors to interpret, question, and understand the natural context of the problem at hand (Guba & Lincoln, 1994). A case study is a methodological approach aimed at an in-depth examination of how a limitedly addressed system operates and functions, utilizing multiple data to systematically gather information about the system (Chmiliar, 2010). The research field consists of undergraduate students enrolled in the tourism faculty. The data for the research were collected through the purposive sampling method. Purposive sampling is the selection of rich cases related to the topic to conduct in-depth research on the subject (Büyüköztürk, Kılıç Çakmak, Akgün, Karadeniz & Demirel, 2012). The research data were collected through the interview technique. The interview technique is a controlled and purposeful verbal communication form between the researcher and the research subject (Cohen and Manion, 1994). The data for the research were collected between December 1st and December 20th, 2023. During the data collection process, it was observed that responses were repeated after the 26th interview. The interviews were concluded after the 32nd person. The interview form was semi-structured, and each lasted approximately 25 minutes. The interview form included questions aimed at revealing information about the participants, followed by questions created within the scope of the research. The questions in the interview form are as follows:

1) Have you used ChatGPT before? (If your answer is yes, specify the purpose for which you used it).
2) Do you believe that examples of such cases would be beneficial after the topics covered in the lessons? Explain how they could contribute to you.

3) Do examples of cases help reinforce topics for exam preparation? Explain in which other areas examples of cases could assist you.
4) Can the created examples of cases be helpful in your professional life? Can they provide you with preliminary information regarding issues you might encounter? Explain how they could assist you in your professional life.
5) "If you were to describe the created scenarios with three words, which three words would you choose?"

Before the interviews were conducted, participants were provided with theoretical information related to the subject. Since there were participants from different classes in tourism education, three different case studies were created through ChatGPT. The example cases are as follows:

Case Study 1

In the rapidly evolving landscape of the tourism sector, Ali has been practicing guiding for many years. However, recent advancements in digitization and technology have deeply impacted traditional guiding practices. Ali has struggled to adapt to these changes, and his business has declined significantly. Tourists' travel habits have shifted, and many have started organizing their trips through online booking platforms. Ali's old customer base has increasingly favored digital platforms for hotel reservations and tour organizations. Ali has lost his old customer base while grappling to adapt to this change. Tourists now use mobile applications and their own guidance platforms during their travels. Ali's traditional approach to guiding has lost competitiveness against these innovative tools. Tourists seek more interactive and personalized guiding experiences, leading them to distance themselves from Ali's services. When planning their travels, tourists actively utilize social media. Shared travel experiences influence the determination of popular destinations among tourists and impact the selection of tour guides. Ali has failed to gain sufficient visibility through social media, resulting in the loss of potential customers.Tourists often prefer to communicate with their guides using online communication tools before and during their travels. Due to language barriers, Ali has fallen short in online communication, leading to decreased customer satisfaction.

Case Study 2

Ali is a professional guide offering services in English in the highly competitive Mediterranean region. However, there has been a decrease in tour participation compared to previous years. Understanding the importance of personal branding and participating in more tours, Ali has decided to market his business more effectively. To strengthen his personal brand, Guide Ali has started using social media effectively. By regularly sharing posts on platforms such as Instagram and Facebook, he showcased his travel experiences and expertise. This allowed potential customers to get to know him better and build trust. Ali aimed to go beyond standard tours by creating unique and interesting tour programs. Offering distinctive themes, interactions with local culture, and unique experiences, he attracted potential tourists. This helped him stand out among the competition and increased demand for his services. To increase customer satisfaction and strengthen his online reputation, Ali started collecting feedback from customers after tours. Positive reviews from satisfied customers helped him gain the trust of potential customers, and Ali's reputation was enhanced. Ali collaborated with other professionals in the tourism sector in the Mediterranean region and strengthened his local network. By partnering with hotels, travel agencies, and other guides, he increased opportunities to participate in more tours.

Case Study 3

Ali, a professional guide offering services in English in the highly competitive Mediterranean region, has experienced a decrease in tour participation compared to previous years. Recognizing the importance of personal branding and participating in more tours, Ali decided to market his business more effectively. To strengthen his personal brand, Guide Ali started using social media effectively. By regularly sharing posts on platforms such as Instagram and Facebook, he showcased his travel experiences and expertise. This allowed potential customers to get to know him better and build trust. Ali aimed to go beyond standard tours by creating unique and interesting tour programs. Offering distinctive themes, interactions with local culture, and unique experiences, he attracted potential tourists. This helped him stand out among the competition and increased demand for his services. To increase customer satisfaction and strengthen his online reputation, Ali started collecting feedback from customers after tours. Positive reviews from satisfied customers helped him gain the trust of potential customers, and Ali's reputation was enhanced. Ali collaborated with other professionals in the tourism sector in the Mediterranean region and strengthened his local network. By partnering with hotels, travel agencies, and other guides, he increased opportunities to participate in more tours.

RESULTS

In the research, an analysis of the demographic characteristics of the 32 participants in total reveals that 18 of them are female, while 14 are male. Regarding the age distribution of the participants, it can be observed that 6 individuals are 20 years old, 12 individuals are 21 years old, 10 individuals are 22 years old, 1 individual is 23 years old, 1 individual is 24 years old, 1 individual is 25 years old, and 1 individual is 27 years old. When looking at the classes of the 32 students included in the study, it is observed that 8 of them are in the first year of tourism guidance, 6 of them are in the second year, 4 of them are in the third year, and 14 of them are in the fourth year of tourism guidance. The participants have been coded as K1, K2, K3…" in accordance with the responses provided by the participants, the items with the highest frequency values are listed below.

Table 1. ChatGPT using experience

Have You Ever Used ChatGPT?	f	%
Yes	18	56.25
No	14	43.75
Total	32	100.0

A total of 56.25% of participating students reported having experience with ChatGPT, while 43.75% indicated that they had not experienced ChatGPT. Among the participants who used ChatGPT, some mentioned benefiting from the application in terms of gaining information about courses K1 and K5, conducting preliminary research before presentations, and generating new ideas while writing stories. Participant K6 specifically mentioned using the program for translation purposes. Another participant, K11, turned to the application to acquire more detailed information about a course. Additionally, K13 reported using the application for drawing purposes. On the other hand, among the participants who did not use ChatGPT, K3 expressed that the program created confusion and that personally researching and finding the necessary information felt more secure.

Table 2. Contributions of case studies to students

Contributions	f	%
Enhancing Memorability	10	32.3
Reinforcing the Subject	5	16.1
Providing Different Perspectives	3	9.7
Gaining New Ideas	3	9.7
Having Foreknowledge	3	9.7
Offering Practical Information	2	6.4
Better Grasping the Subject	2	6.4
Speeding up the Learning Process	1	3.2
Increasing Efficiency	1	3.2
Providing Hands-on Experience	1	3.2
Total	**31**	**100.0**

Table 2 presents the contributions of the case studies given regarding the content of the lesson after the course delivery. After the lesson, students were asked about the contributions of the presented case studies related to the covered topics, and their responses are displayed in Table 2. The highest percentage, with 32.3%, is attributed to enhancing memorability. It was observed that case studies presented in a manner similar to the topic covered in the class contribute to making the subjects more memorable for students. Reinforcing the subject follows with 16.1%. Providing different perspectives on the topic, gaining new ideas, and having foresight are ranked third with 9.7% each. Other responses indicated that the presented case studies accelerated learning, increased work efficiency, provided practical experience, and aided in better understanding the subject. Based on the responses provided by the participants, the highest frequency values are as follows:

K2: *I believe that having examples provided after the topics covered in class will be beneficial for me to better understand the subject matter and to have more examples come to mind. It will also help me gain insight into the types of situations I may encounter in the future.*

K26: *I believe that providing case studies after the topics covered in the lessons enhances memorability.*

K14: *Providing case studies after the topics covered not only reinforces the subject matter but also enhances memorability.*

K13: *Supporting the subject discussed after the lesson with any case study will enhance memorability.*

K11: *Narrating the topics discussed in class in the form of case studies or stories helps the subject stay in my mind more effectively.*

K22: *The case studies provided after the lecture help reinforce the subject for me.*

Table 3. Benefits of case studies

Benefits	f	%
Ensuring the Memorability of Topics	9	41.0
Ease of Comprehension	4	18.2
Developing Foresight	3	13.6
Learning from Experiences	2	9.1
Enhancing Interpretative Skills	2	9.1
Ease of Problem Solving	1	4.5
Idea Generation	1	4.5
Total	**22**	**100.0**

Table 3 presents the benefits of the case studies given after the lesson to reinforce the topics in preparing for exams and the events that contributed to the case studies. Table 3 provides the benefits of the case studies given after the lesson to reinforce the topics in preparing for exams and their contributions to students during the study and in different life events. The rate of making the topics covered in class memorable with the case studies stands at 41.0%, ranking first. Ensuring easy comprehensibility comes in second place with 18.2%. Following these two benefits are learning from experiences, generating ideas about topics and encountered events, ease of problem-solving, developing the ability to interpret, producing ideas related to subjects and events, and being foresighted. Based on the responses provided by the participants, the highest frequency values are as follows:

K28: *Case studies are beneficial for enhancing memorability during the course presentation.*

K32: *Case studies help enhance memorability and facilitate a better understanding of the subject during exam preparation.*

K31: *The case studies provided after the lecture assist in a better understanding during exam preparation and make the topics discussed in class more memorable.*

K12: *Case studies can assist me in preparing for exams and solving problems in our daily lives.*

K2: *I believe that having examples given on topics I'm not familiar with would be helpful for me to gain insights while studying for exams.*

K3: *The examples provided after the lessons can be extremely helpful for me while preparing for exams and reinforcing the topics covered in class. These examples enable me to see creative instances that I might not have thought of, providing clearer insights.*

Table 4. Disadvantages of case studies

Disadvantages	f	%
Creating Confusion	2	100.0
Total	**2**	**100.0**

Table 4 provides the disadvantages of the sample cases given after the course in terms of preparing for exams and different situations in life. It is observed that two students mentioned that the sample cases created confusion for them. Based on the responses provided by the participants, the highest frequency values are as follows:

K6: *I don't think the case studies provided after the lecture will be helpful during exam preparation because they can be confusing for me.*

K25: *The case studies provided after the lecture become confusing for me during exam preparation.*

Table 5. Contributions of case studies to business life

Contributions of Case Studies to Business Life	f	%
Being Prepared for Possible Problems in Advance	11	33.3
Benefit from Experience Sharing	8	24.2
Prior Knowledge	5	15.2
Preparation Based on Anticipation	3	9.1
Ease of Access to Information	3	9.1
Time Saving	2	6.1
Providing Motivation	1	3.0
Total	**33**	**100.0**

Table 5 illustrates the contributions of the sample cases given to students regarding their work life after the course presentation. Students who mentioned that they would be prepared in advance for possible problems after the sample cases ranked first with 33.3%. Following this response, benefiting from experience sharing takes second place with 24.2%. Ease of access to information and preparation based on anticipation ranks third with 9.1%. Based on the responses provided by the participants, the highest frequency values are as follows:

K22: *The created case studies prepare us for the challenges and situations encountered in professional life, making us more ready and assisting us in taking preventive measures against potential issues.*

K31: *The created case studies help me understand how to react to potential issues in professional life before they occur.*

K17: *The created case studies allow me to benefit from the experiences of individuals who have previously encountered similar issues in professional life. Knowing the behaviors to adopt in the face of problems in advance would be advantageous for me.*

K6: *The given case studies provide preliminary information about the potential issues I may encounter in professional life, helping me gain insight into how to react to situations.*

K28: *Through the case studies, we acquire information about potential issues that may arise in professional life and learn how to handle challenges effectively.*

K4: *The examples given to reinforce the subject matter after the lessons help us anticipate and be better prepared for real-life situations in the professional world.*

Students were asked to share three words that come to mind regarding the case studies, and these words have been analyzed using a word cloud.

Figure 1. Word cloud

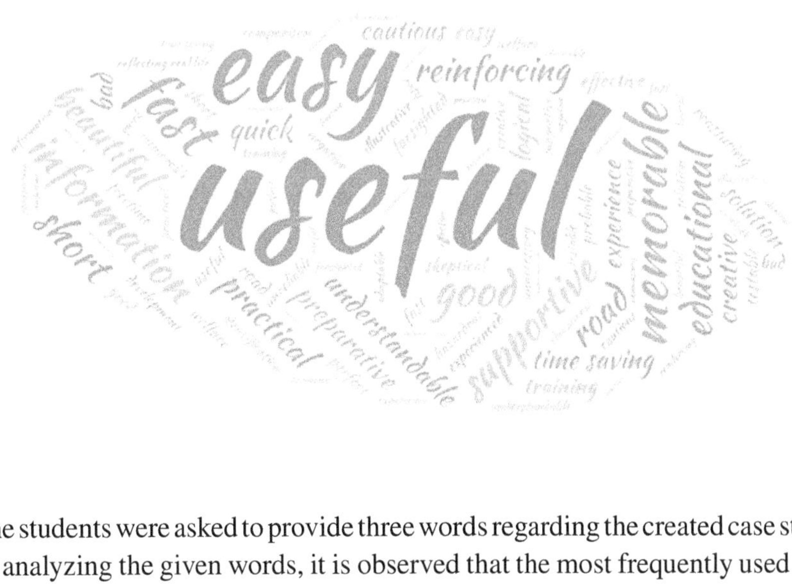

The students were asked to provide three words regarding the created case studies. Upon analyzing the given words, it is observed that the most frequently used words are "useful," "information," "supportive," "instructive," and "memorable." Among 38 words, 8 have a positive connotation, while some of the negative words include "bad," "unnecessary," and "unreliable."

SOLUTIONS AND RECOMMENDATION

The promotion and support of educators to encourage students to familiarize themselves with the ChatGPT program, an artificial intelligence-based application, in their work and educational lives is considered beneficial. Additionally, it is inferred from the responses provided by students that presenting case studies related to the subject after the course helps reinforce the topic more memorably. Based on the research findings, the following recommendations can be made:

- Case studies created through ChatGPT can be deemed important for students to reinforce and later recall the subject. Therefore, educators presenting real-life events that can be experienced through artificial intelligence applications in a narrative form to students can lead to positive outcomes.
- Besides theoretical information, students have a positive perspective on case studies created with artificial intelligence for recalling this information in memory. In conclusion, such applications allow students to approach theoretical information from different perspectives.
- In education, after providing theoretical information, the mention of case studies can also be beneficial in the working environment of the tourism sector, as indicated by tourism students. Due to the deficiencies in practical education, gaining insights into events that may occur in the tourism sector through artificial intelligence applications and developing ideas for different solutions can be facilitated.
- Tourism students find value in and positively evaluate case studies that can be created with artificial intelligence. Educators need to present case studies to students after theoretical information and demonstrate how such case studies can be created.

FUTURE RESEARCH DIRECTIONS

This study evaluated the opinions of tourism students receiving tourism education about case studies created with ChatGPT. The case studies can complement theoretical knowledge by realistically portraying events and phenomena. Artificial intelligence technology, encountered in various aspects of life, has also begun to be utilized in education. Particularly in Turkey, due to the lack of applied education in tourism, exploring the applications that can be implemented with artificial intelligence is essential. Furthermore, research should focus on ChatGPT and explore applications in tourism education using the recently launched Google Gemini. Investigating potential applications that can encourage the use of artificial intelligence-based tools among tourism students is crucial.

CONCLUSION

The literature review indicates that there are studies in the field of education using the ChatGPT artificial intelligence application, but it is observed that these studies do not include case study analyses. This study, therefore, holds an original character in this regard. Lo (2023) found in their study that the ChatGPT artificial intelligence application facilitates students' access to information and supports teachers in creating course materials and making recommendations related to the course content. In the current study, the analysis of the data revealed that students benefit from the ChatGPT application in the pre-class and presentation preparation stages, and it can be said that similar results were obtained in this study. Grassini (2023) examined articles on the subject of ChatGPT in the literature and found that while some educators praised the positive and progress-assisting effects of artificial intelligence technologies on the education sector, other educators criticized them for potentially reducing analytical skills, fostering laziness, and encouraging incorrect behavior. In the present study, positive responses, such as time-saving and assistance in preparing course materials, were obtained, while negative responses, such as getting used to convenience and being unreliable, were also obtained. Sok and Heng (2023) discussed the benefits and risks of using the ChatGPT application in education and research. They argued that ChatGPT has at least five basic benefits, such as helping find article topics or creating a research paper outline and brainstorming as a result of consolidating ideas. However, they also identified risks such as integrity issues in academic honesty, the assessment of unfair learning, the risk of accessing incorrect information, and excessive dependence on AI-based applications. In the current study, similar positive results were found alongside negative responses from students. Students were asked to write the first three words that come to mind, especially in the context of case studies, and when these words were analyzed with a word cloud, it was observed that positive words such as useful, memorable, understandable, and supportive were frequently used. In addition to positive words, it was found that unnecessary, risky, and skeptical words were also used. To change these negative perceptions of students, it is believed that providing case studies related to the subject during and after the course would help students reinforce and remember the course content.

Educators should also encourage students to use the ChatGPT artificial intelligence application when preparing course materials.

REFERENCES

Adeshola, I., & Adepoju, A. P. (2023). The opportunities and challenges of ChatGPT in education. *Interactive Learning Environments*, 1–14. doi:10.1080/10494820.2023.2253858

Al Zuned, A. M. (2017). Effective business leadership styles: A case study of Harriet Green. *Middle East Journal of Business*, *55*(5380), 1–10. doi:10.5742/MEJB.2017.92943

Balas, M., & Ing, E. B. (2023). Conversational AI models for ophthalmic diagnosis: Comparison of Chatgpt and the isabel pro differential diagnosis generator. *JFO Open Ophthalmology*, *1*, 100005. doi:10.1016/j.jfop.2023.100005

Bassey, M. (1999). *Case Study Research in Educational Settings*. Open University Press.

Beckisheva, T. G., Gasparyan, G. A., & Kovalenko, N. A. (2015). Case study as an active method of teaching business English. *Procedia: Social and Behavioral Sciences*, *166*, 292–295. doi:10.1016/j.sbspro.2014.12.526

Božić, V. (2023). *ChatGPT and Education*. Academic Press.

Buil-Fabrega, M., Martínez Casanovas, M., Ruiz-Munzon, N., & Filho, W. L. (2019). Flipped classroom as an active learning methodology in sustainable development curricula. *Sustainability (Basel)*, *11*(17), 4577. doi:10.3390/su11174577

Büyüköztürk, Ş., Kılıç Çakmak, E., Akgün, Ö., Karadeniz, Ş., & Demirel, F. (2008). *Bilimsel araştırma yöntemleri*. Pegem Akademi.

Campbell, M., Hoane, A. J. Jr, & Hsu, F. H. (2002). Deep blue. *Artificial Intelligence*, *134*(1-2), 57–83. doi:10.1016/S0004-3702(01)00129-1

Çelik, B. (2023). Hakikat ötesi dönemde markalara yönelik tüketici algısı: Vaka çalışması. *Ufuk Üniversitesi Sosyal Bilimler Enstitüsü Dergisi*, *12*(23), 21–43. doi:10.58635/ufuksbedergi.1264624

Chen, Y., Chen, Y., & Heffernan, N. (2020). Personalized math tutoring with a conversational agent. *arXiv preprint arXiv:2012.12121*.

Chmiliar, L. (2010). Multiple-case designs. In A. J. Mills, G. Eurepas & E. Wiebe (Eds.), *Encyclopedia of case study research* (pp. 582-583). SAGE Publications.

Cotien, L., & Manion, L. (1994). *Research methods in education* (4th ed.). Routlege.

Deng, L., & Yu, D. (2014). Deep learning: Methods and applications. *Foundations and Trends® in Signal Processing*, *7*(3–4), 197-387.

Erul, E., & Işın, A. (2023). Chatgpt ile sohbetler: Turizmde Chatgpt'nin önemi (Chats With Chatgpt. *Journal of Tourism And Gastronomy Studies*, *11*(1), 780–793. doi:10.21325/jotags.2023.1217

Fırat, M. (2023). *How ChatGPT can transform autodidactic experiences and open education. department of distance education.* Open Education Faculty, Anadolu University.

Fuchs, K. (2023, May). Exploring the opportunities and challenges of NLP models in higher education: Is ChatGPT a blessing or a curse? *Frontiers in Education*, *8*, 1166682. doi:10.3389/feduc.2023.1166682

Gleason, N. (2022). *ChatGPT and the rise of AI writers: How should higher education respond?* THE Campus Learn, Share, Connect.

Goeldner, C. R., & Ritchie, J. B. (2012). *Tourism principles, practices, philosophies.* John Wiley & Sons.

Grassini, S. (2023). Shaping the future of education: Exploring the potential and consequences of ai and chatgpt in educational settings. *Education Sciences*, *13*(7), 692. doi:10.3390/educsci13070692

Guan, C., Mou, J., & Jiang, Z. (2020). Artificial intelligence innovation in education: A Twenty-year data-driven historical analysis. *International Journal of Innovation Studies*, *4*(4), 134–147. doi:10.1016/j.ijis.2020.09.001

Guba, E. G., & Lincoln, Y. S. (1994). Competing paradigms in qualitative research. Handbook of Qualitative Research, 2(105), 163-194.

Gummesson, E. (1988). *Qualitative methods in management research.* Studentlitteratur, Chartwell-Bratt.

Heale, R., & Twycross, A. (2018). What is a case study? *Evidence-Based Nursing*, *21*(1), 7–8. doi:10.1136/eb-2017-102845 PMID:29146764

Health, T. L. D. (2023). ChatGPT: Friend or foe? *The Lancet. Digital Health*, *5*(3), e102. doi:10.1016/S2589-7500(23)00023-7 PMID:36754723

İlaslan, E. (2023). Yapay zeka sohbet robotları ve ChatGPT'nin hemşirelik eğitiminde kullanılması. *Akdeniz Hemşirelik Dergisi*, *2*(2), 73–80. doi:10.59398/ahd.1330341

Iskender, A. (2023). Holy or unholy? Interview with open AI's ChatGPT. *European Journal of Tourism Research*, *34*, 3414–3414. doi:10.54055/ejtr.v34i.3169

İşler, B., & Kiliç, M. (2021). Eğitimde yapay zekâ kullanimi ve gelişimi. *Yeni Medya Elektronik Dergisi*, *5*(1), 1–11.

Kurzweil, R. (1990). *The age of intelligent machines*. MIT Press.

Lawrence, P. R. (1953). In K. R. Andrews (Ed.), *The Case Method of Teaching Human Relations and Administration* (p. 215). Harvard University Press.

Leonard-Barton, D. (1990). A dual methodology for case studies: Synergistic use of a longitudinal single site with replicated multiple sites. *Organization Science*, *1*(3), 248–266. doi:10.1287/orsc.1.3.248

Lo, C. K. (2023). What is the impact of Chatgpt on education? A rapid review of the literature. *Education Sciences*, *13*(4), 410. doi:10.3390/educsci13040410

LundB. (2022). A Chat with ChatGPT: How will AI impact scholarly publishing? doi:10.13140/RG.2.2.34572.18565

Martínez Casanovas, M., Ruíz-Munzón, N., & Buil-Fabregá, M. (2022). Higher education: The best practices for fostering competences for sustainable development through the use of active learning methodologies. *International Journal of Sustainability in Higher Education*, *23*(3), 703–727. doi:10.1108/IJSHE-03-2021-0082

Merriam, S. B. (1998). *Case study research and case study applications in education*. Jossey-Bass Publishers.

Montenegro-Rueda, M., Fernández-Cerero, J., Fernández-Batanero, J. M., & López-Meneses, E. (2023). Impact of the implementation of ChatGPT in education: A systematic review. *Computers*, *12*(8), 153. doi:10.3390/computers12080153

OpenAI (2023). *About ChatGPT*. https://openai.com/about

Patil, A. S., & Abraham, A. (2010). Intelligent and interactive Web-Based tutoring system in engineering education: Reviews, perspectives and development. In *Computational Intelligence for Technology Enhanced Learning* (pp. 79–97). Springer. doi:10.1007/978-3-642-11224-9_4

Pradana, M., Elisa, H. P., & Syarifuddin, S. (2023). Discussing ChatGPT in education: A literature review and bibliometric analysis. *Cogent Education, 10*(2), 2243134. doi:10.1080/2331186X.2023.2243134

Qadir, J. (2022). Engineering education in the era of Chatgpt: Promise and pitfalls of generative AI for education. In *2023 IEEE Global Engineering Education Conference (EDUCON)* (pp. 1-9). IEEE.

Rahman, M. M., & Watanobe, Y. (2023). Chatgpt for education and research: Opportunities, threats, and strategies. *Applied Sciences (Basel, Switzerland), 13*(9), 5783. doi:10.3390/app13095783

Rudolph, J., Tan, S., & Tan, S. (2023). ChatGPT: Bullshit spewer or the end of traditional assessments in higher education? *Journal of Applied Learning and Teaching, 6*(1).

Russel, S., & Norvig, P. (2010). *Artificial intelligence - a modern approach.* Pearson Education.

Sajjad, S. (2010). Effective teaching methods at higher education level. *Pakistan Journal of Special Education, 11*, 29–43.

Skilton, M., & Hovsepian, F. (2017). *The 4th Industrial Revolution: Responding to the Impact of Artificial Intelligence on Business.* Springer.

SokS.HengK. (2023). Chatgpt for education and research: A review of benefits and risks. Available At SSRN 4378735.

Sridhar, G. S. (2018). *Artificial Intelligence: The Future Way of Technology.* Gs Srıdhar.

Swiecki, Z., Khosravi, H., Chen, G., Martinez-Maldonado, R., Lodge, J. M., Milligan, S., Selwyn, N., & Gašević, D. (2022). Assessment in the age of artificial intelligence. *Computers and Education. Artificial Intelligence, 3*, 1–10.

Teng, X. (2019, April). Discussion about artificial intelligence's advantages and disadvantages compete with natural intelligence. *Journal of Physics: Conference Series, 1187*(3), 032083. doi:10.1088/1742-6596/1187/3/032083

Timms, M. J. (2016). Letting artificial intelligence in education out of the box: Educational cobots and smart classrooms. *International Journal of Artificial Intelligence in Education, 26*(2), 701–712. doi:10.1007/s40593-016-0095-y

Tong, Y., & Zhang, L. (2023). Discovering the next decade's synthetic biology research trends with Chatgpt. *Synthetic and Systems Biotechnology*, *8*(2), 220–223. doi:10.1016/j.synbio.2023.02.004 PMID:36923604

Wals, A. E. J., & Alblas, A. H. (1997). School-Based research and development of environmental education: A case study. *Environmental Education Research*, *3*(3), 253–269. doi:10.1080/1350462970030301

ADDITIONAL READING

BiswasS. (2023). Role of Chat GPT in Education. *Available at* SSRN 4369981.

Huallpa, J. J. (2023). Exploring the ethical considerations of using Chat GPT in university education. *Periodicals of Engineering and Natural Sciences*, *11*(4), 105–115.

Ivanov, S., & Soliman, M. (2023). Game of algorithms: ChatGPT implications for the future of tourism education and research. *Journal of Tourism Futures*, *9*(2), 214–221. doi:10.1108/JTF-02-2023-0038

Rakap, S. (2023). Chatting with GPT: Enhancing Individualized Education Program Goal Development for Novice Special Education Teachers. *Journal of Special Education Technology*. doi:10.1177/01626434231211295

Sjoberg, G., Orum, A. M., & Feagin, J. R. (2020). *A case for the case study*. The University of North Carolina Press.

Skavronskaya, L., Hadinejad, A., & Cotterell, D. (2023). Reversing the threat of artificial intelligence to opportunity: A discussion of ChatGPT in tourism education. *Journal of Teaching in Travel & Tourism*, *23*(2), 253–258. doi:10.1080/15313220.2023.2196658

Yu, H. (2023). Reflection on whether Chat GPT should be banned by academia from the perspective of education and teaching. *Frontiers in Psychology*, *14*, 1181712. doi:10.3389/fpsyg.2023.1181712 PMID:37325766

KEY TERMS AND DEFINITIONS

Case Study: It is a narratively presented scenario that is prepared for classroom use, aiming to provide an opportunity for students to discuss, problem-solve, and generate new ideas based on imaginary scenarios created around real-life situations (Sajjad, 2010).

ChatGPT: This application, launched in November 2022, is built upon a pretrained transformer that can comprehend and respond to questions and answers in a manner aligned with the input. ChatGPT is an artificial intelligence model based on a transformer that has been pretrained to generate responses similar to those produced by humans (OpenAI, 2023).

Deep Learning: It is also known as deep structured learning, hierarchical learning, or deep machine learning, is a subset of machine learning that employs a series of algorithms to capture intricate patterns in data. This is achieved by employing multiple layers of processing with sophisticated structures, often comprising numerous non-linear transformations (Deng & Yu, 2014).

Qualitative Research: It is an approach that endeavors to interpret, question, and understand the natural context of the problem at hand (Guba & Lincoln, 1994).

Chapter 8
Examining the Task – Technology Fit of ChatGPT for Healthcare Services

Eli Fianu
https://orcid.org/0000-0003-2308-6831
Ghana Technology University College, Ghana

Fred Amankwah-Sarfo
https://orcid.org/0000-0001-7872-4082
Ghana Communication Technology University, Ghana

Margaret Ofori
https://orcid.org/0000-0002-3840-5949
University of Health and Allied Sciences, Ghana

ABSTRACT

The study sought to examine the task-technology fit of ChatGPT for healthcare services. The research model was based on an integration of the task-technology fit (TTF) model and the technology acceptance model 2 (TAM2). The study used a quantitative research design. Data were collected from 265 health workers who have used ChatGPT in the performance of their work. Data analysis was done using structural equation modelling. Six of the seven hypotheses were accepted. The results show significant positive relationships between task characteristics and task-technology fit, task-technology fit and ChatGPT usage, ChatGPT usage and performance impacts, social influence and perceived usefulness, perceived usefulness and usage intention, as well as usage intention and ChatGPT usage. There was an insignificant positive relationship between task-technology fit and performance impacts.

DOI: 10.4018/979-8-3693-1239-1.ch008

INTRODUCTION

Modern civilization has over the years encountered distressing life events such as dengue fever, avian flu, Ebola virus, and quite recently, the CoVID-19 pandemic. People encounter circumstances every day that could harm their health. According to Abdullah et al. (2023), stressful life events and health are related, and stressors can increase the likelihood of developing serious diseases. Aside from that, the population is aging, and more people have several comorbid conditions (Fan et al., 2021). Such situations highlight the need for developing sophisticated services, tools, equipment, and general high-quality clinical/hospital information systems. Maintenance of the health and wellbeing of the population is of utmost importance (Ivanovic et al., 2023). Enhancements to health-related quality of life (QoL) factors are significant and well acknowledged in treatments and follow-ups for people who have survived major diseases. The quality of life (QoL) of cancer patients is seriously disrupted during the active oncological treatment period or during follow-up care, in addition to the usual health issues such as anxiety, sleep disorders, mental impairment, pain, appetite loss, psychological difficulties, sexual dysfunction, et cetera (Fan et al., 2021).

Artificial intelligence (AI) has enormous and varied implications for the provision of health services. AI has the power to completely transform healthcare by improving the efficacy, accessibility, and efficiency of medical services. Conversational agents have been developed to support a range of health-related activities, such as behaviour modification, treatment support, health monitoring, training, triage, and screening assistance (Abdullah et al., 2023). This is due to the increased demand for healthcare services and the increasing capabilities of AI. Furthermore, the application of AI in healthcare is growing, providing chances to enhance the provision of medical services (Javaid et al., 2023)

Additionally, because AI may supplement or replace the limited processing power of human experts in primary health care, it has the potential to increase the efficacy and efficiency of the delivery of health care services (Javaid et al., 2023). The delivery of health services may change as a result of the advancement of AI mobile communication technology, which can offer a more practical means of attending to the various health needs of locals (Ivanovic et al., 2023). Additionally, the automation of digital health systems and the provision of medical care remotely through tele-interactions, tele-diagnosis, tele-assessment, and tele-monitoring are two more ways that AI technologies have the potential to revolutionize the delivery of healthcare (Javaid et al., 2023).

Conversational AI is facilitating mental health assessments and has been linked to better recovery rates, which is transforming the way mental health care is provided (Nadarzynski et al., 2019). Furthermore, AI techniques may be utilized to lessen the strain on public health, especially in situations like the COVID-19 pandemic (Liu et al., 2021).

The usage of eHealth solutions, which make use of the internet and related technologies to enhance and distribute health services and information, especially in rural regions, thereby expanding the reach of health services, is another way that artificial intelligence (AI) is affecting the delivery of healthcare services (Abdullah et al., 2023). Moreover, the integration of artificial intelligence (AI) into public health education programs highlights the various ways that AI technology might enhance health care delivery.

OpenAI introduced a complimentary trial version of their AI chatbot ChatGPT 3.5 on 30th November 2022. The release resulted in a significant increase in OpenAI's estimated worth, reaching an impressive US$29 billion (Rudolph et al., 2023). A chatbot is a computer program that utilizes artificial intelligence to hold conversations resembling those between humans. Within seconds, users can inquire or request information, receiving prompt responses from the system. Surprisingly, ChatGPT amassed a user base of one million within just five days of its initial release (Rudolph et al., 2023). ChatGPT means Chat Generative Pre-Trained Transformer (Cashman, 2023; Open AI, 2022). GPT refers to a type of AI model known as a language model, specifically developed to comprehend and produce language that resembles that of a human. ChatGPT, constructed using OpenAI's GPT-3 series of extensive language models, incorporates a blend of supervised and reinforcement learning methods during the fine-tuning process. Diverging from search engines like Google, Bing, or Baidu, ChatGPT doesn't explore the internet to gather information about current affairs. Instead, its knowledge is confined to things it learned before 2021.

BACKGROUND

The direct use of artificial intelligence (AI) by various categories of health workers now seems imminent with the launch of ChatGPT, which the New York Times hailed as the best AI chatbot ever made publicly available (Abdullah et al., 2023). Many doctors have expressed dissatisfaction over the last ten years about how their heavy usage of electronic medical records (EMRs) has alienated them from their patients (Abdullah et al., 2023). By reducing the amount of time spent on administrative tasks and increasing the amount of time spent with patients, emerging AI technology may enhance the doctor-patient connection. Skeptics are rightly concerned that greater technology use will continue to disrupt workflows and alienate clinicians from their patients despite any possible advantages. Aside from this debate, it seems certain that medical AI will enhance diagnostic procedures.

There is substantial literature on the impact of the application of ChatGPT and other AI-powered tools in industry. The following are examples of studies conducted for specific sectors: patent generation (Lee & Hsiang, 2020), smart vehicles (Gao et al., 2023), conversational AI services (Chowdhury, 2023), healthcare (Abdullah et al., 2023; Ivanovic et al., 2023; Javaid et al., 2023), hospitality and tourism (Dwivedi et al., 2023; Gursoy et al., 2023; Mich & Garigliano, 2023), education (French et al., 2023; Mhlanga, 2023), finance (Coman et al., 2023; Stears & Deeks, 2023), business in general (Arman & Lamiya, 2023), customer experience (Vijayakumar, 2023), and the global economy (Bhushan, 2021).

These studies are generally literature reviews, viewpoint papers, and case studies. A few studies, for instance Lee & Hsiang (2020) and Coman et al. (2023) adopted an experimental approach, while Vijayakumar (2023) analysed quantitative data. The studies in healthcare involved discussions of reviewed literature and a report on Open AI based medical data management projects. The current study is novel because it uses a quantitative research design by collecting primary data from healthcare professionals regarding the task-technology fit of ChatGPT in the delivery of health care services. The studies reviewed lack the approach adopted in the current study.

MAIN FOCUS OF THE CHAPTER

Theoretical Foundation

Task-Technology Fit Model

Task–technology fit (TTF) is an information systems theory used to define the extent to which technology supports people in completing their portfolio of tasks (Al-rahmi et al., 2023). TTF model was developed by Goodhue and Thompson (1995) to examine the linkage between individual performance and information systems (ISs) (Khan et al., 2021). TTF model proposes that the degree to which a technology's characteristics match the requirements of a task influences the effectiveness of using that technology to perform that task (Al-rahmi et al., 2023). The model aims to explain the correlation between individuals' performance and information technologies (Goodhue & Thompson, 1995).

The TTF model was first proposed by Detmar W. Straub and Gregory Thompson in 1995. They argued that the fit between task characteristics and technology functionalities plays a crucial role in determining the success or failure of technology implementation. The model has gained widespread acceptance in the field of information systems and has been applied in various contexts, including enterprise resource planning (ERP) systems, customer relationship management (CRM) systems, and e-commerce platforms.

Task-technology fit (TTF) aims to explain the relationships between task characteristics, task-technology fit, and individuals' performance (Goodhue & Thompson, 1995). A good fit between the technology and the task that technology is intended to support is crucial for the successful adoption of information systems (IS) in organizations. The technology should be well-suited to the specific needs of the task. When there is a good fit, users are able to complete tasks more easily, quickly, and efficiently (Liang et al., 2021). Goodhue and Thompson (1995) averred that task characteristics encompass the demanding activities that users might face when utilizing IT tools. Technology characteristics, on the other hand, encapsulate the machinery or equipment specifically designed to facilitate the successful completion of diverse tasks.

In the TTF framework, task characteristics directly influence task-technology fit, signifying that the nature and demands of a task can impact how well a technology aligns with fulfilling those requirements. Similarly, technology characteristics also directly influence task-technology fit, highlighting how the attributes and capabilities of a technology affect its suitability for a particular task. This bidirectional relationship emphasizes the interdependence between task and technology factors in achieving alignment.

The task-technology fit, a pivotal construct in the model, directly affects utilization. This indicates that when a technology aligns well with the demands and nature of a task, it is more likely to be used effectively and comprehensively. Moreover, utilization directly impacts performance impacts, underscoring the significance of how extensively and effectively a technology is used in influencing outcomes and performance within an organization.

Furthermore, the task-technology fit also directly influences performance impacts, emphasizing the critical role that the alignment between task demands and technological capabilities plays in determining overall performance outcomes.

Since its inception, several researchers have applied the TTF model in predicting and explaining user behaviour toward adoption of technology (Kang et al., 2022). TTF model has been applied in several research studies conducted to assess the usefulness and ease of use of several technologies, including adoption of digital media in learning (Al-rahmi et al., 2023), examining internet banking user's continuance intention (Rahi & Ghani, 2021), smartwatch utilisation and user satisfaction (Karim & Mustafa, 2023), intelligent tutoring systems and learning performance (Yuce et al., 2019) and the adoption of blockchain technology (Liang et al., 2021).

Al-maatouk et al. (2020) examined the role of task-technology fit in acceptance of e-learning in higher education by integrating TTF model with the information systems success model. According to Al-maatouk et al. (2020), the usefulness of technology in enhancing learning depends on how well its functionalities align with the actual demands of the learning tasks. Their research supports the notion that three key characteristics, namely technology, task, and social influence, impact academic achievement through the Task-Technology Fit (TTF) model. Additionally, Tao et al. (2023) used an integrated model comprising self-determination theory (SDT), task–technology fit, and the technology acceptance model (TAM) to study consumer acceptance and usage behaviours in m-Health. Their study indicated relatedness and competence were significant motivational antecedents of perceived ease of use. Task–technology fit, and the perceived ease of use significantly affected perceived usefulness. The review of the literature showed that there is a lack of studies that use TTF model to explain how ChatGPT can impact the performance of health care delivery tasks.

Technology Acceptance Model 2 (TAM2)

Technology Acceptance Model 2 (TAM2) is an extension of the original TAM. It was proposed by Viswanath Venkatesh and Fred Davis in the year 2000. The current study integrates TAM2 with TTF model to explain how ChatGPT can impact the performance of health care delivery tasks. The original TAM (Davis, 1989; Davis et al., 1989) proposed that two belief constructs, perceived usefulness and perceived ease of use, are primary determinants of an individual's behavioural intention to use an information technology. Behavioural intention was postulated as the predictor of actual usage behaviour. TAM is a widely used model for understanding and predicting user acceptance or rejection of new technologies (Tam et al., 2020; Göktaş & Akgül, 2022; Muchran & Ahmar, 2019).

According to Venkatesh and Davis (2000), an individual's behavioural intention to use an information system is determined by two beliefs: perceived usefulness, defined as the extent to which a person believes that using the system will enhance his or her job performance, and perceived ease of use, defined as the extent to which a person believes that using the system will be free of effort. The model has evolved to become the key model in understanding factors that influence human behaviour towards acceptance or rejection of technology (Maranguni, 2019). The model examines in detail the impact of ''interrelated social forces'' (Venkatesh & Davis, 2000) that would make an individual adopt a particular technology (Zhang et al., 2010). The model is therefore suitable to study health care professionals' use of ChatGPT because these individuals are in a complex network of social relationships (Venkatesh et al., 2003) with their managers, coworkers, and patients. TAM2 has the following additional constructs:

- Subjective norm: expresses the influence of important others, friends, and family
- Image: expresses the status of an individual in the organization
- Job relevance: shows the importance of the technology for the job
- Output quality: reflects the perceived quality of the system's output
- Result demonstrability: expresses the ability of the individual to share with others the results of using the technology.

In TAM2, subjective norm—a measure of social influence—directly impacts perceived usefulness, wherein experience and voluntariness moderate this influence. Additionally, subjective norm affects usage intention, a link moderated by users' experience with the technology. Moreover, subjective norm influences the perceived image associated with using a technology. Furthermore, factors like the relevance of the technology to users' tasks, output quality, result demonstrability, and the perceived ease of use all contribute to the perceived usefulness of the technology. The perceived usefulness, in turn, influences users' intention to use the technology. Notably, the ease of use also directly influences both the perceived usefulness and the intention to use the technology. Lastly, users' intention to use the technology positively correlates with their actual usage behavior, solidifying the connection between intention and action in technology adoption. TAM2 thus outlines a comprehensive framework illustrating how various factors interrelate to influence users' acceptance and utilization of technology.

Research Model

The research model is based on an extension of the Task-Technology Fit model (Goodhue & Thompson, 1995) with constructs from the Technology Acceptance Model 2 (TAM2) (Venkatesh & Bala, 2008). The constructs from TAM2 are social influence, perceived usefulness, and usage intention. The research model is shown in Figure 1.

Figure 1. The research model

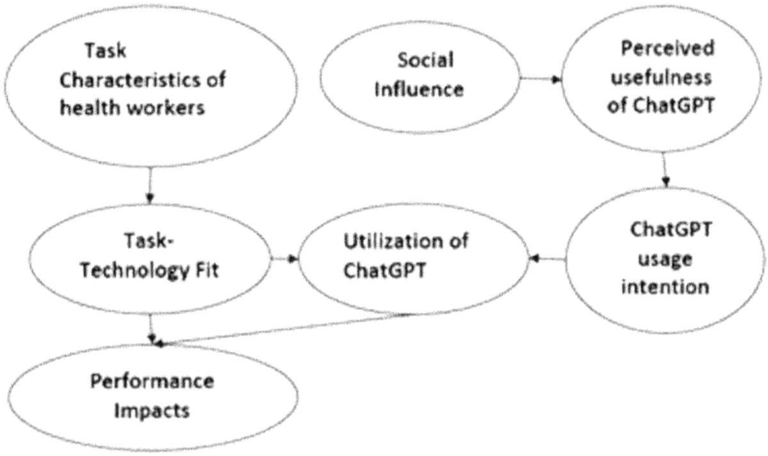

Hypothesis Development

Task Characteristics

The link between task and technology features, which determine task-technology fit, has a major impact on how well technology supports healthcare tasks (Kang et al., 2022). According to O'Grady et al. (2019), the "Fit between Individuals, Task, and Technology" (FITT) framework proposes that the compatibility of technology with clinical activities and procedures is a determining factor in the adoption of technology in a healthcare context. Moreover, task-technology fit is a key factor in the effectiveness of an information system in the healthcare industry, and task-performance is correlated with both individual and group performance (Gebauer & Tang, 2008).

Task-technology fit is influenced by the link between task and technology characteristics, which in turn affects user performance and the efficiency of technology in supporting healthcare tasks (Wanti et al., 2020). Furthermore, the task-technology fit model highlights the significance of task-technology fit in healthcare settings and aims to explain how technology impacts performance (Vatanasakdakul et al., 2020). Task-technology fit is a major determinant in adoption intention, and the link between task features and technology characteristics is critical in influencing the adoption and usage of electronic health technology (Gu et al., 2021).

Based on the tenets of the task-technology fit model and the reviewed literature, the following hypothesis is proposed:

H1: The level of alignment between task characteristics of health workers and the features of ChatGPT significantly impacts the perceived task-technology fit, with a higher alignment leading to a stronger perception of fit among users.

Task-Technology Fit and Task Performance

One of the most important factors influencing the adoption and continued use of technology in healthcare settings is the relationship between task-technology fit and technology usage intention. Technology usage intention has been found to be highly impacted by task-technology fit, which evaluates how well a technology supports the tasks that it is intended to support (Shin & Song, 2022). Perceived ease of use and utilization are positively impacted by this fit, which in turn influences users' intentions to continue with the technology (Shin & Song, 2022). Moreover, it has been demonstrated that task-technology fit significantly influences behavioral intention to utilize technology, which in turn influences perceived satisfaction (Navarro et al., 2021). Furthermore, the Expectancy Confirmation Model's interaction with the Technology Acceptance Model (TAM) and the Task-Technology Fit model has demonstrated that users' continuance usage intention is determined by perceived task-technology fit and confirmation (Zhao & Bação, 2020).

Task-technology fit, which assesses the compatibility between a technology and the tasks it is designed to support, has been found to have a positive effect on performance (Yodha & Nuryakin, 2023). This fit is proposed as the degree of fitness between tasks and technology to assist in the performance of individual daily tasks and the utilization of technology (Zhao & Bação, 2020). Furthermore, the assessment of fit among the individual, task, and technology is crucial to the successful adoption of health information technology, ultimately improving the quality and efficiency of healthcare delivery (Schnall et al., 2012).

Based on the tenets of the task-technology fit model and the reviewed literature, the following hypotheses are proposed:

H2: Task-technology fit has a significant impact on the usage of ChatGPT by health workers

H3: Task-technology fit has a significant impact on the performance of health workers who use ChatGPT

H4: Usage of ChatGPT has a significant impact on the performance of health workers.

Social Influence

The relationship between social influence and perceived usefulness of ChatGPT can be explained using the lenses of innovation diffusion and social norms. Raman et al. (2023) used Rogers' diffusion of innovations framework for a study involving university students to identify factors influencing their intentions to use ChatGPT in higher education. Given that social norms and attributes have an impact on students' inclinations to adopt technology, this study sheds light on the impact of social factors on the perceived usefulness of ChatGPT.

In their mixed-methods study, Nadarzynski et al. (2019) examined the acceptability of AI-led chatbot services in the healthcare industry. They emphasized the significance of taking patients' viewpoints, motivations, and abilities into account when creating and evaluating health chatbots. The impact of social factors, including patient viewpoints, on the perceived usefulness of chatbots in hospital settings is highlighted by this study.

Based on the tenets of the technology acceptance model 2 (TAM2) and the reviewed literature, the following hypothesis is proposed:

H5: Social influence has a significant impact on the perceived usefulness of ChatGPT.

Perceived Usefulness

Goli et al. (2023) found that the intention to use chatbots is positively impacted by perceived usefulness and simplicity of use, highlighting the importance of these aspects in determining users' intents. Furthermore, Giovanis et al. (2012) emphasized that customers' intentions and perceived ease of use are mediated in part by perceived usefulness, underscoring the significance of perceived usefulness in motivating usage intentions.

The Technology Acceptance Model (TAM) and its application in diverse situations can provide insight into the relationship between ChatGPT's perceived usefulness and usage intention. Perceived utility is a major factor in determining whether or not users accept information technology, according to Davis (1989), and it has a significant mediating effect between users' perceptions and social influence. This implies that consumers' motivations to use technology, particularly ChatGPT, are significantly shaped by their perception of its utility.

Based on the tenets of the technology acceptance model 3 (TAM3) and the cited literature, the following hypothesis is proposed:

H6: Perceived usefulness of ChatGPT has a significant impact on the intention of health workers to use ChatGPT

Usage Intention

According to research by Rad et al. (2022), having a positive attitude towards technology and intending to utilize it are important factors that influence how much technology is actually used. Nguyen et al. (2022) also addressed the acceptance of technology, highlighting the connection between intention and actual usage by suggesting that the intention to use technology might be interpreted as acceptance of it.

According to Setiawati et al. (2019), behavioral intention to use technology is influenced by perceived utility, while real technology utilization is influenced by behavioral intention to use. Suwannapusit (2021) further supported the idea that intention has an impact on real usage by pointing out that the behavioral intention of utilizing technology influences the actual use behavior of technology choices.

The following hypothesis is thus proposed:

H7: The intention of health workers to use ChatGPT has a significant impact on the actual usage of ChatGPT.

Methodology

Research Design

The study uses a quantitative research design. The quantitative research design is chosen because the researchers want to statistically test the influence of independent latent constructs on mediating latent constructs and dependent latent constructs via path analysis.

Population

The population for the study comprises Ghanaian health workers who have installed and used ChatGPT or similar AI tools. The actual size of the population is unknown.

Sampling Technique

A purposive sampling method was be used; health workers who had installed and used the app were targeted.

Sample Size Calculation

The Cochran (1963) formula for calculating the sample size for an unknown population size (large populations) is used. The formula is shown below:

$$n_0 = \frac{Z^2 pq}{e^2}$$

where:

n_0 = sample size
Z = the Z score. A z-score describes the position of a raw score in terms of its distance from the mean when measured in standard deviation units.
p = the estimated proportion of an attribute that is present in the population. This is also known as the prevalence rate.
q = 1-p
e = margin of error

A 95% confidence interval is chosen; thus, the margin of error is 0.05. The Z-score at 95% is 1.96. Based on a pilot study, a value of 0.2 was chosen for p.

From equation (1) $n_0 = \frac{3.8416 * 0.2 * 0.6}{0.0025}$

n_0= 246

The minimum sample size is therefore 246.

Data Collection Methods

The survey instrument was developed from the research model. The instrument had two main parts. The first part comprised questions on the demographic details of respondents. The second part comprised 5-point Likert scale questions based on the constructs in the model. Measurement items for the constructs were derived from Venkatesh & Bala (2008) and Thompson (1995). The instrument was constructed on Google forms and the link was shared to respondents who had used ChatGPT. Data were collected from two hundred and sixty-five (265) respondents.

Data Analysis and Results

Data analysis was done using Confirmatory Factor Analysis (CFA) and structural equation modelling (SEM) technique via JASP 0.18.1.0. SEM is appropriate for the non-parametric modelling of complex cause-effect relationships between latent variables (Hair et al., 2012). The two-step approach to PLS-SEM proposed by

Chin (1998) is used. The measurement model (outer model) was initially assessed, followed by the assessment of the structural model (inner model). Data cleaning was done before PLS-SEM. The data was checked for missing values and outliers; two hundred and fifty-six (256) responses were retained after data cleaning. Table 1 shows the descriptive statistics of the constructs.

Table 1. Descriptive statistics of constructs

Construct	Item	Valid	Missing	Mean	Std. Deviation	Minimum	Maximum
Task Characteristics	TChar1	256	0	2.855	0.982	1	5
	TChar2	256	0	3.059	0.895	1	5
	TChar3	256	0	3.227	0.909	1	5
	TChar4	256	0	3.398	0.857	1	5
Task-Technology Fit	TTF1	256	0	3.918	0.571	2	5
	TTF2	256	0	3.695	0.614	2	5
	TTF3	256	0	3.688	0.764	1	5
	TTF4	256	0	3.953	0.592	2	5
	TTF5	256	0	3.898	0.661	2	5
	TTF6	256	0	4.031	0.552	2	5
	TTF7	256	0	3.328	0.913	1	5
Social Influence	SInf1	256	0	3.086	0.994	1	5
	SInf2	256	0	3.008	0.998	1	5
	SInf3	256	0	3.176	0.935	1	5
	SInf4	256	0	3.465	0.88	1	5
Perceived Usefulness	PU1	256	0	3.684	0.69	1	5
	PU2	256	0	3.645	0.688	1	5
	PU3	256	0	3.66	0.734	1	5
	PU4	256	0	3.77	0.661	1	5
Usage Intention	UsInt1	256	0	3.676	0.692	1	5
	UsInt2	256	0	3.574	0.743	1	5
	UsInt3	256	0	3.586	0.797	1	5
Actual Use	Use1	256	0	3.34	0.906	1	5
	Use2	256	0	3.379	0.803	1	5
	Use3	256	0	3.516	0.863	1	5
Task Performance	Perf1	256	0	3.523	0.767	1	5
	Perf2	256	0	3.57	0.779	1	5

The reliability and validity of the constructs are shown in Table 2. Across the constructs, both Cronbach's alpha and McDonald's Omega scores demonstrate high levels of reliability, generally above the recommended threshold of 0.7. For instance, constructs like Task Performance, Perceived Usefulness, and Social Influence exhibit notably high reliability, with Cronbach's alpha and McDonald's Omega scores consistently above 0.9. This suggests a strong degree of internal consistency in the items used to measure these constructs. Constructs like Task Characteristics and Task-Technology Fit display good reliability with scores above 0.8.

Validity, assessed through the Average Variance Extracted (AVE), measures the amount of variance captured by the constructs relative to the measurement error. In the table, most constructs display AVE values above the acceptable threshold of 0.5, indicating a reasonable level of convergent validity. Constructs such as Perceived Usefulness, Usage Intention, and Task Performance stand out with notably high AVE scores, suggesting that a substantial portion of their variance is due to the underlying constructs rather than measurement error. Task Characteristics and Task-Technology Fit also demonstrate good validity.

Table 2. Construct validity and reliability

Construct	Cronbach Alpha	McDonald's Omega	Average Variance Extracted (AVE)
Task Characteristics	0.8	0.81	0.522
Task-Technology Fit	0.873	0.869	0.5
Social Influence	0.913	0.923	0.737
Perceived Usefulness	0.952	0.948	0.835
Usage Intention	0.925	0.928	0.814
Actual Usage	0.886	0.876	0.716
Task Performance	0.931	0.931	0.872

Additionally, the measurement model was assessed using the heterotrait-monotrait ratio of correlations ($HTMT^{0.90}$). The heterotrait-monotrait ratio of correlations ($HTMT^{0.90}$) measures discriminant validity. If the HTMT value is below 0.90, discriminant validity has been established between two constructs (Hair et al., 2014). Table 3 shows that all the constructs exhibit discriminant validity.

Table 3. Heterotrait-monotrait ratio of correlations (HTMT)

	Task Characteristics	Task-Technology Fit	Social Influence	Perceived Usefulness	Usage Intention	Actual Usage	Task Performance
Task Characteristics	1						
Task-Technology Fit	0.244	1					
Social Influence	0.117	0.508	1				
Perceived Usefulness	0.294	0.814	0.613	1			
Usage Intention	0.103	0.659	0.691	0.799	1		
Actual Usage	0.315	0.706	0.625	0.856	0.772	1	
Task Performance	0.169	0.69	0.527	0.766	0.776	0.833	1

A bootstrapping procedure was used to assess the structural model to determine the significance of each estimated path. Bootstrapping is the process of drawing a large number of re-samples with replacements from the original sample and then estimating the model parameters for each bootstrap re-sample. The results of the bootstrapping procedure are shown in Table 4.

Table 4. Hypothesis testing results

Hypothesis	Hypothesized Path	Path Coefficient	P Value	Result
H1	Task Characteristics -> Task-Technology Fit	0.174	0.000	Supported
H2	Task-Technology Fit -> Actual Usage	0.460	0.000	Supported
H3	Task-Technology Fit -> Task Performance	0.109	0.171	Not supported
H4	Actual Usage -> Task Performance	0.808	0.000	Supported
H5	Social Influence -> Perceived Usefulness	0.401	0.000	Supported
H6	Perceived Usefulness -> Usage Intention	0.874	0.000	Supported
H7	Usage Intention -> Actual Usage	0.878	0.000	Supported
R^2 (Task-Technology Fit) = 0.108 R^2 (Task Performance) = 0.693 R^2 (Actual Usage) = 0.733 SRMR = 0.226				

The results from the structural equation modeling (Table 4) reveal distinct patterns in the hypothesized paths between constructs. Firstly, the relationship from Task Characteristics to Task-Technology Fit demonstrates a significant positive path coefficient of 0.174 (p = 0.000), supporting the notion that task characteristics influence the fit of technology for performing tasks. Secondly, the path from Task-

Technology Fit to Actual Usage exhibits a substantial positive coefficient of 0.460 ($p = 0.000$), confirming that a better fit of technology with tasks leads to increased actual usage—a supported relationship. However, the path from Task-Technology Fit to Task Performance, while showing a positive coefficient of 0.109, does not achieve statistical significance ($p = 0.171$), suggesting that in this model, the technology-task fit does not significantly impact task performance.

Moving to the social factors, the path from Social Influence to Perceived Usefulness manifests a notable positive coefficient of 0.401 ($p = 0.000$), indicating that social influences positively affect the perceived usefulness of the technology. Furthermore, the relationship from Perceived Usefulness to Usage Intention displays a strong positive path coefficient of 0.874 ($p = 0.000$), indicating a robust influence of perceived usefulness on the intention to use. Finally, the path from Usage Intention to Actual Usage demonstrates a substantial positive coefficient of 0.878 ($p = 0.000$), supporting the premise that the intention to use strongly predicts actual usage. Overall, the structural equation modeling supports several relationships, highlighting the influential paths between these constructs in the model, while indicating nuances in the impact of certain variables on others.

The proposed model explained 10.8% of the variance in Task-Technology Fit, 69.3% of the variance in Task Performance, and 73.3% of the variance in Actual Usage. The R square values are shown in Table 3. The standardized root mean square residual (SRMR) was used to assess model fit. Hu & Bentler (1999) proposed that models that have SRMR values less than 0.08 have a good model fit. Table 3 shows SRMR value of 0.226 which implies the model does not have a good fit; however, lack of a good fit does not imply a bad model because of the model possesses good internal consistency, validity (convergent and discriminant), and reliability.

The wording of the measurement items is shown in Table 5.

Table 5. Wording of the measurement items

Construct	Item	Wording
Task Characteristics	TChar1	I frequently perform tasks that are not well-defined
	TChar2	I frequently perform ad-hoc, non-routine tasks
	TChar3	Frequently the tasks I perform involve answering questions that have never been asked in quite that form before
	TChar4	The tasks I perform frequently involve more that one unit/department
Task-Technology Fit	TTF1	The responses I get from ChatGPT are current
	TTF2	The responses I get from ChatGPT are what I need to carry out my tasks
	TTF3	The responses I get from ChatGPT are sufficiently detailed
	TTF4	ChatGPT, to my knowledge, delivers responses in a timely manner
	TTF5	I can count on ChatGPT to be "up" and available when I need it
	TTF6	It is easy to learn how to use ChatGPT
	TTF7	I am getting the training I need to use ChatGPT effectively
Social Influence	SInf1	People who influence my behaviour think that I should use ChatGPT
	SInf2	People who are important to me think that I should use ChatGPT
	SInf3	Friends and family are helpful in the use of ChatGPT
	SInf4	In general, friends and family support the use of ChatGPT
Perceived Usefulness	PU1	Using ChatGPT improves my performance of my job
	PU2	Using ChatGPT in my job increases my productivity
	PU3	Using ChatGPT enhances my effectiveness in my job
	PU4	I find ChatGPT to be useful in my job
Usage Intention	UsInt1	I intend to frequently use ChatGPT
	UsInt2	I predict I will frequently use ChatGPT
	UsInt3	I plan to frequently use ChatGPT
Actual Use	Use1	I frequently use ChatGPT for information on standard operating procedures
	Use2	I frequently use ChatGPT while performing ad-hoc tasks
	Use3	I frequently use ChatGPT for general healthcare research
Task Performance	Perf1	Largely, ChatGPT has a positive impact on my effectiveness and productivity in my job
	Perf2	ChatGPT is an important and valuable aid to me in the performance of my job

DISCUSSION

The results provide support for most of the relationships in the task-technology fit model and TAM2. Regarding the significant positive relationship between task-technology fit and task characteristics, it points to the fact that there is significant fit between the tasks performed by the respondents (health workers) and the technological aspects of ChatGPT. The level of alignment between task characteristics of health workers and the features of ChatGPT significantly impacts the perceived task-technology fit, with a higher alignment leading to a stronger perception of fit among users. The items used to measure task-technology fit were based on how current, useful, detailed, and timely ChatGPT responses are. The items also included the availability of ChatGPT as a platform, and how easy it is to learn the software. The responses for the measurement items collectively show that the features of ChatGPT (currency, usefulness, level of detail, timeliness, accessibility, and ease of use) provide a good fit for the tasks performed by the respondents (health workers). It is also important to note that ChatGPT in the context of this study provides assistance to perform tasks, and thus, is not the major tool used to perform tasks.

The positive and statistically significant relationship between task-technology fit and actual usage is as expected. It provides support for studies conducted by Shin & Song (2022), Navarro et al. (2021), and Zhao & Bacao (2020a). The task-technology fit dimensions, especially ease of use and usefulness have been found to directly impact actual system usage (Shin & Song, 2022). The relationship between task-technology fit and task performance though positive, was statistically insignificant. This result shows that the respondents are of the opinion that task-technology fit positively impacts task performance; however, the impact of this fit may be diminished by other factors such as job characteristics, leadership, organizational factors, and training. The factors influencing task performance by workers are multifaceted and encompass various dimensions (Basit, 2019). Actual usage of ChatGPT was found to have a positive and statistically significant impact of task performance, although task-technology fit was insignificant. This result provides support for the task-technology fit model, and it is as expected. Utilization of ChatGPT has a direct positive impact on the task performance of the health workers.

As expected, social influence was found to have a positive and statistically significant influence on perceived usefulness. Influence from important others, friends, and family regarding the use of ChatGPT has a positive and significant influence on the perceived usefulness of ChatGPT. Perceived usefulness in the context of this study refers to elements of productivity, effectiveness, performance, and usefulness. Additionally, perceived usefulness was found to have a positive and statistically significant influence on intention to use ChatGPT. This result provides support for TAM2. Perceptions of improved productivity, effectiveness, performance, and usefulness will directly impact intentions to use ChatGPT to support the delivery of health services.

SOLUTIONS AND RECOMMENDATIONS

Theoretical Implications

The study's conclusions have important theoretical ramifications for the fields of technology adoption and human-computer interaction, especially when it comes to ChatGPT use by healthcare professionals. The task-technology fit and task characteristics were shown to be positively correlated. This is consistent with ideas that highlight the significance of matching technology to particular task requirements. This is consistent with the Task-Technology Fit (TTF) model, which posits that improved performance outcomes result from a better fit between the features of technology and the intrinsic qualities of tasks. The Technology Acceptance Model (TAM), which holds that perceived usefulness and ease of use affect technology adoption, is further supported by the study's validation of a positive association between task-technology fit and ChatGPT usage.

Moreover, the identified positive association between ChatGPT usage and performance impacts aligns with the Extended Technology Acceptance Model (TAM2), which posits that actual system use impacts individual and organizational outcomes.

The study found no significant positive relationship between task-technology fit and the impact on performance. This casts doubt on long-held beliefs about the TTF model and raises the possibility that better performance outcomes aren't always ensured by a perfect match between task and technology. This break from the predicted relationship calls into question the suitability of the TTF model in healthcare environments and emphasizes the necessity for careful analysis when determining how task-technology fit affects performance.

Furthermore, the established positive link between perceived usefulness and usage intention aligns with the TAM, reinforcing the notion that individuals are more likely to adopt technology if they perceive it as beneficial to their tasks. The concluding relationship between usage intention and ChatGPT usage echoes the idea that behavioral intention is a significant predictor of actual system use, reinforcing the TAM's predictive validity.

Practical Implications

The study's results present actionable insights for healthcare practitioners, policymakers, and developers aiming to implement ChatGPT in healthcare settings. Firstly, the significant positive relationship between task characteristics and task-technology fit underscores the importance of tailoring ChatGPT functionalities to align with specific healthcare tasks. Customization of ChatGPT can enhance its integration into healthcare workflows, improving overall task-technology fit.

Recognizing the impact of social influence on perceived usefulness, policymakers and healthcare leaders should prioritize strategies that foster positive social influence within the health service workforce. Encouraging collaborative discussions, training programs, and knowledge-sharing platforms can contribute to increased acceptance and utilization of ChatGPT among healthcare professionals.

The study's findings also emphasize the need to highlight the practical benefits of ChatGPT for health service workers. Policymakers and developers should focus on demonstrating its positive impact on efficiency, accuracy, and workflow optimization to enhance healthcare practitioners' perception of its usefulness, thus fostering greater acceptance and adoption.

Addressing the discrepancy between task-technology fit and performance impacts is crucial. While there is a positive relationship between task-technology fit and ChatGPT usage, an insignificant relationship with performance impacts suggests a potential misalignment. Developers and healthcare stakeholders should assess how well ChatGPT aligns with specific performance outcomes and make necessary adjustments to ensure measurable improvements.

FUTURE RESEARCH DIRECTIONS

The study revealed a positive relationship between task characteristics and task-technology fit. Future research could delve deeper into the customization of ChatGPT to specific healthcare tasks and assess its impact on task-specific outcomes.

Additionally, the study highlighted the importance of social influence, perceived usefulness, and usage intention in the adoption of ChatGPT by health service workers. Future research could involve longitudinal studies to track the evolving perceptions and utilization patterns of ChatGPT over time. This would provide a deeper understanding of how healthcare practitioners' attitudes and behaviors towards ChatGPT change as they gain more experience with the technology.

REFERENCES

Abdullah, I. S., Loganathan, A., & Lee, R. W. (2023). *ChatGPT & Doctors: The Medical Dream Team.* Health Sciences Commons. https://hsrc.himmelfarb.gwu.edu/smhs_URGENT_Matters

Arman, M., & Lamiya, U. R. (2023). Exploring the Implication of ChatGPT AI for Business: Efficiency and Challenges. *Journal of Innovation Information Technology and Application*, *5*(1), 52–64. doi:10.35970/jinita.v5i1.1828

Basit, A. A. (2019). Examining how respectful engagement affects task performance and affective organizational commitment. *Personnel Review*, *48*(3), 644–658. doi:10.1108/PR-02-2018-0050

Bhushan, S. (2021). The impact of artificial intelligence and machine learning on the global economy and its implications for the hospitality sector in India. *Worldwide Hospitality and Tourism Themes*, *13*(2), 252–259. doi:10.1108/WHATT-09-2020-0116

Cashman, C. (2023). *What is ChatGPT. HP Tech Takes*. https://www.hp.com/us-en/shop/tech-takes/what-is-chatgpt#:~:text="weak" AI.-,Development,and generate human-like language.

Chowdhury, N. A. (2023). *Unlocking the power of ChatGPT: An in-depth look at ChatAI's business model*. Academic Press.

Coman, D. M., State, V., Voinea, M. C., & Cucui, G. (2023). *Impacts of chatbots on the accounting service industry*. https://univagora.ro/jour/index.php/aijes

Dwivedi, Y. K., Pandey, N., Currie, W., & Micu, A. (2023). Leveraging ChatGPT and other generative artificial intelligence (AI)-based applications in the hospitality and tourism industry: Practices, challenges and research agenda. *International Journal of Contemporary Hospitality Management*. Advance online publication. doi:10.1108/IJCHM-05-2023-0686

Fan, Z. Y., Yang, Y., Zhang, C. H., Yin, R. Y., Tang, L., & Zhang, F. (2021). Prevalence and patterns of comorbidity among middle-aged and elderly people in China: A cross-sectional study based on CHARLS data. *International Journal of General Medicine*, *14*, 1449–1455. doi:10.2147/IJGM.S309783 PMID:33907449

French, F., Levi, D., Maczo, C., Simonaityte, A., Triantafyllidis, S., & Varda, G. (2023). Creative Use of OpenAI in Education: Case Studies from Game Development. *Multimodal Technologies and Interaction*, *7*(8), 81. Advance online publication. doi:10.3390/mti7080081

Gao, Y., Tong, W., Wu, E. Q., Chen, W., Zhu, G. Y., & Wang, F. Y. (2023). Chat With ChatGPT on Interactive Engines for Intelligent Driving. *IEEE Transactions on Intelligent Vehicles*, *8*(3), 2034–2036. doi:10.1109/TIV.2023.3252571

Gebauer, J., & Tang, Y. (2008). Applying the theory of task-technology fit to mobile technology: The role of user mobility. *International Journal of Mobile Communications*, *6*(3), 321. doi:10.1504/IJMC.2008.017514

Giovanis, A., Binioris, S., & Polychronopoulos, G. (2012). An Extension of TAM Model With IDT and Security/Privacy Risk in the Adoption of Internet Banking Services in Greece. Euromed Journal of Business. doi:10.1108/14502191211225365

Goli, M., Sahu, A. K., Bag, S., & Dhamija, P. (2023). Users' Acceptance of Artificial Intelligence-Based Chatbots. International Journal of Technology and Human Interaction. doi:10.4018/IJTHI.318481

Goodhue, D. L., & Thompson, R. L. (1995). Task-Technology Fit and Individual Performance. *Management Information Systems Quarterly*, *19*(2), 213–236. doi:10.2307/249689

Gu, D., Khan, S., Khan, I. U., Khan, S. U., Xie, Y., Li, X., & Zhang, G. (2021). Assessing the Adoption of e-Health Technology in a Developing Country: An Extension of the UTAUT Model. *SAGE Open*, *11*(3). doi:10.1177/21582440211027565

Gursoy, D., Li, Y., & Song, H. (2023). ChatGPT and the hospitality and tourism industry: An overview of current trends and future research directions. *Journal of Hospitality Marketing & Management*, *32*(5), 579–592. doi:10.1080/19368623.2023.2211993

Ivanovic, M., Autexier, S., Kokkonidis, M., & Rust, J. (2023). Quality medical data management within an open AI architecture-cancer patients case. *Connection Science*, *35*(1), 2194581. Advance online publication. doi:10.1080/09540091.2023.2194581

Javaid, M., Haleem, A., & Singh, R. P. (2023). ChatGPT for healthcare services: An emerging stage for an innovative perspective. BenchCouncil Transactions on Benchmarks. *Standards and Evaluations*, *3*(1), 100105. doi:10.1016/j.tbench.2023.100105

Kang, H.-J., Han, J., & Kwon, G. H. (2022). The Acceptance Behavior of Smart Home Health Care Services in South Korea: An Integrated Model of UTAUT and TTF. *International Journal of Environmental Research and Public Health*, *19*(20), 13279. doi:10.3390/ijerph192013279 PMID:36293859

Lee, J.-Sh., & Hsiang, J. (2020). Patent Claim Generation by Fine-Tuning OpenAI GPT-2. *World Patent Information*, *62*, 101983. doi:10.1016/j.wpi.2020.101983

Mhlanga, D. (2023). The Value of Open AI and Chat GPT for the Current Learning Environments and the Potential Future Uses. SSRN *Electronic Journal*. https://doi.org/ doi:10.2139/ssrn.4439267

Mich, L., & Garigliano, R. (2023). ChatGPT for e-Tourism: A technological perspective. *Information Technology & Tourism*, *25*(1), 1–12. doi:10.1007/s40558-023-00248-x

Nadarzynski, T., Miles, O., Cowie, A., & Ridge, D. (2019). Acceptability of artificial intelligence (AI)-led chatbot services in healthcare: A mixed-methods study. *Digital Health*, *5*. doi:10.1177/2055207619871808 PMID:31467682

Navarro, M. M., Prasetyo, Y. T., Young, M. N., Nadlifatin, R., & Redi, A. A. N. P. (2021). The Perceived Satisfaction in Utilizing Learning Management System among Engineering Students during the COVID-19 Pandemic: Integrating Task Technology Fit and Extended Technology Acceptance Model. *Sustainability (Basel)*, *13*(19), 10669. doi:10.3390/su131910669

Nguyen, Q. N., & Mai, V. N. (2022). Technology Acceptance in Seeking Jobs Among University Graduates in Vietnam. *International Journal of Emerging Technologies in Learning*, *17*(20), 49–61. doi:10.3991/ijet.v17i20.33229

O'Grady, M., Kapoor, S., Gilmer, E., Neighbors, C., Conigliaro, J., Kwon, N., & Morgenstern, J. (2019). Point-of-Care Mobile Application to Guide Health Care Professionals in Conducting Substance Use Screening and Intervention: A Mixed-Methods User Experience Study. *ACI Open*, *03*(01), e1–e12. doi:10.1055/s-0039-1684002

Open, A. I. (2022). *Introducing ChatGPT*. Open AI. https://openai.com/blog/chatgpt

Rad, D., Egerau, A., Roman, A., Dughi, T., Balas, E., Maier, R., Ignat, S., & Rad, G. (2022). A Preliminary Investigation of the Technology Acceptance Model (TAM) in Early Childhood Education and Care. BRAIN. *Broad Research in Artificial Intelligence and Neuroscience*, *13*(1), 518–533. doi:10.18662/brain/13.1/297

Raman, R. Das, P., Kaur, T., JP, S., & Nedungadi, P. (2023). *University Students as Early Adopters of ChatGPT: Innovation Diffusion Study*. doi:10.21203/rs.3.rs-2734142/v1

Rudolph, J., Tan, S., & Tan, S. (2023). ChatGPT: Bullshit spewer or the end of traditional assessments in higher education? *Journal of Applied Learning & Teaching*, *6*(1). Advance online publication. doi:10.37074/jalt.2023.6.1.9

Schnall, R., Smith, A. B., Sikka, M., Gordon, P., Camhi, E., Kanter, T., & Bakken, S. (2012). Employing the FITT framework to explore HIV case managers' perceptions of two electronic clinical data (ECD) summary systems. *International Journal of Medical Informatics*, *81*(10), e56–e62. doi:10.1016/j.ijmedinf.2012.07.002 PMID:22841702

Setiawati, E., Trisnawati, R., & Diana, U. (2019). The analysis of acceptance of hospital information management system (HIMS) using technology acceptance model method. *Riset Akuntansi Dan Keuangan Indonesia*, *4*(2), 186–195. doi:10.23917/reaksi.v4i2.8652

Shin, A., & Song, H.-D. (2022). The Effects of Basic Psychological Needs, Task-Technology Fit, and Student Engagement on MOOC Learners' Continuance Intention to Use. *Human Behavior and Emerging Technologies*, *2022*, 1–12. doi:10.1155/2022/6444509

Stears, C., & Deeks, J. (2023). Editorial: The use of artificial intelligence in fighting financial crime, for better or worse? In Journal of Money Laundering Control (Vol. 26, Issue 3, pp. 433-435). Emerald Publishing. https://doi.org/ doi:10.1108/JMLC-05-2023-174

Suwannapusit, U. (2021). The UTAUT Model Analysis in the Technology Use of Generation-Z Users in Cambodia during COVID-19 Situation. *International Journal of Current Science Research and Review*, *04*(07). Advance online publication. doi:10.47191/ijcsrr/V4-i7-06

Vatanasakdakul, S., Aoun, C., & Putra, Y. H. S. (2020). Social Media in Micro-Enterprises. *Journal of Global Information Management*, *28*(3), 184–203. doi:10.4018/JGIM.2020070110

Venkatesh, V., & Bala, H. (2008). Technology acceptance model 3 and a research agenda on interventions. *Decision Sciences*, *39*(2), 273–315. doi:10.1111/j.1540-5915.2008.00192.x

Vijayakumar, H. (2023). Revolutionizing Customer Experience with AI: A Path to Increase Revenue Growth Rate. *15th International Conference on Electronics, Computers and Artificial Intelligence, ECAI 2023 - Proceedings*. https://doi.org/10.1109/ECAI58194.2023.10194016

Wanti, L. P., Insan, H. F. M., & Prasetya, N. W. A. (2020). End User Satisfaction for Location Health Service Application with Analysis of Task Technology Fit. Lontar Komputer? *Jurnal Ilmiah Teknologi Informasi*, *11*(2), 76. doi:10.24843/LKJITI.2020.v11.i02.p02

Zhao, Y., & Bacao, F. (2020a). What factors determining customer continuingly using food delivery apps during 2019 novel coronavirus pandemic period? *International Journal of Hospitality Management*, *91*, 102683. doi:10.1016/j.ijhm.2020.102683 PMID:32929294

Zhao, Y., & Bacao, F. (2020b). What factors determining customer continuingly using food delivery apps during 2019 novel coronavirus pandemic period? *International Journal of Hospitality Management*, *91*, 102683. doi:10.1016/j.ijhm.2020.102683 PMID:32929294

ADDITIONAL READING

Abdaljaleel, M. (2024). *A multinational study on the factors influencing university students ' attitudes and usage of ChatGPT, Scientific Reports*. Nature Publishing Group UK. doi:10.1038/s41598-024-52549-8

Asch, D. A. (2024). An Interview with ChatGPT About. *Health Care*, 1–8. doi:10.1056/CAT.23.0043

Hodge, J. G. Jr, Gostin, L. O., & Jacobson, P. D. (1999). Legal issues concerning electronic health information: Privacy, quality, and liability. *Journal of the American Medical Association*, *282*(15), 1466–1471. doi:10.1001/jama.282.15.1466 PMID:10535438

Koubaa, A., Boulila, W., Ghouti, L., Alzahem, A., & Latif, S. (2023). Exploring ChatGPT Capabilities and Limitations : A Survey. *IEEE Access : Practical Innovations, Open Solutions*, *11*(September), 118698–118721. doi:10.1109/ACCESS.2023.3326474

Meskó, B., & Topol, E. J. (2023). The imperative for regulatory oversight of large language models (or generative AI) in healthcare. *Digital Medicine*, *6*(1), 1–6. doi:10.1038/s41746-023-00873-0 PMID:37414860

Rahimzadeh, V., Kostick-Quenet, K., Blumenthal Barby, J., & McGuire, A. L. (2023). Ethics Education for Healthcare Professionals in the Era of ChatGPT and Other Large Language Models : Do We Still Need It? Ethics Education for Healthcare Professionals in the Era of ChatGPT and. *The American Journal of Bioethics*, *23*(10), 17–27. doi:10.1080/15265161.2023.2233358 PMID:37487184

Sallam, M., Salim, N. A., Barakat, M., Al-Mahzoum, K., Al-Tammemi, A. B., Malaeb, D., Hallit, R., & Hallit, S. (2023). 'Assessing health students' attitudes and usage of ChatGPT in Jordan: Validation study'. *JMIR Medical Education*, *9*(1), e48254. doi:10.2196/48254 PMID:37578934

Zhang, X., Liu, S., Chen, X., Wang, L., Gao, B., & Zhu, Q. (2018). Health information privacy concerns, antecedents, and information disclosure intention in online health communities. *Information & Management*, *55*(4), 482–493. doi:10.1016/j.im.2017.11.003

KEY TERMS AND DEFINITION

Artificial Intelligence (AI): The intelligence demonstrated by machines, contrasted with the natural intelligence displayed by humans (Hwang & Kim, 2021; Klimova et al., 2023; Samala et al., 2022).

ChatGPT: A large language model chatbot developed by OpenAI, trained on a massive dataset of text and code. Its key characteristics include generative, large language model, dialogue format, and machine learning based. It is can generate text, translate languages, write different kinds of creative content, and answers questions in an informative way (Wu et al., 2023; Herbold et al., 2023).

Conversational Agents: Computer programs or systems, like ChatGPT, designed to engage in natural language conversations with users. In health services, conversational agents can be employed to interact with patients, answer queries, provide information, and assist in various healthcare-related tasks (Allouch et al., 2021).

Ethical AI: The responsible and fair development and deployment of artificial intelligence technologies (Mittelstadt, 2019). In the context of ChatGPT and health services, ethical considerations include privacy protection, unbiased decision-making, and transparency in the use of AI in healthcare interactions.

Health Information Privacy: Involves safeguarding individuals' personal and health-related data (Hodge, 2003; Zhang et al., 2018). In the context of using ChatGPT in health services, maintaining privacy is crucial to ensure the confidentiality and security of sensitive health information shared during conversations.

Health Services: The actions taken to maintain and improve the health of individuals and communities. They can be provided by a variety of professionals, including doctors, nurses, therapists, and pharmacists. Health services can be preventative, diagnostic, therapeutic, or rehabilitative.

Machine Learning (ML): A type of artificial intelligence that learns from data without being explicitly programmed (Binkhonain & Zhao, 2019; Bunod et al., 2022; Mahesh, 2020).

Natural Language Processing (NLP): The ability of computers to understand and process human language (Galassi et al., 2020; Khurana et al., 2023; Meera & Geerthik, 2022).

Telehealth: The use of technology, such as video calls, chat platforms, and remote monitoring, to provide healthcare services and information remotely (Gajarawala & Pelkowski, 2021). ChatGPT can potentially contribute to telehealth by serving as a conversational interface in virtual healthcare interactions.

User Experience (UX): Encompasses the overall experience a person has when interacting with a system or service (Alomari et al., 2020; Luther & Tiberius, 2020). In the context of ChatGPT and health services, UX involves evaluating the ease of use, effectiveness, and satisfaction of users engaging with the model for healthcare-related communication.

Chapter 9
Successful Footprints of ChatGPT Deployments in the Education Sector:
Pros Outweigh Cons by Embracing Ethics and Etiquette

Shivi Khanna
https://orcid.org/0000-0002-4410-5694
CHRIST University, Bangalore, India

Sunita Kumar
https://orcid.org/0000-0002-0628-1873
CHRIST University, Bangalore, India

F. C. M. A. Nabanita Ghosh
https://orcid.org/0000-0001-5176-7314
CHRIST University, Bangalore, India

ABSTRACT

Artificial intelligence (AI) is essential in all aspects of life. One crucial area to examine is the integration of artificial intelligence in education. The true essence is in providing individuals with the necessary knowledge, skills, and values needed to have a fulfilling and meaningful life. Education must adapt to equip students with essential abilities to navigate life's challenges while upholding integrity in a dynamic world. Artificial intelligence (AI), shown by technologies such as ChatGPT, exhibits significant promise in educational environments. This chapter

DOI: 10.4018/979-8-3693-1239-1.ch009

explores personalized learning enabled by artificial intelligence (AI). Furthermore, intelligent tutoring systems are also analyzed. The text delves into various facets of the educational system where ChatGPT might offer help. Additionally, offering explanations for the prohibition of Chat GPT in many countries and educational institutions. The discussion has focused on how AI affects the socio-economic gap in the education sector.

INTRODUCTION

Artificial intelligence (AI) refers to the cognitive abilities exhibited by computers or software, in contrast to the cognitive abilities displayed by humans or other animals. Artificial Intelligence is a discipline within computer science that focuses on the development and analysis of intelligent machines. AI technology is extensively utilized across various sectors, including industry, government, and science. Artificial Intelligence (AI) is a crucial factor in all areas of life. An essential sector to consider is artificial intelligence in education. The function of education is frequently misunderstood as solely a means to obtain work. Yet, its genuine core is in equipping individuals with the knowledge, abilities, and principles essential for guiding a satisfying and purposeful existence. In a constantly changing world, education needs to adjust in order to provide students with the necessary skills to negotiate the complexities of life while maintaining integrity. Artificial Intelligence (AI), as demonstrated by technologies like as ChatGPT shows great potential in the educational setting.

Artificial Intelligence (AI) is currently transforming educational approaches, improving learning experiences, and facilitating personalized education, rather than being a concept that belongs to the future. This chapter seeks to investigate the varied and developing role of AI, specifically Chat GPT, in education, analyzing its potential to fundamentally transform the methods of teaching and learning. This chapter delves into the examination of individualized learning facilitated by artificial intelligence (AI). Additionally, Intelligent Tutoring Systems are also examined. It also explores different aspects of the school system where Chat GPT can provide assistance. Also providing insights into the reasons why Chat GPT has been prohibited in several countries and a few educational institutions. The impact of AI on the socio-economic divide in the education sector has been deliberated.

BACKGROUND

The education sector has undergone sea changes modes of teaching and learning practices. The launching of new tools and techniques has made the education sector reach new heights with merits and demerits Alan (android developer (androiddeveloper.co.in, 2023). The learners and educators made the implementation of ChatGPT into the system to make the process readymade. Ideal ways of utilizing the features to make the learning more engaging and interactive and save considerable time by avoiding the routine tasks. Encouragement arose among many to explore the opportunities to make use of the advantages of these chatbots to reduce the repeated tasks or tasks with similar lines of monotony(Gursoy et al., 2023). The landscape of education faced reformatory phases as the demand for digitized education went up the need for personalized coaching became prominent, and further, and further the paramount significance became pertinent with the advent of the demon Covid 2019. Unlike the 18th century and before, today education has become accessible to many due to the technological moves. This rise in the e-education system has democratized education regardless of geographical boundaries. Artificial Intelligence (AI) has revolutionized numerous industries, and its integration into education holds immense promise for transforming learning methodologies. AI encompasses the development of intelligent machines capable of performing tasks that typically require human intelligence, such as learning, problem-solving, and decision-making. The integration of AI in the classroom promotes curiosity, customization, and profound learning experiences, equipping students to manage a rapidly changing world while revolutionizing teaching techniques, evaluations, and personalized learning paths.

ChatGPT is one of the most famous artificial intelligence based tools being developed in the recent years. Chat GPT appeared to be a bridging link between the availability of traditional education and the need for system-driven education by empowering educators and learners alike. ChatGPT emerged as a game changer in the realm of education sector (Fütterer et al., 2023; Iskender, 2023). Over the excitement of the educators became rampant and they grabbed the benefits of the release and diffusion of this new technology-driven information availability.

The educational landscape is undergoing a significant transformation, driven by the rapid advancement of AI tools like ChatGPT. AI is no longer a futuristic concept; it is actively reshaping educational methodologies, enhancing learning experiences, and paving the way for personalized education. This article aims to explore AI's (specifically ChatGPT) diverse and evolving role in education, examining its potential to revolutionize the way we teach and learn. AI technologies aim to enhance teaching methods, personalize learning experiences, and optimize educational outcomes within the educational sector. In section two of this chapter personalized learning through AI has been explored, here we have also explored

Intelligent Tutoring Systems. Section three of this chapter focuses on the role of ChatGPT in the education sector, here we have focused on various dimensions of the education system in which ChatGPT can be helpful. This section also provides of glimpse of reasons for ChatGPT being banned in certain countries and few educational institutions. We have looked at bigger picture in section four by providing possible serious consequences of rampant usage of AI in education sector. Can AI increase or reduce the socio economic divide in education sector has been discussed in section five. While section six of this chapter provides the future of AI enabled education.

THE MAIN FOCUS OF THE CHAPTER

Personalized Learning Through AI

One of the most significant contributions of AI is the possibility of personalized learning. AI algorithms can analyze vast amounts of student data, including learning styles, performance data, and individual needs, to tailor educational content and instruction to each student. This personalized approach can lead to improved engagement, deeper understanding, and more effective learning outcomes (Afzal et al., 2023). Personalized learning is a pedagogical approach aimed at tailoring education to individual student needs, preferences, and learning styles. AI facilitates personalized learning experiences by analyzing students' learning patterns, preferences, and abilities. Adaptive learning platforms leverage AI algorithms to tailor educational content and pacing, allowing students to learn at their own pace (Zhang et al., 2020). Research by Zhang et al., 2020 highlights the importance of personalized learning in fostering student engagement and academic achievement. Personalized learning enhances student motivation and deeper understanding by adapting content, pace, and learning pathways to individual student abilities and interests.

Various strategies have been proposed for implementing personalized learning. Adaptive learning platforms, as researched by Gligorea et al., 2023, utilize artificial intelligence to analyze student performance data and deliver customized content and assessments. Additionally, differentiated instruction, as explored by Triantoro, 2013, involves tailoring teaching methods and materials to accommodate diverse learning needs within a classroom.

Studies suggest that personalized learning positively impacts student outcomes. Zheng et al., 2022 found that students engaged in personalized learning experiences demonstrated increased academic growth compared to those in traditional classroom settings. Moreover, personalized learning fosters a sense of ownership and autonomy in students, leading to higher levels of self-efficacy and perseverance (Gligorea et al., 2023). Despite its potential, personalized learning faces challenges in implementation.

Ensuring equitable access to technology and resources for all students remains a concern (Afzal et al., 2023). Additionally, effective teacher training and support are crucial for successfully integrating personalized learning approaches into classrooms (Makhambetova et al., 2021).

Personalized learning in improving student engagement, motivation, and academic outcomes. Strategies like adaptive learning platforms and differentiated instruction have shown promise in tailoring education to individual student needs. However, challenges related to accessibility, teacher training, and equitable implementation need to be addressed for the widespread success of personalized learning initiatives. AI-powered adaptive learning platforms are a powerful tool for personalized learning. These platforms use AI algorithms to adjust the difficulty of learning materials and provide targeted instruction in response to each student's progress and understanding. This can help to ensure that students are challenged appropriately and receive the support they need to succeed (Shemshack & Spector, 2020).

AN INNOVATIVE APPROACH TO PERSONALIZED LEARNING

Intelligent Tutoring Systems (ITS) represent an innovative approach to personalized learning, leveraging artificial intelligence to provide tailored and interactive guidance to students. Intelligent Tutoring Systems (ITS) utilize AI to provide customized and interactive guidance to students. These systems adapt their teaching strategies based on real-time feedback, offering personalized assistance to address individual learning needs.

Figure 1. ITS for personalized learning

Studies have shown the efficacy of ITS in enhancing learning outcomes across various subjects. For instance, a meta-analysis Baidoo-Anu & Owusu Ansah, 2023 found that students using ITS exhibited significantly higher academic achievement than those using traditional methods. The adaptive nature of ITS, which adjusts content and pacing based on individual student responses, contributes to improved retention and understanding of materials as depicted in figure 1. ITS significantly influences student engagement by fostering active participation and personalized interactions. Research (Shemshack & Spector, 2020) indicated that students using ITS demonstrated higher levels of motivation and engagement due to the system's ability to provide instant feedback and adaptive challenges aligned with their learning pace and preferences. Furthermore, the interactive nature of ITS contributes to a more immersive and engaging learning experience, positively impacting student interest and commitment to learning (Makhambetova et al., 2021).

ITS applications span various educational domains, from mathematics and science to language learning and programming. Recent advancements in natural language processing have enabled ITS to provide personalized language learning experiences. Some studies have, (Kumar et al., 2023; Smale-Jacobse et al., 2019) highlighted the effectiveness of an ITS in teaching foreign languages by adapting content and exercises to individual linguistic proficiency levels, resulting in enhanced language acquisition.

ROLE OF CHATGPT IN EDUCATION

The entry of ChatGPT into the education system gained substantial recognition among the learners and educators too. The simplicity of getting ready-made outputs with zero-time involvement at the cost of tarnishing the reputation of the self and education system has become a known practice. The quick-go-lucky approach thoughts among the reader's minds fail to consider the impetus of self-learning and self-efficacy, and the layers of automated outputs diminish the brightness of human willpower. The San Francisco-based research laboratory, with its founder, twitter CEO Elon Musk and Silicon Valley megadonor Peter Thiel, was the propagator in devising the technology of the ChatGPT used by the masses.

The ChatGPT tool is not at all infallible as the inherent capacity to generate limited algorithm-centric output. The intensity of feeds that went into the tool would be deciding the capability of bringing out the outputs in terms of responses asked by the users. In the field of artificial intelligence, the effectiveness of responses is strongly linked to the ability to create clear and contextually relevant queries or inquiries. AI, like ChatGPT, promotes the cultivation of inquiry skills, the critical evaluation of responses, and the ethical application of AI among students. This method improves students' abilities to ask insightful questions, analyze information critically, and adjust to the changing landscape of artificial intelligence. Promoting the utilization of AI in investigations fosters a need for more profound discovery and inquiry-driven learning among students.

USED CASES OF AI IN EDUCATION SYSTEM

Students can utilize ChatGPT as a substitute for a specific persona, such as a debate partner who can identify flaws in their arguments, a recruiter who conducts job interviews, or a new boss who provides feedback in a particular manner. This might aid students in comprehending their material with enhanced subtlety and fresh outlook. ChatGPT serves as a valuable tool for assisting in the creation of quizzes, exams, and lesson plans for educational classes. ChatGPT can assist educators in ensuring that the questions they create are both inclusive and tailored to the students' learning level, hence promoting accessibility. When you request ChatGPT to generate five question exams regarding the recruiting and selection process implemented by organizations in the United States, the outcomes are remarkably up-to-date. You have the ability to adopt these concepts and personalize them. AI tools can also assist pupils who are not proficient in communicating in English. Teachers can motivate these students to utilize AI tools for translation aid, enhancing their English composition skills, and honing their conversational abilities.Artificial intelligence systems can assist pupils in utilizing the internet in a responsible manner. The teacher's responsibility is to caution students about the potential lack of credibility and accuracy in the answers provided by AI. They should encourage students to engage in critical thinking to determine whether they should place trust in the response. Additionally, students should verify the information using other reliable sources.

ChatGPT can be used by the students for composing their biodata, letter of recommendation when they apply for higher education in different other nations of high repute. In case of the professional who are closely knitted with the field of digital marketing, writers, content developers, bloggers, social media agents and such other experts can make a good use of ChatGPT to create the write up by giving prompt such as "Once upon a time" or "Long long ago there lived" and many other allied stuff.

ChatGPT can be used as a translator specially for those who have creative ideas but not able to shape in the language of their choice and at that juncture ChatGPT can be tremendously instrumental in translating the text and paragraphs into the desired language.

The writers can be popular with their pieces of writing in the other languages where they are not proficient in terms of spelling, grammar. The typicality of the research gets dominated by the parameters namely proof reading, writing skills and the ChatGPT can be a solution to this as the feedback and act as a catalyst in enhancing the quality of the written work.

For the educators who are imparting education can create course content, design multiple choice questions without any typical manual effort. The designing of the curriculum can be made by the smart use of ChatGPT. Also, the grading system of the students can be done by evaluation of the assignment, can provide the rubrics for evaluation and thus the teaching community can harness the potential of artificial intelligence tools to enhance the quality of the assignment or work generated. The students can make use of this platform to complete the timely prototype assignment where the mind works at a compromising rate.

ChatGPT helps in developing academic projects, assignments and also the tasks of personal interest. The research processes can be made smooth by adopting the use of the GPT tool in the lines of topic selection, background selection, identifying relevant resources and assists in organizing research and citation requirements. ChatGPT can also be considered in framing a catchy title for the project or research. By giving a command to ChatGPT based on the requirement, an array of ready made- inputs will be appearing on the screen and the user can pick up at his/her convenience the most suitable one keeping in mind the need of the study and thereby making adequate fitment.

Various research designs can be generated by the use of ChatGPT, such as to analyze the customer specific database such as change in the behaviour of the customers, post purchase attitude, dynamicity in the tastes and preferences and so on.

DIMENSIONS OF LEARNING BY USING CHATGPT

The table below shows the various dimensions of learning where the tool ChatGPT was deployed.

Table 1. Dimensions of learning through ChatGPT

Language Learning	Writing Assistance	Automated Grading	Personalized Learning
Can produce chatbots and artificial language tutors who can mend the gaps of the vocabularies. It generates real life like conversations and provides instant feedback on the grammar, spelling and pronunciation too.	Chatbots can also be instrumental in giving feedbacks on the writing style of the students and thereafter the learners can amicably educate themselves and improve the quality of their writing. Also assists in identifying errors in punctuation.	GPT can be an aid not only to the learners but also to the educators as teachers can save their valuable time by getting system based automated grading for the assignments of their students. Also provides feedback on the quality of the inputs submitted.	GPT works as an instructor in advising the type of the material to be considered, the resources such as videos, textbooks, articles to be used for improving the skills. GPT analyses the learning patterns and preferences of the students.

ROLE OF CHAT GPT IN THE EDUCATION SECTOR

ChatGPT is a pre-trained transformer language model that helps automate manual inputs, potentially transforming education. Chatbots facilitate the provision of human-like responses through the utilization of deep learning algorithms integrated into the system. It enriches educational experiences by combining critical thinking and judgment. In the age of advanced technology, it serves as a tool that has the inherent ability to revolutionize traditional methods of education and instruction. By reinventing educational methods, it introduces new perspectives to both learners and educators, invigorating their minds with fresh ideas.

The use of augmented reality and simulations in the learning process allows learners to engage in dynamic and immersive learning experiences. It enables students to focus on the importance of projects or assignments, significantly reducing the time required for decision-making. Through incremental advancements across various editions, ChatGPT has showcased its proficiency in producing desired outcomes in very sophisticated domains. These include capabilities such as interpreting visual visuals and art, recognizing noises, generating flow charts for recipes, and various other similar tasks. The utilization of technology got increasingly prominent in all areas of academic demands, however not flawless. GPT disseminated pedagogical materials to the educational community. The incorporation of ChatGPT in education offers numerous benefits that could potentially transform the learning process. Utilizing the full potential of artificial intelligence and natural language processing, ChatGPT technology offers various advantages in the realm of education. These benefits enable pupils, enhance teaching methodologies, and cultivate a more captivating and efficient educational setting.

ChatGPT offers significant benefits for teachers. Firstly, improved instructional support provides immediate suggestions, resources, and recommendations. The system's analysis of lesson planning, material generation, and instructional design can provide lessons that are more captivating and impactful. Furthermore, ChatGPT facilitates customized learning experiences by adjusting to the specific requirements of each student. The system examines student data, identifies strengths and weaknesses, and produces customized content or interventions to target specific learning deficiencies, hence improving student engagement and results. ChatGPT technology streamlines teachers' workload by automating mundane administrative processes such as evaluating coursework or producing reports. The enhanced time efficiency enables educators to prioritize educational activities, deliver prompt feedback, and actively interact with students. Lastly, it provides access to a wide range of educational resources, such as textbooks, articles, films, and interactive stuff. This enables educators to enhance their instructional materials, integrate current information, and provide exceptional teaching.

ISSUES ASSOCIATED WITH CHATGPT

The use of tools in the education sector should neither be detrimental to the growth path of the students nor should be a hindrance towards mental development. The education of the traditional days in contrast with the modern days became prominently different due to the augmentation of the technologies which though appear to be blissful but at times sheerly fail to magnify the spontaneous process of human thinking. Technologies are welcomed to be instrumental in reducing the mundane work structure, repetitive tasks with zero utilization of intelligence but bounded by creativity and innovation and nature driven outputs can't be trusted with automatic algorithm-based machine-driven outputs. Over dependence on the gadgets, on technological outputs to ease out the burden of the task and assignments will slowly erode the vitality of the brain and would become non-functional. As known the brain can sustain without oxygen for only three to six minutes in terms of pathological dictums but in utilization factor the brain should not be dormant for long hours. Apart from the scientific reason which explains the possibility of the brain getting damaged it also makes the humans inclined to borrow a source of knowledge instead of making an attempt to explore things on their own. It leads to gradual dilapidation of the inbuilt capacity of hunting for the unknown due to the ease and convenience of all time available machine made resources.

The comfort of using ChatGPT by the students and learning took its new heights recently. Human minds are connected with the ready-made approaches at the cost of the knowledge burn, ethical issues and mental inertia. The countries New South Wales, Queensland, and Tasmania, have already banned the use on the grounds of generating sparks of cheating by the tool and turning off the student's core capability and critical thinking approaches. Concern arises as to how the judicious use of technology would be aligned with the flawless pure and filtered composition and as ChatGPT generates using its tool power the sophisticated outputs the learners' community lacks to invest their valuable time in producing their output (Gill et al., 2024; Memarian & Doleck, 2023). The substantial savings in time due to immediacy and availability at ease is poisoning the entire student community's high-order thinking skills and also posing a subtle threat to the educators as their existence would be challenged in the future. The countries that banned the use of ChatGPT are Italy, Russia, China, North Korea, Cuba, Iran, and Syria (Paul et al., 2023; Stahl & Eke, 2024).

Table 2. Reasons for ChatGPT banned in some countries

Name of the Country	Reasons
Italy	ChatGPT's non compliance with the European General Data Protection (GDPR)
China	ChatGPT's noncompliance with the China's strict censorship laws, generation of irrelevant information, blocking of country's great firewall,
Russia	Banned due to nefarious reasons, the use of Chat GPT scaled up the unethical activities at a rapid rate.
North Korea	Banned due to rampant spread of misinformation.
Cuba	Banned due to the wrong movement of information.
Iran	Banned due to the deteriorating relation with United States of America
Syria	Banned to shield its populace from potential threats.

Some countries banned ChatGPT to arrest the malpractices exercised by the learners and also to harness the noble practice of learning. India banned in February 2023 the use of ChatGPT by the students of the Central Board of Secondary Education (CBSE) as the GPT-generated write-ups and outputs are massively utilized by the students and becoming indistinguishable from human work. The teaching community can verify the use of the tool by making the application of plagiarism detection tool, a tool named GPT Zero, conducting research in exam rooms to check the use of devices if any. The use of ChatGPT also intrudes into the privacy of the masses and disrupts the confidentiality of the facts as it can propel the continued growth of scams and scandals. It also creates phishing attacks. ChatGPT also leads to the development of bias. It creates outputs that are dominated by genders and races (Fütterer et al., 2023). The banning of the tool in the education sector is also followed by various schools of different countries which are outlined in a tabular manner below:

Table 3. Schools that have banned ChatGPT

Name of the Schools	Reasons for Banning the Use
New York City Department of Education	Concerns with regards to the bot's accuracy and also due to plagiarism.
Seattle Public Schools and Los Angeles Unified School District	To protect the academic integrity and to nurture the academic excellence.
Seattle Public Schools	The school rests on the original thoughts and genuine work from students
Baltimore County Public Schools in Maryland	Negated the access to the tool though technology not compromised.

SEVERE CONSEQUENCES OF AI IN EDUCATION

Educators and experts are increasingly concerned that the rising adoption of AI language models such as ChatGPT in educational settings may result in a dearth of intellectual curiosity and self-directed learning among pupils. The accessibility and efficiency of AI-powered text generation may dissuade students from cultivating their own concepts and engaging in autonomous investigation, resulting in a dearth of ingenuity and uniqueness in their academic endeavors. This issue is especially pertinent in disciplines that necessitate the use of discerning thought and examination, such as historical research, writing, and doctrines. Within these disciplines, students are required to actively interact with intricate concepts and viewpoints, as well as cultivate their own assertions and interpretations grounded in substantiated facts and thorough analysis. Excessive dependence on AI language models may erode these abilities and result in a dearth of intellectual curiosity and autonomous thinking. Additionally, the utilization of AI language models can give rise to ethical considerations regarding academic honesty and the act of plagiarizing. Although there may be debates regarding the classification of utilizing AI for text generation as plagiarism, it is crucial for students to acquire the skill of appropriately referencing sources and acknowledging the contributions of others.

The difficulty arises from the AI's deficiency in emotional intelligence, which hinders its comprehension and provision of support for students' emotional and psychological requirements. Human educators demonstrate exceptional proficiency in providing emotional support, empathy, and comprehension, which continue to be crucial components of education. Amidst a time of escalating automation, the teacher's responsibility in offering emotional support becomes increasingly crucial.

WILL AI CHANGE SOCIO ECONOMIC DIVIDE IN EDUCATION SECTOR?

An eminent obstacle in the realm of education presently is the task of confronting bias. Prejudice can appear in several forms, such as in the development of educational programs, instructional methods, and standardized assessments. AI can mitigate these prejudices by offering data-driven insights into potential areas of bias. Through the examination of data encompassing the entirety of the educational system, artificial intelligence (AI) can assist educators in recognizing and resolving prejudices present in their instructional techniques, curriculum development, and evaluation approaches. The digital divide is a substantial obstacle for numerous underprivileged communities. Insufficient availability of technology and internet connectivity might pose substantial obstacles to accessing educational opportunities. Nevertheless, AI has the potential to narrow the gap between those who have access to digital resources and those who do not by offering tailored educational routes that can be accessed from any internet-enabled device. This can facilitate equitable access to educational resources for kids in underprivileged groups, enabling them to enjoy the same opportunities as their more affluent peers. Over the past century, the concept of a bleak dystopian future dominated by artificial intelligence has been widely disseminated through science fiction films and novels. Given that the corporate sector plays a significant role in advancing AI research and implementation, concerns arise regarding their capacity to prioritize responsible and ethical behavior over profit-seeking, in addition to the widespread automation and resulting job displacement. Due to the rapid increase in data and computing capabilities, AI has garnered widespread attention, reached the peak of its popularity, and is influencing all aspects of life. Nevertheless, with the transfer of human cognitive abilities to robots, what will ensue? We have not yet witnessed. Will it result in unemployment or create additional employment opportunities? Will it enhance societal cohesion or promote prejudice? These questions arise in society as a result of the advancement of AI technology. Policy adjustments are necessary to mitigate the potential socio-economic disparity that may arise as a result of artificial intelligence. It is crucial to build upon the existing rules, regulations, standards, and concepts. The preparedness to accept AI is becoming more unequal between wealthy and poor nations. Advanced economies possess the necessary resources and are inclined to embrace automation due to the significant expenses associated with labor. Three key factors to tackle this gap include enhancing capabilities, facilitating technology transfer, and exploring international funding prospects.

FUTURE OF AI-ENABLED EDUCATION

There have been categories of the current AI software applications in education into three groups: a) customized coaches, b) competent assistance with learning through collaboration, and c) sophisticated augmented reality (AR) (Luckin & Holmes, 2016). Intelligent teaching systems (ITS) can replicate the experience of individualized human tutoring. Utilizing learner models, algorithms, and neural networks, a form of AI, these systems can determine the optimal learning trajectory for each learner and select appropriate information. They also offer cognitive support and facilitate discussion to engage the student actively. Intelligent teaching systems (ITS) possess immense potential, particularly at educational institutions that offer distance learning on a big scale (Touretzky et al., 2019). These schools sometimes have modules with thousands of students, making it impractical to provide individualized human coaching. Extensive research demonstrates that learning is inherently social, with interaction and collaboration playing a central role in the learning process (Jonassen et al., 1995).

LEARNERS CLASSIFICATION

Learner models or profiles serve as the foundation for numerous AI applications. These models enable the predicting of various outcomes, such as the probability of a student withdrawing from a course or gaining admission to a program. This prediction allows for timely support feedback and guidance on content-related issues during the learning process. Classification, modeling, and prediction are integral components of educational data mining. Precisely forecasting of students' academic performance is crucial for making admission decisions and enhancing educational services.

Many universities use Support Vector Machines (SVM) to predict admission accuracy of more than 95%. This technique can also indicate on prospective students from various geographical areas. Research focused on drop-out and retention aims to create early detection techniques to identify students who are in danger of leaving school within their initial year. AI can also support understanding the cognitive and noncognitive traits of students to predict their academic behavior.

For effective communication and collaboration with AI technologies in all aspects of life, education, and employment, it is essential to prioritize pedagogical approaches that focus on developing human abilities such as creativity, complex problem-solving, critical thinking, and teamwork. We thus propose developing a capacity approach as a reaction to this humanistic perspective. The problem field of designing for learning in an AI world encompasses humanistic methods, agency, co-creation, and welfare.

In education, AI-as-a-service applications can be identified by providing back-end infrastructure services by global technology companies to educational institutions or Edtech startups. Pearson, for instance, has collaborated with IBM to integrate Watson APIs into their courseware products as part of their initial efforts to develop AI-powered applications. Google's G Suite is well recognized as a collection of user-friendly applications designed for classroom use, as well as Google's infrastructure and APIs that extract data and allow for the integration of third-party products. Microsoft has recently initiated the promotion of its Power Platform for educational purposes. The Power Platform is a cohesive platform that allows organizations to seamlessly integrate multiple applications and data sources into a unified data model for analysis. It also offers standardized models and templates for organizations to develop their services and applications, all backed by Microsoft's Azure cloud computing service. Microsoft Education Team (2020) states that the software package consists of Power Apps, which allow educators to create their low-code applications, and Power Virtual Agents, which facilitate the creation and management of intelligent chatbots. These chatbots, such as the intelligent Question Bot, can autonomously provide answers to students, thereby promoting student independence and personalized learning. The Power Platform as an infrastructure technology that supports and strengthens the adoption of AI by educators and institutions (Kirschner & Stoyanov, 2020). In addition, Amazon has commenced promoting several educational services and technologies associated with its cloud architecture, Amazon Web Services (AWS).

These examples emphasize the significance of seeing AI in education as a product of past technology sector endeavors to expand AI systems into many businesses and behaviors. Significantly, they illustrate the growing integration of education with multinational private digital companies and the business principles of platform capitalism. They demonstrate the integration of AI into education through ordinary AI-as-a-service plugins that operate behind the scenes, rather than using more impressive automated teaching agents or tutoring systems. The genealogical progression of AI in education is markedly different from the endeavors of academic specialists and the specialized edtech industry. The significance of these infrastructural arrangements in schools and universities is currently still being determined. However, these arrangements will likely be increasingly used to manage and analyze data for institutional performance management. They may also be required for processes of governance and accountability (Garrett et al., 2020).

Figure 2. Fields of study which can be explored by AI

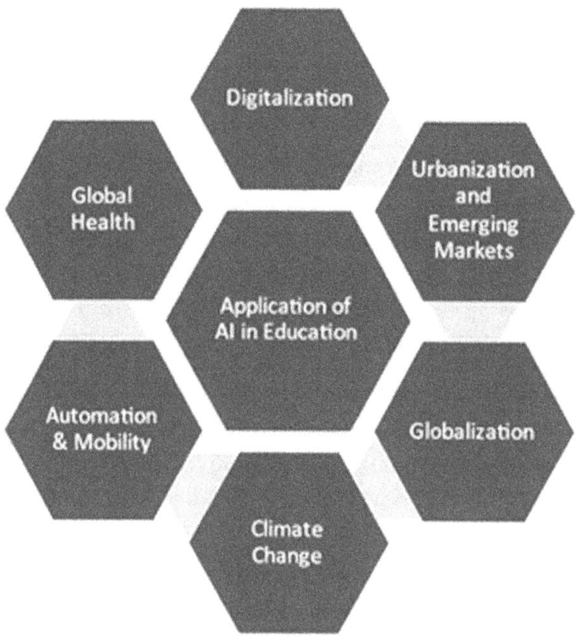

Artificial intelligence (AI) can be utilized to evaluate data from diverse sources and discern trends that can enhance the efficiency of cities, mitigate crime, and enhance public services. Artificial intelligence (AI) is a precious instrument for managing the risks and opportunities of globalization, and may be utilized to foster wealthier and fairer world (Demír & Demír, 2023). AI can assist in analyzing and forecasting the consequences of climate change on both the environment and society. AI technologies can enhance our capacity to predict weather patterns and climatic conditions. Artificial intelligence (AI) can automate numerous tasks that previously relied on human effort, hence allowing for the allocation of resources towards more innovative and high-value endeavors (Carvalho et al., 2022). A prominent advantage of AI in automation is its ability to generate cost savings. AI utilizes real-time data to forecast traffic patterns and enhance routes for both drivers and passengers, enabling individuals to evade crowded areas or select other paths during peak periods(Haluza & Jungwirth, 2023). Artificial intelligence can enhance significantly global health outcomes. A significant benefit of AI is its capacity to rapidly integrate vast quantities of data from many sources, such as electronic medical records, genomic data, imaging tests, and patient questionnaires (Demir & Demir, 2023; Goodyear et al., 2021). AI can also aid the aging population by offering support in performing daily tasks that may progressively become challenging for senior folks (Williamson & Eynon, 2020). AI-powered robots or virtual assistants can support elderly individuals in organizing their prescription routines, completing simple household tasks, and notifying them when it is necessary to pause from their regular activities.

SOLUTIONS AND RECOMMENDATIONS

The introduction of artificially intelligent content in educational tasks requires the revision of evaluation techniques and institutional rules. Teachers should enhance the design of tests and assignments by incorporating interactive tools to reduce the likelihood of plagiarism. ChatGPT's first version lacked the capability to process photographs and videos, resulting in a lack of context. This hindered learners who intended to utilize it for inappropriate activities. OpenAI's GPT-4, a large multimodal model, is capable of analyzing images. Learners are required to be physically present and demonstrate their skills in person for these components. AI-powered writing analysis technology could be provided to instructors at the institutional level. Defining the boundaries of ChatGPT's involvement in students' learning requires establishing guidelines to prevent plagiarism. Responding to the impact of ChatGPT also necessitates teacher training and education for students . It is essential to instruct educators on how to eliminate opportunities for plagiarism in assessments. Training can be offered to identify the use of ChatGPT in learner activities using AI content identification toolkits. Teachers should undergo training to utilize ChatGPT in their lesson planning and program assessment effectively. Educating learners about ChatGPT's limitations is crucial, such as its dependence on biased data, outdated information, and potential to generate inaccurate or deceptive results. Verify, assess, and confirm the accuracy of ChatGPT's content by consulting other credible sources such reference books, as recommended by educators . Enhancing students' understanding of academic integrity policies and consequences for academic dishonesty is crucial.

FUTURE RESEARCH DIRECTIONS

Prohibiting or restricting ChatGPT will not resolve the issue. It is better to acknowledge it and create clear guidelines for its use in academic environments. ChatGPT poses a significant threat to existing evaluation methodologies. Future evaluation models should prioritize autonomous and introspective thinking, logical reasoning, sophisticated problem-solving utilizing AI tools, inventive thinking, and rigorous data validation. Increased monitoring and transparency will be necessary as ChatGPT advances to differentiate between content generated by humans and artificial intelligence. Regulators are lagging behind technological progress, but the ongoing conversation among all stakeholders will likely result in legislative measures. In quick engineering, creative ways are needed to improve and optimize the queries given to ChatGPT in order to ensure accurate, engaging, and relevant responses. Students with special needs may face extra obstacles when trying to use a chatbot. Individuals with intellectual limitations may need further assistance with chatbot material. Instructors must ensure that learners who have challenges can receive the necessary support to comprehend and utilize chatbots, whereas learners with visual impairments may encounter difficulties in viewing chatbot information. Instructors must ensure that learners facing difficulties receive the necessary help.Today, learning and assessment are continuous processes that extend beyond the school sector into the commercial world. Concurrent possibilities and problems emerge, such as evaluating and recruiting a software engineer through a coding challenge or assimilating a new hire into an organization's business and technical functions. ChatGPT could be highly advantageous if it helps developers produce more reliable software in less time. It is our duty as educators to instruct software engineers on how to effectively handle and evaluate technology for the best outcomes, requiring a clear record of actions.

CONCLUSION

Despite the potential of ITS, several challenges persist. Ethical concerns regarding data privacy and algorithm biases require careful consideration (Gligorea et al., 2023). Additionally, equitable access to ITS remains a challenge, particularly for students in underserved communities or with limited technological resources.

The effectiveness of Intelligent Tutoring Systems in education, particularly in enhancing learning outcomes, promoting engagement, and offering personalized learning experiences across diverse subjects. While promising, further research is needed to address ethical concerns, ensure accessibility, and explore the long-term effects of ITS on educational practices.

With the ongoing advancement of AI, it is imperative for the job of a teacher in the classroom to undergo a constructive evolution. Although AI efficiently disseminates information, educators provide distinct expertise and capabilities, enhancing the educational experience. Teachers who actively embrace ongoing learning and flexibility are essential. They adapt to the evolving educational landscape, continuously improving their abilities and keeping up with technological innovations and teaching approaches.

A teacher's responsibility encompasses more than just the transmission of information. They offer advice, mentorship, inspiration, and the cultivation of critical thinking abilities. In the current era, AI is responsible for handling monotonous tasks, while educators focus on fostering distinctly human qualities such as creativity, empathy, and flexibility.

Teachers not only transmit knowledge but also play a crucial role in molding students' character and values. They provide the necessary ethical and social guidance for safely navigating the digital realm, highlighting the significance of ethical conduct and responsible utilization of AI.

Integrating AI in education represents a transformative shift towards personalized, efficient, and inclusive learning environments. While AI presents numerous opportunities for enhancing education, challenges related to ethical considerations, data privacy, and equitable access must be addressed. As research and development in AI continue, its potential to revolutionize education remains a promising frontier.

REFERENCES

androiddeveloper.co.in. (2023, July 20). *The Transformative Impact of ChatGPT in the Education Sector*. Android Developer. https://www.androiddeveloper.co.in/blog/impact-of-chatgpt-in-the-education-sector/

Afzal, A., Khan, S., Daud, S., Ahmed, Z., & Butt, A. (2023). Addressing the Digital Divide. *Access and Use of Technology in Education.*, *3*(2), 883–895. doi:10.54183/jssr.v3i2.326

Baidoo-Anu, D., & Owusu Ansah, L. (2023). Education in the Era of Generative Artificial Intelligence (AI): Understanding the Potential Benefits of ChatGPT in Promoting Teaching and Learning. SSRN *Electronic Journal*. doi:10.2139/ssrn.4337484

Carvalho, L., Martinez-Maldonado, R., Tsai, Y.-S., Markauskaite, L., & De Laat, M. (2022). How can we design for learning in an AI world? *Computers and Education: Artificial Intelligence*, *3*, 100053. doi:10.1016/j.caeai.2022.100053

Demir, M., & Demir, Ş. Ş. (2023). Is ChatGPT the right technology for service individualization and value co-creation? Evidence from the travel industry. *Journal of Travel & Tourism Marketing*, *40*(5), 383–398. doi:10.1080/10548408.2023.2255884

Demír, Ş. Ş., & Demír, M. (2023). Professionals' perspectives on ChatGPT in the tourism industry: Does it inspire awe or concern? *Journal of Tourism Theory and Research*, *9*(2), 61–77. doi:10.24288/jttr.1313481

Fütterer, T., Fischer, C., Alekseeva, A., Chen, X., Tate, T., Warschauer, M., & Gerjets, P. (2023). ChatGPT in education: Global reactions to AI innovations. *Scientific Reports*, *13*(1), 15310. doi:10.1038/s41598-023-42227-6 PMID:37714915

Garrett, N., Beard, N., & Fiesler, C. (2020). More Than "If Time Allows": The Role of Ethics in AI Education. *Proceedings of the AAAI/ACM Conference on AI, Ethics, and Society*, 272–278. 10.1145/3375627.3375868

Gligorea, I., Cioca, M., Oancea, R., Gorski, A.-T., Gorski, H., & Tudorache, P. (2023). Adaptive Learning Using Artificial Intelligence in e-Learning: A Literature Review. *Education Sciences*, *13*(12), 12. Advance online publication. doi:10.3390/educsci13121216

Goodyear, P., Carvalho, L., & Yeoman, P. (2021). Activity-Centred Analysis and Design (ACAD): Core purposes, distinctive qualities and current developments. *Educational Technology Research and Development*, *69*(2), 445–464. doi:10.1007/s11423-020-09926-7 PMID:33456288

Gursoy, D., Li, Y., & Song, H. (2023). ChatGPT and the hospitality and tourism industry: An overview of current trends and future research directions. *Journal of Hospitality Marketing & Management*, *32*(5), 579–592. doi:10.1080/19368623.2023.2211993

HaluzaD.JungwirthD. (2023). Artificial Intelligence and Ten Societal Megatrends: A GPT-3 Case Study [Preprint]. doi:10.20944/preprints202301.0474.v1

Iskender, A. (2023). Holy or Unholy? Interview with Open AI's ChatGPT. *European Journal of Tourism Research, 34*, 3414. doi:10.54055/ejtr.v34i.3169

Jonassen, D., Davidson, M., Collins, M., Campbell, J., & Bannan, B. (1995). Constructivism and Computer-Mediated Communication in Distance Education. *American Journal of Distance Education, 9*(2), 7–26. doi:10.1080/08923649509526885

Kirschner, P. A., & Stoyanov, S. (2020). Educating Youth for Nonexistent/Not Yet Existing Professions. *Educational Policy, 34*(3), 477–517. doi:10.1177/0895904818802086

Kumar, A., Gupta, N., & Bapat, G. (2023). Who is making the decisions? How retail managers can use the power of ChatGPT. *The Journal of Business Strategy*. Advance online publication. doi:10.1108/JBS-04-2023-0067

Leu. (2023). *Summary of ChatGPT-Related Research and Perspective Towards the Future of Large Language Models*. . doi:10.1016/j.metrad.2023.100017

Luckin, R., & Holmes, W. (2016). Intelligence Unleashed: An argument for AI in Education. In *UCL Knowledge Lab: London, UK*. UCL Knowledge Lab. https://www.pearson.com/content/dam/corporate/global/pearson-dot-com/files/innovation/Intelligence-Unleashed-Publication.pdf

Makhambetova, A., Zhiyenbayeva, N., & Ergesheva, E. (2021). Personalized Learning Strategy as a Tool to Improve Academic Performance and Motivation of Students. *International Journal of Web-Based Learning and Teaching Technologies, 16*(6), 1–17. doi:10.4018/IJWLTT.286743

Memarian, B., & Doleck, T. (2023). ChatGPT in education: Methods, potentials, and limitations. *Computers in Human Behavior: Artificial Humans, 1*(2), 100022. doi:10.1016/j.chbah.2023.100022

Paul, J., Ueno, A., & Dennis, C. (2023). ChatGPT and consumers: Benefits, Pitfalls and Future Research Agenda. *International Journal of Consumer Studies, 47*(4), 1213–1225. doi:10.1111/ijcs.12928

Shemshack, A., & Spector, J. M. (2020). A systematic literature review of personalized learning terms. *Smart Learning Environments, 7*(1), 33. doi:10.1186/s40561-020-00140-9

Smale-Jacobse, A. E., Meijer, A., Helms-Lorenz, M., & Maulana, R. (2019). Differentiated Instruction in Secondary Education: A Systematic Review of Research Evidence. *Frontiers in Psychology, 10*, 2366. doi:10.3389/fpsyg.2019.02366 PMID:31824362

Stahl, B. C., & Eke, D. (2024). The ethics of ChatGPT – Exploring the ethical issues of an emerging technology. *International Journal of Information Management*, *74*, 102700. doi:10.1016/j.ijinfomgt.2023.102700

Touretzky, D., Gardner-McCune, C., Martin, F., & Seehorn, D. (2019). Envisioning AI for K-12: What Should Every Child Know about AI? *Proceedings of the AAAI Conference on Artificial Intelligence*, *33*(01), 01. Advance online publication. doi:10.1609/aaai.v33i01.33019795

Triantoro, S. (2013). Effects of Self-Efficacy on Students' Academic Performance. *Journal of Educational. Health and Community Psychology*, *2*, 19–25.

Von Garrel, J., & Mayer, J. (2023). Artificial Intelligence in studies—Use of ChatGPT and AI-based tools among students in Germany. *Humanities & Social Sciences Communications*, *10*(1), 799. doi:10.1057/s41599-023-02304-7

Williamson, B., & Eynon, R. (2020). Historical threads, missing links, and future directions in AI in education. *Learning, Media and Technology*, *45*(3), 223–235. doi:10.1080/17439884.2020.1798995

Zhang, L., Basham, J., & Yang, S. (2020). Understanding the implementation of personalized learning: A research synthesis. *Educational Research Review*, *31*, 100339. doi:10.1016/j.edurev.2020.100339

Zheng, L., Long, M., Zhong, L., & Gyasi, J. F. (2022). The effectiveness of technology-facilitated personalized learning on learning achievements and learning perceptions: A meta-analysis. *Education and Information Technologies*, *27*(8), 11807–11830. doi:10.1007/s10639-022-11092-7

ADDITIONAL READING

Akgun, S., & Greenhow, C. (2022). Artificial intelligence in education: Addressing ethical challenges in K-12 settings. *AI and Ethics*, *2*(3), 431–440. doi:10.1007/s43681-021-00096-7 PMID:34790956

AymanS. E.El-SeoudS.NagatyK.KaramO. (2023). The Impact of ChatGPT on Student Learning/performing. doi:10.13140/RG.2.2.28890.11205

Chaudhry, M. A., & Kazim, E. (2022). Artificial Intelligence in Education (AIEd): A high-level academic and industry note 2021. *AI and Ethics*, *2*(1), 157–165. doi:10.1007/s43681-021-00074-z PMID:34790953

Demir, M., & Demir, Ş. Ş. (2023). Is ChatGPT the right technology for service individualization and value co-creation? Evidence from the travel industry. *Journal of Travel & Tourism Marketing*, *40*(5), 383–398. doi:10.1080/10548408.2023.2255884

Dwivedi, Y. K., Kshetri, N., Hughes, L., Slade, E. L., Jeyaraj, A., Kar, A. K., Baabdullah, A. M., Koohang, A., Raghavan, V., Ahuja, M., Albanna, H., Albashrawi, M. A., Al-Busaidi, A. S., Balakrishnan, J., Barlette, Y., Basu, S., Bose, I., Brooks, L., Buhalis, D., ... Wright, R. (2023). Opinion Paper: "So what if ChatGPT wrote it?" Multidisciplinary perspectives on opportunities, challenges and implications of generative conversational AI for research, practice and policy. *International Journal of Information Management*, *71*, 102642. doi:10.1016/j.ijinfomgt.2023.102642

Glaser, N. (2023). Exploring the Potential of ChatGPT as an Educational Technology: An Emerging Technology Report. *Tech Know Learn*, *28*(4), 1945–1952. doi:10.1007/s10758-023-09684-4

Gursoy, D., Li, Y., & Song, H. (2023). ChatGPT and the hospitality and tourism industry: An overview of current trends and future research directions. *Journal of Hospitality Marketing & Management*, *32*(5), 579–592. doi:10.1080/19368623.2023.2211993

Iskender, A. (2023). Holy or Unholy? Interview with Open AI's ChatGPT. *European Journal of Tourism Research*, *34*, 3414. doi:10.54055/ejtr.v34i.3169

Lo, C. K. (2023). What Is the Impact of ChatGPT on Education? A Rapid Review of the Literature. *Education Sciences*, *13*(4), 410. doi:10.3390/educsci13040410

Tlili, A., Shehata, B., Adarkwah, M. A., Bozkurt, A., Hickey, D. T., Huang, R., & Agyemang, B. (2023). What if the devil is my guardian angel: ChatGPT as a case study of using chatbots in education. *Smart Learn. Environ.*, *10*(1), 15. doi:10.1186/s40561-023-00237-x

Yu, H. (2023). Reflection on whether Chat GPT should be banned by academia from the perspective of education and teaching. *Frontiers in Psychology*, *14*, 1181712. doi:10.3389/fpsyg.2023.1181712 PMID:37325766

Zhang. (2021). *AI technologies for education: Recent research & future directions.* doi:10.1016/j.caeai.2021.100025

KEY TERMS AND DEFINITIONS

Artificial Intelligence: Refers to the cognitive abilities exhibited by computers or software, in contrast to the cognitive abilities displayed by humans or other animals. Artificial Intelligence is a discipline within computer science that focuses on the development and analysis of intelligent machines.

Intelligent Tutoring Systems: Represent an innovative approach to personalized learning, leveraging artificial intelligence to provide tailored and interactive guidance to students. Intelligent Tutoring Systems (ITS) utilize AI to provide customized and interactive guidance to students.

Personalized Learning: Is a pedagogical approach aimed at tailoring education to individual student needs, preferences, and learning styles. AI facilitates personalized learning experiences by analyzing students' learning patterns, preferences, and abilities. Adaptive learning platforms leverage AI algorithms to tailor educational content and pacing, allowing students to learn at their own pace (Zhang et al., 2020).

Chapter 10
Building Trust and Credibility:
Ethical Use of AI in the Service Industry

Mahmut Demir
Isparta University of Applied Sciences, Turkey

ABSTRACT

This chapter aims to elucidate the ethical imperatives in deploying AI technologies within the service sector. By examining a spectrum of ethical dimensions, ranging from transparency and fairness to privacy and accountability, this study provides a comprehensive framework for fostering trust and credibility in AI-driven service offerings. This chapter offers actionable guidance to stakeholders seeking to navigate the ethical complexities of AI integration. Furthermore, it aims to contribute to the ongoing discourse surrounding the development of ethical AI guidelines and policies tailored to the unique challenges and opportunities within the service industry. The progression of this chapter is structured around a holistic exploration of ethical considerations pertinent to AI deployment in the service industry.

INTRODUCTION

Integrating Artificial Intelligence (AI) into the service industry has ushered in transformative opportunities, revolutionizing customer experiences, operational efficiencies, and business strategies (Demir & Demir, 2023a). However, amidst the proliferation of AI-driven solutions, concerns surrounding ethics and responsible use have emerged as paramount considerations. The delicate balance between innovation and ethical stewardship emphasizes that organizations must navigate the ethical environment with vigilance and integrity (Dalgıç et al., 2024).

DOI: 10.4018/979-8-3693-1239-1.ch010

In pursuing ethical AI deployment, transparency emerges as a foundational principle, enabling stakeholders to comprehend the inner workings of AI systems and the rationale behind their decisions (Memarian & Doleck, 2023). By promoting transparency, organizations can build trust and confidence among users, mitigating concerns surrounding algorithmic opacity and unpredictability. Likewise, explainability is pivotal, particularly in service industries where AI influences critical outcomes such as healthcare diagnoses and financial decisions. Through transparent and explainable AI systems, organizations can empower users to make informed choices, fostering a culture of accountability and ethical stewardship.

Fairness and bias mitigation represent another critical dimension of ethical AI deployment, particularly when AI algorithms significantly influence human lives and livelihoods (Ferrara, 2023). The pervasiveness of algorithmic bias underscores organizations' need to identify and mitigate biases that may perpetuate discriminatory outcomes proactively. Moreover, accountability and oversight mechanisms ensure AI systems operate under ethical norms and regulatory standards. By establishing robust governance frameworks and oversight mechanisms, organizations can uphold accountability and mitigate the risks associated with AI deployment in service contexts.

This chapter aims to elucidate the ethical imperatives in deploying AI technologies within the service sector. By examining a spectrum of ethical dimensions, ranging from transparency and fairness to privacy and accountability, this study provides a comprehensive framework for fostering trust and credibility in AI-driven service offerings. This chapter offers actionable guidance to stakeholders seeking to navigate the ethical complexities of AI integration. Furthermore, it aims to contribute to the ongoing discourse surrounding the development of ethical AI guidelines and policies tailored to the unique challenges and opportunities within the service industry. The progression of this chapter is structured around a holistic exploration of ethical considerations pertinent to AI deployment in the service industry.

BACKGROUND

Literature Review

Understanding Ethical AI in Service Industries

In contemporary discourse, as AI continues to permeate diverse industries such as healthcare, finance, retail, and customer service, the ethical implications of its implementation become increasingly paramount. The burgeoning presence of AI in service industries necessitates a parallel focus on its ethical implications (Demir & Demir, 2023b). This necessitates a multifaceted approach, encompassing not only the technology itself but also its development, deployment, and societal impact. Several core ethical principles underpin responsible AI development in service industries. These principles, often outlined in industry codes or academic frameworks, provide a foundation for building trust and mitigating risks (Habbal et al., 2024; Unver, 2023). Some prominent examples include transparency and explainability, fairness and bias mitigation, accountability, and oversight, protecting privacy and data security, empowering human oversight and intervention, developing ethical ai guidelines and policies, and ethical technology practices.

One prominent ethical framework in AI development is utilitarianism (Sebo, 2023), which evaluates actions based on their outcomes and seeks to maximize overall societal welfare. Utilitarianism may guide AI developers and service providers in the context of service industries to prioritize solutions that optimize benefits for the greatest number of stakeholders while minimizing harm. For instance, in healthcare, AI-powered diagnostic tools can improve patient outcomes by enhancing accuracy and efficiency in disease detection and treatment planning. Deontological ethics emphasizes the importance of adhering to moral principles and duties irrespective of consequences (Boddington, 2023; Schurr & Moran, 2023). Applied to AI in service industries, this framework underscores the significance of respecting individual rights, autonomy, and privacy. For example, AI algorithms for financial credit scoring must ensure fairness and transparency to avoid perpetuating biases or discrimination against certain demographic groups. Virtue ethics focuses on cultivating virtuous character traits and intentions in decision-making (Heyder et al., 2023; Smith & Vickers, 2024). In AI ethics, this perspective encourages developers and practitioners to embody virtues such as fairness, honesty, and empathy. In customer service, AI chatbots can be programmed to exhibit empathy and emotional intelligence when interacting with users, fostering positive customer experiences and relationships.

Drawing upon theoretical frameworks and real-world examples, ethical considerations in AI implementation can vary across service industries.

Education: In education, AI-powered tools offer opportunities for personalized learning, adaptive assessment, and administrative optimization (Dalgıç et al., 2024). However, ethical challenges include data privacy concerns, algorithmic transparency, and equitable access to educational resources. For example, AI tutors must ensure fairness and inclusivity by adapting teaching strategies to accommodate diverse learning styles and backgrounds, thereby avoiding exacerbating educational inequalities.

Tourism: AI applications in the tourism industry range from chatbots for customer service to recommendation systems for personalized travel itineraries (Demir & Demir, 2023b). Ethical considerations encompass data privacy, cultural sensitivity, and the preservation of authentic travel experiences. For instance, AI-driven recommendation engines must balance commercial interests with promoting lesser-known destinations to mitigate over-tourism and support sustainable tourism practices.

Transportation: Autonomous vehicles (AVs) represent a significant advancement in transportation, promising enhanced safety, efficiency, and accessibility (Kumar, 2024). Ethical considerations in AV deployment encompass liability issues, algorithmic decision-making, and societal implications such as job displacement. Ensuring the ethical design of AV algorithms is crucial to prioritizing human safety, minimizing accidents, and navigating moral dilemmas in emergencies (Resnik & Andrews, 2023).

Arts: AI technologies are increasingly employed in creating, curating, and disseminating artistic content, raising questions about authorship, creativity, and cultural appropriation (Radanliev & De Roure, 2023). For instance, AI-generated artworks challenge traditional notions of artistic expression and intellectual property rights, necessitating critical reflection on the role of AI as a creative collaborator or tool.

Healthcare: IBM's Watson for Oncology provides oncologists with AI-driven insights and treatment recommendations based on vast medical literature and patient data (Chaurasia, 2023; Baihakki & Qutayan, 2023). However, concerns have been raised regarding the transparency of Watson's recommendations and potential biases in its algorithms, highlighting ethical challenges related to accountability and patient safety. AI-assisted medical diagnosis requires explainability. Doctors should understand the reasoning behind an AI's conclusions to ensure accurate diagnoses and treatment plans. Additionally, ensuring patient data privacy in AI-powered healthcare systems is paramount.

Finance: Automated algorithmic trading systems in the financial industry have raised ethical questions about market manipulation, fairness, and systemic risks (Meneceur, 2023; Römer et al., 2023). High-frequency trading algorithms, for instance, can execute trades at speeds imperceptible to human traders, potentially exacerbating market volatility and disparities in market access. AI-powered credit scoring algorithms must be demonstrably fair and unbiased to avoid discriminatory lending practices. Additionally, transparency in interest rate calculations and risk assessments based on AI models is crucial.

Retail: Personalized recommendation systems employed by e-commerce platforms utilize AI algorithms to analyze consumer behavior and preferences, enhancing user experience and driving sales (Lund et al., 2023; Pappas et al., 2023). Nevertheless, there are ethical considerations surrounding data privacy, as these systems often collect and utilize vast amounts of personal data without adequate consent or transparency. Recommendation engines that leverage customer data raise privacy concerns. Balancing personalization with user privacy by offering opt-out options and anonymized data analysis is an ethical imperative.

Customer Service: AI chatbots can improve customer service efficiency, but over-reliance on them can lead to frustration if human support is unavailable for complex issues (Chen et al., 2023; Rivas & Zhao, 2023). Striking a balance between AI automation and human interaction is an ethical consideration.

Navigating the ethical dimensions of AI in service industries requires a nuanced understanding of ethical frameworks, real-world implications, and proactive strategies for ethical AI development and governance. By prioritizing ethical considerations alongside technological advancements, stakeholders can harness the transformative potential of AI while upholding fundamental principles of fairness, accountability, and respect for human values and dignity.

Transparency and Explainability

In service industries, where AI increasingly shapes customer interactions and decision-making processes, transparency and explainability become cornerstones of ethical and trustworthy AI implementation (Aranovich & Matulionyte, 2023; Yordanova, 2023). However, concerns regarding AI algorithms' opaque decision-making processes have underscored the importance of transparency and explainability. Transparency refers to the openness and accessibility of AI algorithms, data sources, and decision-making processes to stakeholders, including end-users, regulators, and affected communities (Balasubramaniam et al., 2023; Kawamleh, 2023). Explainability pertains to the ability of AI systems to provide understandable rationales for their decisions or recommendations, enabling users to comprehend the underlying logic and potential biases (Cortese et al., 2023; Fernandez-Quilez, 2023). Despite their importance, achieving transparency and explainability in AI presents multifaceted challenges. These challenges include the complexity of AI algorithms, proprietary concerns among technology developers, regulatory ambiguity, and the potential trade-offs between transparency and performance.

Promoting transparency and explainability in AI systems yields several benefits for both service providers and end-users (Aranovich & Matulionyte, 2023; Balasubramaniam et al., 2023). Transparent AI systems enhance accountability, facilitate regulatory compliance, mitigate algorithmic biases, and empower users to make informed decisions. Explainable AI fosters user trust, improves user satisfaction, and enables effective human-AI collaboration in service delivery. Implementing best practices is crucial for promoting transparency and explainability in AI-driven service environments. These practices include adopting open-source AI frameworks, documenting AI development processes, providing user-friendly explanations of AI decisions, conducting algorithmic audits, and fostering a culture of ethical AI governance within organizations (Aranovich & Matulionyte, 2023; Fernandez-Quilez, 2023).

Transparency and explainability are indispensable pillars for fostering trust and credibility in AI-driven service environments (Fernandez-Quilez, 2023; Kawamleh, 2023; Yordanova, 2023). Service providers enhance user trust, mitigate risks, and uphold ethical principles by prioritizing transparency and explainability in AI development and deployment. Continued research and collaboration are essential for advancing best practices and regulatory frameworks that promote transparent and explainable AI in the service industry (Aranovich & Matulionyte, 2023). Transparency and explainability are not simply technical hurdles but ethical imperatives in developing trustworthy AI for service industries. By embracing these concepts and developing effective explanation techniques, businesses can build customer trust and ensure that AI drives positive change within this crucial sector.

When customers understand how AI systems work, they will make informed decisions about interacting with them. Explaining how a recommendation engine personalizes suggestions can build user trust in the service. Explainable AI empowers human service providers to understand the reasoning behind AI decisions and intervene when necessary (Balasubramaniam et al., 2023; Cortese et al., 2023). For instance, a healthcare professional could review an AI-assisted diagnosis and provide a more nuanced interpretation based on their expertise. Improved understanding of an AI model's inner workings facilitates identifying and addressing potential biases in the training data. This helps build fairer and more equitable service experiences. AI systems trained on biased data can perpetuate discriminatory practices (Cortese et al., 2023; Kawamleh, 2023). Without transparency, such biases can go unnoticed, leading to unfair outcomes in service delivery.

Fairness and Bias Mitigation

Ensuring fairness and mitigating biases in AI systems is imperative for fostering trust and credibility within the service industry. Fairness in AI refers to the equitable treatment of individuals or groups across diverse demographic categories, such as race, gender, or socioeconomic status (Ferrara, 2023; Guimarães et al., 2023). Conversely, bias occurs when AI algorithms systematically favor or disadvantage certain groups, leading to unfair outcomes. Addressing biases in AI requires identifying sources of bias, assessing their impact, and implementing mitigation strategies.

The service industry thrives on trust. Customers expect interactions to be fair, unbiased, and based on their unique needs. AI systems can perpetuate or amplify biases in the data they are trained on. These biases can lead to discriminatory outcomes in service delivery, eroding trust and creating ethical dilemmas. Fairness and bias mitigation are not afterthoughts in service industry AI; they are fundamental ethical considerations (Deho et al., 2022; Pagano et al., 2023). By prioritizing these aspects and actively mitigating bias, businesses can build trust, ensure equitable service delivery, and contribute to a more ethical and inclusive service industry. Achieving fairness and bias mitigation in AI poses numerous challenges, including the inherent complexity of AI algorithms, the scarcity of diverse and representative training data, and the potential amplification of societal biases encoded in historical data (Guimarães et al., 2023; Hagendorff et al., 2023). Moreover, trade-offs between fairness and other performance metrics, such as accuracy or efficiency, further complicate the pursuit of fairness in AI systems.

Implementing best practices is essential for promoting fairness and mitigating biases in AI-driven service environments. These practices include collecting diverse and representative training data, conducting bias audits and impact assessments, implementing fairness-aware algorithms, and fostering interdisciplinary collaborations between data scientists, ethicists, and domain experts (Hagendorff et al., 2023; John-Mathews et al., 2022). Numerous examples from the service industry illustrate the significance of fairness and bias mitigation in AI applications. In hiring and recruitment, AI-powered resume screening tools must mitigate biases to ensure equal opportunities for job candidates from diverse backgrounds. Similarly, AI-driven risk assessment tools in criminal justice must avoid perpetuating racial or socioeconomic biases in sentencing decisions. Fairness and bias mitigation are critical pillars for upholding trust and credibility in AI-driven service environments (Deho et al., 2022; Guimarães et al., 2023). By prioritizing fairness and implementing bias mitigation strategies, service providers can enhance user trust, promote social justice, and mitigate potential harms associated with algorithmic biases. Research and collaboration are essential for advancing ethical AI practices and regulatory frameworks that promote fairness in the service industry (John-Mathews et al., 2022; Pagano et al., 2023).

Accountability and Oversight

Accountability and oversight mechanisms are crucial in promoting the ethical use of AI within the service industry. The challenges and opportunities associated with accountability and oversight provide insights into fostering trust and credibility in AI-driven service environments (Almeida et al., 2022; Attard-Frost et al., 2023). In recent years, the proliferation of AI technologies in the service industry has raised concerns about accountability and oversight. Ensuring that AI systems are used ethically and responsibly requires robust mechanisms for accountability and oversight (Burr & Leslie, 2023; Gardner et al., 2022). Accountability entails the responsibility of AI developers, service providers, and stakeholders to ensure that AI systems operate ethically and transparently (Sand et al., 2022; Tóth et al., 2022). Oversight refers to the mechanisms, regulations, and governance structures designed to monitor and regulate AI deployment to mitigate risks and ensure compliance with ethical standards and legal requirements (Demir & Demir, 2023b; Gardner et al., 2022).

Ethical frameworks provide guiding principles for promoting accountability and oversight in AI development and deployment (Almeida et al., 2022; Sand et al., 2022;). This emphasizes the importance of adherence to moral principles and duties, urging AI stakeholders to prioritize transparency, fairness, and accountability in their decision-making processes (Attard-Frost et al., 2023). Achieving accountability and oversight in AI applications presents multifaceted challenges, including the complexity of AI algorithms, the lack of transparency in proprietary AI systems, the rapid pace of technological advancements, and the global nature of AI deployment, which complicates regulatory harmonization and enforcement (Burr & Leslie, 2023; Tóth et al., 2022).

Accountability and oversight are fundamental components of ethical AI use in the service industry (Almeida et al., 2022; Burr & Leslie, 2023). By prioritizing accountability and implementing robust oversight mechanisms, service providers can enhance trust and credibility, mitigate risks, and uphold ethical principles in AI-driven service environments. These practices include establishing clear guidelines and standards for AI development and deployment, conducting regular audits and evaluations of AI systems, fostering transparency and stakeholder engagement, and ensuring robust mechanisms for reporting and addressing ethical concerns (Attard-Frost et al., 2023; Sand et al., 2022). Accountability and oversight are not burdensome for service industry AI; they are essential safeguards for building trust and ensuring ethical service delivery. By establishing clear lines of responsibility, implementing robust oversight mechanisms, and fostering collaboration amongst stakeholders, the service industry can harness the power of AI for positive change and build a future where AI serves customers fairly and ethically.

Protecting Privacy and Data Security

Service industry AI systems often operate on vast customer data, encompassing personal information, purchase history, and online behavior. Leveraging this data effectively unlocks opportunities for personalization, improved service delivery, and targeted marketing. However, this reliance on data comes with a critical responsibility: protecting customer privacy and data security. Privacy refers to individuals' rights to control their personal information's collection, use, and dissemination (Saeed et al., 2024). Data security encompasses measures and protocols to protect data from unauthorized access, disclosure, or modification (Wang, 2024). Ensuring privacy and data security in AI applications involves implementing robust safeguards to mitigate risks and uphold ethical standards.

Protecting privacy and ensuring data security in AI applications presents multifaceted challenges, including the vast amounts of data collected and processed by AI systems, the complexity of AI algorithms, the proliferation of cyber threats and vulnerabilities, and the evolving regulatory environment governing data protection and privacy rights (e.g., Kolhar & Aldossary, 2023; Saeed et al., 2024). New data collection methods and security threats emerge constantly. Businesses need to adapt their data protection strategies to keep pace with technological advancements. On the other hand, overly stringent security measures can hinder user experience. Striking the right balance between robust security and user-friendly interfaces is crucial.

Implementing best practices is crucial for protecting privacy and ensuring data security in AI-driven service environments. These practices include adopting privacy-preserving AI algorithms, implementing encryption and access controls, conducting regular data audits and risk assessments, and fostering a culture of data ethics and compliance within organizations. Many examples (e.g., Kolhar & Aldossary, 2023; Saeed et al., 2024; Wong, 2024) from the service industry illustrate the importance of privacy protection and data security in AI applications. AI-driven medical diagnosis systems must comply with stringent privacy regulations such as the Health Insurance Portability and Accountability Act (HIPAA) to safeguard patient confidentiality (Bender & Price II, 2024; Tomar & Sharma, 2024). Similarly, in e-commerce, robust data encryption and authentication mechanisms protect consumers' financial information from cyber threats and unauthorized access.

Protecting privacy and ensuring data security are essential for ethical AI use in the service industry. Protecting customer privacy and data security is not an afterthought in the service industry AI but an ethical imperative (Wang, 2024; Wong, 2024). By prioritizing data protection, implementing robust security measures, and fostering a culture of privacy awareness, businesses can build trust, ensure responsible AI development, and contribute to a service industry where customer data is respected and secure. By prioritizing privacy protection and implementing robust data security measures, service providers can enhance trust and credibility, mitigate risks, and uphold ethical principles in AI-driven service environments.

Empowering Human Oversight and Intervention

"Empowering Human Oversight and Intervention" is a critical aspect of ensuring the ethical use of AI in the service industry (Endsley, 2023; Fanni et al., 2023). In the context of AI applications, human oversight refers to the active involvement of human agents in monitoring, controlling, and intervening in AI-driven processes to ensure they align with ethical standards, legal requirements, and organizational values (Fanni et al., 2023; Zhang, 2024). This concept is particularly pertinent given the increasing reliance on AI systems across various service sectors, ranging from customer support and recommendation systems to financial analysis and healthcare diagnostics.

Human-in-the-loop (HITL) systems directly integrate human judgment and intervention into AI workflows (Mosqueira-Rey et al., 2023). These systems leverage the strengths of both AI algorithms and human cognition, allowing humans to review AI-generated outputs, provide feedback, and intervene when errors or ethical concerns arise (Amugongo et al., 2023; Zhang, 2024). HITL approaches are particularly valuable in high-stakes domains where the consequences of AI errors can be severe, such as healthcare diagnosis or autonomous vehicle operation (Mosqueira-Rey et al., 2023).

Research on AI ethics (e.g., Endsley, 2023; Moore et al., 2023; Pisoni & Díaz-Rodríguez, 2023) has led to the development of various ethical frameworks and guidelines that inform the design, deployment, and oversight of AI systems in the service industry. These frameworks, such as fairness, accountability, transparency, and explainability (FATE), provide principled approaches to address ethical challenges in AI (Fanni et al., 2023; Moore et al., 2023). By adhering to established ethical principles, service providers can empower human oversight and intervention to uphold ethical standards and mitigate potential harms associated with AI deployment. Human-centric design approaches prioritize human stakeholders' needs, preferences, and values throughout the AI development lifecycle (Endsley, 2023; Moore et al., 2023). By involving end-users, domain experts, ethicists, and other relevant stakeholders in the design process, service providers can better anticipate the potential impacts of AI systems and design interfaces that facilitate human oversight and intervention. User-friendly dashboards, decision support tools, and alert mechanisms empower humans to monitor AI performance and intervene proactively when necessary (Fanni et al., 2023; Zhang, 2024).

Effective human oversight requires ongoing monitoring and evaluation of AI systems to assess their performance, identify biases or errors, and ensure compliance with ethical standards and regulatory requirements (Amugongo et al., 2023; Endsley, 2023). This entails establishing robust monitoring mechanisms, conducting regular audits, and soliciting feedback from human stakeholders. Service providers can detect issues early by continuously evaluating AI systems in real-world contexts and taking corrective actions to maintain trust and credibility. While AI excels at pattern recognition and data analysis, it lacks the human capacity for critical thinking, empathy, and nuanced understanding. Complex situations, ethical dilemmas, and unforeseen circumstances often require human judgment to navigate effectively (Fanni et al., 2023; Pisoni & Díaz-Rodríguez, 2023). Transparency in accountability mechanisms, including mechanisms for redress and recourse in the event of AI-related harms, reinforces trust and ensures that human oversight effectively upholds ethical standards.

Education and training institutions play a crucial role in equipping professionals with the knowledge, skills, and ethical awareness necessary to effectively oversee AI systems in the service industry (Dalgıç et al., 2024). Interdisciplinary education programs integrating technical training with ethical reasoning and critical thinking prepare individuals to navigate the complex ethical challenges associated with AI deployment. Continuous professional development and training initiatives help ensure that human overseers can effectively fulfill their roles in an evolving technological environment (Demir & Demir, 2023b). Empowering human oversight and intervention is essential for promoting the ethical use of AI in the service industry (Amugongo et al., 2023; Pisoni & Díaz-Rodríguez, 2023). By prioritizing transparency, accountability, human-centric design, and continuous monitoring, service providers can leverage the complementary strengths of AI algorithms and human judgment to uphold ethical standards, build trust with stakeholders, and mitigate potential risks and harms associated with AI deployment. Research and collaboration are vital in developing the theoretical foundations, practical tools, and educational resources necessary to support effective human oversight in an AI-driven world (Demir et al., 2022).

Developing Ethical AI Guidelines and Policies

Developing ethical AI guidelines and policies within the service industry is paramount for fostering trust, credibility, and responsible deployment of artificial intelligence technologies (Adams et al., 2023; Chan, 2023). As AI becomes increasingly integrated into various service sectors such as healthcare, finance, customer support, and more, ethical considerations become critical to protect individuals' rights, uphold moral values, and mitigate potential risks associated with AI applications. Developing ethical AI guidelines and policies involves a multifaceted approach that considers various stakeholders, ethical frameworks, legal regulations, and technological capabilities. Engaging stakeholders from diverse backgrounds, including ethicists, policymakers, industry experts, technologists, and end-users, is fundamental for gathering insights, identifying concerns, and fostering collaborative efforts toward ethical AI development (Dhirani et al., 2023; Huh et al., 2023). Stakeholder engagement ensures that diverse perspectives are considered, leading to more comprehensive and inclusive guidelines. Drawing upon established ethical frameworks such as utilitarianism, deontology, virtue ethics, and consequentialism provides a foundational basis for guiding AI development and deployment (Adams et al., 2023; Demir & Demir, 2023b). These frameworks help identify ethical principles such as fairness, transparency, accountability, privacy, and autonomy, which should be upheld throughout the AI lifecycle.

Conducting thorough risk assessments to identify potential ethical, societal, and legal risks associated with AI applications is essential (Nguyen et al., 2023; Zhou & Chen, 2023). This involves evaluating biases in datasets, potential discriminatory outcomes, risks to privacy and security, and the impact on human autonomy (Chan, 2023; Nguyen et al., 2023). Strategies for mitigating these risks should be incorporated into the guidelines to ensure responsible AI deployment. Safeguarding individuals' data privacy and ensuring data security are ethical considerations in AI development. Guidelines should emphasize obtaining informed consent, minimizing data collection, implementing robust security measures, and adhering to relevant data protection regulations such as GDPR (General Data Protection Regulation). Despite the autonomy of AI systems, human oversight and control are essential for ensuring accountability and ethical decision-making (Adams et al., 2023; Dhirani et al., 2023). Ethical AI guidelines should not be static but evolve in response to technological advancements, societal changes, and emerging ethical dilemmas. Continuous monitoring and evaluation of AI systems, along with feedback mechanisms from stakeholders, enable iterative improvements and ensure ongoing adherence to ethical standards (Chan, 2023; Huh et al., 2023).

Establishing mechanisms for compliance with ethical guidelines and enforcing ethical standards is crucial for holding organizations accountable for their AI practices (Dhirani et al., 2023; Zhou & Chen, 2023). This may involve certification programs, regulatory oversight, auditing processes, and penalties for non-compliance, thereby incentivizing adherence to ethical norms. Promoting education and awareness about ethical AI principles and guidelines among developers, policymakers, and end-users is essential for fostering a culture of responsible AI use. Training programs, workshops, and public awareness campaigns can empower stakeholders to make informed decisions and advocate for ethical AI practices. Developing ethical AI guidelines and policies in the service industry requires a comprehensive approach integrating stakeholder engagement, ethical frameworks, risk assessment, transparency, data privacy, human oversight, continuous monitoring, compliance mechanisms, and education initiatives (Huh et al., 2023; Nguyen et al., 2023). By prioritizing ethical considerations in AI development and deployment, organizations can build trust, credibility, and societal acceptance of AI technologies while minimizing potential harms and maximizing their benefits. AI guidelines and policies should be enforced organization-wide and shared with all stakeholders to ensure widespread ethical compliance.

Ethical Technology Practices

The service industry highlights several core ethical principles that should underpin technology ethical practices based on AI (Demir et al., 2023). Ethical practices necessitate vigilance in mitigating bias throughout the AI development lifecycle. This principle is not limited to service industries. Bias in AI-powered facial recognition software or hiring algorithms can have far-reaching societal consequences. The vast amounts of data collected for AI development and operation necessitate robust data protection measures (Bleher & Braun, 2023; Chen, 2023). Ethical practices require obtaining informed consent, ensuring data security, and adhering to data protection regulations. Ethical technology development practices establish clear lines of accountability for decisions made by AI systems (Munn, 2023; Palladino, 2023). However, ethical practices necessitate aligning AI applications with societal good. This requires considering the potential impact of AI on employment, social structures, and individual rights across all technological sectors. Transparency in AI-powered robots working alongside humans is crucial for safety and trust. Fairness considerations extend to algorithmic decision-making in organizations' resource allocation or job scheduling.

Transparent and explainable AI empowers users to understand and participate in AI-driven interactions, fostering trust and a sense of control (Demir et al., 2023). Ethical AI development fosters responsible innovation, ensuring technological advancements benefit society (Palladino, 2023; Stahl & Eke, 2024). This strengthens the reputation of the technology sector and encourages public support for AI research and development. Proactive adherence to ethical principles helps mitigate legal and reputational risks associated with biased or discriminatory AI practices. This creates a more sustainable foundation for long-term technological progress. Research in technology ethical practices assesses the societal impact of AI technologies and identifies ethical risks associated with their deployment in the service industry (Munn, 2023; Stahl & Eke, 2024). Scholars conduct ethical risk assessments to evaluate AI applications' potential harms and benefits, considering societal values, cultural norms, and distributional effects.

Developing ethical decision-making and governance frameworks is essential for ensuring the responsible use of AI in the service industry (Bleher & Braun, 2023; Palladino, 2023). Academic studies (e.g., Chen, 2023; Demir et al., 2023; Stahl & Eke, 2024) explore ethical decision-making models, guidelines, and governance structures that guide organizations in navigating ethical dilemmas and making morally sound choices regarding AI technologies. Researchers establish transparent and participatory governance mechanisms to promote ethical awareness, accountability, and trustworthiness in AI-driven services. Technology ethical practices based on AI encompass a broad range of considerations, including ethical frameworks, transparency, accountability, fairness, privacy, and societal impact (Bleher & Braun, 2023; Munn, 2023). Academic research in this field aims to develop guidelines, principles, and tools that promote the responsible development, deployment, and utilization of AI technologies in the service industry, thereby building trust, credibility, and societal acceptance of AI-driven services.

CONCLUSION

This chapter has delved into the intricate relationship between artificial intelligence (AI) and trust within the service industry. Building trust necessitates a multi-faceted approach that integrates ethical considerations throughout the entire AI lifecycle-from the initial stages of design and development to deployment and ongoing monitoring. A foundational understanding of ethical AI principles is indispensable for stakeholders in service industries. Ethical AI entails not only the development of technically proficient algorithms but also the alignment of AI systems with societal values and norms.

Transparency and explainability serve as cornerstones of ethical AI, enabling stakeholders to comprehend the inner workings of AI systems and the rationale behind their decisions (Aranovich & Matulionyte, 2023; Fernandez-Quilez, 2023). Transparent AI systems foster trust by demystifying the black-box nature of algorithms, empowering users to evaluate the fairness and reliability of AI-generated outcomes. Implementing explainable AI techniques offers a solution by demystifying the decision-making process and rebuilding trust in instances where bias might be suspected. Addressing algorithmic bias and ensuring fairness in AI decision-making processes are imperative for upholding ethical standards in service industries (Ferrara, 2023; Hagendorff et al., 2023). By employing techniques such as fairness-aware machine learning and bias mitigation strategies, service providers can mitigate the adverse impacts of biased algorithms and promote equitable outcomes for all stakeholders. If not meticulously designed and monitored, AI algorithms can perpetuate societal biases. Identifying and mitigating potential biases in both data sets and algorithms is paramount to guaranteeing fair treatment for all users. Techniques such as data debiasing and fairness audits contribute to constructing inclusive AI systems.

Accountability mechanisms are pivotal in ensuring that AI systems operate ethically and responsibly (Almeida et al., 2022; Tóth et al., 2022). Establishing clear lines of accountability, implementing robust governance structures, and fostering a culture of accountability within organizations are essential steps toward enhancing the accountability of AI systems in service provision. The question of who holds accountability for the actions of AI systems within the service sector requires a clear definition. Mechanisms for redress must be established, empowering users to challenge unfair or biased outcomes generated by AI. The service industry's use of AI often involves collecting and analyzing personal data. Safeguarding privacy and data security is paramount in the ethical use of AI within service industries (Kolhar & Aldossary, 2023; Saeed et al., 2024). Adhering to data protection regulations, implementing privacy-preserving technologies, and adopting privacy-by-design principles are crucial for mitigating privacy risks and earning consumers' trust in AI-enabled services. Implementing robust privacy and security measures safeguards user data from unauthorized access or misuse.

Despite the advancements in AI technologies, human oversight and intervention remain indispensable for ensuring ethical AI deployment (Amugongo et al., 2023; Fanni et al., 2023). Human-in-the-loop approaches enable experts to supervise AI systems, intervene when necessary, and mitigate the potential negative consequences of AI errors or biases (Mosqueira-Rey et al., 2023). Service providers must retain control over critical decision-making processes, ensuring AI systems are harnessed responsibly and ethically. Industry leaders are responsible for cultivating a culture of ethical AI development and deployment. This necessitates the establishment of ethical AI guidelines and policies that prioritize user trust alongside advancements in technology. The formulation of ethical AI guidelines and policies is essential for guiding industry practices and promoting responsible AI deployment. Collaborative efforts between policymakers, industry stakeholders, academia, and civil society are indispensable in crafting comprehensive regulatory frameworks that balance innovation and ethical considerations. Embracing ethical technology practices entails integrating ethical considerations into every stage of the AI lifecycle, from design and development to deployment and monitoring. By embracing ethical AI principles, stakeholders can build trust and credibility, foster societal acceptance of AI technologies, and harness the transformative potential of AI for the betterment of society.

Building trust in service-oriented AI is an ongoing process. Ongoing research and development efforts are essential for augmenting AI systems' transparency, fairness, and accountability. Industry leaders must foster a culture of ethical AI development and deployment, prioritizing user trust in tandem with achieving technological advancement. Regulatory bodies are pivotal in establishing and enforcing ethical AI development and implementation frameworks, guaranteeing this powerful technology's responsible use (Demir & Demir, 2023b). By prioritizing ethical considerations, service providers can leverage the potential of AI to revolutionize service delivery while cultivating trust and securing sustainable customer loyalty. The future of service-oriented AI hinges on a collaborative effort between researchers, developers, businesses, and policymakers. This collaborative approach will ensure that AI is designed and utilized for the greater good, leading to a service environment that is both efficient, personalized, and ethical.

Theoretical Implications

The theoretical implications of exploring the ethical use of AI in the service industry are manifold. Firstly, this research contributes to advancing the understanding of ethical AI frameworks within the specific context of service industries. Delving into transparency, fairness, accountability, and privacy protection offers theoretical insights into how these principles can be integrated into AI systems operating within service-oriented settings. This study provides a theoretical foundation for examining the intricate interplay between ethical considerations and technological advancements. It offers a nuanced understanding of how ethical AI practices can be embedded into the design, deployment, and operation of AI systems in service industries, thereby enriching the theoretical discourse on the ethical implications of AI adoption. Furthermore, by emphasizing the importance of human oversight and intervention in AI-driven service environments, this research underscores the significance of maintaining human agency and responsibility amidst technological proliferation. This theoretical exploration sheds light on the complex dynamics between automated decision-making processes and human judgment, thereby contributing to theoretical discussions surrounding the symbiotic relationship between humans and AI in service contexts.

Practical Implications

This study's practical implications are profound for industry practitioners and policymakers alike. Firstly, by elucidating the significance of transparency and explainability in AI systems, this research provides actionable insights for service industry professionals to enhance the trust and credibility of their AI-driven services. Practical strategies such as employing interpretable AI models and facilitating transparent communication with users can be adopted to foster greater trust and acceptance of AI technologies. Similarly, by addressing fairness and bias mitigation issues, this study offers practical recommendations for service industry stakeholders to ensure equitable outcomes in AI-driven decision-making processes. Implementing bias detection and mitigation techniques and conducting regular audits of AI systems can help mitigate the risk of perpetuating discriminatory practices within service environments. This research underscores the importance of accountability and oversight mechanisms in governing AI systems within service industries. Organizations can mitigate the potential risks associated with AI deployment by establishing clear lines of responsibility and implementing robust oversight mechanisms while upholding ethical standards and regulatory compliance. This study underscores the practical importance of safeguarding privacy and data security in AI-enabled services. By adhering to stringent data protection protocols and leveraging privacy-preserving techniques, service providers can mitigate the risk of data breaches and uphold the privacy rights of their customers. Furthermore, by advocating for the development of ethical AI guidelines and policies tailored to the specific needs of service industries, this research offers practical guidance for industry stakeholders to navigate the ethical complexities of AI adoption. By proactively formulating ethical frameworks and industry standards, organizations can foster a culture of responsible AI innovation while mitigating potential ethical risks.

Limitations and Future Directions

Despite its contributions, this study has some limitations. Firstly, the scope of this research may be constrained by the evolving nature of AI technologies and the diverse service industries. Future studies could benefit from a more comprehensive analysis encompassing a wider range of AI applications and service sectors. While this study emphasizes the importance of ethical considerations in AI deployment, the practical implementation of ethical AI principles may vary across organizational contexts and regulatory environments. Future research could explore the contextual factors influencing the adoption and effectiveness of ethical AI practices in diverse service settings. The efficacy of existing ethical frameworks and guidelines in addressing emerging challenges in AI governance warrants further investigation. Future studies could focus on evaluating the effectiveness of current ethical frameworks in mitigating ethical risks and promoting responsible AI practices within service industries. The role of stakeholders, including governments, regulatory bodies, industry associations, and civil society organizations, in shaping the ethical environment of AI in service industries warrants closer examination. Future research could explore the collaborative efforts needed to develop and enforce ethical standards and regulatory frameworks that align with all stakeholders' interests.

REFERENCES

Adams, C., Pente, P., Lemermeyer, G., & Rockwell, G. (2023). Ethical principles for artificial intelligence in K-12 education. *Computers and Education: Artificial Intelligence*, *4*, 1–18. doi:10.1016/j.caeai.2023.100131

Almeida, D., Shmarko, K., & Lomas, E. (2022). The ethics of facial recognition technologies, surveillance, and accountability in an age of artificial intelligence: A comparative analysis of US, EU, and UK regulatory frameworks. *AI and Ethics*, *2*(3), 377–387. doi:10.1007/s43681-021-00077-w PMID:34790955

Amugongo, L. M., Kriebitz, A., Boch, A., & Lütge, C. (2023). Operationalising AI ethics through the agile software development lifecycle: A case study of AI-enabled mobile health applications. *AI and Ethics*, 1–18. doi:10.1007/s43681-023-00331-3

Aranovich, T. D. C., & Matulionyte, R. (2023). Ensuring AI explainability in healthcare: Problems and possible policy solutions. *Information & Communications Technology Law*, *32*(2), 259–275. doi:10.1080/13600834.2022.2146395

Attard-Frost, B., De los Ríos, A., & Walters, D. R. (2023). The ethics of AI business practices: A review of 47 AI ethics guidelines. *AI and Ethics*, *3*(2), 389–406. doi:10.1007/s43681-022-00156-6

Baihakki, M. A., & Qutayan, S. M. S. B. (2023). Ethical issues of artificial intelligence (AI) in the healthcare. *Journal of Science. Technology and Innovation Policy*, *9*(1), 32–38. doi:10.11113/jostip.v9n1.129

Balasubramaniam, N., Kauppinen, M., Rannisto, A., Hiekkanen, K., & Kujala, S. (2023). Transparency and explainability of AI systems: From ethical guidelines to requirements. *Information and Software Technology*, *159*, 107197. Advance online publication. doi:10.1016/j.infsof.2023.107197

Bender, S. M., & Price, W. N. II. (2024). Legal aspects of artificial intelligence in medical practice. In *Artificial Intelligence in Clinical Practice* (pp. 401–411). Academic Press. doi:10.1016/B978-0-443-15688-5.00046-2

Bleher, H., & Braun, M. (2023). Reflections on putting AI ethics into practice: How three AI ethics approaches conceptualize theory and practice. *Science and Engineering Ethics*, *29*(3), 21–33. doi:10.1007/s11948-023-00443-3 PMID:37237246

Boddington, P. (2023). Normative Ethical Theory and AI Ethics. In A. I. Ethics (Ed.), *A Textbook* (pp. 229–276). Springer Nature Singapore.

Burr, C., & Leslie, D. (2023). Ethical assurance: A practical approach to the responsible design, development, and deployment of data-driven technologies. *AI and Ethics*, *3*(1), 73–98. doi:10.1007/s43681-022-00178-0

Chan, C. K. Y. (2023). A comprehensive AI policy education framework for university teaching and learning. *International Journal of Educational Technology in Higher Education*, *20*(1), 38–51. doi:10.1186/s41239-023-00408-3

Chaurasia, A. (2023). Algorithmic Precision Medicine: Harnessing Artificial Intelligence for Healthcare Optimization. *Asian Journal of Biotechnology and Bioresource Technology*, *9*(4), 28–43. doi:10.9734/ajb2t/2023/v9i4190

Chen, Y., Jensen, S., Albert, L. J., Gupta, S., & Lee, T. (2023). Artificial intelligence (AI) student assistants in the classroom: Designing chatbots to support student success. *Information Systems Frontiers*, *25*(1), 161–182. doi:10.1007/s10796-022-10291-4

Chen, Z. (2023). Ethics and discrimination in artificial intelligence-enabled recruitment practices. *Humanities & Social Sciences Communications*, *10*(1), 1–12. doi:10.1057/s41599-023-02079-x

Cortese, J. F. N. B., Cozman, F. G., Lucca-Silveira, M. P., & Bechara, A. F. (2023). Should explainability be a fifth ethical principle in AI ethics? *AI and Ethics*, *3*(1), 123–134. doi:10.1007/s43681-022-00152-w

Dalgıç, A., Yaşar, E., & Demir, M. (2024). ChatGPT and learning outcomes in tourism education: The role of digital literacy and individualized learning. *Journal of Hospitality, Leisure, Sport and Tourism Education*, *34*, 1–13. doi:10.1016/j.jhlste.2024.100481

Deho, O. B., Zhan, C., Li, J., Liu, J., Liu, L., & Duy Le, T. (2022). How do the existing fairness metrics and unfairness mitigation algorithms contribute to ethical learning analytics? *British Journal of Educational Technology*, *53*(4), 822–843. doi:10.1111/bjet.13217

Demir, M., & Demir, Ş. Ş. (2023a). Is ChatGPT the right technology for service individualization and value co-creation? evidence from the travel industry. *Journal of Travel & Tourism Marketing*, *40*(5), 383–398. doi:10.1080/10548408.2023.2255884

Demir, M., Demir, Ş. Ş., & Yaşar, E. (2022). Big data and innovative organizational performance: Evidence from a moderated-mediated model. *Creativity and Innovation Management*, *31*(4), 696–709. doi:10.1111/caim.12525

Demir, M., Yaşar, E., & Demir, Ş. Ş. (2023). Digital transformation and human resources planning: The mediating role of innovation. *Journal of Hospitality and Tourism Technology*, *14*(1), 21–36. doi:10.1108/JHTT-04-2021-0105

Demir, Ş. Ş., & Demir, M. (2023b). Professionals' perspectives on ChatGPT in the tourism industry: Does it inspire awe or concern? *Journal of Tourism Theory and Research*, *9*(2), 61–77. doi:10.24288/jttr.1313481

Dhirani, L. L., Mukhtiar, N., Chowdhry, B. S., & Newe, T. (2023). Ethical dilemmas and privacy issues in emerging technologies: A review. *Sensors (Basel)*, *23*(3), 1–15. doi:10.3390/s23031151 PMID:36772190

Endsley, M. R. (2023). Supporting Human-AI Teams: Transparency, explainability, and situation awareness. *Computers in Human Behavior*, *140*, 1–15. doi:10.1016/j.chb.2022.107574

Fanni, R., Steinkogler, V. E., Zampedri, G., & Pierson, J. (2023). Enhancing human agency through redress in Artificial Intelligence Systems. *AI & Society*, *38*(2), 537–547. doi:10.1007/s00146-022-01454-7 PMID:35692234

Fernandez-Quilez, A. (2023). Deep learning in radiology: Ethics of data and on the value of algorithm transparency, interpretability and explainability. *AI and Ethics*, *3*(1), 257–265. doi:10.1007/s43681-022-00161-9

Ferrara, E. (2023). Fairness and bias in artificial intelligence: A brief survey of sources, impacts, and mitigation strategies. *Sci*, *6*(1), 1–15. doi:10.3390/sci6010003

Gardner, A., Smith, A. L., Steventon, A., Coughlan, E., & Oldfield, M. (2022). Ethical funding for trustworthy AI: Proposals to address the responsibilities of funders to ensure that projects adhere to trustworthy AI practice. *AI and Ethics*, *2*(2), 1–15. doi:10.1007/s43681-021-00069-w PMID:34790951

Habbal, A., Ali, M. K., & Abuzaraida, M. A. (2024). Artificial Intelligence Trust, Risk and Security Management (AI TRiSM): Frameworks, applications, challenges and future research directions. *Expert Systems with Applications*, *240*, 1–14. doi:10.1016/j.eswa.2023.122442

Hagendorff, T., Bossert, L. N., Tse, Y. F., & Singer, P. (2023). Speciesist bias in AI: How AI applications perpetuate discrimination and unfair outcomes against animals. *AI and Ethics*, *3*(3), 717–734. doi:10.1007/s43681-022-00199-9

Heyder, T., Passlack, N., & Posegga, O. (2023). Ethical management of human-AI interaction: Theory development review. *The Journal of Strategic Information Systems*, *32*(3), 1–50. doi:10.1016/j.jsis.2023.101772

Huh, J., Nelson, M. R., & Russell, C. A. (2023). ChatGPT, AI advertising, and advertising research and education. *Journal of Advertising*, *52*(4), 477–482. doi:10.1080/00913367.2023.2227013

John-Mathews, J. M., Cardon, D., & Balagué, C. (2022). From reality to world. A critical perspective on AI fairness. *Journal of Business Ethics*, *178*(4), 945–959. doi:10.1007/s10551-022-05055-8

Kawamleh, S. (2023). Against explainability requirements for ethical artificial intelligence in health care. *AI and Ethics*, *3*(3), 901–916. doi:10.1007/s43681-022-00212-1

Kolhar, M., & Aldossary, S. M. (2023). Privacy-Preserving Convolutional Bi-LSTM Network for Robust Analysis of Encrypted Time-Series Medical Images. *AI*, *4*(3), 706–720. doi:10.3390/ai4030037

Kumar, A. (2024). Exploring Ethical Considerations in AI-driven Autonomous Vehicles: Balancing Safety and Privacy. *Journal of Artificial Intelligence General science, 2*(1), 125-138.

Lund, B. D., Wang, T., Mannuru, N. R., Nie, B., Shimray, S., & Wang, Z. (2023). ChatGPT and a new academic reality: Artificial Intelligence-written research papers and the ethics of the large language models in scholarly publishing. *Journal of the Association for Information Science and Technology*, *74*(5), 570–581. doi:10.1002/asi.24750

Memarian, B., & Doleck, T. (2023). Fairness, Accountability, Transparency, and Ethics (FATE) in Artificial Intelligence (AI), and higher education: A systematic review. Computers and Education. *Artificial Intelligence*, *5*, 1–12. doi:10.1016/j.caeai.2023.100152

Meneceur, Y. (2023). Artificial Intelligence, Public Administration, and the Rule of Law: Towards the Uncertainties of a New "Rule of Algorithms". In *The Rule of Law and Automated Decision-Making: Exploring Fundamentals of Algorithmic Governance* (pp. 117–145). Springer International Publishing. doi:10.1007/978-3-031-30142-1_6

Moore, S., Tong, R., Singh, A., Liu, Z., Hu, X., Lu, Y., . . . Stamper, J. (2023, June). Empowering education with llms-the next-gen interface and content generation. In *International Conference on Artificial Intelligence in Education* (pp. 32-37). Cham: Springer Nature Switzerland. 10.1007/978-3-031-36336-8_4

Mosqueira-Rey, E., Hernández-Pereira, E., Alonso-Ríos, D., Bobes-Bascarán, J., & Fernández-Leal, Á. (2023). Human-in-the-loop machine learning: A state of the art. *Artificial Intelligence Review*, *56*(4), 3005–3054. doi:10.1007/s10462-022-10246-w

Munn, L. (2023). The uselessness of AI ethics. *AI and Ethics*, *3*(3), 869–877. doi:10.1007/s43681-022-00209-w

Nguyen, A., Ngo, H. N., Hong, Y., Dang, B., & Nguyen, B. P. T. (2023). Ethical principles for artificial intelligence in education. *Education and Information Technologies*, *28*(4), 4221–4241. doi:10.1007/s10639-022-11316-w PMID:36254344

Pagano, T. P., Loureiro, R. B., Lisboa, F. V., Peixoto, R. M., Guimarães, G. A., Cruz, G. O., Araujo, M. M., Santos, L. L., Cruz, M. A. S., Oliveira, E. L. S., Winkler, I., & Nascimento, E. G. (2023). Bias and unfairness in machine learning models: A systematic review on datasets, tools, fairness metrics, and identification and mitigation methods. *Big Data and Cognitive Computing*, *7*(1), 15–25. doi:10.3390/bdcc7010015

Palladino, N. (2023). A 'biased' emerging governance regime for artificial intelligence? How AI ethics get skewed moving from principles to practices. *Telecommunications Policy*, *47*(5), 1–12. doi:10.1016/j.telpol.2022.102479

Pappas, A., Fumagalli, E., Rouziou, M., & Bolander, W. (2023). More than Machines: The Role of the Future Retail Salesperson in Enhancing the Customer Experience. *Journal of Retailing*, *99*(4), 518–531. doi:10.1016/j.jretai.2023.10.004

Pisoni, G., & Díaz-Rodríguez, N. (2023). Responsible and human centric AI-based insurance advisors. *Information Processing & Management*, *60*(3), 1–14. doi:10.1016/j.ipm.2023.103273

Radanliev, P., & De Roure, D. (2023). Review of the state of the art in autonomous artificial intelligence. *AI and Ethics*, *3*(2), 497–504. doi:10.1007/s43681-022-00176-2

Resnik, D. B., & Andrews, S. L. (2023). A precautionary approach to autonomous vehicles. *AI and Ethics*, 1–16.

Rivas, P., & Zhao, L. (2023). Marketing with chatgpt: Navigating the ethical terrain of gpt-based chatbot technology. *AI*, *4*(2), 375–384. doi:10.3390/ai4020019

Römer, J., Rana, Z., Sickmann, J., Pitz, T., & Goldbach, C. (2023). Mobility and Trust in Algorithms: Attitude of Consumers towards Algorithmic Decision-making Systems in the Mobility Sector. In *Towards the New Normal in Mobility: Technische und betriebswirtschaftliche Aspekte* (pp. 569–594). Springer Fachmedien Wiesbaden. doi:10.1007/978-3-658-39438-7_33

Saeed, M. M. A., Saeed, R. A., & Ahmed, Z. E. (2024). Data Security and Privacy in the Age of AI and Digital Twins. In *Digital Twin Technology and AI Implementations in Future-Focused Businesses* (pp. 99–124). IGI Global. doi:10.4018/979-8-3693-1818-8.ch008

Sand, M., Durán, J. M., & Jongsma, K. R. (2022). Responsibility beyond design: Physicians' requirements for ethical medical AI. *Bioethics*, *36*(2), 162–169. doi:10.1111/bioe.12887 PMID:34089625

Schurr, A., & Moran, S. (2023). The presence of automation enhances deontological considerations in moral judgments. *Computers in Human Behavior*, *140*, 1–10. doi:10.1016/j.chb.2022.107590

Sebo, J. (2023). The rebugnant conclusion: Utilitarianism, insects, microbes, and AI systems. *Ethics, Policy & Environment*, *26*(2), 249–264. doi:10.1080/21550085.2023.2200724

Smith, N., & Vickers, D. (2024). Living well with AI: Virtue, education, and artificial intelligence. *Theory and Research in Education*, *21*(2), 19–44. doi:10.1177/14778785241231561

Stahl, B. C., & Eke, D. (2024). The ethics of ChatGPT–Exploring the ethical issues of an emerging technology. *International Journal of Information Management*, *74*, 1–14. doi:10.1016/j.ijinfomgt.2023.102700

Tomar, K., & Sharma, S. (2024). A proposed artificial intelligence and blockchain technique for solving health insurance challenges. In *Data-Driven Technologies and Artificial Intelligence in Supply Chain* (pp. 31–57). CRC Press.

Tóth, Z., Caruana, R., Gruber, T., & Loebbecke, C. (2022). The dawn of the AI robots: Towards a new framework of AI robot accountability. *Journal of Business Ethics*, *178*(4), 895–916. doi:10.1007/s10551-022-05050-z

Unver, M. B. (2023). Governing fiduciary relationships or building up a governance model for trust in AI? Review of healthcare as a socio-technical system. *International Review of Law Computers & Technology*, *37*(2), 198–226. doi:10.1080/13600869.2023.2192569

Wang, W. (2024). Research on Data Security and Privacy Protection in the Context of Big Data. *Frontiers in Computing and Intelligent Systems*, *7*(1), 29–33. doi:10.54097/astapa66

Wong, S. K. Y. (2024). Privacy and confidentiality. In *Artificial Intelligence in Medicine* (pp. 45–58). Academic Press. doi:10.1016/B978-0-323-95068-8.00004-2

Yordanova, Z. (2023). Ethical Implications of Transparency and Explainability of Artificial Intelligence for Managing Value-Added Tax (VAT) in Corporations. In *International Conference on Advanced Research in Technologies, Information, Innovation and Sustainability* (pp. 344-353). Cham: Springer Nature Switzerland.

Zhang, L. A. (2024). How does artificial intelligence affect reliable engineering? *Advances in Operation Research and Production Management*, *1*(1), 7–18. doi:10.54254/3006-1210/direct/0718

Zhou, J., & Chen, F. (2023). AI ethics: From principles to practice. *AI & Society*, *38*(6), 2693–2703. doi:10.1007/s00146-022-01602-z

ADDITIONAL READING

Chi, N. T. K., & Hoang Vu, N. (2023). Investigating the customer trust in artificial intelligence: The role of anthropomorphism, empathy response, and interaction. *CAAI Transactions on Intelligence Technology*, *8*(1), 260–273. doi:10.1049/cit2.12133

Choung, H., David, P., & Ross, A. (2023). Trust in AI and its role in the acceptance of AI technologies. *International Journal of Human-Computer Interaction*, *39*(9), 1727–1739. doi:10.1080/10447318.2022.2050543

Demir, M., Dalgıç, A., & Yaşar, E. (2022). How Perceived Overqualification Affects Task Performance and Proactive Behavior: The Role of Digital Competencies and Job Crafting. *International Journal of Hospitality & Tourism Administration*, 1–23. doi:10.1080/15256480.2022.2135665

Figueroa-Armijos, M., Clark, B. B., & da Motta Veiga, S. P. (2023). Ethical perceptions of AI in hiring and organizational trust: The role of performance expectancy and social influence. *Journal of Business Ethics*, *186*(1), 179–197. doi:10.1007/s10551-022-05166-2

Habbal, A., Ali, M. K., & Abuzaraida, M. A. (2024). Artificial Intelligence Trust, Risk and Security Management (AI TRiSM): Frameworks, applications, challenges and future research directions. *Expert Systems with Applications*, *240*, 122442. Advance online publication. doi:10.1016/j.eswa.2023.122442

Wong, L. W., Tan, G. W. H., Ooi, K. B., & Dwivedi, Y. (2023). The role of institutional and self in the formation of trust in artificial intelligence technologies. *Internet Research*, *34*(2), 343–370. doi:10.1108/INTR-07-2021-0446

KEY TERMS AND DEFINITIONS

Accountability and Oversight: Establishing mechanisms to hold stakeholders accountable for AI decisions and outcomes, enhancing transparency and trustworthiness in service provision.

Ethical AI: The conscientious developing and deploying artificial intelligence systems, adhering to moral principles and societal values to build trust and credibility.

Ethical AI Guidelines and Policies: Frameworks and regulations that outline ethical standards and best practices for developing and deploying AI in the service industry, guiding stakeholders to ensure responsible and trustworthy AI use.

Ethical Technology Practices: Comprehensive approaches to integrating ethical considerations throughout the lifecycle of AI technology development and implementation in service delivery, promoting trust and credibility by prioritizing ethical behavior in all aspects of technology usage.

Fairness and Bias Mitigation: Strategies and practices employed to detect, address, and minimize biases in AI systems, promoting equitable treatment and bolstering credibility in service delivery.

Human Oversight and Intervention: Incorporating human judgment and intervention in critical AI processes, emphasizing human values and ethical considerations to enhance trust in AI systems.

Privacy and Data Security: Prioritizing personal data protection, ensuring compliance with privacy regulations, and fostering trust by safeguarding sensitive information in AI applications.

Transparency and Explainability: Ensuring that AI algorithms and processes are transparent and understandable to stakeholders, facilitating trust by providing insights into decision-making mechanisms.

Compilation of References

Abdul-Kader, S. (2021). Application Of Speech-To-Text synthesizer by using Natural Language Processing (NLP). *Turkish Online Journal of Qualitative Inquiry, 12*(10).

Abdullah, I. S., Loganathan, A., & Lee, R. W. (2023). *ChatGPT & Doctors: The Medical Dream Team.* Health Sciences Commons. https://hsrc.himmelfarb.gwu.edu/smhs_URGENT_Matters

Abrams, D., Wetherell, M., Cochrane, S., Hogg, M. A., & Turner, J. C. (1990). Knowing what to think by knowing who you are: Self-categorization and the nature of norm formation, conformity and group polarization. *British Journal of Social Psychology*, *29*(2), 97–119. doi:10.1111/j.2044-8309.1990.tb00892.x PMID:2372667

Adamopoulou, E., & Moussiades, L. (2020). Chatbots: History, technology, and applications. *Machine Learning with Applications*, *2*, 100006. doi:10.1016/j.mlwa.2020.100006

Adams, C., Pente, P., Lemermeyer, G., & Rockwell, G. (2023). Ethical principles for artificial intelligence in K-12 education. *Computers and Education: Artificial Intelligence*, *4*, 1–18. doi:10.1016/j.caeai.2023.100131

Adeshola, I., & Adepoju, A. P. (2023). The opportunities and challenges of ChatGPT in education. *Interactive Learning Environments*, 1–14. doi:10.1080/10494820.2023.2253858

Adl, A., & Elfergany, A. K. (2020). Tracking How a Change in a Telecom Service Affects Its Customers Using Sentiment Analysis and Personality Insight. *International Journal of Service Science, Management, Engineering, and Technology*, *11*(3), 33–46. doi:10.4018/IJSSMET.2020070103

Afzal, A., Khan, S., Daud, S., Ahmed, Z., & Butt, A. (2023). Addressing the Digital Divide. *Access and Use of Technology in Education.*, *3*(2), 883–895. doi:10.54183/jssr.v3i2.326

Ahmed, R. R., Romeika, G., Kauliene, R., Streimikis, J., & Dapkus, R. (2020). ES-QUAL model and customer satisfaction in online banking: Evidence from multivariate analysis techniques. *Oeconomia Copernicana*, *11*(1), 59–93. doi:10.24136/oc.2020.003

Ajzen, I. (1980). Understanding attitudes and predicting social behavior. Academic Press.

Ajzen, I. (1991). The theory of planned behavior. *Organizational Behavior and Human Decision Processes*, *50*(2), 179–211. doi:10.1016/0749-5978(91)90020-T

Akakpo, M. G. (2023). Skilled for the Future: Information Literacy for AI Use by University Students in Africa and the Role of Librarians. *Internet Reference Services Quarterly*, 1–8.

Akhtar, M., & Neidhardt, J. (2019). The Potential of Chatbots : Analysis of Chatbot Conversations. *2019 IEEE 21st Conference on Business Informatics (CBI), 1*, 397–404. 10.1109/CBI.2019.00052

Akter, S., Hossain, M. A., Sajib, S., Sultana, S., Rahman, M., Vrontis, D., & McCarthy, G. (2023). A framework for AI-powered service innovation capability: Review and agenda for future research. *Technovation, 125*, 1–17. doi:10.1016/j.technovation.2023.102768

Al Shboul, M. K. I., Alwreikat, A., & Alotaibi, F. A. (2023). Investigating the Use of ChatGpt as a Novel Method for Seeking Health Information: A Qualitative Approach. *Science & Technology Libraries*, •••, 1–10. doi:10.1080/0194262X.2023.2250835

Al Zuned, A. M. (2017). Effective business leadership styles: A case study of Harriet Green. *Middle East Journal of Business*, *55*(5380), 1–10. doi:10.5742/MEJB.2017.92943

Alawida, M., Mejri, S., Mehmood, A., Chikhaoui, B., & Isaac Abiodun, O. (2023). A Comprehensive Study of ChatGPT: Advancements, Limitations, and Ethical Considerations in Natural Language Processing and Cybersecurity. *Information (Basel)*, *14*(8), 462. Advance online publication. doi:10.3390/info14080462

Albayrak, N., Özdemir, A., & Zeydan, E. (2018). An Overview of Artificial Intelligence Based Chatbots and An Example Chatbot Application. *2018 26th Signal Processing and Communications Applications Conference (SIU)*, 1–4.

Ali, F. (2023, April 11). *GPT-1 to GPT-4: Each of OpenAI's GPT Models Explained and Compared*. MakeUseOf. Retrieved November 9, 2023, from https://www.makeuseof.com/gpt-models-explained-and-compared/

Ali, F. (2023). Let the devil speak for itself: Should ChatGPT be allowed or banned in hospitality and tourism schools? *Journal of Global Hospitality and Tourism*, *2*(1), 1–6. doi:10.5038/2771-5957.2.1.1016

Ali, F., Yasar, B., Ali, L., & Dogan, S. (2023). Antecedents and consequences of travelers' trust towards personalized travel recommendations offered by ChatGPT. *International Journal of Hospitality Management, 114*, 1–9. doi:10.1016/j.ijhm.2023.103588

Aljanabi, M. (2023). ChatGPT: Future directions and open possibilities. *Mesopotamian Journal of Cybersecurity, 2023*, 16-17.

Al-Maskari, A., & Sanderson, M. (2010). A review of factors influencing user satisfaction in information retrieval. *Journal of the American Society for Information Science and Technology*, *61*(5), 859–868. doi:10.1002/asi.21300

Almeida, D., Shmarko, K., & Lomas, E. (2022). The ethics of facial recognition technologies, surveillance, and accountability in an age of artificial intelligence: A comparative analysis of US, EU, and UK regulatory frameworks. *AI and Ethics*, *2*(3), 377–387. doi:10.1007/s43681-021-00077-w PMID:34790955

Al-Okaily, A., Al-Okaily, M., Ai Ping, T., Al-Mawali, H., & Zaidan, H. (2021). An empirical investigation of enterprise system user satisfaction antecedents in Jordanian commercial banks. *Cogent Business & Management, 8*(1), 1918847. Advance online publication. doi:10.1080/23311975.2021.1918847

Alt, M.-A., Vizeli, I., & Săplăcan, Z. (2021). Banking with a Chatbot – A Study on Technology Acceptance. *Studia Universitatis Babes-Bolyai Oeconomica, 66*(1), 13–35. doi:10.2478/subboec-2021-0002

Amugongo, L. M., Kriebitz, A., Boch, A., & Lütge, C. (2023). Operationalising AI ethics through the agile software development lifecycle: A case study of AI-enabled mobile health applications. *AI and Ethics*, 1–18. doi:10.1007/s43681-023-00331-3

androiddeveloper.co.in . (2023, July 20). *The Transformative Impact of ChatGPT in the Education Sector.* Android Developer. https://www.androiddeveloper.co.in/blog/impact-of-chatgpt-in-the-education-sector/

Aoki, N. (2020). An experimental study of public trust in AI chatbots in the public sector. *Government Information Quarterly, 37*(4), 101490. doi:10.1016/j.giq.2020.101490

Apple. (n.d.). *Siri.* Apple. Retrieved November 8, 2023, from https://www.apple.com/ca/siri/

Aranovich, T. D. C., & Matulionyte, R. (2023). Ensuring AI explainability in healthcare: Problems and possible policy solutions. *Information & Communications Technology Law, 32*(2), 259–275. doi:10.1080/13600834.2022.2146395

Arman, M., & Lamiya, U. R. (2023). Exploring the Implication of ChatGPT AI for Business: Efficiency and Challenges. *Journal of Innovation Information Technology and Application, 5*(1), 52–64. doi:10.35970/jinita.v5i1.1828

Arndt, J. (1967). Role of product-related conversations in the diffusion of a new product. *JMR, Journal of Marketing Research, 4*(3), 291–295. doi:10.1177/002224376700400308

Ashfaq, M., Yun, J., Waheed, A., Khan, M. S., & Farrukh, M. (2019). *Customers' Expectation, Satisfaction, and Repurchase Intention of Used Products Online: Empirical Evidence From China.* doi:10.1177/2158244019846212

Ashfaq, M., Yun, J., Yu, S., & Maria, S. (2020). I, Chatbot : Modeling the Determinants of Users ' Satisfaction and Continuance Intention of AI-Powered Service Agents. *Telematics and Informatics, 101473*, 101473. Advance online publication. doi:10.1016/j.tele.2020.101473

Atkins, S., Badrie, I., & van Otterloo, S. (2021). *Applying Ethical AI Frameworks in practice: Evaluating conversational AI chatbot solutions.* Computers and Society Research Journal.

Attaran, M. (2023). The impact of 5G on the evolution of intelligent automation and industry digitization. *Journal of Ambient Intelligence and Humanized Computing, 14*(5), 5977–5993. doi:10.1007/s12652-020-02521-x PMID:33643481

Attard-Frost, B., De los Ríos, A., & Walters, D. R. (2023). The ethics of AI business practices: A review of 47 AI ethics guidelines. *AI and Ethics*, *3*(2), 389–406. doi:10.1007/s43681-022-00156-6

Ausat, A. M. A., Azzaakiyyah, H. K., Permana, R. M., Riady, Y., & Suherlan, S. (2023). The Role of ChatGPT in Enabling MSMEs to Compete in the Digital Age. *Innovative: Journal Of Social Science Research*, *3*(2), 622–631.

Ayoola, O. O., Alenoghena, R., & Adeniji, S. (2023). ChatGPT impacts on access-efficiency, employment, education and ethics: The socio-economics of an AI language model. *BizEcons Quarterly*, *16*, 1–17.

Bagozzi, R. P. (1981). Attitudes, intentions, and behavior: A test of some key hypotheses. *Journal of Personality and Social Psychology*, *41*(4), 607–627. doi:10.1037/0022-3514.41.4.607

Bahrini, A., Khamoshifar, M., Abbasimehr, H., Riggs, R. J., Esmaeili, M., Majdabadkohne, R. M., & Pasehvar, M. (2023, April). ChatGPT: Applications, opportunities, and threats. In *2023 Systems and Information Engineering Design Symposium (SIEDS)* (pp. 274-279). IEEE. 10.1109/SIEDS58326.2023.10137850

Baidoo-Anu, D., & Owusu Ansah, L. (2023). Education in the Era of Generative Artificial Intelligence (AI): Understanding the Potential Benefits of ChatGPT in Promoting Teaching and Learning. SSRN *Electronic Journal*. doi:10.2139/ssrn.4337484

Baihakki, M. A., & Qutayan, S. M. S. B. (2023). Ethical issues of artificial intelligence (AI) in the healthcare. *Journal of Science. Technology and Innovation Policy*, *9*(1), 32–38. doi:10.11113/jostip.v9n1.129

Balas, M., & Ing, E. B. (2023). Conversational AI models for ophthalmic diagnosis: Comparison of Chatgpt and the isabel pro differential diagnosis generator. *JFO Open Ophthalmology*, *1*, 100005. doi:10.1016/j.jfop.2023.100005

Balasubramaniam, N., Kauppinen, M., Rannisto, A., Hiekkanen, K., & Kujala, S. (2023). Transparency and explainability of AI systems: From ethical guidelines to requirements. *Information and Software Technology*, *159*, 107197. Advance online publication. doi:10.1016/j.infsof.2023.107197

Bansal, G., Chamola, V., Hussain, A., Guizani, M., & Niyato, D. (2024). Transforming Conversations with AI—A Comprehensive Study of ChatGPT. *Cognitive Computation*, 1–24. doi:10.1007/s12559-023-10236-2

Banu, S., & Patil, S. D. (2020). An intelligent web app chatbot. *Proceedings of the International Conference on Smart Technologies in Computing, Electrical and Electronics, ICSTCEE 2020*, 309–315. 10.1109/ICSTCEE49637.2020.9276948

Barnett, A., Savic, M., Pienaar, K., Carter, A., Warren, N., Sandral, E., Manning, V., & Lubman, D. I. (2021). International Journal of Drug Policy Enacting ' more-than-human ' care : Clients ' and counsellors ' views on the multiple affordances of chatbots in alcohol and other drug counselling. *The International Journal on Drug Policy*, *94*, 102910. doi:10.1016/j.drugpo.2020.102910 PMID:33059955

Barr, K. (2023). *Expedia Wants You to Trust ChatGPT With Your Travel Plans*. Retrieved from: https://gizmodo.com/expedia-chatgpt-travel-hotels-ai-vrbo-1850302553

Baruah, H., Singh, S. R., & Sarmah, P. (2024). *Transliteration Characteristics in Romanized Assamese Language Social Media Text and Machine Transliteration*. ACM Transactions on Asian and Low-Resource Language Information Processing. doi:10.1145/3639565

Basit, A. A. (2019). Examining how respectful engagement affects task performance and affective organizational commitment. *Personnel Review*, *48*(3), 644–658. doi:10.1108/PR-02-2018-0050

Bassey, M. (1999). *Case Study Research in Educational Settings*. Open University Press.

Beckisheva, T. G., Gasparyan, G. A., & Kovalenko, N. A. (2015). Case study as an active method of teaching business English. *Procedia: Social and Behavioral Sciences*, *166*, 292–295. doi:10.1016/j.sbspro.2014.12.526

Ben Saad, S., & Abida, F. C. (2016). Social Interactivity and Its Impact on a User ' s Approach Behavior in Commercial Web Sites : A Study Case of Virtual Agent Presence. *Journal of Marketing Management*, *4*(2), 63–80. doi:10.15640/jmm.v4n2a6

Bender, S. M., & Price, W. N. II. (2024). Legal aspects of artificial intelligence in medical practice. In *Artificial Intelligence in Clinical Practice* (pp. 401–411). Academic Press. doi:10.1016/B978-0-443-15688-5.00046-2

Bernard, H. R. (2017). *Research methods in anthropology: Qualitative and quantitative approaches*. Rowman & Littlefield.

Bhardwaz, S., & Kumar, J. (2023). An Extensive Comparative Analysis of Chatbot Technologies - ChatGPT, Google BARD and Microsoft Bing. *2023 2nd International Conference on Applied Artificial Intelligence and Computing (ICAAIC)*, 673–679. 10.1109/ICAAIC56838.2023.10140214

Bhattacherjee, A. (2001). Understanding information systems continuance: An expectation-confirmation model. *Management Information Systems Quarterly*, *25*(3), 351–370. doi:10.2307/3250921

Bhushan, S. (2021). The impact of artificial intelligence and machine learning on the global economy and its implications for the hospitality sector in India. *Worldwide Hospitality and Tourism Themes*, *13*(2), 252–259. doi:10.1108/WHATT-09-2020-0116

Bicchieri, C., & Mercier, H. (2014). Norms and beliefs: How change occurs. *The complexity of social norms*, 37-54.

Bleher, H., & Braun, M. (2023). Reflections on putting AI ethics into practice: How three AI ethics approaches conceptualize theory and practice. *Science and Engineering Ethics*, *29*(3), 21–33. doi:10.1007/s11948-023-00443-3 PMID:37237246

Boddington, P. (2023). Normative Ethical Theory and AI Ethics. In A. I. Ethics (Ed.), *A Textbook* (pp. 229–276). Springer Nature Singapore.

Bolton, R. N., McColl-Kennedy, J. R., Cheung, L., Gallan, A., Orsingher, C., Witell, L., & Zaki, M. (2018). Customer experience challenges: bringing together digital, physical and social realms. In Journal of Service Management (Vol. 29, Issue 5). doi:10.1108/JOSM-04-2018-0113

Boshoff, C. (2007). A psychometric assessment of e-s-qual : A scale to measure electronic service quality. *Journal of Electronic Commerce Research*, *8*(1), 101–114.

Bowman, J. (2023). *How AI Is Being Used in the Travel Industry*. https://www.fool.com/investing/stock-market/market-sectors/information-technology

Božić, V. (2023). *ChatGPT and Education*. Academic Press.

Braun, V., & Clarke, V. (2006). Using thematic analysis in psychology. *Qualitative Research in Psychology*, *3*(2), 77–101. doi:10.1191/1478088706qp063oa

Brinkmann, S. (2014). Unstructured and semi-structured interviewing. The Oxford handbook of qualitative research, 2, 277-299.

Brynjolfsson, E., & McAfee, A. (2014). *The second machine age: Work, progress, and prosperity in a time of brilliant technologies*. WW Norton & Company.

Buil-Fabrega, M., Martínez Casanovas, M., Ruiz-Munzon, N., & Filho, W. L. (2019). Flipped classroom as an active learning methodology in sustainable development curricula. *Sustainability (Basel)*, *11*(17), 4577. doi:10.3390/su11174577

Burger, B., Kanbach, D. K., Kraus, S., Breier, M., & Corvello, V. (2023). On the use of AI-based tools like ChatGPT to support management research. *European Journal of Innovation Management*, *26*(7), 233–241. doi:10.1108/EJIM-02-2023-0156

Burr, C., & Leslie, D. (2023). Ethical assurance: A practical approach to the responsible design, development, and deployment of data-driven technologies. *AI and Ethics*, *3*(1), 73–98. doi:10.1007/s43681-022-00178-0

Büyüköztürk, Ş., Kılıç Çakmak, E., Akgün, Ö., Karadeniz, Ş., & Demirel, F. (2008). *Bilimsel araştırma yöntemleri*. Pegem Akademi.

Campbell, M., Hoane, A. J. Jr, & Hsu, F. H. (2002). Deep blue. *Artificial Intelligence*, *134*(1-2), 57–83. doi:10.1016/S0004-3702(01)00129-1

Cannas, V. G., Ciano, M. P., Saltalamacchia, M., & Secchi, R. (2023). Artificial intelligence in supply chain and operations management: A multiple case study research. *International Journal of Production Research*, 1–28.

Cano, C. A. G., Castillo, V. S., & Gallego, T. A. C. (2023). Unveiling the Thematic Landscape of Generative Pre-trained Transformer (GPT) Through Bibliometric Analysis. *Metaverse Basic and Applied Research*, *2*, 33–33. doi:10.56294/mr202333

Cao, Y., Li, S., Liu, Y., Yan, Z., Dai, Y., Yu, P. S., & Sun, L. (2023). A comprehensive survey of ai-generated content (aigc): A history of generative ai from gan to chatgpt. *arXiv preprint arXiv:2303.04226*. https://doi.org//arXiv.2303.04226 doi:10.48550

Carvalho, I., & Ivanov, S. (2023). ChatGPT for tourism: Applications, benefits, and risks. *Tourism Review*, 1–14. doi:10.1108/TR-02-2023-0088

Carvalho, L., Martinez-Maldonado, R., Tsai, Y.-S., Markauskaite, L., & De Laat, M. (2022). How can we design for learning in an AI world? *Computers and Education: Artificial Intelligence*, *3*, 100053. doi:10.1016/j.caeai.2022.100053

Cashman, C. (2023). *What is ChatGPT. HP Tech Takes*. https://www.hp.com/us-en/shop/tech-takes/what-is-chatgpt#:~:text="weak" AI.-,Development,and generate human-like language.

Çelik, B. (2023). Hakikat ötesi dönemde markalara yönelik tüketici algısı: Vaka çalışması. *Ufuk Üniversitesi Sosyal Bilimler Enstitüsü Dergisi*, *12*(23), 21–43. doi:10.58635/ufuksbedergi.1264624

Chan, C. K. Y. (2023). A comprehensive AI policy education framework for university teaching and learning. *International Journal of Educational Technology in Higher Education*, *20*(1), 38–51. doi:10.1186/s41239-023-00408-3

Chao, C. M. (2019). Factors determining the behavioral intention to use mobile learning: An application and extension of the UTAUT model. *Frontiers in Psychology*, *10*, 1652. doi:10.3389/fpsyg.2019.01652 PMID:31379679

Chatterjee, J., & Dethlefs, N. (2023). This new conversational AI model can be your friend, philosopher, and guide... and even your worst enemy. *Patterns (New York, N.Y.)*, *4*(1), 1–3. doi:10.1016/j.patter.2022.100676 PMID:36699746

Chaturvedi, R., Verma, S., Das, R., & Dwivedi, Y. K. (2023). Social companionship with artificial intelligence: Recent trends and future avenues. *Technological Forecasting and Social Change*, *193*, 1–20. doi:10.1016/j.techfore.2023.122634

Chaurasia, A. (2023). Algorithmic Precision Medicine: Harnessing Artificial Intelligence for Healthcare Optimization. *Asian Journal of Biotechnology and Bioresource Technology*, *9*(4), 28–43. doi:10.9734/ajb2t/2023/v9i4190

Chen, Y., Chen, Y., & Heffernan, N. (2020). Personalized math tutoring with a conversational agent. *arXiv preprint arXiv:2012.12121*.

Cheng, X., & Zhou, M. (2010, August). Study on effect of eWOM: A literature review and suggestions for future research. In *2010 International conference on management and service science* (pp. 1-4). IEEE. 10.1109/ICMSS.2010.5576663

Chen, J.-S., Le, T.-T.-Y., & Florence, D. (2021). Usability and responsiveness of artificial intelligence chatbot on online customer experience in e-retailing. *International Journal of Retail & Distribution Management*, *49*(11), 1512–1531. doi:10.1108/IJRDM-08-2020-0312

Chen, S., Zhang, K., Li, X., Ye, H., Lin, K. J., & Law, R. (2023). ChatGPT: Cross-cultural tourism research imperative. *Journal of Economics and Management*, *45*(1), 137–146. doi:10.22367/jem.2023.45.07

Chen, Y., Jensen, S., Albert, L. J., Gupta, S., & Lee, T. (2023). Artificial intelligence (AI) student assistants in the classroom: Designing chatbots to support student success. *Information Systems Frontiers*, *25*(1), 161–182. doi:10.1007/s10796-022-10291-4

Chen, Y., & Xie, J. (2008). Online consumer review: Word-of-mouth as a new element of marketing communication mix. *Management Science*, *54*(3), 477–491. doi:10.1287/mnsc.1070.0810

Chen, Z. (2023). Ethics and discrimination in artificial intelligence-enabled recruitment practices. *Humanities & Social Sciences Communications*, *10*(1), 1–12. doi:10.1057/s41599-023-02079-x

Chhabria, K. (2022). Evolving Journey of Chatbots : Insights into Business Decisions. *2022 International Interdisciplinary Humanitarian Conference for Sustainability (IIHC)*, 102–107. 10.1109/IIHC55949.2022.10060780

Chin, W. W. (1998). The partial least squares approach to structural equation modeling. *Modern Methods for Business Research*, *295*(2), 295–336.

Chmiliar, L. (2010). Multiple-case designs. In A. J. Mills, G. Eurepas & E. Wiebe (Eds.), *Encyclopedia of case study research* (pp. 582-583). SAGE Publications.

Choi, H., Kim, Y., & Kim, J. (2011). Driving factors of post adoption behavior in mobile data services. *Journal of Business Research*, *64*(11), 1212–1217. doi:10.1016/j.jbusres.2011.06.025

Chowdhury, N. A. (2023). *Unlocking the power of ChatGPT: An in-depth look at ChatAI's business model*. Academic Press.

Chui, M., Roberts, R., & Yee, L. (2022). *Generative AI is here: How tools like ChatGPT could change your business*. Quantum Black AI by McKinsey.

Ciesla, R. (2024). *The Book of Chatbots: From ELIZA to ChatGPT*. Springer Nature. doi:10.1007/978-3-031-51004-5

Cochran, W. G. (1963). *Sampling Techniques* (2nd ed.). John Wiley & Sons.

Colby, K. M. (2013). *Artificial paranoia: A computer simulation of paranoid processes* (Vol. 49). Elsevier.

Coman, D. M., State, V., Voinea, M. C., & Cucui, G. (2023). *Impacts of chatbots on the accounting service industry*. https://univagora.ro/jour/index.php/aijes

Cordero, J., Barba-Guaman, L., & Guamán, F. (2022). *Use of chatbots for customer service in MSMEs*. Applied Computing and Informatics., doi:10.1108/ACI-06-2022-0148

Cortana. (n.d.). *Microsoft*. Retrieved November 8, 2023, from https://www.microsoft.com/en-us/cortana

Cortese, J. F. N. B., Cozman, F. G., Lucca-Silveira, M. P., & Bechara, A. F. (2023). Should explainability be a fifth ethical principle in AI ethics? *AI and Ethics*, *3*(1), 123–134. doi:10.1007/s43681-022-00152-w

Cotien, L., & Manion, L. (1994). *Research methods in education* (4th ed.). Routlege.

Creswell, J. W. (2013). *Qualitative inquiry and research design: Choosing among five approaches*. Sage publications.

Dalgıç, A. (2023). Restoran İşletmelerine Yapılan Olumsuz Yorumları ChatGPT Değerlendirebilir Mi? TripAdvisor'da Bir Uygulama. *İşletme Araştırmaları Dergisi, 15*(4), 3069-3080.

Dalgıç, A., Yaşar, E., & Demir, M. (2024). ChatGPT and learning outcomes in tourism education: The role of digital literacy and individualized learning. *Journal of Hospitality, Leisure, Sport and Tourism Education*, *34*, 1–13. doi:10.1016/j.jhlste.2024.100481

DataHorizzon Research. (2019, March 9). *Chatbot Market Size to Reach USD 32.4 Billion By 2032 CAGR: 21.6%. Report By DataHorizzon Research*. Yahoo!Finance. Retrieved October 29, 2023, from https://finance.yahoo.com/news/chatbot-market-size-reach-usd-235000000.html?guccounter=1

Davis, F. D. (1985). *A technology acceptance model for empirically testing new end-user information systems: Theory and results* [Doctoral dissertation]. Massachusetts Institute of Technology.

Davis, F. D. (1989). Perceived usefulness, perceived ease of use, and user acceptance of information technology. *Management Information Systems Quarterly*, *13*(3), 319–340. doi:10.2307/249008

De Bock, K. W., Coussement, K., De Caigny, A., Slowiński, R., Baesens, B., Boute, R. N., ... Weber, R. (2023). Explainable AI for Operational Research: A defining framework, methods, applications, and a research agenda. *European Journal of Operational Research*, 1–24. doi:10.1016/j.ejor.2023.09.026

Deho, O. B., Zhan, C., Li, J., Liu, J., Liu, L., & Duy Le, T. (2022). How do the existing fairness metrics and unfairness mitigation algorithms contribute to ethical learning analytics? *British Journal of Educational Technology*, *53*(4), 822–843. doi:10.1111/bjet.13217

Demir, M., & Demir, Ş. Ş. (2015). *Otel işletmelerinde yenilik yönetimi: ilkeler ve örnekler*. Detay Yayıncılık.

Demir, M., & Demir, Ş. Ş. (2023b). Is ChatGPT the right technology for service individualization and value co-creation? Evidence from the travel industry. *Journal of Travel & Tourism Marketing*, *40*(5), 383–398. doi:10.1080/10548408.2023.2255884

Demir, M., Demir, Ş. Ş., Dalgıç, A., & Ergen, F. D. (2021). Impact of COVID-19 pandemic on the tourism industry: An evaluation from the hotel managers' perspective. *Journal of Tourism Theory and Research*, *7*(1), 44–57. doi:10.24288/jttr.857610

Demir, M., Demir, Ş. Ş., & Yaşar, E. (2022). Big data and innovative organizational performance: Evidence from a moderated-mediated model. *Creativity and Innovation Management*, *31*(4), 696–709. doi:10.1111/caim.12525

Demir, M., & Günaydın, Y. (2023). A digital job application reference: How do social media posts affect the recruitment process? *Employee Relations*, *45*(2), 457–477. doi:10.1108/ER-05-2022-0232

Demir, M., Yaşar, E., & Demir, Ş. Ş. (2023). Digital transformation and human resources planning: The mediating role of innovation. *Journal of Hospitality and Tourism Technology*, *14*(1), 21–36. doi:10.1108/JHTT-04-2021-0105

Demir, Ş. Ş., & Demir, M. (2023a). Professionals' perspectives on ChatGPT in the tourism industry: Does it inspire awe or concern? *Journal of Tourism Theory and Research*, *9*(2), 61–77. doi:10.24288/jttr.1313481

Deng, L., & Yu, D. (2014). Deep learning: Methods and applications. *Foundations and Trends® in Signal Processing*, *7*(3–4), 197-387.

Deng, L., Turner, D. E., Gehling, R., & Prince, B. (2010). User experience, satisfaction, and continual usage intention of IT. *European Journal of Information Systems*, *19*(1), 60–75. doi:10.1057/ejis.2009.50

Dhirani, L. L., Mukhtiar, N., Chowdhry, B. S., & Newe, T. (2023). Ethical dilemmas and privacy issues in emerging technologies: A review. *Sensors (Basel)*, *23*(3), 1–15. doi:10.3390/s23031151 PMID:36772190

Dichter, E. (1966). How word-of-mouth advertising works. *Harvard Business Review*, *44*, 147–166.

Dogru, T., Line, N., Mody, M., Hanks, L., Abbott, J. A., Acikgoz, F., Assaf, A., Bakir, S., Berbekova, A., Bilgihan, A., Dalton, A., Erkmen, E., Geronasso, M., Gomez, D., Graves, S., Iskender, A., Ivanov, S., Kizildag, M., Lee, M., ... Zhang, T. (2023). Generative Artificial Intelligence in the Hospitality and Tourism Industry: Developing a Framework for Future Research. *Journal of Hospitality & Tourism Research (Washington, D.C.)*, 1–19. doi:10.1177/10963480231188663

Donthu, N., Kumar, S., Pandey, N., Pandey, N., & Mishra, A. (2021). Mapping the electronic word-of-mouth (eWOM) research: A systematic review and bibliometric analysis. *Journal of Business Research*, *135*, 758–773. doi:10.1016/j.jbusres.2021.07.015

Dwivedi, Y. K., Pandey, N., Currie, W., & Micu, A. (2023b). Leveraging ChatGPT and other generative artificial intelligence (AI)-based applications in the hospitality and tourism industry: practices, challenges and research agenda. *International Journal of Contemporary Hospitality Management*. doi:10.1108/IJCHM-05-2023-0686

Dwivedi, Y. K., Kshetri, N., Hughes, L., Slade, E. L., Jeyaraj, A., Kar, A. K., Baabdullah, A. M., Koohang, A., Raghavan, V., Ahuja, M., Albanna, H., Albashrawi, M. A., Al-Busaidi, A. S., Balakrishnan, J., Barlette, Y., Basu, S., Bose, I., Brooks, L., Buhalis, D., ... Wright, R. (2023). "So what if ChatGPT wrote it?" Multidisciplinary perspectives on opportunities, challenges, and implications of generative conversational AI for research, practice, and policy. *International Journal of Information Management*, *71*, 1–63. doi:10.1016/j.ijinfomgt.2023.102642

Dwivedi, Y. K., Rana, N. P., Jeyaraj, A., Clement, M., & Williams, M. D. (2019). Re-examining the unified theory of acceptance and use of technology (UTAUT): Towards a revised theoretical model. *Information Systems Frontiers*, *21*(3), 719–734. doi:10.1007/s10796-017-9774-y

Egbemhenghe, A., Ojeyemi, T., Iwuozor, K. O., Emenike, E. C., Ogunsanya, T. I., Anidiobi, S. U., & Adeniyi, A. G. (2023). Revolutionizing Water Treatment, Conservation, and Management: Harnessing the Power of AI-Driven ChatGPT Solutions. *Environmental Challenges*, *13*, 100782. Advance online publication. doi:10.1016/j.envc.2023.100782

Ellison, G., & Fudenberg, D. (1995). Word-of-mouth communication and social learning. *The Quarterly Journal of Economics*, *110*(1), 93–125. doi:10.2307/2118512

Elmohandes, N., & Marghany, M. (2024). Effective or ineffective? Using ChatGPT for staffing in the hospitality industry. *European Journal of Tourism Research*, *36*, 3617–3627. doi:10.54055/ejtr.v36i.3286

Endsley, M. R. (2023). Supporting Human-AI Teams: Transparency, explainability, and situation awareness. *Computers in Human Behavior*, *140*, 1–15. doi:10.1016/j.chb.2022.107574

Eren, B. A. (2021). Determinants of customer satisfaction in chatbot use: Evidence from a banking application in Turkey. *International Journal of Bank Marketing*, *39*(2), 294–311. doi:10.1108/IJBM-02-2020-0056

Erul, E., & Işın, A. (2023). Chatgpt ile sohbetler: Turizmde Chatgpt'nin önemi (Chats With Chatgpt. *Journal of Tourism And Gastronomy Studies*, *11*(1), 780–793. doi:10.21325/jotags.2023.1217

Fanni, R., Steinkogler, V. E., Zampedri, G., & Pierson, J. (2023). Enhancing human agency through redress in Artificial Intelligence Systems. *AI & Society*, *38*(2), 537–547. doi:10.1007/s00146-022-01454-7 PMID:35692234

Fan, Z. Y., Yang, Y., Zhang, C. H., Yin, R. Y., Tang, L., & Zhang, F. (2021). Prevalence and patterns of comorbidity among middle-aged and elderly people in China: A cross-sectional study based on CHARLS data. *International Journal of General Medicine*, *14*, 1449–1455. doi:10.2147/IJGM.S309783 PMID:33907449

Fares, O. H., Butt, I., & Lee, S. H. M. (2023). Utilization of artificial intelligence in the banking sector: A systematic literature review. *Journal of Financial Services Marketing*, *28*(4), 835–852.

Fernandez-Quilez, A. (2023). Deep learning in radiology: Ethics of data and on the value of algorithm transparency, interpretability and explainability. *AI and Ethics*, *3*(1), 257–265. doi:10.1007/s43681-022-00161-9

Ferrara, E. (2023). Fairness and bias in artificial intelligence: A brief survey of sources, impacts, and mitigation strategies. *Sci*, *6*(1), 1–15. doi:10.3390/sci6010003

Fırat, M. (2023). *How ChatGPT can transform autodidactic experiences and open education. department of distance education.* Open Education Faculty, Anadolu University.

Fishbein, M., & Ajzen, I. (1977). *Belief, attitude, intention, and behavior: An introduction to theory and research.* Academic Press.

Fisher, R. J., & Price, L. L. (1992). An investigation into the social context of early adoption behavior. *The Journal of Consumer Research*, *19*(3), 477–486. doi:10.1086/209317

Fornell, C., & Larcker, D. F. (1981). Evaluating structural equation models with unobservable variables and measurement error. *JMR, Journal of Marketing Research*, *18*(1), 39–50. doi:10.1177/002224378101800104

Frąckiewicz, M. (2023). *Chat GPT-4 in Travel and Tourism: Enhancing Experiences with AI.* https://ts2.space/en/chat-gpt-4-in-travel-and-tourism-enhancing-experiences-with-ai/#:~:text=Overall%2C%20AI%2Dpowered%20chat%20GPT,and%20automate%20customer%20support%20tasks

Fraiwan, M., & Khasawneh, N. (2023). A Review of ChatGPT Applications in Education, Marketing, Software Engineering, and Healthcare: Benefits, Drawbacks, and Research Directions. *arXiv preprint arXiv:2305.00237.*

French, F., Levi, D., Maczo, C., Simonaityte, A., Triantafyllidis, S., & Varda, G. (2023). Creative Use of OpenAI in Education: Case Studies from Game Development. *Multimodal Technologies and Interaction*, *7*(8), 81. Advance online publication. doi:10.3390/mti7080081

Fuchs, K. (2023, May). Exploring the opportunities and challenges of NLP models in higher education: Is ChatGPT a blessing or a curse? *Frontiers in Education*, *8*, 1166682. doi:10.3389/feduc.2023.1166682

Fui-Hoon Nah, F., Zheng, R., Cai, J., Siau, K., & Chen, L. (2023). Generative AI and ChatGPT: Applications, challenges, and AI-human collaboration. *Journal of Information Technology Case and Application Research*, *25*(3), 277–304. doi:10.1080/15228053.2023.2233814

Fusté-Forné, F., & Orea-Giner, A. (2023). Gastronomy in tourism management and marketing: An interview with ChatGPT. ROBONOMICS. *The Journal of the Automated Economy*, *4*, 42–42.

Fusté-Forné, F., & Orea-Giner, A. (2023). Gastronomy in tourism management and marketing: An interview with ChatGPT. *ROBONOMICS: The Journal of the Automated Economy*, *4*, 1–13.

Fütterer, T., Fischer, C., Alekseeva, A., Chen, X., Tate, T., Warschauer, M., & Gerjets, P. (2023). ChatGPT in education: Global reactions to AI innovations. *Scientific Reports*, *13*(1), 15310. doi:10.1038/s41598-023-42227-6 PMID:37714915

Ganesa, P., Sanjana, J., & Mane, A. S. (2020). Behavioural Intention of AI-Chatbots by Telecom Customers – UTAUT2 Perspective with Trust. *04th International Conference on Marketing. Technology in Society*, *2020*, 1–2.

Gao, Y., Tong, W., Wu, E. Q., Chen, W., Zhu, G. Y., & Wang, F. Y. (2023). Chat With ChatGPT on Interactive Engines for Intelligent Driving. *IEEE Transactions on Intelligent Vehicles*, *8*(3), 2034–2036. doi:10.1109/TIV.2023.3252571

Gardner, A., Smith, A. L., Steventon, A., Coughlan, E., & Oldfield, M. (2022). Ethical funding for trustworthy AI: Proposals to address the responsibilities of funders to ensure that projects adhere to trustworthy AI practice. *AI and Ethics*, *2*(2), 1–15. doi:10.1007/s43681-021-00069-w PMID:34790951

Garrett, N., Beard, N., & Fiesler, C. (2020). More Than "If Time Allows": The Role of Ethics in AI Education. *Proceedings of the AAAI/ACM Conference on AI, Ethics, and Society*, 272–278. 10.1145/3375627.3375868

Gebauer, J., & Tang, Y. (2008). Applying the theory of task-technology fit to mobile technology: The role of user mobility. *International Journal of Mobile Communications*, *6*(3), 321. doi:10.1504/IJMC.2008.017514

Gefen, D., Karahanna, E., & Straub, D. W. (2003a). Trust and TAM in online shopping: An integrated model. *Management Information Systems Quarterly*, *27*(1), 51–90. doi:10.2307/30036519

Gefen, D., Karahanna, E., & Straub, D. W. (2003b). Inexperience and experience with online stores: The importance of TAM and trust. *IEEE Transactions on Engineering Management*, *50*(3), 307–321. doi:10.1109/TEM.2003.817277

George, A. S., & George, A. H. (2023). A review of ChatGPT AI's impact on several business sectors. *Partners Universal International Innovation Journal*, *1*(1), 9–23.

Giovanis, A., Binioris, S., & Polychronopoulos, G. (2012). An Extension of TAM Model With IDT and Security/Privacy Risk in the Adoption of Internet Banking Services in Greece. Euromed Journal of Business. doi:10.1108/14502191211225365

Gleason, N. (2022). *ChatGPT and the rise of AI writers: How should higher education respond?* THE Campus Learn, Share, Connect.

Gligorea, I., Cioca, M., Oancea, R., Gorski, A.-T., Gorski, H., & Tudorache, P. (2023). Adaptive Learning Using Artificial Intelligence in e-Learning: A Literature Review. *Education Sciences*, *13*(12), 12. Advance online publication. doi:10.3390/educsci13121216

Godwin-Jones, R. (2019). In a world of SMART technology, why learn another language? *Journal of Educational Technology & Society*, *22*(2), 4–13.

Goeldner, C. R., & Ritchie, J. B. (2012). *Tourism principles, practices, philosophies*. John Wiley & Sons.

Goli, M., Sahu, A. K., Bag, S., & Dhamija, P. (2023). Users' Acceptance of Artificial Intelligence-Based Chatbots. International Journal of Technology and Human Interaction. doi:10.4018/IJTHI.318481

Goodhue, D. L., & Thompson, R. L. (1995). Task-Technology Fit and Individual Performance. *Management Information Systems Quarterly*, *19*(2), 213–236. doi:10.2307/249689

Goodyear, P., Carvalho, L., & Yeoman, P. (2021). Activity-Centred Analysis and Design (ACAD): Core purposes, distinctive qualities and current developments. *Educational Technology Research and Development*, *69*(2), 445–464. doi:10.1007/s11423-020-09926-7 PMID:33456288

Google Now. (2020). https://www.google.co.uk/landing/now/

Grassini, S. (2023). Shaping the future of education: Exploring the potential and consequences of AI and ChatGPT in educational settings. *Education Sciences*, *13*(7), 692. doi:10.3390/educsci13070692

Guan, C., Mou, J., & Jiang, Z. (2020). Artificial intelligence innovation in education: A Twenty-year data-driven historical analysis. *International Journal of Innovation Studies*, *4*(4), 134–147. doi:10.1016/j.ijis.2020.09.001

Guba, E. G., & Lincoln, Y. S. (1994). Competing paradigms in qualitative research. Handbook of Qualitative Research, 2(105), 163-194.

Gu, D., Khan, S., Khan, I. U., Khan, S. U., Xie, Y., Li, X., & Zhang, G. (2021). Assessing the Adoption of e-Health Technology in a Developing Country: An Extension of the UTAUT Model. *SAGE Open*, *11*(3). doi:10.1177/21582440211027565

Gummesson, E. (1988). *Qualitative methods in management research*. Studentlitteratur, Chartwell-Bratt.

Guo, Y. M., Ng, W. L., Hao, F., Zhang, C., Liu, S. X., & Aman, A. M. (2023). Trust in Virtual Interaction: The Role of Avatars in Sustainable Customer Relationships. *Sustainability (Basel)*, *15*(18), 1–11. doi:10.3390/su151814026

Gupta, A., Yousaf, A., & Mishra, A. (2020). How pre-adoption expectancies shape post-adoption continuance intentions: An extended expectation-confirmation model. *International Journal of Information Management*, *52*, 102094. doi:10.1016/j.ijinfomgt.2020.102094

GuptaB.MuftiT.SohailS. S.MadsenD. Ø. (2023). *ChatGPT: A Brief Narrative Review*. Preprints.org. doi:10.20944/preprints202304.0158.v1

Gursoy, D., Li, Y., & Song, H. (2023). ChatGPT and the hospitality and tourism industry: An overview of current trends and future research directions. *Journal of Hospitality Marketing & Management*, *32*(5), 1–14. doi:10.1080/19368623.2023.2211993

Habbal, A., Ali, M. K., & Abuzaraida, M. A. (2024). Artificial Intelligence Trust, Risk and Security Management (AI TRiSM): Frameworks, applications, challenges and future research directions. *Expert Systems with Applications*, *240*, 1–14. doi:10.1016/j.eswa.2023.122442

Hagendorff, T., Bossert, L. N., Tse, Y. F., & Singer, P. (2023). Speciesist bias in AI: How AI applications perpetuate discrimination and unfair outcomes against animals. *AI and Ethics*, *3*(3), 717–734. doi:10.1007/s43681-022-00199-9

Haile, T. T. (2024). Web's Progression: Moving from Passive Content Consumption to Active Content Creation and Content Validation. *International Journal of Business and Management*, *18*(6), 135–135. doi:10.5539/ijbm.v18n6p135

Hair, J. F., Black, W. C., Babin, B. J., & Anderson, R. E. (2014). *Multivariate data analysis* (7th ed.). Pearson Education International.

Hair, J. F., Sarstedt, M., Pieper, T. M., & Ringle, C. M. (2012). The Use of Partial Least Squares Structural Equation Modeling in Strategic Management Research : A Review of Past Practices and Recommendations for Future Applications. *Long Range Planning*, *45*(5–6), 320–340. doi:10.1016/j.lrp.2012.09.008

Hair, J. Jr, Hair, J. F. Jr, Hult, G. T. M., Ringle, C. M., & Sarstedt, M. (2021). *A primer on partial least squares structural equation modeling (PLS-SEM)*. Sage Publications. doi:10.1007/978-3-030-80519-7

Haleem, A., Javaid, M., & Singh, R. P. (2022). An era of ChatGPT as a significant futuristic support tool: A study on features, abilities, and challenges. *Bench Council Transactions on Benchmarks, Standards and Evaluations, 2*(4), 100089.

Haleem, A., Javaid, M., & Singh, R. P. (2022). An era of ChatGPT as a significant futuristic support tool: A study on features, abilities, and challenges. *Bench Council Transactions on Benchmarks, Standards and Evaluations, 2*(4), 100089. doi:10.1016/j.tbench.2023.100089

HaluzaD.JungwirthD. (2023). Artificial Intelligence and Ten Societal Megatrends: A GPT-3 Case Study [Preprint]. doi:10.20944/preprints202301.0474.v1

Haque, M. U., Dharmadasa, I., Sworna, Z. T., Rajapakse, R. N., & Ahmad, H. (2022). "I think this is the most disruptive technology": Exploring Sentiments of ChatGPT Early Adopters using Twitter Data. *arXiv preprint arXiv:2212.05856.*

Harahap, M. A. K., Ausat, A. M. A., Rachman, A., Riady, Y., & Azzaakiyyah, H. K. (2023). Overview of ChatGPT Technology and its Potential in Improving Tourism Information Services. *Jurnal Minfo Polgan*, *12*(2), 424–431. doi:10.33395/jmp.v12i1.12416

Hashem, T. N. (2023). Can Aggressive Marketing Cause an Ethical Dilemma? *International Journal (Toronto, Ont.)*, *10*(4), 1216–1229.

Hassani, H., & Silva, E. S. (2023). The role of ChatGPT in data science: How ai-assisted conversational interfaces are revolutionizing the field. *Big Data and Cognitive Computing*, *7*(2), 1–16. doi:10.3390/bdcc7020062

Heale, R., & Twycross, A. (2018). What is a case study? *Evidence-Based Nursing*, *21*(1), 7–8. doi:10.1136/eb-2017-102845 PMID:29146764

Health, T. L. D. (2023). ChatGPT: Friend or foe? *The Lancet. Digital Health*, *5*(3), e102. doi:10.1016/S2589-7500(23)00023-7 PMID:36754723

Heavin, C., & Power, D. J. (2018). Challenges for digital transformation – towards a conceptual decision support guide for managers. *Journal of Decision Systems*, *0125*(sup1), 1–8. doi:10.1080/12460125.2018.1468697

Heitmann, M., Donald, R. L., & Andreas, H. (2007). Choice Goal Attainment and Decision and Consumption Satisfaction. *JMR, Journal of Marketing Research*, *44*(2), 234–250. doi:10.1509/jmkr.44.2.234

Helberger, N., & Diakopoulos, N. (2023). ChatGPT and the AI Act. *Internet Policy Review*, *12*(1), 1–6. doi:10.14763/2023.1.1682

Henseler, J., Ringle, C. M., & Sarstedt, M. (2015). A new criterion for assessing discriminant validity in variance-based structural equation modeling. *Journal of the Academy of Marketing Science*, *43*(1), 115–135. doi:10.1007/s11747-014-0403-8

Hernandez-Ortega, B. (2011). The role of post-use trust in the acceptance of a technology: Drivers and consequences. *Technovation*, *31*(10-11), 523–538. doi:10.1016/j.technovation.2011.07.001

Heyder, T., Passlack, N., & Posegga, O. (2023). Ethical management of human-AI interaction: Theory development review. *The Journal of Strategic Information Systems*, *32*(3), 1–50. doi:10.1016/j.jsis.2023.101772

HosameldeenO.AbousamraN. K.Al-AqrabiH.EmbarakO.DurraniU. (2023). *Improving the Accuracy of Customer Service Seq2Seq Chatbots Through Dataset Pruning*. doi:10.20944/preprints202303.0070.v1

How GPT will change the way we interact with Chatbots. (n.d.). Botpress Blog. https://botpress.com/blog/how-gpt-will-change-the-way-we-interact-with-chatbots

Hsiao, K.-L., & Chen, C.-C. (2022). What drives continuance intention to use a food-ordering chatbot? An examination of trust and satisfaction. *Library Hi Tech*, *40*(4), 929–946. doi:10.1108/LHT-08-2021-0274

Hsu, J. S.-C., Lin, T.-C., Fu, T.-W., & Hung, Y.-W. (2015). The effect of unexpected features on app users' continuance intention. *Electronic Commerce Research and Applications*, *14*(6), 418–430. doi:10.1016/j.elerap.2015.06.003

Huang, M. H., & Rust, R. T. (2018). Artificial intelligence in service. *Journal of Service Research*, *21*(2), 155–172. doi:10.1177/1094670517752459

Huete-Alcocer, N. (2017). A literature review of word of mouth and electronic word of mouth: Implications for consumer behavior. *Frontiers in Psychology*, *8*, 1256. doi:10.3389/fpsyg.2017.01256 PMID:28790950

Huh, J., Nelson, M. R., & Russell, C. A. (2023). ChatGPT, AI advertising, and advertising research and education. *Journal of Advertising*, *52*(4), 477–482. doi:10.1080/00913367.2023.2227013

Hu, L., & Bentler, P. M. (1999). Cutoff criteria for fit indexes in covariance structure analysis: Conventional criteria versus new alternatives. *Structural Equation Modeling, 6*(1), 1–55. doi:10.1080/10705519909540118

Hung, K. H., & Li, S. Y. (2007). The influence of eWOM on virtual consumer communities: Social capital, consumer learning, and behavioral outcomes. *Journal of Advertising Research, 47*(4), 485–495. doi:10.2501/S002184990707050X

Huseynov, F. (2023). Chatbots in digital marketing: Enhanced customer experience and reduced customer service costs. In *Contemporary Approaches of Digital Marketing and the Role of Machine Intelligence* (pp. 46–72). IGI Global. doi:10.4018/978-1-6684-7735-9.ch003

İlaslan, E. (2023). Yapay zeka sohbet robotları ve ChatGPT'nin hemşirelik eğitiminde kullanılması. *Akdeniz Hemşirelik Dergisi, 2*(2), 73–80. doi:10.59398/ahd.1330341

Ingle, S., & Connolly, R. (2006). Methodological and Research Issues Using ES-QUAL to Measure Online Service Quality in Irish SMEs. *Irish Journal of Management, 27*(2).

Iskender, A. (2023). Holy or unholy? Interview with open AI's ChatGPT. *European Journal of Tourism Research, 34*, 3414–3414. doi:10.54055/ejtr.v34i.3169

İşler, B., & Kiliç, M. (2021). Eğitimde yapay zekâ kullanimi ve gelişimi. *Yeni Medya Elektronik Dergisi, 5*(1), 1–11.

Ivanov, S. H. (2023). Automated decision-making. *Foresight, 25*(1), 4-19. doi:10.1108/FS-09-2021-0183

Ivanov, S., & Soliman, M. (2023). Game of algorithms: ChatGPT implications for the future of tourism education and research. *Journal of Tourism Futures*, 1-8. doi:10.1108/JTF-02-2023-0038

Ivanovic, M., Autexier, S., Kokkonidis, M., & Rust, J. (2023). Quality medical data management within an open AI architecture-cancer patients case. *Connection Science, 35*(1), 2194581. Advance online publication. doi:10.1080/09540091.2023.2194581

Jain, V., Rai, H., Subash, P., & Mogaji, E. (2023). The Prospects and Challenges of ChatGPT on Marketing Research and Practices. *Emmanuel, The Prospects and Challenges of ChatGPT on Marketing Research and Practices.*

Jalilvand, M. R., & Samiei, N. (2012). The effect of electronic word of mouth on brand image and purchase intention An empirical study in the automobile. *Marketing Intelligence & Planning, 30*(4), 460–476. doi:10.1108/02634501211231946

Jansson, J., Pettersson, T., Mannberg, A., Brännlund, R., & Lindgren, U. (2017). Adoption of alternative fuel vehicles: Influence from neighbors, family and coworkers. *Transportation Research Part D, Transport and Environment, 54*, 61–73. doi:10.1016/j.trd.2017.04.012

Jarrahi, M. H., Kenyon, S., Brown, A., Donahue, C., & Wicher, C. (2023). Artificial intelligence: A strategy to harness its power through organizational learning. *The Journal of Business Strategy, 44*(3), 126–135. doi:10.1108/JBS-11-2021-0182

Javaid, M., Haleem, A., & Singh, R. P. (2023). ChatGPT for healthcare services: An emerging stage for an innovative perspective. *BenchCouncil Transactions on Benchmarks. Standards and Evaluations*, *3*(1), 100105.

Jin, S. V., & Youn, S. (2023). Social Presence and Imagery Processing as Predictors of Chatbot Continuance Intention in Human-AI-Interaction Social Presence and Imagery Processing as Predictors of Chatbot Continuance. *International Journal of Human-Computer Interaction*, *39*(9), 1874–1886. doi:10.1080/10447318.2022.2129277

John, M. M., Olsson, H. H., & Bosch, J. (2023). Towards an AI-driven business development framework: A multi-case study. *Journal of Software (Malden, MA)*, *35*(6), e2432. doi:10.1002/smr.2432

John-Mathews, J. M., Cardon, D., & Balagué, C. (2022). From reality to world. A critical perspective on AI fairness. *Journal of Business Ethics*, *178*(4), 945–959. doi:10.1007/s10551-022-05055-8

Johnston, R., Jones, K., & Manley, D. (2018). Confounding and collinearity in regression analysis: A cautionary tale and an alternative procedure, illustrated by studies of British voting behaviour. *Quality & Quantity*, *52*(4), 1957–1976. doi:10.1007/s11135-017-0584-6 PMID:29937587

Jonassen, D., Davidson, M., Collins, M., Campbell, J., & Bannan, B. (1995). Constructivism and Computer-Mediated Communication in Distance Education. *American Journal of Distance Education*, *9*(2), 7–26. doi:10.1080/08923649509526885

Joo, Y. J., Park, S., & Shin, E. K. (2017). Students' expectation, satisfaction, and continuance intention to use digital textbooks. *Computers in Human Behavior*, *69*, 83–90. doi:10.1016/j.chb.2016.12.025

Jusman, I. A., Ausat, A. M. A., & Sumarna, A. (2023). Application of ChatGPT in Business Management and Strategic Decision Making. *Jurnal Minfo Polgan*, *12*(2), 1688–1697. doi:10.33395/jmp.v12i2.12956

Kang, D., Jang, W., & Park, Y. (2016). Evaluation of e-commerce websites using fuzzy hierarchical TOPSIS based on ES-QUAL. *Applied Soft Computing*, *42*, 53–65. doi:10.1016/j.asoc.2016.01.017

Kang, H.-J., Han, J., & Kwon, G. H. (2022). The Acceptance Behavior of Smart Home Health Care Services in South Korea: An Integrated Model of UTAUT and TTF. *International Journal of Environmental Research and Public Health*, *19*(20), 13279. doi:10.3390/ijerph192013279 PMID:36293859

Kasneci, E., Seßler, K., Küchemann, S., Bannert, M., Dementieva, D., Fischer, F., Gasser, U., Groh, G., Günnemann, S., Hüllermeier, E., Krusche, S., Kutyniok, G., Michaeli, T., Nerdel, C., Pfeffer, J., Poquet, O., Sailer, M., Schmidt, A., Seidel, T., ... Kasneci, G. (2023). ChatGPT for good? On opportunities and challenges of large language models for education. *Learning and Individual Differences*, *103*, 102274. doi:10.1016/j.lindif.2023.102274

Kawamleh, S. (2023). Against explainability requirements for ethical artificial intelligence in health care. *AI and Ethics*, *3*(3), 901–916. doi:10.1007/s43681-022-00212-1

Keiper, M. C. (2023). ChatGPT in practice: Increasing event planning efficiency through artificial intelligence. *Journal of Hospitality, Leisure, Sport and Tourism Education, 33*, 100454. doi:10.1016/j.jhlste.2023.100454

Khurana, D., Koli, A., Khatter, K., & Singh, S. (2023). Natural language processing: State of the art, current trends and challenges. *Multimedia Tools and Applications, 82*(3), 3713–3744. doi:10.1007/s11042-022-13428-4 PMID:35855771

Kim, J. H., Kim, J., Kim, S., & Hailu, T. B. (2023). Effects of AI ChatGPT on travelers' travel decision-making. *Tourism Review*. Advance online publication. doi:10.1108/TR-07-2023-0489

Kim, M., Kim, J., & Lennon, S. J. (2006). Online service attributes available on apparel retail web sites : An E-S-QUAL approach. *Managing Service Quality, 16*(1), 51–77. doi:10.1108/09604520610639964

King, M. R., & Chat, G. P. T. (2023). A conversation on artificial intelligence, chatbots, and plagiarism in higher education. *Cellular and Molecular Bioengineering, 16*(1), 1–2. doi:10.1007/s12195-022-00754-8 PMID:36660590

King, R. A., Racherla, P., & Bush, V. D. (2014). What we know and don't know about online word-of-mouth: A review and synthesis of the literature. *Journal of Interactive Marketing, 28*(3), 167–183. doi:10.1016/j.intmar.2014.02.001

Kirschner, P. A., & Stoyanov, S. (2020). Educating Youth for Nonexistent/Not Yet Existing Professions. *Educational Policy, 34*(3), 477–517. doi:10.1177/0895904818802086

KirtaniaD. K. (2023). OpenAI ChatGPT for Library and Information Science (LIS) Professionals. *Available at* SSRN 4404903. doi:10.2139/ssrn.4404903

Koc, E., Hatipoglu, S., Kivrak, O., Celik, C., & Koc, K. (2023). Houston, we have a problem!: The use of ChatGPT in responding to customer complaints. *Technology in Society, 74*, 102333. doi:10.1016/j.techsoc.2023.102333

Kohli, B., Choudhury, T., Sharma, S., & Kumar, P. (2018). A Platform for Human-Chatbot Interaction Using Python. *2018 Second International Conference on Green Computing and Internet of Things (ICGCIoT)*, 439–444. 10.1109/ICGCIoT.2018.8753031

Kolhar, M., & Aldossary, S. M. (2023). Privacy-Preserving Convolutional Bi-LSTM Network for Robust Analysis of Encrypted Time-Series Medical Images. *AI, 4*(3), 706–720. doi:10.3390/ai4030037

Korzynski, P., Mazurek, G., Altmann, A., Ejdys, J., Kazlauskaite, R., Paliszkiewicz, J., Wach, K., & Ziemba, E. (2023). Generative artificial intelligence as a new context for management theories: analysis of ChatGPT. *Central European Management Journal*, 1-11. doi:10.1108/CEMJ-02-2023-0091

Kshetri, N., Dwivedi, Y. K., Davenport, T. H., & Panteli, N. (2023). Generative artificial intelligence in marketing: Applications, opportunities, challenges, and research agenda. *International Journal of Information Management*, 102716.

Kumar, A. (2024). Exploring Ethical Considerations in AI-driven Autonomous Vehicles: Balancing Safety and Privacy. *Journal of Artificial Intelligence General science, 2*(1), 125-138.

Kumar, A., Gupta, N., & Bapat, G. (2023). Who is making the decisions? How retail managers can use the power of ChatGPT. *The Journal of Business Strategy*, 1–9. doi:10.1108/JBS-04-2023-0067

Kumar, K., Nikhil, N., Singh, K., & Shivshanker, V. (2022). A survey on providing customer and public administration based services using AI : chatbot. In *Multimedia Tools and Applications*. Springer US. doi:10.1007/s11042-021-11458-y

Kung, T. H., Cheatham, M., Medenilla, A., Sillos, C., De Leon, L., Elepaño, C., Madriaga, M., Aggabao, R., Diaz-Candido, G., Maningo, J., & Tseng, V. (2023). Performance of ChatGPT on USMLE: Potential for AI-assisted medical education using large language models. *PLOS Digital Health, 2*(2), e0000198. doi:10.1371/journal.pdig.0000198 PMID:36812645

Kurzweil, R. (1990). *The age of intelligent machines*. MIT Press.

Kusal, S., Patil, S., Choudrie, J., Kotecha, K., Mishra, S., & Abraham, A. (2022). AI-based Conversational Agents: A Scoping Review from Technologies to Future Directions. *IEEE Access : Practical Innovations, Open Solutions, 10*, 92337–92356. doi:10.1109/ACCESS.2022.3201144

Lai, H., Chen, C., & Chang, Y. (2016). Expectation-Confirmation Model of Information System Continuance : A Meta-Analysis. *World Academy of Science. Engineering and Technology International Journal of Educational and Pedagogical Sciences, 10*(7), 2325–2330.

Larkin, J., Ballatore, A., & Mityurova, E. (2023). Museums, COVID-19 and the pivot to social media. *Curator (New York, N.Y.), 66*(4), 629–646. doi:10.1111/cura.12558

Lawrence, P. R. (1953). In K. R. Andrews (Ed.), *The Case Method of Teaching Human Relations and Administration* (p. 215). Harvard University Press.

Lee, D., Hosanagar, K., & Nair, H. S. (2018). Advertising content and consumer engagement on social media: Evidence from Facebook. *Management Science, 64*(11), 5105–5131. doi:10.1287/mnsc.2017.2902

Lee, J.-Sh., & Hsiang, J. (2020). Patent Claim Generation by Fine-Tuning OpenAI GPT-2. *World Patent Information, 62*, 101983. doi:10.1016/j.wpi.2020.101983

Lee, M. K., & Turban, E. (2001). A trust model for consumer internet shopping. *International Journal of Electronic Commerce, 6*(1), 75–91. doi:10.1080/10864415.2001.11044227

Lee, M., & Park, J. (2022). Do parasocial relationships and the quality of communication with AI shopping chatbots determine middle-aged women consumers' continuance usage intentions? *Journal of Consumer Behaviour, 21*(4), 842–854. doi:10.1002/cb.2043

Lee, S., & Kim, B. G. (2009). Factors affecting the usage of intranet: A confirmatory study. *Computers in Human Behavior, 25*(1), 191–201. doi:10.1016/j.chb.2008.08.007

Lee, W., Xiong, L., & Hu, C. (2012). The effect of Facebook users' arousal and valence on intention to go to the festival: Applying an extension of the technology acceptance model. *International Journal of Hospitality Management*, *31*(3), 819–827. doi:10.1016/j.ijhm.2011.09.018

Leonard-Barton, D. (1990). A dual methodology for case studies: Synergistic use of a longitudinal single site with replicated multiple sites. *Organization Science*, *1*(3), 248–266. doi:10.1287/orsc.1.3.248

Leu. (2023). *Summary of ChatGPT-Related Research and Perspective Towards the Future of Large Language Models.* . doi:10.1016/j.metrad.2023.100017

Levy, M., Ferrand, P., & Chirat, V. (1989). SESAM-DIABETE, an expert system for insulin-requiring diabetic patient education. *Computers and Biomedical Research, an International Journal*, *22*(5), 442–453. doi:10.1016/0010-4809(89)90037-2 PMID:2776447

Li, L., Lee, K. Y., Emokpae, E., & Yang, S.-B. (2021). What makes you continuously use chatbot services? Evidence from chinese online travel agencies. *Electronic Markets*, *31*(3), 575–599. doi:10.1007/s12525-020-00454-z PMID:35603227

Ling, K. C., Chai, L. T., & Piew, T. H. (2010). The effects of shopping orientations, online trust and prior online purchase experience toward customers' online purchase intention. *International Business Research*, *3*(3), 63. doi:10.5539/ibr.v3n3p63

Liu, X., Zheng, Y., Du, Z., Ding, M., Qian, Y., Yang, Z., & Tang, J. (2021). GPT understands, too. arXiv. *arXiv preprint arXiv:2103.10385.*

Liu, Y., Li, X., & Xiang, Z. (2022). The Effect of Chatbot-customer Interaction on Consumer Brand Advocacy: Exploring the Role of Chatbots. *ICEIEC 2022 - Proceedings of 2022 IEEE 12th International Conference on Electronics Information and Emergency Communication*, 185–190. 10.1109/ICEIEC54567.2022.9835050

Liu, Y., & Lopez, R. A. (2016). The impact of social media conversations on consumer brand choices. *Marketing Letters*, *27*(1), 1–13. doi:10.1007/s11002-014-9321-2

Lo, C. K. (2023). What is the impact of Chatgpt on education? A rapid review of the literature. *Education Sciences*, *13*(4), 410. doi:10.3390/educsci13040410

Loureiro, S. M. C., Ali, F., & Ali, M. (2022). Symmetric and asymmetric modeling to understand drivers and consequences of hotel chatbot engagement. *International Journal of Human-Computer Interaction*, 1–13. doi:10.1080/10447318.2022.2124346

Lubbe, I., & Ngoma, N. (2021). Useful chatbot experience provides technological satisfaction: An emerging market perspective. *South African Journal of Information Management*, *23*(1). Advance online publication. doi:10.4102/sajim.v23i1.1299

Lu, C.-C., Wu, L., & Hsiao, W.-H. (2019). Developing customer product loyalty through mobile advertising: Affective and cognitive perspectives. *International Journal of Information Management*, *47*, 101–111. doi:10.1016/j.ijinfomgt.2018.12.020

Luckin, R., & Holmes, W. (2016). Intelligence Unleashed: An argument for AI in Education. In *UCL Knowledge Lab: London, UK.* UCL Knowledge Lab. https://www.pearson.com/content/dam/corporate/global/pearson-dot-com/files/innovation/Intelligence-Unleashed-Publication.pdf

LundB. (2022). A Chat with ChatGPT: How will AI impact scholarly publishing? doi:10.13140/RG.2.2.34572.18565

Lund, B. D., & Wang, T. (2023). Chatting about ChatGPT: How may AI and GPT impact academia and libraries? *Library Hi Tech News*, *40*(3), 26–29. doi:10.1108/LHTN-01-2023-0009

Lund, B. D., Wang, T., Mannuru, N. R., Nie, B., Shimray, S., & Wang, Z. (2023). ChatGPT and a new academic reality: Artificial Intelligence-written research papers and the ethics of the large language models in scholarly publishing. *Journal of the Association for Information Science and Technology*, *74*(5), 570–581. doi:10.1002/asi.24750

Magno, F., & Dossena, G. (2023). The effects of chatbots' attributes on customer relationships with brands: PLS-SEM and importance–performance map analysis. *The TQM Journal*, *35*(5), 1156–1169. doi:10.1108/TQM-02-2022-0080

Makhambetova, A., Zhiyenbayeva, N., & Ergesheva, E. (2021). Personalized Learning Strategy as a Tool to Improve Academic Performance and Motivation of Students. *International Journal of Web-Based Learning and Teaching Technologies*, *16*(6), 1–17. doi:10.4018/IJWLTT.286743

Marimon, F., Vidgen, R., Barnes, S., & Cristobal, E. (2009). Purchasing behaviour in an online supermarket The applicability of E-S-QUAL. *International Journal of Market Research*, *1*(January), 111–129.

Marshall, M. N. (1996). Sampling for qualitative research. *Family Practice*, *13*(6), 522–526. doi:10.1093/fampra/13.6.522 PMID:9023528

Martínez Casanovas, M., Ruíz-Munzón, N., & Buil-Fabregá, M. (2022). Higher education: The best practices for fostering competences for sustainable development through the use of active learning methodologies. *International Journal of Sustainability in Higher Education*, *23*(3), 703–727. doi:10.1108/IJSHE-03-2021-0082

Maxham, J. G. III. (2001). Service recovery's influence on consumer satisfaction, positive word-of-mouth, and purchase intentions. *Journal of Business Research*, *54*(1), 11–24. doi:10.1016/S0148-2963(00)00114-4

Mehrolia, S., Alagarsamy, S., Moorthy, V., & Jeevananda, S. (2023). Will Users Continue Using Banking Chatbots? The Moderating Role of Perceived Risk. *FIIB Business Review*, 1-19. doi:10.1177/23197145231169900

Memarian, B., & Doleck, T. (2023). ChatGPT in education: Methods, potentials, and limitations. *Computers in Human Behavior: Artificial Humans*, *1*(2), 100022. doi:10.1016/j.chbah.2023.100022

Memarian, B., & Doleck, T. (2023). Fairness, Accountability, Transparency, and Ethics (FATE) in Artificial Intelligence (AI), and higher education: A systematic review. Computers and Education. *Artificial Intelligence*, *5*, 1–12. doi:10.1016/j.caeai.2023.100152

Meneceur, Y. (2023). Artificial Intelligence, Public Administration, and the Rule of Law: Towards the Uncertainties of a New "Rule of Algorithms". In *The Rule of Law and Automated Decision-Making: Exploring Fundamentals of Algorithmic Governance* (pp. 117–145). Springer International Publishing. doi:10.1007/978-3-031-30142-1_6

Mercier, M. (2023, February 15). *How GPT Will Change The Way We Interact With Chatbots.* Botpress. Retrieved November 9, 2023, from https://botpress.com/blog/how-gpt-will-change-the-way-we-interact-with-chatbots

Merriam, S. B. (1998). *Case study research and case study applications in education.* Jossey-Bass Publishers.

Meyer-Waarden, L., & Cloarec, J. (2022). "Baby, you can drive my car": Psychological antecedents that drive consumers' adoption of AI-powered autonomous vehicles. *Technovation, 109*, 102348. doi:10.1016/j.technovation.2021.102348

Mhlanga, D. (2023). The Value of Open AI and Chat GPT for the Current Learning Environments and the Potential Future Uses. SSRN *Electronic Journal.* https://doi.org/ doi:10.2139/ssrn.4439267

Mich, L., & Garigliano, R. (2023). ChatGPT for e-Tourism: A technological perspective. *Information Technology & Tourism, 25*(1), 1–12. doi:10.1007/s40558-023-00248-x

Miles, M. B., & Huberman, A. M. (1994). *Qualitative data analysis: An expanded sourcebook.* Sage.

Molnár, G., & Szüts, Z. (2018, September). The role of chatbots in formal education. In *2018 IEEE 16th International Symposium on Intelligent Systems and Informatics (SISY)* (pp. 197-202). IEEE. 10.1109/SISY.2018.8524609

Mondal, S., Das, S., & Vrana, V. G. (2023). How to bell the cat? A theoretical review of generative artificial intelligence towards digital disruption in all walks of life. *Technologies, 11*(2), 1–17. doi:10.3390/technologies11020044

Montenegro-Rueda, M., Fernández-Cerero, J., Fernández-Batanero, J. M., & López-Meneses, E. (2023). Impact of the implementation of ChatGPT in education: A systematic review. *Computers, 12*(8), 153. doi:10.3390/computers12080153

Moore, S., Tong, R., Singh, A., Liu, Z., Hu, X., Lu, Y., . . . Stamper, J. (2023, June). Empowering education with llms-the next-gen interface and content generation. In *International Conference on Artificial Intelligence in Education* (pp. 32-37). Cham: Springer Nature Switzerland. 10.1007/978-3-031-36336-8_4

Mosqueira-Rey, E., Hernández-Pereira, E., Alonso-Ríos, D., Bobes-Bascarán, J., & Fernández-Leal, Á. (2023). Human-in-the-loop machine learning: A state of the art. *Artificial Intelligence Review, 56*(4), 3005–3054. doi:10.1007/s10462-022-10246-w

Munn, L. (2023). The uselessness of AI ethics. *AI and Ethics, 3*(3), 869–877. doi:10.1007/s43681-022-00209-w

Muñoz, K. E., & Chen, L. H. (2023). Can dating app users' self-disclosure foster travel intentions? An appnography approach. *Journal of Hospitality and Tourism Management*, *55*, 493–501. doi:10.1016/j.jhtm.2023.05.020

Murtarelli, G., Collina, C., & Romenti, S. (2023). "Hi! How can I help you today?": Investigating the quality of chatbots–millennials relationship within the fashion industry. *The TQM Journal*, *35*(3), 719–733. doi:10.1108/TQM-01-2022-0010

Mutoffar, M. M., Kuswayati, S., Anggraeny, F. T., & Sumarni, T. (2023). Exploring the Potential of ChatGPT in Improving Online Marketing and Promotion of MSMEs. *Jurnal Minfo Polgan*, *12*(2), 480–489. doi:10.33395/jmp.v12i1.12440

Nadarzynski, T., Miles, O., Cowie, A., & Ridge, D. (2019). Acceptability of artificial intelligence (AI)-led chatbot services in healthcare: A mixed-methods study. *Digital Health*, *5*. doi:10.1177/2055207619871808 PMID:31467682

Navarro, M. M., Prasetyo, Y. T., Young, M. N., Nadlifatin, R., & Redi, A. A. N. P. (2021). The Perceived Satisfaction in Utilizing Learning Management System among Engineering Students during the COVID-19 Pandemic: Integrating Task Technology Fit and Extended Technology Acceptance Model. *Sustainability (Basel)*, *13*(19), 10669. doi:10.3390/su131910669

Nguyen, A., Ngo, H. N., Hong, Y., Dang, B., & Nguyen, B. P. T. (2023). Ethical principles for artificial intelligence in education. *Education and Information Technologies*, *28*(4), 4221–4241. doi:10.1007/s10639-022-11316-w PMID:36254344

Nguyen, D. M., Chiu, Y.-T. H., & Le, H. D. (2021). Determinants of Continuance Intention towards Banks' Chatbot Services in Vietnam: A Necessity for Sustainable Development. *Sustainability (Basel)*, *13*(14), 7625. doi:10.3390/su13147625

Nguyen, Q. N., & Mai, V. N. (2022). Technology Acceptance in Seeking Jobs Among University Graduates in Vietnam. *International Journal of Emerging Technologies in Learning*, *17*(20), 49–61. doi:10.3991/ijet.v17i20.33229

O'Grady, M., Kapoor, S., Gilmer, E., Neighbors, C., Conigliaro, J., Kwon, N., & Morgenstern, J. (2019). Point-of-Care Mobile Application to Guide Health Care Professionals in Conducting Substance Use Screening and Intervention: A Mixed-Methods User Experience Study. *ACI Open*, *03*(01), e1–e12. doi:10.1055/s-0039-1684002

Oliver, R. L. (1980). A cognitive model of the antecedents and consequences of satisfaction decisions. *JMR, Journal of Marketing Research*, *17*(4), 460–469. doi:10.1177/002224378001700405

Open, A. I. (2022). *Introducing ChatGPT*. Open AI. https://openai.com/blog/chatgpt

Open, A. I. (2023, March 14). *GPT*-4. OpenAI. Retrieved November 9, 2023, from https://openai.com/research/gpt-4

OpenA. I. (2023). *ChatGPT*. https:// openai.com

OpenA. I. (2023). *ChatGPT*. https://openai.com

OpenAI (2023). *About ChatGPT*. https://openai.com/about

Overby, M. A. (1987). Psyxpert: An expert system prototype for aiding psychiatrists in the diagnosis of psychotic disorders. *Computers in Biology and Medicine*, *17*(6), 383–393. doi:10.1016/0010-4825(87)90056-4 PMID:3319379

Pagano, T. P., Loureiro, R. B., Lisboa, F. V., Peixoto, R. M., Guimarães, G. A., Cruz, G. O., Araujo, M. M., Santos, L. L., Cruz, M. A. S., Oliveira, E. L. S., Winkler, I., & Nascimento, E. G. (2023). Bias and unfairness in machine learning models: A systematic review on datasets, tools, fairness metrics, and identification and mitigation methods. *Big Data and Cognitive Computing*, *7*(1), 15–25. doi:10.3390/bdcc7010015

Palladino, N. (2023). A 'biased'emerging governance regime for artificial intelligence? How AI ethics get skewed moving from principles to practices. *Telecommunications Policy*, *47*(5), 1–12. doi:10.1016/j.telpol.2022.102479

Palmeira, M., Spassova, G., & Quoidbach, J. (2020). You're not yelping your case: The unexpected social consequences of word of mouth. *European Journal of Marketing*, *54*(2), 419–447. doi:10.1108/EJM-08-2018-0551

Pappas, A., Fumagalli, E., Rouziou, M., & Bolander, W. (2023). More than Machines: The Role of the Future Retail Salesperson in Enhancing the Customer Experience. *Journal of Retailing*, *99*(4), 518–531. doi:10.1016/j.jretai.2023.10.004

Parasuraman, A., Zeithaml, V. A., & Malhotra, A. (2005). ES-QUAL: A multiple-item scale for assessing electronic service quality. *Journal of Service Research*, *7*(3), 213–233. doi:10.1177/1094670504271156

Park, E. (2020a). Telematics and Informatics User acceptance of smart wearable devices: An expectation-confirmation model approach. *Telematics and Informatics, 47*. doi:10.1016/j.tele.2019.101318

Park, G., Chung, J., & Lee, S. (2023). Effect of AI chatbot emotional disclosure on user satisfaction and reuse intention for mental health counseling: A serial mediation model. *Current Psychology (New Brunswick, N.J.)*, *42*(32), 28663–28673. doi:10.1007/s12144-022-03932-z PMID:36406852

Park, J., Amendah, E., Lee, Y., & Hyun, H. (2019). M-payment service: Interplay of perceived risk, benefit, and trust in service adoption. *Human Factors and Ergonomics in Manufacturing*, *29*(1), 31–43. doi:10.1002/hfm.20750

Parry, M. E., Kawakami, T., & Kishiya, K. (2012). The effect of personal and virtual word-of-mouth on technology acceptance. *Journal of Product Innovation Management*, *29*(6), 952–966. doi:10.1111/j.1540-5885.2012.00972.x

Patil, A. S., & Abraham, A. (2010). Intelligent and interactive Web-Based tutoring system in engineering education: Reviews, perspectives and development. In *Computational Intelligence for Technology Enhanced Learning* (pp. 79–97). Springer. doi:10.1007/978-3-642-11224-9_4

Patil, P. P., Dwivedi, Y. K., & Rana, N. P. (2017). Digital payments adoption: an analysis of literature. *Digital Nations–Smart Cities, Innovation, and Sustainability: 16th IFIP WG 6.11 Conference on E-Business, E-Services, and E-Society, I3E 2017, Delhi, India, November 21–23, 2017 Proceedings*, *16*, 61–70.

Paul, J., Ueno, A., & Dennis, C. (2023). ChatGPT and consumers: Benefits, pitfalls and future research Agenda. *International Journal of Consumer Studies*, *47*(4), 1–13. doi:10.1111/ijcs.12928

Pepitone, A. (1976). Toward a normative and comparative biocultural social psychology. *Journal of Personality and Social Psychology*, *34*(4), 641–653. doi:10.1037/0022-3514.34.4.641

Peres, R., Schreier, M., Schweidel, D. A., & Sorescu, A. (2023). Blockchain meets marketing: Opportunities, threats, and avenues for future research. *International Journal of Research in Marketing*, *40*(1), 1–11. doi:10.1016/j.ijresmar.2022.08.001

Persada, S. F., Miraja, B. A., Nadlifatin, R., Belgiawan, P. F., Redi, A. A. N. P., & Lin, S. (2021). Determinants of Students ' Intention to Continue Using Online Private Tutoring : An Expectation - Confirmation Model. *Technology. Knowledge and Learning*. Advance online publication. doi:10.1007/s10758-021-09548-9

Pesonen, J. A. (2021). 'Are You OK?' Students' Trust in a Chatbot Providing Support Opportunities. doi:10.1007/978-3-030-77943-6_13

Pisoni, G., & Díaz-Rodríguez, N. (2023). Responsible and human centric AI-based insurance advisors. *Information Processing & Management*, *60*(3), 1–14. doi:10.1016/j.ipm.2023.103273

Pradana, A., Sing, G. O., & Kumar, Y. J. (2017). SamBot-intelligent conversational bot for interactive marketing with consumer-centric approach. *International Journal of Computer Information Systems and Industrial Management Applications, 6*(2014), 265-275.

Pradana, M., Elisa, H. P., & Syarifuddin, S. (2023). Discussing ChatGPT in education: A literature review and bibliometric analysis. *Cogent Education*, *10*(2), 2243134. doi:10.1080/2331186X.2023.2243134

Pricope Vancia, A. P., Băltescu, C. A., Brătucu, G., Tecău, A. S., Chițu, I. B., & Duguleană, L. (2023). Examining the Disruptive Potential of Generation Z Tourists on the Travel Industry in the Digital Age. *Sustainability (Basel)*, *15*(11), 1–19. doi:10.3390/su15118756

Prieto, M., Baltas, G., & Stan, V. (2017). Car sharing adoption intention in urban areas: What are the key sociodemographic drivers? *Transportation Research Part A, Policy and Practice*, *101*, 218–227. doi:10.1016/j.tra.2017.05.012

Qadir, J. (2022). Engineering education in the era of Chatgpt: Promise and pitfalls of generative AI for education. In *2023 IEEE Global Engineering Education Conference (EDUCON)* (pp. 1-9). IEEE.

Qureshi, R., Shaughnessy, D., Gill, K. A., Robinson, K. A., Li, T., & Agai, E. (2023). Are ChatGPT and large language models "the answer" to bringing us closer to systematic review automation? *Systematic Reviews*, *12*(1), 1–4. doi:10.1186/s13643-023-02243-z PMID:37120563

Radanliev, P., & De Roure, D. (2023). Review of the state of the art in autonomous artificial intelligence. *AI and Ethics*, *3*(2), 497–504. doi:10.1007/s43681-022-00176-2

Rad, D., Egerau, A., Roman, A., Dughi, T., Balas, E., Maier, R., Ignat, S., & Rad, G. (2022). A Preliminary Investigation of the Technology Acceptance Model (TAM) in Early Childhood Education and Care. BRAIN. *Broad Research in Artificial Intelligence and Neuroscience*, *13*(1), 518–533. doi:10.18662/brain/13.1/297

Radford, A., Narasimhan, K., Salimans, T., & Sutskever, I. (2018). *Improving language understanding by generative pre-training*. https://www.mikecaptain.com/resources/pdf/GPT-1.pdf

Radford, A., Wu, J., Child, R., Luan, D., Amodei, D., & Sutskever, I. (2019). Language models are unsupervised multitask learners. *OpenAI Blog, 1*(8), 9.

Rahman, M. M., & Watanobe, Y. (2023). Chatgpt for education and research: Opportunities, threats, and strategies. *Applied Sciences (Basel, Switzerland)*, *13*(9), 5783. doi:10.3390/app13095783

Ramaditiya, A., Rahmatia, S., Munawar, A., & Samijayani, O. N. (2021). Implementation chatbot whatsapp using python programming for broadcast and reply message automatically. *Proceeding - 2021 International Symposium on Electronics and Smart Devices: Intelligent Systems for Present and Future Challenges, ISESD 2021*, 1–4. 10.1109/ISESD53023.2021.9501523

Raman, R. Das, P., Kaur, T., JP, S., & Nedungadi, P. (2023). *University Students as Early Adopters of ChatGPT: Innovation Diffusion Study*. doi:10.21203/rs.3.rs-2734142/v1

Rathore, B. (2023). Digital Transformation 4.0: A Case Study of LK Bennett from Marketing Perspectives. *International Journal of Enhanced Research in Management & Computer Applications*, *10*(11), 45–54.

Raven, B. H., & Rubin, J. Z. (1976). *Social psychology: People in groups*. Academic Press.

Ray, P. P. (2023). ChatGPT: A comprehensive review on background, applications, key challenges, bias, ethics, limitations and future scope. *Internet of Things and Cyber-Physical Systems*, 121-154. doi:10.1016/j.iotcps.2023.04.003

Ray, P. P. (2023). ChatGPT: A comprehensive review on background, applications, key challenges, bias, ethics, limitations and future scope. *Internet of Things and Cyber-Physical Systems*.

Ray, P. P. (2023). AI in Sensor Research: A Reality Check and the Underestimated Potential of ChatGPT. *ACS Sensors*, *8*(4), 1371–1372. doi:10.1021/acssensors.3c01045 PMID:37318550

Reiss, M. V. (2023). Testing the reliability of chatgpt for text annotation and classification: A cautionary remark. *arXiv preprint arXiv:2304.11085*. /arXiv.2304.11085 doi:10.31219/osf.io/rvy5p

Resnik, D. B., & Andrews, S. L. (2023). A precautionary approach to autonomous vehicles. *AI and Ethics*, 1–16.

Riikkinen, M., Saarijärvi, H., & Sarlin, P. (2018). *Using artificial intelligence to create value in insurance in insurance*. doi:10.1108/IJBM-01-2017-0015

Rimal, R. N., & Real, K. (2005). How behaviors are influenced by perceived norms: A test of the theory of normative social behavior. *Communication Research*, *32*(3), 389–414. doi:10.1177/0093650205275385

Rivas, P., & Zhao, L. (2023). Marketing with chatgpt: Navigating the ethical terrain of gpt-based chatbot technology. *AI*, *4*(2), 375–384. doi:10.3390/ai4020019

Römer, J., Rana, Z., Sickmann, J., Pitz, T., & Goldbach, C. (2023). Mobility and Trust in Algorithms: Attitude of Consumers towards Algorithmic Decision-making Systems in the Mobility Sector. In *Towards the New Normal in Mobility: Technische und betriebswirtschaftliche Aspekte* (pp. 569–594). Springer Fachmedien Wiesbaden. doi:10.1007/978-3-658-39438-7_33

Rudolph, J., Tan, S., & Tan, S. (2023). ChatGPT: Bullshit spewer or the end of traditional assessments in higher education? *Journal of Applied Learning & Teaching*, *6*(1). Advance online publication. doi:10.37074/jalt.2023.6.1.9

Rudolph, J., Tan, S., & Tan, S. (2023). ChatGPT: Bullshit spewer or the end of traditional assessments in higher education? *Journal of Applied Learning and Teaching*, *6*(1).

Russell, S. J., & Norvig, P. (2010). Artificial intelligence a modern approach. Academic Press.

Russel, S., & Norvig, P. (2010). *Artificial intelligence - a modern approach*. Pearson Education.

Saeed, M. M. A., Saeed, R. A., & Ahmed, Z. E. (2024). Data Security and Privacy in the Age of AI and Digital Twins. In *Digital Twin Technology and AI Implementations in Future-Focused Businesses* (pp. 99–124). IGI Global. doi:10.4018/979-8-3693-1818-8.ch008

Sajjad, S. (2010). Effective teaching methods at higher education level. *Pakistan Journal of Special Education*, *11*, 29–43.

Saka, A., Taiwo, R., Saka, N., Salami, B. A., Ajayi, S., Akande, K., & Kazemi, H. (2023). GPT models in construction industry: Opportunities, limitations, and a use case validation. *Developments in the Built Environment*, 100300.

Sallam, M. (2023, March). ChatGPT utility in healthcare education, research, and practice: systematic review on the promising perspectives and valid concerns. In Healthcare (Vol. 11, No. 6, p. 887). MDPI. doi:10.3390/healthcare11060887

Sánchez-Prieto, J. C., Olmos-Migueláñez, S., & García-Peñalvo, F. J. (2017). MLearning and pre-service teachers: An assessment of the behavioral intention using an expanded TAM model. *Computers in Human Behavior*, *72*, 644–654. doi:10.1016/j.chb.2016.09.061

Sand, M., Durán, J. M., & Jongsma, K. R. (2022). Responsibility beyond design: Physicians' requirements for ethical medical AI. *Bioethics*, *36*(2), 162–169. doi:10.1111/bioe.12887 PMID:34089625

Sands, S., Ferraro, C., Campbell, C., & Tsao, H.-Y. (2021). Managing the human–chatbot divide: How service scripts influence service experience. *Journal of Service Management*, *32*(2), 246–264. doi:10.1108/JOSM-06-2019-0203

Sanny, L., Susastra, A. C., Roberts, C., & Yusramdaleni, R. (2020). The analysis of customer satisfaction factors which influence chatbot acceptance in Indonesia. *Management Science Letters*, 1225–1232. doi:10.5267/j.msl.2019.11.036

Saqib, N. (2020). Positioning–a literature review. *PSU Research Review*, *5*(2), 141–169. doi:10.1108/PRR-06-2019-0016

Sarkar, S., Aleali, A., Shakarian, P., Armenta, M., Sanchez, D., & Lakkaraju, K. (2019, August). Impact of social influence on adoption behavior: An online controlled experimental evaluation. In *Proceedings of the 2019 IEEE/ACM International Conference on Advances in Social Networks Analysis and Mining* (pp. 226-233). 10.1145/3341161.3342882

Schnall, R., Smith, A. B., Sikka, M., Gordon, P., Camhi, E., Kanter, T., & Bakken, S. (2012). Employing the FITT framework to explore HIV case managers' perceptions of two electronic clinical data (ECD) summary systems. *International Journal of Medical Informatics*, *81*(10), e56–e62. doi:10.1016/j.ijmedinf.2012.07.002 PMID:22841702

Schurr, A., & Moran, S. (2023). The presence of automation enhances deontological considerations in moral judgments. *Computers in Human Behavior*, *140*, 1–10. doi:10.1016/j.chb.2022.107590

Sebo, J. (2023). The rebugnant conclusion: Utilitarianism, insects, microbes, and AI systems. *Ethics, Policy & Environment*, *26*(2), 249–264. doi:10.1080/21550085.2023.2200724

Setiawati, E., Trisnawati, R., & Diana, U. (2019). The analysis of acceptance of hospital information management system (HIMS) using technology acceptance model method. *Riset Akuntansi Dan Keuangan Indonesia*, *4*(2), 186–195. doi:10.23917/reaksi.v4i2.8652

Sezgin, E., Sirrianni, J., & Linwood, S. L. (2022). Operationalizing and implementing pretrained, large artificial intelligence linguistic models in the US health care system: Outlook of generative pretrained transformer 3 (GPT-3) as a service model. *JMIR Medical Informatics*, *10*(2), e32875. doi:10.2196/32875 PMID:35142635

Shawar, B. A., & Atwell, E. (2007). Different measurements metrics to evaluate a chatbot system. *Bridging the Gap: Academic and Industrial Research in Dialog Technologies Workshop Proceedings,* 89–96.

Shemshack, A., & Spector, J. M. (2020). A systematic literature review of personalized learning terms. *Smart Learning Environments*, *7*(1), 33. doi:10.1186/s40561-020-00140-9

Shin, A., & Song, H.-D. (2022). The Effects of Basic Psychological Needs, Task-Technology Fit, and Student Engagement on MOOC Learners' Continuance Intention to Use. *Human Behavior and Emerging Technologies*, *2022*, 1–12. doi:10.1155/2022/6444509

Shin, D., Chotiyaputta, V., & Zaid, B. (2022). The effects of cultural dimensions on algorithmic news: How do cultural value orientations affect how people perceive algorithms? *Computers in Human Behavior*, *126*, 107007. doi:10.1016/j.chb.2021.107007

Shin, H., & Kang, J. (2023). Bridging the gap of bibliometric analysis: The evolution, current state, and future directions of tourism research using ChatGPT. *Journal of Hospitality and Tourism Management*, *57*, 40–47. doi:10.1016/j.jhtm.2023.09.001

Singh, S., Thakur, P., & Singh, S. (2023). How Does the Use of AI in HRM Contribute to Improved Business Performance?: A Systematic Review. *Advances in Human Resources Management and Organizational Development*, *5*(0), 131–139. doi:10.4018/978-1-6684-6745-9.ch008

Skavronskaya, L., Hadinejad, A., & Cotterell, D. (2023). Reversing the threat of artificial intelligence to opportunity: A discussion of ChatGPT in tourism education. *Journal of Teaching in Travel & Tourism*, *23*(2), 253–258. doi:10.1080/15313220.2023.2196658

Skilton, M., & Hovsepian, F. (2017). *The 4th Industrial Revolution: Responding to the Impact of Artificial Intelligence on Business*. Springer.

Smale-Jacobse, A. E., Meijer, A., Helms-Lorenz, M., & Maulana, R. (2019). Differentiated Instruction in Secondary Education: A Systematic Review of Research Evidence. *Frontiers in Psychology*, *10*, 2366. doi:10.3389/fpsyg.2019.02366 PMID:31824362

Smith, A. N., Fischer, E., & Yongjian, C. (2012). How does brand-related user-generated content differ across YouTube, Facebook, and Twitter? *Journal of Interactive Marketing*, *26*(2), 102–113. doi:10.1016/j.intmar.2012.01.002

Smith, N., & Vickers, D. (2024). Living well with AI: Virtue, education, and artificial intelligence. *Theory and Research in Education*, *21*(2), 19–44. doi:10.1177/14778785241231561

Sohail, S. S., Farhat, F., Himeur, Y., Nadeem, M., Madsen, D. Ø., Singh, Y., Atalla, S., & Mansoor, W. (2023). Decoding ChatGPT: A taxonomy of existing research, current challenges, and possible future directions. *Journal of King Saud University. Computer and Information Sciences*, *35*(8), 1–23. doi:10.1016/j.jksuci.2023.101675

SokS.HengK. (2023). Chatgpt for education and research: A review of benefits and risks. Available At SSRN 4378735.

Soliman, M., & Al Balushi, M. K. (2023). Unveiling destination evangelism through generative AI tools. *ROBONOMICS: The Journal of the Automated Economy*, *4*(54), 1.

Sridhar, G. S. (2018). *Artificial Intelligence: The Future Way of Technology*. Gs Srıdhar.

Stahl, B. C., & Eke, D. (2024). The ethics of ChatGPT – Exploring the ethical issues of an emerging technology. *International Journal of Information Management*, *74*, 102700. doi:10.1016/j.ijinfomgt.2023.102700

Stears, C., & Deeks, J. (2023). Editorial: The use of artificial intelligence in fighting financial crime, for better or worse? In Journal of Money Laundering Control (Vol. 26, Issue 3, pp. 433-435). Emerald Publishing. https://doi.org/ doi:10.1108/JMLC-05-2023-174

Suárez, A., Jiménez, J., de Pedro, M. L., Andreu-Vázquez, C., García, V. D. F., Sánchez, M. G., & Freire, Y. (2024). Beyond the Scalpel: Assessing ChatGPT's potential as an auxiliary intelligent virtual assistant in oral surgery. *Computational and Structural Biotechnology Journal*, *24*, 46–52. doi:10.1016/j.csbj.2023.11.058 PMID:38162955

Subagja, A. D., Ausat, A. M. A., Sari, A. R., Wanof, M. I., & Suherlan, S. (2023). Improving Customer Service Quality in MSMEs through the Use of ChatGPT. *Jurnal Minfo Polgan*, *12*(2), 380–386. doi:10.33395/jmp.v12i1.12407

Sudirjo, F., Diawati, P., Riady, Y., Ausat, A. M. A., & Suherlan, S. (2023). The Role of ChatGPT in Enhancing the Information Search and Decision-Making Process of Travellers. *Jurnal Minfo Polgan*, *12*(2), 500–507. doi:10.33395/jmp.v12i1.12443

Suta, P., Lan, X., Wu, B., Mongkolnam, P., & Chan, J. H. (2020). An overview of machine learning in chatbots. *International Journal of Mechanical Engineering and Robotics Research*, *9*(4), 502–510. doi:10.18178/ijmerr.9.4.502-510

Sutrisno, S., Ausat, A. M. A., Permana, B., & Harahap, M. A. K. (2023). Do Information Technology and Human Resources Create Business Performance: A Review. *International Journal of Professional Business Review: Int. J. Prof. Bus. Rev.*, *8*(8), 14.

Suwannapusit, U. (2021). The UTAUT Model Analysis in the Technology Use of Generation-Z Users in Cambodia during COVID-19 Situation. *International Journal of Current Science Research and Review*, *04*(07). Advance online publication. doi:10.47191/ijcsrr/V4-i7-06

Swiecki, Z., Khosravi, H., Chen, G., Martinez-Maldonado, R., Lodge, J. M., Milligan, S., Selwyn, N., & Gašević, D. (2022). Assessment in the age of artificial intelligence. *Computers and Education. Artificial Intelligence*, *3*, 1–10.

Talwar, S., Dhir, A., Khalil, A., Mohan, G., & Islam, A. N. (2020). Point of adoption and beyond. Initial trust and mobile-payment continuation intention. *Journal of Retailing and Consumer Services*, *55*, 102086. doi:10.1016/j.jretconser.2020.102086

Talwar, S., Talwar, M., Kaur, P., & Dhir, A. (2020). Consumers' resistance to digital innovations: A systematic review and framework development. *Australasian Marketing Journal*, *28*(4), 286–299. doi:10.1016/j.ausmj.2020.06.014

Tam, C., Santos, D., & Oliveira, T. (2020). Exploring the influential factors of continuance intention to use mobile Apps: Extending the expectation confirmation model. *Information Systems Frontiers*, *22*(1), 243–257. doi:10.1007/s10796-018-9864-5

Taylor, S., & Todd, P. (1995). Assessing IT usage: The role of prior experience. *Management Information Systems Quarterly*, *19*(4), 561–570. doi:10.2307/249633

Tegmark, M. (2018). *Life 3.0: Being human in the age of artificial intelligence*. Vintage.

Teng, X. (2019, April). Discussion about artificial intelligence's advantages and disadvantages compete with natural intelligence. *Journal of Physics: Conference Series*, *1187*(3), 032083. doi:10.1088/1742-6596/1187/3/032083

Thomson, M. (2006). Human Brands: Investigating Antecedents to Consumers' Strong Attachments to Celebrities. *Journal of Marketing, 70*(3), 104–119. doi:10.1509/jmkg.70.3.104

Thorp, H. H. (2023). ChatGPT is fun, but not an author. *Science, 379*(6630), 313–313. doi:10.1126/science.adg7879 PMID:36701446

Timms, M. J. (2016). Letting artificial intelligence in education out of the box: Educational cobots and smart classrooms. *International Journal of Artificial Intelligence in Education, 26*(2), 701–712. doi:10.1007/s40593-016-0095-y

Tomar, K., & Sharma, S. (2024). A proposed artificial intelligence and blockchain technique for solving health insurance challenges. In *Data-Driven Technologies and Artificial Intelligence in Supply Chain* (pp. 31–57). CRC Press.

Tong, Y., & Zhang, L. (2023). Discovering the next decade's synthetic biology research trends with Chatgpt. *Synthetic and Systems Biotechnology, 8*(2), 220–223. doi:10.1016/j.synbio.2023.02.004 PMID:36923604

Tóth, Z., Caruana, R., Gruber, T., & Loebbecke, C. (2022). The dawn of the AI robots: Towards a new framework of AI robot accountability. *Journal of Business Ethics, 178*(4), 895–916. doi:10.1007/s10551-022-05050-z

Touretzky, D., Gardner-McCune, C., Martin, F., & Seehorn, D. (2019). Envisioning AI for K-12: What Should Every Child Know about AI? *Proceedings of the AAAI Conference on Artificial Intelligence, 33*(01), 01. Advance online publication. doi:10.1609/aaai.v33i01.33019795

Tran, A. D., Pallant, J. I., & Johnson, L. W. (2021). Exploring the impact of chatbots on consumer sentiment and expectations in retail. *Journal of Retailing and Consumer Services, 63*, 102718. doi:10.1016/j.jretconser.2021.102718

Triantoro, S. (2013). Effects of Self-Efficacy on Students' Academic Performance. *Journal of Educational. Health and Community Psychology, 2*, 19–25.

Turing, A. (1950). Computing machinery and intelligence. *Mind, 59*(236), 433–460. doi:10.1093/mind/LIX.236.433

Tussyadiah, I. (2020). A review of research into automation in tourism: Launching the Annals of Tourism Research Curated Collection on Artificial Intelligence and Robotics in Tourism. *Annals of Tourism Research, 81*, 102883. doi:10.1016/j.annals.2020.102883

Unver, M. B. (2023). Governing fiduciary relationships or building up a governance model for trust in AI? Review of healthcare as a socio-technical system. *International Review of Law Computers & Technology, 37*(2), 198–226. doi:10.1080/13600869.2023.2192569

Van Dis, E. A., Bollen, J., Zuidema, W., van Rooij, R., & Bockting, C. L. (2023). ChatGPT: Five priorities for research. *Nature, 614*(7947), 224–226. doi:10.1038/d41586-023-00288-7 PMID:36737653

Varadarajan, R. (2010). Strategic marketing and marketing strategy: Domain, definition, fundamental issues and foundational premises. *Journal of the Academy of Marketing Science*, *38*(2), 119–140. doi:10.1007/s11747-009-0176-7

Vărzaru, A. A., Bocean, C. G., Rotea, C. C., & Budică-Iacob, A. F. (2021). Assessing antecedents of behavioral intention to use mobile technologies in e-commerce. *Electronics (Basel)*, *10*(18), 2231. doi:10.3390/electronics10182231

Vatanasakdakul, S., Aoun, C., & Putra, Y. H. S. (2020). Social Media in Micro-Enterprises. *Journal of Global Information Management*, *28*(3), 184–203. doi:10.4018/JGIM.2020070110

Veiga, C., Santos, M. C., Águas, P., & Santos, J. A. C. (2017). Are millennials transforming global tourism? Challenges for destinations and companies. *Worldwide Hospitality and Tourism Themes*, *9*(6), 603–616. doi:10.1108/WHATT-09-2017-0047

Venkatesan, R. (2017). Executing on a customer engagement strategy. *Journal of the Academy of Marketing Science*, *45*(3), 289–293. doi:10.1007/s11747-016-0513-6

Venkatesh, V., & Bala, H. (2008). Technology acceptance model 3 and a research agenda on interventions. *Decision Sciences*, *39*(2), 273–315. doi:10.1111/j.1540-5915.2008.00192.x

Venkatesh, V., & Brown, S. A. (2001). A longitudinal investigation of personal computers in homes: Adoption determinants and emerging challenges. *Management Information Systems Quarterly*, *25*(1), 71–102. doi:10.2307/3250959

Vijayakumar, H. (2023). Revolutionizing Customer Experience with AI: A Path to Increase Revenue Growth Rate. *15th International Conference on Electronics, Computers and Artificial Intelligence, ECAI 2023 - Proceedings*. https://doi.org/10.1109/ECAI58194.2023.10194016

Von Garrel, J., & Mayer, J. (2023). Artificial Intelligence in studies—Use of ChatGPT and AI-based tools among students in Germany. *Humanities & Social Sciences Communications*, *10*(1), 799. doi:10.1057/s41599-023-02304-7

Vorobeva, D., Costa Pinto, D., António, N., & Mattila, A. S. (2023). The augmentation effect of artificial intelligence: Can AI framing shape customer acceptance of AI-based services? *Current Issues in Tourism*, •••, 1–21. doi:10.1080/13683500.2023.2214353

Wals, A. E. J., & Alblas, A. H. (1997). School-Based research and development of environmental education: A case study. *Environmental Education Research*, *3*(3), 253–269. doi:10.1080/1350462970030301

Wang, C., Harris, J., & Patterson, P. (2013). The Roles of Habit, Self-Efficacy, and Satisfaction in Driving Continued Use of Self-Service Technologies. *Journal of Service Research*, *16*(3), 400–414. doi:10.1177/1094670512473200

Wang, W. (2024). Research on Data Security and Privacy Protection in the Context of Big Data. *Frontiers in Computing and Intelligent Systems*, *7*(1), 29–33. doi:10.54097/astapa66

Wanti, L. P., Insan, H. F. M., & Prasetya, N. W. A. (2020). End User Satisfaction for Location Health Service Application with Analysis of Task Technology Fit. Lontar Komputer? *Jurnal Ilmiah Teknologi Informasi*, *11*(2), 76. doi:10.24843/LKJITI.2020.v11.i02.p02

Weizenbaum, J. (1966). ELIZA—A computer program for the study of natural language communication between man and machine. *Communications of the ACM*, *9*(1), 36–45. doi:10.1145/365153.365168

What exactly is alexa? where does she come from? and how does she work ? (2019). Digital Trends website: https://www.digitaltrends.com/home/what-is-amazonsalexa-and-what-can-it-do/

Williamson, B., & Eynon, R. (2020). Historical threads, missing links, and future directions in AI in education. *Learning, Media and Technology*, *45*(3), 223–235. doi:10.1080/17439884.2020.1798995

Wong, K. K. K. (2019). *Mastering partial least squares structural equation modeling (PLS-Sem) with Smartpls in 38 Hours.* IUniverse.

Wong, S. K. Y. (2024). Privacy and confidentiality. In *Artificial Intelligence in Medicine* (pp. 45–58). Academic Press. doi:10.1016/B978-0-323-95068-8.00004-2

Wu, T., He, S., Liu, J., Sun, S., Liu, K., Han, Q. L., & Tang, Y. (2023). A brief overview of ChatGPT: The history, status quo and potential future development. *IEEE/CAA Journal of Automatica Sinica, 10*(5), 1122-1136.

Wu, C. S., Cheng, F. F., Yen, D. C., & Huang, Y. W. (2011). User acceptance of wireless technology in organizations: A comparison of alternative models. *Computer Standards & Interfaces*, *33*(1), 50–58. doi:10.1016/j.csi.2010.03.002

Xiong, W., Wang, C., & Ma, L. (2023). Partner or subordinate? Sequential risky decision-making behaviors under human-machine collaboration contexts. *Computers in Human Behavior*, *139*, 107556. doi:10.1016/j.chb.2022.107556

Yaşar, E., Demir, M., & Taşdemir, T. (2023). Embedded big data in packaged foods: Examining consumer sentiment during the purchasing process post-COVID-19. *British Food Journal*, *125*(10), 1–17. doi:10.1108/BFJ-12-2022-1124

Yenduri, G., Ramalingam, M., Chemmalar Selvi, G., Supriya, Y., Srivastava, G., Maddikunta, P. K. R., ... Athanasios, V. (n.d.). *GPT (Generative Pre-trained Transformer)–A Comprehensive Review on Enabling Technologies, Potential Applications, Emerging Challenges, and Future Directions*. Academic Press.

Yordanova, Z. (2023). Ethical Implications of Transparency and Explainability of Artificial Intelligence for Managing Value-Added Tax (VAT) in Corporations. In *International Conference on Advanced Research in Technologies, Information, Innovation and Sustainability* (pp. 344-353). Cham: Springer Nature Switzerland.

Yoshikuni, A. C., Dwivedi, R., Dultra-de-Lima, R. G., Parisi, C., & Oyadomari, J. C. T. (2023). Role of Emerging Technologies in Accounting Information Systems for Achieving Strategic Flexibility through Decision-Making Performance: An Exploratory Study Based on North American and South American Firms. *Global Journal of Flexible Systems Management*, 1-20.

Yun, J., & Park, J. (2022). The Effects of Chatbot Service Recovery With Emotion Words on Customer Satisfaction, Repurchase Intention, and Positive Word-Of-Mouth. *Frontiers in Psychology*, *13*, 922503. Advance online publication. doi:10.3389/fpsyg.2022.922503 PMID:35712132

Zerbini, C., Bijmolt, T. H., Maestripieri, S., & Luceri, B. (2022). Drivers of consumer adoption of e-Commerce: A meta-analysis. *International Journal of Research in Marketing*, *39*(4), 1186–1208. doi:10.1016/j.ijresmar.2022.04.003

Zhang, L. A. (2024). How does artificial intelligence affect reliable engineering? *Advances in Operation Research and Production Management*, *1*(1), 7–18. doi:10.54254/3006-1210/direct/0718

Zhang, L., Basham, J., & Yang, S. (2020). Understanding the implementation of personalized learning: A research synthesis. *Educational Research Review*, *31*, 100339. doi:10.1016/j.edurev.2020.100339

Zhao, Y., & Bacao, F. (2020a). What factors determining customer continuingly using food delivery apps during 2019 novel coronavirus pandemic period? *International Journal of Hospitality Management*, *91*, 102683. doi:10.1016/j.ijhm.2020.102683 PMID:32929294

Zheng, L., Long, M., Zhong, L., & Gyasi, J. F. (2022). The effectiveness of technology-facilitated personalized learning on learning achievements and learning perceptions: A meta-analysis. *Education and Information Technologies*, *27*(8), 11807–11830. doi:10.1007/s10639-022-11092-7

Zheng, X., Zhang, C., & Woodland, P. C. (2021, December). Adapting GPT, GPT-2 and BERT language models for speech recognition. In *2021 IEEE Automatic Speech Recognition and Understanding Workshop (ASRU)* (pp. 162-168). IEEE. 10.1109/ASRU51503.2021.9688232

Zhou, W., Zhang, C., Wu, L., & Shashidhar, M. (2023). ChatGPT and marketing: Analyzing public discourse in early Twitter posts. *Journal of Marketing Analytics*, 1-14.

Zhou, J., & Chen, F. (2023). AI ethics: From principles to practice. *AI & Society*, *38*(6), 2693–2703. doi:10.1007/s00146-022-01602-z

Zhu, Q., & Luo, J. (2022). Generative pre-trained transformer for design concept generation: an exploration. *Proceedings of the design society, 2*, 1825-1834. 10.1017/pds.2022.185

Zhu, Y., Janssen, M., Wang, R., & Liu, Y. (2022). It Is Me, Chatbot: Working to Address the COVID-19 Outbreak-Related Mental Health Issues in China. User Experience, Satisfaction, and Influencing Factors. *International Journal of Human-Computer Interaction*, *38*(12), 1182–1194. doi:10.1080/10447318.2021.1988236

Zhu, Y., Wang, R., & Pu, C. (2022). "I am chatbot, your virtual mental health adviser." What drives citizens' satisfaction and continuance intention toward mental health chatbots during the COVID-19 pandemic? An empirical study in China. *Digital Health*, *8*. doi:10.1177/20552076221090031 PMID:35381977

About the Contributors

Mahmut Demir graduated from Cukurova University Mersin School of Tourism and Hotel Management in 1993. He earned his master's degree (2002) and Ph.D. degree (2009) from Dokuz Eylül University, Department of Tourism Management. He started to work as an academic at Mugla University in 1997. He has been working at the Isparta University of Applied Sciences, Tourism Faculty as a professor since 2012. In 2011 he was invited by The Sheffield Hallam University in the UK, where he worked as a visiting scholar for three months. He is the president, board member, and founder member of the International Center of Social Sciences and Education Research (ICSER). Along with ICSER, Prof. Dr. Mahmut DEMIR organized fifteen international conferences between 2015-2020. He is editor in chief of both "Journal of Tourism Theory and Research" and "International Journal of Social Sciences and Education Research". His research interest includes tourism, travel and Hospitality management, organizational behavior, human research management, digitalization and innovation in tourism.

Ali Dalgıç was born in Antalya, Turkey in 1987. He was a research assistant in the Department of Tourism Management at Mersin University. He completed his MSc degree in Management at Adnan Menderes University, Aydin/Turkey in December 2013. He got PhD in Tourism Management at Mersin University. He is working at Isparta University of Applied Sciences Faculty of Tourism as an Assistant Professor. His research interests include event management, alternative tourism and strategic management.

* * *

Ernest Kwame Affum (Dr EK) is Management Consultant, Author, Public Speaker, Mentor, Life Coach, Conference Speaker and Lecturer at the Department of Management Studies, University of Mines and Technology, Tarkwa. He is also a certified trainer with the Ghana Statistical Service. Dr Affum possesses PhD in Economics (with specialization in Industrial Economics) and MBA (Strategic Management), both obtained from Zhongnan University of Economics and Law (ZUEL), Wuhan, Hubei, China, and a BSc. in Business Administration (Accounting) from the University of Ghana Business School. Dr Affum has wide experience in business management and administration, sales and marketing, business development and operations from industries such as healthcare, banking and finance, food and beverage, automobile and real estate having worked with Devtraco Limited, Valkom Enterprise, E K Bonsu Limited, Rakes Company (Barclays Bank), Ajeks Company Limited and the Sunyani Regional Hospital. Dr Affum has tutored, as fulltime and Part-time lecturer, in courses such as communication, economics, financial and management accounting, auditing, marketing, corporate finance, business law, principles of project management, and strategic management in the Wuhan Textiles University (WTU), Birmingham Institute of Fashion and Creative Arts (BIFCA), Wuhan, China Universities Summer School Association (CUSSA) China, University of Ghana and the Ghana Institute of Management and Public Administration (GIMPA). As a public speaker and trainer, he has spoken in several conferences across China and Ghana on Institutional Leadership Development, Relationships, Business Start-Up and Development, Events Planning and Management, academic research, SMEs and AfCFTA, among others. Dr Affum was National Trainer and Team Leader, Center Lead and District Field Supervisor for Ghana's 2021 Population and Housing Census. As author, Dr Affum has written several motivational, educational and inspirational articles for magazines, blogs and conferences. Dr Affum is the author of the books, EKs Quotes: LIFE Tunes Vol I and II', an inspiration read. Dr Affum is both supervisor and reviewer for master's and doctoral degree candidates, as well as Emerald Publishing's International Journal of Workplace Health Management. Dr Affum's research interests cover areas such as SMEs, Innovation, Technology Transfer, Industrial Organisations, Business Development, Leadership Development, Human Resources and Economic Growth.

George Cudjoe Agbemabiese is a senior lecturer at the Faculty of Management Studies and presently the Vice Dean, School of Graduate Studies at the University of Professional Studies Accra. He holds a PhD from Putra Business School, University Putra Malaysia and an MPhil from the University of Ghana Business School, University of Ghana. He has co-authored and published academic papers including book chapters in peer reviewed journals including Scopus indexed and high impact factor journals. His areas of interest include Customer Relationship Management, Service Quality, Relationship Marketing, Customer Perceived Value, Service Recovery and Customer Loyalty.

Fred Amankwah-Sarfo is a highly accomplished professional in the field of Information Systems, recognized for his extensive academic achievements and leadership roles within academic and research circles. Education: Dr. Amankwah-Sarfo earned his Doctor of Philosophy (Ph.D.) in Information Systems from the University of Ghana. During his doctoral studies from September 2016 to December 2020, he exhibited exceptional dedication and leadership as the President of the Doctoral Researchers Association of Ghana. His commitment extended to various societies, including the Association of Information Systems, where he actively participated and contributed to the academic community. Additionally, he completed a Doctoral Certificate in Leadership Skills and Career Development for the Emerging Scholar from the Pan African Doctoral Academy in 2017, further enhancing his expertise in leadership and career development. Earlier in his academic journey, Dr. Amankwah-Sarfo pursued a Master of Business Administration (MBA) in Management Information Systems at the University of Ghana, graduating between 2005 and 2007. He laid the foundation for his academic pursuits with a Bachelor of Science (BSc) in Business Administration and Management, General, obtained from the same institution between 2000 and 2003.

Patrick Amfo Anim is a Marketing lecturer at Lancaster University Ghana. He is a Ph.D. Candidate at the University of Ghana Business School. He also holds M.Phil. and a B.Sc. in Marketing from the University of Ghana and University of Professional Studies Accra respectively. His research areas include B2B marketing, Branding, Political marketing, Service innovation, Digital & Social Media Marketing, Environmental Sustainability, and Entrepreneurship. His research works have been published in internationally peer-reviewed journals including Journal of Business and Industrial Marketing, Journal of Consumer Marketing, European Journal of Innovation Management, and Journal of Enterprising Communities: People and Places in the Global Economy. He serves as a reviewer for the Journal of Small Business and Enterprise Development, European Journal of Marketing, and Journal of Sustainable Business and Management Solutions in Emerging Economies. He has also presented competitive papers at reputable international conferences.

Emmanuel Arthur is a Senior lecturer in Marketing, and currently the Provost at Lancaster University Ghana. He holds a B.A (Hons) degree from the University of Ghana Legon, a Postgraduate Diploma in Marketing from the Chartered Institute of Marketing U.K, a Postgraduate Cert in Academic Practice from Lancaster University U.K, an M.A from Birmingham City University and a PhD from London Metropolitan University. He is a chartered marketer and a full member of both the Chartered Institute of Marketing UK and Ghana. He has specialized research interest in market orientation, service marketing, international and export marketing, general application of strategic marketing principles, Ghana's mobile telecommunications, aviation and oil and gas industries with several publications in reputable journals.

Joseph Aversa is an Assistant Professor at Toronto Metropolitan University's Ted Rogers School of Retail Management in Toronto, Canada. His current research interests include retail location decision-making, big data analytics, retail planning and location strategy. He received his PhD from Wilfrid Laurier University, Department of Geography and Environmental Studies.

Nesrin Aydın Alakuş graduated from Ordu Perşembe Tourism Vocational High School Hospitality Management department in 2015. Then she graduated from Süleyman Demirel University Eğirdir Tourism and Hotel Management School Hospitality and Travel Management Department in 2019. She has been in the sector theoretically and practically since my high school years.

William Brown-Acquaye is a seasoned professional in Information Systems and Technology, renowned for his extensive experience and leadership within academia and the field of industrial technological processes. For over 15 years, Dr. Brown-Acquaye has been an integral part of the Ghana Technology University College (GTUC), currently serving as the Head of the Information Systems Department since March 2018. His tenure has been marked by significant contributions in curriculum development, instructional design, and the implementation of learning management systems. As a Senior Lecturer since August 2017, he has demonstrated adeptness in training delivery, utilizing his expertise to enhance learning experiences. His responsibilities extended to the coordination of the Faculty of Computing and Information Systems since January 2016, where he has played a pivotal role in shaping the academic landscape and fostering growth within this domain. Dr. Brown-Acquaye holds a Doctor of Philosophy (Ph.D.) in Automation of Industrial Technological Processes and Productions, which he earned from Tambov State Technical University between 2012 and 2015. This academic pursuit showcases his dedication to merging industrial processes with technological advancements. Prior to his Ph.D., he obtained a Master of Science (M.Sc.) in Information Systems and Technologies from Tver State Technical University, solidifying his foundational knowledge in Information Systems and Technology between 2002 and 2008. His skill set encompasses a wide array of expertise including training and development, learning management systems, instructional design, curriculum development, and training delivery. Dr. Brown-Acquaye's proficiency in these areas has been instrumental in shaping educational programs and improving learning outcomes within his academic sphere.

Şirvan Şen Demir is a Professor of Tourism Management at the Faculty of Economic and Administrative Sciences, Suleyman Demirel University, Turkey. She received his Ph.D. in 2010 from the Dokuz Eylul University, Turkey. Her research interests include tourism marketing, tourist behavior, digitalization, and innovation in tourism. Her most recent publication is "Demir, Ş.Ş., & Demir, M. (2023). Professionals' perspectives on ChatGPT in the tourism industry: Does it inspire awe or concern? Journal of Tourism Theory and Research, 9(2), 61-76. ".

Ayşegül Simge Demircioğlu Dalgıç graduated from the Tourism Faculty of Adnan Menderes University in 2018. She got her master's degree in Tourism Management from the Social Sciences Institute of Süleyman Demirel University in 2021. Currently, she is continuing her doctoral studies in the field of Tourism Management. Her main areas of interest include tourism marketing, tourism economy, and health tourism.

Omar H. Fares is a Ted Rogers School of Retail Management Lecturer. Omar earned his Bachelor of Commerce and Master of Science in Management from Toronto Metropolitan University. Omar's main research interest is in the consumer behaviour area, particularly focusing on consumers' interaction with novel digital innovations and the impact of digital innovations on retailers. Omar published his research in different journals, including Computers in Human Behavior, the Journal of Financial Services Marketing, and the Journal of Global Scholars of Marketing Science. Omar's professional background combines expertise in sales, market research and planning, corporate strategizing, and leadership & training in the banking and retail sectors. Omar worked for different leading institutions such as Walmart, CIBC, and Fairstone Bank.

Eli Fianu is a Lecturer, and Managing Director of Liscious Services Ltd. He has over seven years' experience as a Lecturer. He also has over seven years' experience in the banking industry and over a decade experience in the telecommunications industry. Dr Eli Fianu has a PhD in Information Systems and Technology from the University of KwaZulu-Natal in South Africa and a MSc in Management Information Systems from Coventry University in the United Kingdom. He has a specialty in Educational Technology. His research interests are in the areas of technology adoption, e-learning, social media, learning analytics and business analytics. He has co-authored several published articles in these areas. Dr Eli Fianu is an advocate of blended learning and strives to conduct research that facilitates the development of effective e-learning models.

Shivi Khanna is an Associate Professor in School of Business and Management at CHRIST University, Banerghatta Road, Bangalore, India. She has completed her PhD in corporate structure determinants in Indian companies. She has published articles in various international and national refereed journals. Her areas of research interests include Corporate Finance, environmental sustainability and social media usage.

Sunita Kumar is a passionate educationist with 17+ years of experience (Industry: 5+ years and Teaching: 12+ years) experience. Dr Sunita area of expertise/ specialization including advertising, branding, digital Marketing, consumer behaviour, Marketing Analytics. Over the last 12 years, she has taught and received positive evaluations for many marketing units, including Brand Management, Marketing Research, International Marketing, Fundamental of Marketing, Consumer Behaviour, Marketing Management, Social Media and Digital Marketing, Data Analysis using SPSS both postgraduate and undergraduate level. She has also been actively supervising master's and Ph.D. candidates from Christ university in Bangalore. Dr Sunita also often shares her industry experience and research findings with different audiences and stakeholders, both locally and internationally. she has been actively leading and involved in numerous research project and consultancies projects, as well as published numerous indexed journals/ articles, book, chapters in a book, conference proceedings, and industry reports.

Seung Hwan (Mark) Lee is a Professor and Associate Dean of Engagement & Inclusion at Ted Rogers School of Management at Toronto Metropolitan University. He earned his Ph.D. in Business Administration from the Ivey School of Business at Western University. He completed his MBA at the University of Windsor and Bachelor's degree in Arts & Science at McMaster University. Dr. Lee's primary research interests are in the consumer behavior discipline, specifically focusing on the structural dynamics of social networks and its impact on retail consumers. Professor Lee also contributes to the topic of branding, marketing education, and sensory marketing. He has published in top tier journals which include Journal of Consumer Research, Journal of Consumer Psychology, Journal of Business Ethics, and Journal of Business Research.

Mahmoud Abdulai Mahmoud is an Associate Professor of Marketing in the Department of Marketing and Entrepreneurship, University of Ghana Business School. Professor Mahmoud's main research interest is in market orientation, tourism, and sustainability marketing. He has published extensively in internationally peer-reviewed academic ranked journals and presented many papers at international conferences.

Michael Boadi Nyamekye holds two doctorate degrees in Business Administration and Marketing. He also holds a couple of master's degrees in diverse fields. He is currently a Senior Lecturer of Marketing at the School of Graduate Studies,

University of Professional Studies Accra. He has published extensive in international referred journals with Scopus index and high impact factors. His research interest spans in areas of Strategic Management, Entrepreneurial Development, and Marketing. With almost three decades of pastoral ministry, he has immense experience in managing both the spiritual and physical needs of diverse people.

Margaret Ofori is a faculty member in the Department of Nursing at the School of Nursing and Midwifery, University of Health and Allied Sciences (UHAS) in Ho, Ghana. Previously, she held the position of First Volta and Oti Regional Officer at the Nursing and Midwifery Council of Ghana. Additionally, she served as a Nurse Educator at the Ho Nurses Training College. Her clinical experience spans various healthcare institutions including the Ho Teaching Hospital, Korle Bu Teaching Hospital, 37 Military Hospital, Volta Regional Hospital, Ho Municipal Hospital, Ketu South Municipal Hospital, and Jasikan District Hospital. Margaret is currently pursuing a Ph.D. in Nursing at York University, Canada. She holds a Master of Philosophy in Nursing, a Diploma in Nursing, and a Bachelor of Education from the University of Ghana and the University of Cape Coast respectively. Margaret is a Registered General Nurse.

Fidelis Quansah is a Senior Lecturer with the Faculty of Management Studies, UPSA. She is currently the Dean of the Faculty of Management Studies. She holds a PhD in Business Administration from OUM-AiT, MBA in Marketing from the University of Ghana, Legon and a BSc in Renewable Natural resources (Wood Science) from KNUST. She has supervised a significant number of dissertations from the undergraduate level through to the PhD level since her engagement with the university. Prof. Quansah's research areas are in the field of international business and marketing.

Wasswa Shafik (Member, IEEE) received the Bachelor of Science degree in information technology engineering with a minor in mathematics from Ndejje University, Kampala, Uganda, in 2016, and the Master of Engineering degree in information technology engineering (MIT) from Yazd University, Yazd, Iran and a Ph.D. degree in computer science at Universiti Brunei Darussalam, Brunei Darussalam. He is also the Founder and a Principal Investigator of the Dig Connectivity Research Laboratory (DCRLab) after serving as a Research Associate at Network Interconnectivity Research Laboratory, Yazd University. Prior to this, he worked as a Community Data Analyst at Population Services International (PSI-Uganda), Community Data Officer at Programme for Accessible Health Communication (PACE-Uganda), Research Assistant at the Socio-Economic Data Centre (SEDC-Uganda), Prime Minister's Office, Kampala, Uganda, an Assistant Data Officer at

TechnoServe, Kampala, IT Support at Thurayya Islam Media, Uganda, and Asmaah Charity Organization. He has more than 60 publications in renowned journals and conferences. His research interests include Ecological Informatics, Computer Vision, AI-enabled IoT/IoMTs, Smart Cities, Cyber Security, and Privacy.

Gloria Ama Konadu Sraha is Senior lecturer in Marketing and currently the Head of Business Studies Department at Lancaster University, Ghana. She holds a bachelor's degree in marketing from All Nations University Ghana, an MSc in International Marketing from the University of the West of Scotland, UK and a PhD in International Business from Victoria University of Wellington, New Zealand. She has attended many AIB conferences in different countries and a reviewer of many academic manuscripts for journals and conferences. Her research interest includes international business, export promotion programmes, gender studies in entrepreneurship and export marketing strategies in emerging countries.

Emre Yaşar completed his master's degree in Tourism Management at Süleyman Demirel University in 2020. After his master's degree, he worked in the field of 100/2000 Intangible Cultural Heritage at Nevşehir Hacı Bektaş Veli University Faculty of Tourism for a year. In 2020, he started my doctorate education in tourism management. Since 2022, he has been working as a research assistant at Isparta University of Applied Sciences Faculty of Tourism.

|**Eda Yayla** was born in 1996 in Istanbul/Beykoz. She started her master's degree after graduating from Nevşehir Hacı Bektaş Veli University, Faculty of Tourism in 2019. She studies on smart tourism, smart destination and cultural heritage. She is currently continuing her doctoral studies at the same university.

Index

L

M

N

O

P

Q

S

T

U

W

www.ingramcontent.com/pod-product-compliance
Lightning Source LLC
LaVergne TN
LVHW081338300926
849161LV00008B/2009
* 9 7 9 8 3 6 9 3 1 2 3 9 1 *